FOCUS: MUSIC OF SOUTH AFRICA

Second Edition

Carol A. Muller

University of Pennsylvania

Routledge
Taylor & Francis Group
NEW YORK AND LONDON

First edition published 2004 by ABC-CLIO, Inc

This edition published 2008
by Routledge
270 Madison Ave, New York, NY 10016

Simultaneously published in the UK
by Routledge
2 Park Square, Milton Park, Abingdon, Oxon OX14 4RN

Routledge is an imprint of the Taylor & Francis Group, an informa business

Typeset in Minion Pro by The Running Head Limited, Cambridge, www.therunninghead.com
Printed and bound in the United States of America on acid-free paper by Sheridan Books, Inc.

Library of Congress Cataloging in Publication Data
Muller, Carol Ann.
Focus: Music of South Africa / Carol A. Muller. — 2nd ed.
p. cm. — (Focus on world music)
1. Music—South Africa—History and criticism. I. Title. II. Title: Music of South Africa.
ML3760.M85 2008
780.968—dc22

2008006968

ISBN10: 0-415-96069-X (hbk)
ISBN10: 0-415-96071-1 (pbk)
ISBN10: 0-203-93063-0 (ebk)
ISBN13: 978-0-415-96069-4 (hbk)
ISBN13: 978-0-415-96071-7 (pbk)
ISBN13: 978-0-203-93063-2 (ebk)

Contents

List of Figures vii
About the Author xi
Series Foreword by Michael B. Bakan xiii
Preface xv

PART I Creating Connections **1**
Introduction 3
1 South African Music: The Lion Sleeps Tonight 5
2 Twentieth-Century Political History 23
3 Twentieth-Century Entertainment History: Live and Mediated 33
4 *Graceland* (1986): World Music Collaboration 53

PART II Twentieth-Century Musical Styles: Music in Migration **71**
Introduction 73
5 Representing the Past in South African Music 75
6 South African Music: Brief Definitions 83
7 Labor Migration: *Isicathamiya* 99
8 Labor Migration: *Maskanda* 113
9 Labor Migration: Gumboot Dance 129

PART III Focusing In: Two Case Studies **153**
Introduction 155
First Case Study: Cape Jazz 157
10 Post-World War II Cape Town 157

11 Sathima Bea Benjamin's Cape Town: Popular Culture in the Post-World War II Era 173
12 Sathima Bea Benjamin as Jazz Musician 185
Second Case Study: Shembe Hymns 203
13 Mission Hymns and the Founding of the Shembe Community 203
14 Shembe Hymns 227

AFTERWORD **259**
15 Final Reflections 261

Appendices **269**
1 A Guide to African Music: A Music of Encounters, North, South, East, and West 269
2 Key Dates in South African History 275
3 Selected Websites and Guide to Recordings: South Africa and Its Music 281
4 Themes Common to the Study of African Music: 1980s to Present 295
5 Discussion of Musical Examples on CD 299

Glossary 311
References 315
Notes 323
Index 327

Figures

	Map of South Africa.	2
2.1	South African women sing their national anthem, wearing robes printed with the South African flag. Photo © David Turnley/CORBIS.	24
7.1	Group leaders sign up for an all-night *isicathamiya* choir competition and pay an entrance fee, the proceeds of which contribute to the monetary prize at the end of the evening. Beatrice Street YMCA, Durban, September 1996, taken by Carol Muller.	103
7.2	Men heating up in the circle at the back of the hall before parading down to the front to perform in front of the judge. Beatrice Street YMCA, Durban, September 1996, taken by Carol Muller.	104
7.3	Women supporters standing on the sideline, showing their admiration for the group of male *isicathamiya* performers, and staking claim to their lovers! Beatrice Street YMCA, Durban, September 1996, taken by Carol Muller.	104
7.4	Same group doing "*isteps*" this time joined by one of the female supporters, who lays claim to her male partner in the group. This takes place in the *praktisa* part of the evening. Beatrice Street YMCA, Durban, September 1996, taken by Carol Muller.	105
7.5	Same group parades around in front of the judge and back onto the small stage in front of the hall, still accompanied by their female supporters. Beatrice Street YMCA, Durban, September 1996, taken by Carol Muller.	105
7.6	The *isicathimiya* group has prayed and warmed up at the back of the hall in a circle now proceeds down alongside the audience members to the front where they will perform in front of the judge. Beatrice Street YMCA, Durban, September 1996, taken by Carol Muller.	107
7.7	*Isicathamiya* group enters the stage in the competition, Beatrice Street YMCA, Durban, September 1996, taken by Carol Muller.	108

7.8	*Isicathamiya* group stand in a line ready to start singing. They will later do the lifted leg dancing or *isteps*. Two women supporters make themselves known to the audience. Beatrice Street YMCA, Durban, September 1996, taken by Carol Muller.	108
7.9	*Isicathamiya* group doing "*isteps*" for the competition at Beatrice Street YMCA, Durban, September 1996,taken by Carol Muller.	109
7.10	Same group "gets down" as the singing and dancing intensify. They make clear eye contact with the judge of the competition as they do so. Beatrice Street YMCA, Durban, September 1996, taken by Carol Muller.	109
8.1	Zulu mouth bow, drawn by Daphne Maree.	114
8.2	Zulu *umakweyana* bow, drawn by Daphne Maree.	114
8.3	A group of Basotho men living in the mountains of Lesotho gather together on a misty morning to listen to the sound of the *lesiba* mouth bow and homemade guitar, or *ramkie*. June 1994, taken by Carol Muller.	116
8.4	Basotho shepherds entertained by a *ramkie* player, early morning in the mountains of Lesotho, June 1994. Blankets are commonly used for warmth in the winter months in this region. Photo taken by Carol Muller.	117
9.1	Blanket Mkhize (guitarist on right), and his 1985 team, including Janet Topp Fargion (on left) and Carol Muller (to the right), perform at a school function in KwaZulu Natal, taken by Douglas Muller.	133
9.2	Blanket Mkhize (guitar) and his sons gumboot dance at a community celebration in rural KwaZulu Natal, September 1996, taken by Carol Muller.	133
9.3	Blanket Mkhize (guitarist on the right side) plays for his team who arrive to perform at the community celebration in rural KwaZulu Natal, September 1996.	135
9.4	Gumboot team of Steven Shelembe competes against the team brought by Blanket Mkhize to celebrate the visit of researchers Janet Topp Fargion and Carol Muller, Creighton, KwaZulu Natal, January 1995, taken by Carol Muller.	135
10.1	Three participants in the New Year's Carnival, Bo-Kaap, Cape Town, January 1996, taken by Carol Muller.	167
10.2	Marching through the streets in the center of Cape Town, New Year's Carnival, January 1996, taken by Carol Muller.	168
13.1	Zionist followers baptized in the Indian Ocean, early Sunday morning, July 1995, Durban, taken by G. C. E. Oosthuizen and used with permission.	204
13.2	Mvangeli Magubane (in green evangelist gown) stands in front of the administrative office where members purchase the hymnal and maps of the holy mountain of Nhlangakaze (both seen behind), as well as marriage and baptismal certificates. Ebuhleni, September 1996, taken by Carol Muller.	205
13.3	Procession of Shembe members on the annual pilgrimage to the Holy Mountain of Nhlangakaze, January 1992, taken by Carol Muller.	206

13.4 Young Shembe boys playing the Shembe bugles at a wedding celebration in Kwa Mashi, Durban, c. October 1995, taken by Carol Muller. 207

13.5 Unmarried female followers of Shembe prepare for the service that precedes the ritual cleansing of the graves of Shembe members by virgin girls, July 1991, Ekuphakameni, KwaZulu Natal, taken by Carol Muller. 208

13.6 Male leaders, three *abavangeli* (evangalists) with leopard-skin shoulder covers waiting between Sabbath services at Ebuhleni, Febrauary 1996, taken by Carol Muller. 209

13.7 Shembe girls' procession with umbrellas to the tample, Paradis, in their special ritual attire. Ebuhleni, KwaZulu Natal, September 1991, taken by Carol Muller. 210

13.8 Shembe boys make an offering to their leader, Ebuhleni, July 1991, taken by Carol Muller. 210

13.9 Married women members march to the beat of the drum to make an offering to Shembe, Ebuhleni, August 1991, taken by Carol Muller. 216

13.10 Shembe male follower sitting on his prayer mat in the Paradis temple at Ebuhleni with his Shembe hymnal and Zulu Bible, waiting for the service, Ebuhleni, August 1991, taken by Carol Muller. 216

13.11 Woman member drums the rhythm of *ukusina* at the Ama 14s' all-night meeting, KwaMashu F Section, November 1991, taken by Carol Muller. 218

13.12 Woman shakes the bells to add to the rhythm of the dance, KwaMashu August 1991, taken by Carol Muller. 220

13.13 Mrs. Nthini (at left) claps to the rhythm of the dance, KwaMashu August 1991, taken by Carol Muller. 221

13.14 Shembe Youth Choir performs at Amos Shembe's funeral, October 1995, at Ebuhleni, taken by Carol Muller. 222

13.15 A Shembe member and her friend with ice-creams. Ebuhleni, September 1996, taken by Carol Muller. 223

13.16 Married women with beaded design on their hats. These women are from the southern part of KwaZulu Natal (the cylindrical shape of the hat indicates their place of origin). Women from the northern part of the province wear hats that flare outwards; some of these can be seen in figure 14.12. Photo: Carol Muller. 224

14.1 A woman sells goods on the side of the road at Ebuhleni: these include vaseline petroleum jelly and sunlight soap, both important for purification purposes, September 1996. Photo by Carol Muller. 228

14.2 Shembe member sells ice-cream cones out of her cooler at Ebuhleni, September 1996. Photo by Carol Muller. 229

14.3 Shembe woman gets married at home in KwaMashu, surrounded by gifts wrapped in woven grass mats, 1995, taken by Carol Muller. 231

14.4 Shembe women attend marriage at home of KwaMashu bride, 1995, taken by Carol Muller. 231

14.5 Beadwork on hat of married woman, KwaMashu, 1995, taken by Carol Muller. 233

14.6	Married women waiting for the inauguration of fourth leader Rev. Vimbeni Shembe, at Gospel, December 2005, taken by Carol Muller.	233
14.7	The installation of fourth leader Rev. Vimbeni Shembe, Gospel, southern KwaZulu Natal, December 1995, taken by Carol Muller.	235
14.8	Installation of Rev. Vimbeni Shembe, December 1995. These are the married women who attended the ceremony. Photo: Carol Muller.	235
14.9	Nazarite virgin with flowers at the installation of fourth leader, Rev. Vimbeni Shembe. Gospel, December 1995, taken by Carol Muller.	236
14.10	Shembe members walk towards the site where Rev. Vimbeni Shembe is to be installed as fourth leader of *ibandla lamaNazaretha* in December 1995, taken by Carol Muller.	237
14.11	Mvangeli Magubane at the installation of Rev. Vimbeni Shembe, December 1995, taken by Carol Muller.	238
14.12	Married women singing at Rev. Vimbeni Shembe's installation as fourth leader of *ibandla lamaNazaretha*, December 2005. The woman with the glasses in the right corner just off center is Ntombemhlope Mthethwa, wife of (now deceased) organist Bongani Mthethwa. Photo: Carol Muller.	239
14.13	Carol Muller stands at the "gate" to Ebuhleni (though there was no fence at the time), which marks the entrance to the holy site and church headquarters of *ibandla lamaNazaretha*. Ebuhleni, September 1996. Photo by Carol Muller.	241
14.14	Funeral service of third leader, Rev. Amos Shembe. Members crowd around the statue of church founder Rev. Isaiah Shembe at Ebuhleni, the church headquarters, October 1995, taken by Carol Muller.	242
14.15	Many videographers and photographers capture the moment of Amos Shembe's funeral and Nelson Mandela's presence at Ebuhleni, October 1995. Photo by Carol Muller.	243
14.16	Shembe member purchases the poster of the holy mountain of Nhlangakaze, updated with the four heads of *ibandla lamaNazaretha*: founder Isaiah; successor Galilee; third leader Amos; and his son, Vimbeni. Ebuhleni, September 1996. Photo by Carol Muller.	245
14.17	Two married women followers of Shembe, the woman on the left has her white *imiNazaretha* prayer gown and the white *inansook* (prayer shawl) covering her body. She is also wearing a photographic image of Shembe on a chain around her neck. Both women wear the characteristic beadwork that covers their hats. The shape of the hats indicates both women come from south of the Tugela River, i.e., the Natal part of KwaZulu Natal. September 1996, Ebuhleni. Photo by Carol Muller.	246
14.18	Married women dance toward Shembe with great joy, Ebuhleni, August 1991, taken by Carol Muller.	250
14.19	Beadwork on a married woman's hat; the design is frequently in the shape of the mountain. Ebuhleni, September 1996, taken by Carol Muller.	253

About the Author

Carol Muller is Professor of Music (Ethnomusicology) and Director of Graduate Studies in Music at the University of Pennsylvania. Born in Cape Town, South Africa, Carol Muller spent her teenage years in KwaZulu Natal. She completed a Bachelor of Music degree in Ethnomusicology at the University of Natal, where she joined a black male migrant worker gumboot dance team along with fellow ethnomusicologist Janet Topp-Fargion. They wrote an honors thesis on the subject. Muller earned her Ph.D. at New York University in 1994 with a dissertation on song, dance, ritual, and dreaming amongst the female followers of South African prophet Isaiah Shembe. While at NYU, Muller initiated a project on Cape Town born, New York based jazz singer Sathima Bea Benjamin. She taught at the University of KwaZulu Natal from 1992–1996, during which time she generated much of the research that formed the core of this book.

Muller returned to the USA in 1996, teaching at New York University, and the University of North Carolina at Chapel Hill. She has been in Philadelphia since 1998. She has published numerous articles and several books, including *Rituals of Fertility and the Sacrifice of Desire* (Chicago 1999), Shembe Hymns (2008), *Musically Connected* (Oxford, forthcoming), and *Musical Echoes,* with Sathima Bea Benjamin (Duke, forthcoming).

Series Foreword

The past decade has witnessed extraordinary growth in the areas of ethnomusicology and world music publishing. With the publication of both the ten-volume *Garland Encyclopedia of World Music* (1998) and the second edition of the *New Grove Dictionary of Music and Musicians* (2001), we now have access to general reference resources that ethnomusicologists and world music enthusiasts of even just a few years ago could only have dreamed of. University and other academic presses—Chicago, Oxford, Cambridge, Illinois, Temple, Wesleyan, Indiana, California, Routledge—have produced excellent ethnomusicological monographs, edited volumes, and smaller-scale reference works in ever-increasing numbers, many accompanied by CDs, DVDs, and other media that bring the musics described vividly to life. A host of new introductory-level textbooks for freshman/sophomore-level world music survey courses have come out too, along with new editions of long-established textbooks catering to that market. New instructional resources for teaching these same kinds of introductory survey courses have been created in addition, the Oxford Global Music Series perhaps most notable among them. And the Internet has of course revolutionized everything, with thousands upon thousands of web-based resources—from superb scholarly and educational resources such as Smithsonian Global Sound (www.smithsonianglobalsound.org) and *Grove Music Online* to the wild frontiers of YouTube and myriad commercial online music providers—all now available from your desktop at the click of a mouse.

Yet for all of this profuse and diverse publishing activity, there remains a conspicuous gap in the literature. We still lack a solid corpus of high quality textbooks designed specifically for area courses in world music, ethnomusicology, and interdisciplinary programs with a strong music component. The need for such texts is greatest where courses for upper-division undergraduate and entry-level graduate students are taught, but it extends to courses at the freshman and sophomore levels as well, especially those enrolling music majors and other students who are serious and motivated.

What has been needed for such courses are books that balance sound pedagogy with exemplary scholarship, and that are substantive in content yet readily accessible to specialist and non-specialist readers alike. These books would be written in a lively and engaging style by leading ethnomusicologists and educators, bringing wide interdisciplinary scope and relevance to the contemporary concerns of their readership. They would, moreover, provide a telescopic view of the musics and cultures they addressed, zooming in from broad-based surveys of expansive music-culture areas and topics toward compelling, in-depth case studies of specific musicultural traditions and their myriad transformations in the modern world.

This is precisely what Routledge's *Focus on World Music* series delivers, with books that are authoritative, accessible, pedagogically strong, richly illustrated, and accompanied by a compelling compact disk of musical examples linked integrally to the text. I am delighted to be part of the team that has brought this exciting and important series to fruition. I hope you enjoy reading these books as much as I have!

Michael B. Bakan
The Florida State University
Series Editor

Preface

In the first edition of this book, titled *South African Music*, the preface focused on what Africa and its music was not. Having taught about African music in both South Africa (the mid-1990s) and the United States (since then) it seemed like my project was to dispel stereotypes about the music of Africa that students often bring to the classroom. First, many talk about Africa as if it is a country like the United States, and not an entire continent with a complex history, and richly textured fabric of musical expression; second, we assume that African music is only about drumming and complex rhythms when it is about so much more; and third, Africa is conceptualized as a place without history—it exists largely as the site of a vague form of cultural memory for those who were sold into slavery and ended up living in other parts of the world, and it has no real presence in the minds of many in the contemporary world. The South African case study was set up to reinforce the fact that these three ideas about African music were completely wrong, and they certainly didn't fit the music of South Africa, the country at the southernmost tip of the African continent.

In this revised edition, *Focus: Music of South Africa*, I reconfigure the framing of the book in ways I couldn't imagine doing in the first edition published by ABC-CLIO in 2004. While I did make some attempt to at least represent pieces of the African continent in the first edition's preface and Appendices, as per the guidelines for the original book series, it is almost impossible to reduce a continent as large and diverse as Africa to bookends—which is what happened in the first edition.[1] I could more effectively talk about the impact of England and the United States on South African music and culture in the twentieth century than I could talk about its relationship to the rest of the African continent because English and American influences overlapped with the narratives of colonization and encounters with northern hemisphere or "Western" cultural forms in other parts of Africa. These narratives traveled to South Africa with greater ease than the music, or knowledge about it, from the rest of Africa.

In the early 1990s, when I wrote the first drafts of this book, like many South Africans,

I lacked a palpable feel for the Southern African subcontinent, and the superficial continental generalizations about "African music" were clearly the outcomes of my having grown up White in apartheid South Africa. Born in the early 1960s, the era of Grand Apartheid, when the apartheid regime began to enforce the laws it had put in place in the 1950s, I had very little experience of the neighboring states—in fact the South African Defense Force effectively declared war on those states in the apartheid era (see Chapman 1996, Introduction). Certainly, with a South African passport travel into any significant part of the African continent was almost impossible. At that time, it was easier to get to Europe, Britain, or the United States than it was to travel to Kenya, Tanzania, or Nigeria.

It was not just the music of the larger continent that was hard to cover in a single volume, but in the post-apartheid era it seems it is just as much of a challenge to represent the complexity of South Africa's twentieth-century musical past as a single narrative. While in the 1990s, South Africans were desperately seeking ways to articulate a sense of national unity, a decade later we are possibly less concerned about defining the internal connections than about rearticulating the ties that bind us to the rest of the world. In response, I suggest in this revised edition that we learn about South African music through four frames—in terms of South Africa as a recently formed national entity, South Africa in the Southern African region, on the African continent, and in the world at large. I have taken this position in this book because much has changed in regard to South Africa's relationship to the rest of Africa and the world in the last decade; and because there is so much more music and writing about music from South Africa than there was even five years ago. In addition, as I explain later in the book, the Internet is radically changing the way we access acoustical and video images of music of the world's peoples, and this is definitely the case with South African music. In other words, how we think about music in South Africa and elsewhere in the world will shift accordingly.

Having opened the discussion of South African music to literally a global perspective, I should underscore that it is absolutely impossible for a single author like myself to provide any kind of complete representation of the twentieth century in South African music. As the Series Editor, Michael Bakan, has suggested, comprehensive treatment of a country's present and past in music was never the intention. Rather, in this book, I make a small beginning by sharing the knowledge I have gained through my own research as a South African ethnomusicologist over the past twenty-five years. It is a perspective on South African music informed first by the fact that I was born in South Africa and lived there until ten years ago, and travel back regularly; but it is also a perspective that has been shaped by living at some distance from the place, by addressing the kinds of questions asked and concerns raised about South African music by those I have encountered in the United States.

Both because of the strong impact of American, British, and European music and culture in the shaping of contemporary South African practices, and because of my own diasporic existence, I am sure that as you study the materials in this book, you will find yourself making comparative observations. When you read about the ways in which "Coloured" South Africans absorbed American jazz and popular music, you no doubt will realize that this process might not be that different for many who grew up in post-World War II America or England. Conversely, you might be surprised at the ways in which African American gospel or the largely White contemporary Christian music have been absorbed into the Zulu-language religious ritual and song-practices amongst the followers of Shembe in KwaZulu Natal. Creating connections, discovering parallel practices, and inserting your own experience into this material on South African music is an important part of understanding the place and power of music in the contemporary world.

How This Book Is Organized

The second edition is greatly revised from the first published with ABC-CLIO. My focus here is on the book's use as a textbook for undergraduate world music students, those interested in the music of Africa, or first year graduate students in ethnomusicology. The book is divided into three parts, and each part is divided again into several chapters. There is a substantial body of newly written material. The overall shape of the book starts wide, with general contextual information, first on South Africa in relationship to the region and African continent, and then becomes increasingly focused. Each chapter ends with a set of keywords and definitions drawn from the chapter's text that work as a kind of summary of core contents as well. Visual images relevant to the discussions at hand are included throughout the volume. A CD of field recordings is inserted at the back of the book and discussed in the appendices.

Part I: "Creating Connections" provides introductory materials for the study of South African music. Chapter 1 begins with a discussion of the globally popular, but South African originating song with three names: "Mbube"/"Wimoweh"/"The Lion Sleeps Tonight." We use that song and its accompanying story to open up a conversation about key characteristics of South African music and culture, and to discuss the challenges we face in thinking about South African music as a single entity. Chapter 2 provides a discussion of the three phases of twentieth-century political history in South Africa: segregation, apartheid, and the post-apartheid periods. Chapter 3 is an overview of South African media history, with a particular focus on radio, the most widely used medium in South Africa today. Chapter 4 moves into a detailed discussion of *Graceland*, the album produced by American musician Paul Simon in collaboration with South African (and other world) musicians, a project frequently assumed to represent a turning point in South African music history.

Part II: "Twentieth-Century Musical Styles: Music in Migration" moves to a more focused overview of significant musical styles in twentieth-century South Africa—particularly those known through world music circuits. Chapter 5 suggests ways in which we might create specific periods for stylistic development and transformations. Chapter 6 provides a series of snapshots of key musical styles. Chapters 7 through 9 are three more in-depth discussions of three different South African music-dance cultures that emerged with the migration of Black South Africans from rural to more urbanized places of employment in the twentieth century. Chapter 7 looks at *isicathamiya*, the music transmitted globally by Joseph Shabalala and Ladysmith Black Mambazo; Chapter 8 examines *maskanda*, a Zulu-language music and dance style, focused largely on the guitar and extended into a "band format" with bass, drums, and rhythm guitar; and Chapter 9 zooms in on gumboot dance.

Part III: "Focusing In: Two Case Studies" takes the reader into the heart of two musical cultures that I have researched in greater depth than previous chapters. Chapters 10–12 examine South African jazz as it was created in the port city of Cape Town in the post-World War II era, amongst people called "Coloured" and to a lesser extent those called "Bantu/African." It expands on the experiences of one individual, singer Sathima Bea Benjamin, and her musical cohorts. Chapters 13 and 14 take us up the Indian Ocean coastline of South Africa to Durban, another port city, and into the sacred world of the Zulu-language followers of Black prophet Isaiah Shembe who received a new style of song in dreams in the early twentieth century. The chapters consider the musical style, words of the songs, and the transformations of style over the course of the twentieth century. Chapter 15 is an afterword that highlights key cultural themes embedded in the study of South African music.

There are five appendices in this book: Appendix 1 is a historical overview of outsider encounters with African Music; Appendix 2 provides an overview of South African history; Appendix 3 gives a useful list of commercially available recordings of South African music (which may be found on iTunes and other song lists for download), and website recommendations; Appendix 4 provides a general outline of themes in the study of African Music, and Appendix 5 is a discussion of the music examples on the accompanying CD. There is a glossary of South African terms and musical keywords; and finally a list of references cited. All South African-related music and video recordings cited in the text can be found listed in Appendix 3.

Supplements

As with the first edition, the book includes an audio CD with examples of the music of South Africa. In addition, there is a companion website, **www.routledge.com/textbooks/focusonworldmusic**, for instructors and students. It includes further resources, lecture notes, and quizzes for student practice.

Acknowledgments

This is a project that has been a long time in the making, and along the way, many people have participated in the conversations about South Africa, its politics, and its music. Some have done so in very general ways, others through quite specific gestures. Those who shaped the early contours were acknowledged in the first edition published by ABC-CLIO in 2004. In this edition, I would like to thank the graduate students who have passed through the Music Department at the University of Pennsylvania since 1998; my colleagues in the Department, Tim Rommen, Emily Dolan, Emma Dillon, Gary Tomlinson, Jeff Kallberg, and Guy Ramsey in particular; Margie and Maryellen, the ever helpful administrative staff; Associate Dean in the School of Arts and Sciences at Penn, Joe Farrell, who ensured I had the leave necessary to think through this text; Phil Bohlman for passing my name on to ABC-CLIO for the original series; Series Editor, Michael Bakan, for his tremendous enthusiasm and gentle prodding; the two anonymous reviewers of the revised edition, and Routledge editor, Constance Ditzel. I almost want to call her Constance Angel because she has been an editor out of this world. Also at Routledge, Denny Tek was enormously supportive in preparing the manuscript and CD; University of Pennsylvania graduate students Roger Grant compiled the index, and Gavin Steingo and Ian MacMillen created the Powerpoint notes for the accompanying website; and Charlotte Davies at The Running Head was a superb copy-editor.

Few books are written without the unfailing love and support of those close to an author. My parents asked regularly about the progress of the revisions; as did my friends in Yardley, PA; but most of all, I cherish the depth of support and selfless giving that has come from Eric, Zachary, and Jasmine as I have sent them into the exile of theme parks, baseball games, and other amusement sites so that I had the time and space to meet the final deadlines. It is indeed to the three of you that I dedicate this volume with the deepest sense of love and appreciation for all you have become in my life.

PART I

Creating Connections

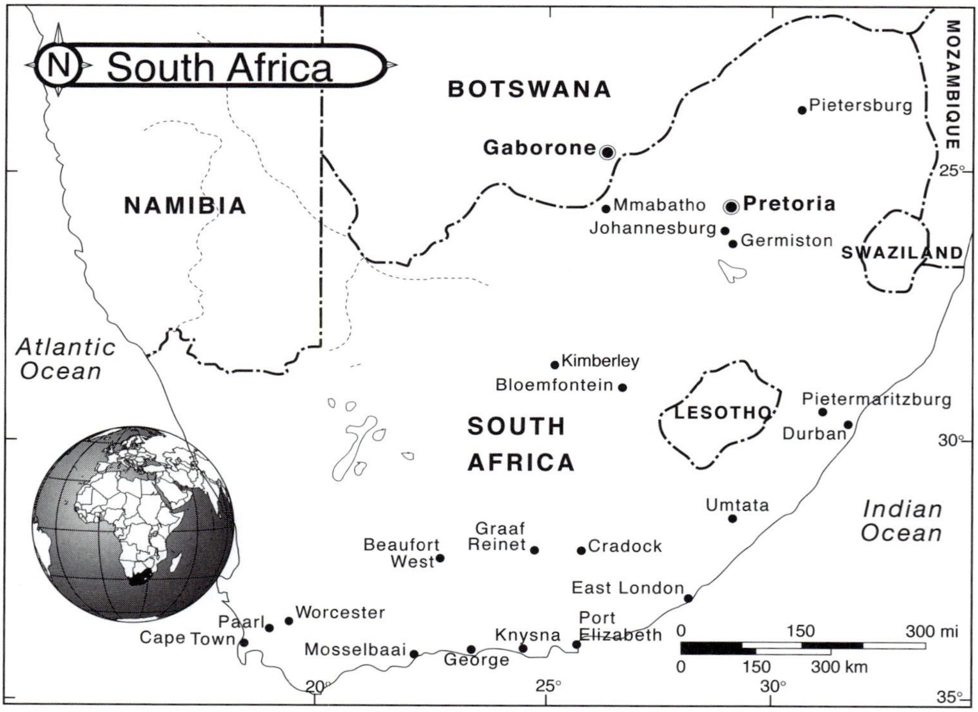
South Africa
N
BOTSWANA
NAMIBIA
MOZAMBIQUE
Gaborone
Pietersburg
Mmabatho
Pretoria
Johannesburg
Germiston
SWAZILAND
Atlantic Ocean
Kimberley
Bloemfontein
LESOTHO
Pietermaritzburg
Durban
SOUTH AFRICA
Umtata
Indian Ocean
Beaufort West
Graaf Reinet
Cradock
East London
Worcester
Paarl
Cape Town
Mosselbaai
George
Knysna
Port Elizabeth
0 150 300 mi
0 150 300 km
20°
25°
30°
35°

Introduction to Part I

Part I provides a wide-angle view on twentieth-century South Africa: its history, politics, and media, and the ways in which they have shaped and been shaped by two specific music recordings: "The Lion Sleeps Tonight" (its first iteration recorded in 1939) and the *Graceland* album (1986). It begins in Chapter 1 with a discussion of "The Lion Sleeps Tonight," a song that is widely known in many languages around the world, but which, until recently, was rarely recognized as a song coming from South Africa. We briefly address the "South African" musical elements of the original tune, "Mbube," and move into a more general discussion of South African music in relationship to the Southern African region (South Africa and the countries on her borders); of South Africa's relationship to the African continent as a whole, and then to the world at large. Chapter 2 outlines South Africa's political history, focused on the twentieth century: beginning with the era of racial segregation (in the early twentieth century) through the apartheid era (1948–1990), and into the post-apartheid era (1994 to the present). The years 1990–1994 are generally termed the "transitional period" from apartheid to Black majority rule. In Chapter 3 we take a quick look at South Africa's media history, with a particular focus on radio as the most widespread broadcast medium. And finally, in Chapter 4, we examine *Graceland* (1986) in some detail. This was a collaborative, and at the time, extremely controversial recording with American popular musician Paul Simon and South Africans including Ladysmith Black Mambazo, Ray Phiri, and extending out to Miriam Makeba and Hugh Masekela. Musical examples of all this music are readily downloadable from iTunes, and other commercial archives of world music, and YouTube has numerous clips of performances by these musicians, some remarkably old and rare, others more recent.

CHAPTER **1**

South African Music

The Lion Sleeps Tonight

"African music was, and remains, a music of encounters." Manu Dibango (cited in Stewart 1993)

Introduction

"In the jungle, the mighty jungle, the lion sleeps tonight." You probably recognize the words and are already humming the melody quietly to yourself as you visualize the jungle and the lion, but you may not know the real story behind the song. That story is a long and complicated one . . .[1]

In short, it begins with the boyhood experiences of Solomon Linda, a Zulu-speaking South African, who inscribed his memory of lion chasing in a song titled "Mbube"[2] (which means "lion" in the Zulu language).[3] In 1939, he recorded the song in Johannesburg, South Africa, with his group of male **close-harmony singers**, the Solomon Linda Evening Birds. To the surprise of the record company, **Gallo**, the song sold over 100,000 copies in the 1940s in Southern Africa. Recordings of "Mbube" were then sent to Decca Records in the United States. It was probably **Hugh Tracey**, African music collector and radio broadcaster, who mailed the records. Tracey began recording the music of Africa with financing from recording entrepreneur Eric Gallo, and broadcasting the music for the **South African Broadcast Corporation (SABC)** in the late 1930s (see further discussion of Tracey below). Decca Records wasn't interested, but folksong collector Alan Lomax, who was working for Decca at the time, passed it on with a box of other discarded records to Pete Seeger of the folk group The Weavers. In 1952, The Weavers, who had heard the word "*mbube*" as "*wimoweh*," arranged and recorded the song with its new name, taking it into the American pop charts. Its fame gathered momentum with The Weavers' 1957 performance in Carnegie Hall in New York City.[4] The Kingston Trio, who covered "Wimoweh" in 1959, attributed the songwriting credits to "Campbell–Linda"

("Paul Campbell" was the pseudonym The Weavers used as a shorthand so the group could be paid royalties without naming each person individually on the recording). Songwriter George Weiss then wrote new words for the song. "The Lion Sleeps Tonight" made the ***Billboard* Top 100** when The Tokens sang the song in 1961. Over the next five decades the "Mbube"/"Wimoweh"/"The Lion Sleeps Tonight" song would undergo hundreds of **covers**, **copies**, and **arrangements**, and be used in the film scores of numerous movies, including most recently Disney's *Lion King* (1994 for the film, 1997 for the staged musical). Despite its repeated successes, however, almost no money was channeled back to Solomon Linda or his family for their father's songwriting contribution to the financial success of "The Lion Sleeps Tonight." Part of this was because Black South Africans had no legal rights in the late 1930s, and while he was alive Solomon Linda, unaware of what **royalties** were, repeatedly gave up his rights to ownership.

In a remarkable turn of events, in February 2006 the heirs of Solomon Linda concluded a legal settlement with American songwriter George Weiss's Abilene Music Company in which the company agreed to pay the family for Linda's part in the creation of the original song "Mbube." It was Weiss, ironically the President of the Songwriters Guild (USA) for many years, who had written the new words to Linda's original tune in the 1960s for The Tokens.[5] They turned "The Lion Sleeps Tonight" and Linda's melody into a worldwide hit. The South African lawyer had found a loophole in British law that enabled them to pursue the legal battle. Yet, despite it being one of the most popular and recorded songs of the twentieth century, a song that has earned more money for those claiming to have written it than almost any other in recorded history—one writer estimated that it had generated $15 million from the *Lion King* alone—Linda died a pauper in South Africa in the early 1960s. Forty years later his daughter died in poverty of HIV/AIDS, unable to afford the antiretroviral drugs that could have prolonged her life.

Dense in legal and emotional issues, copyright matters, local–global themes, even a rags to riches narrative that I will not address in any further detail here, the "Lion Sleeps Tonight" story provides a powerful opening to a book on the last century of South African music. The triumphant end to the legal battles on behalf of Solomon Linda, initiated in the 1990s and finally settled in 2006, is quite a different "world music" story from those that ethnomusicologists usually tell—of the failures of globalization, the betrayals from inappropriate use of Third World music in First World studios, and the insatiable thirst for profit of the uncaring entertainment industry. This story speaks to the newfound sense of place and position of South Africa and its music in the early twenty-first century, not only amongst South Africans inside the nation-state, in the region of Southern Africa, or even the African continent, but also in the world at large. The Black South African **migrant worker** turned recording musician in the 1930s, who posthumously gets his financial due almost seventy years after the fact, parallels the political triumphs of the early 1990s, the place of a now democratic South Africa in the **global economy**, and the audibility of South African sounds in the **world music** mix, in a post-*Graceland* (see Chapter 4), post-apartheid era (see Chapter 2).

Several themes emerge in the "Lion Sleeps Tonight" account, which speak of the character of South African music as a category of "world music." From a traditional song, sung in communal gatherings such as weddings, in a style that was the result of prior forms of musical travel but a language (Zulu) that didn't travel internationally, "Mbube" had transmuted into a one-hit wonder in the **transnational** world of popular music. In so many ways "The Lion Sleeps Tonight" is a song that began opening the doors to South African music and musicians abroad in the twentieth century, particularly from 1960. This was the year Miriam Makeba sang it in New York City's Town Hall, shortly after leaving South Africa for Europe and the United States,[6] and it is one of the songs she would soon record with Caribbean film star and folksinger Harry Belafonte. American folk/popular singer-songwriter Paul Simon would function in a similar curatorial role for *mbube*'s (the song and the style's) historical successor, the ***isicathamiya*** genre of Ladysmith Black Mambazo, in the collaborative *Graceland* project released in 1986 (see Chapter 4 for *Graceland* discussion, and Chapter 7 for *isicathamiya*). Miriam Makeba would perform with the *Graceland* project when it played live on the "African Tour" in Zimbabwe, and later in South Africa.

Though the song was written by one individual and it is his descendants who benefit from the profits earned, "Mbube" has come to symbolize something much larger than itself for South Africans. While it seems to have been the song's use in Disney's *The Lion King*[7] that rekindled the ownership and royalty payment issues, it was an article in *Billboard* magazine (2001) written by White South African Rian Malan, and an Emmy award-winning (2006) documentary film made by another White South African, François Verster, on behalf of the South African Broadcast Corporation (SABC), that highlighted the contentious history of "The Lion Sleeps Tonight" to a wider South African and international public.[8] Finally, the copyright lawyer Owen Dean, who took the case on behalf of Solomon Linda, is a White South African, who had the backing of both the South African government and Gallo Records.

As you read the story, you might be wondering why you don't recognize "The Lion Sleeps Tonight" as "African." There are none of the complex drumming rhythms or drum ensembles accompanying the singing that one might expect of "African" music, and the vocal inflections sound more like church, or **doo-wop** from the 1950s than you might imagine "African" music to be. Part of the purpose of this book is to interrogate just what we mean when we use the word "African" in a South and Southern African context.[9] The "Mbube" parts of the "Lion Sleeps Tonight" provide a useful point of entry because, while there are elements of familiarity in the song in the familiar use of African musical traits, like **call and response** and a **cyclical structure**, it contains clear evidence of Southern African, and specifically **Nguni** song style as outlined in the 1970s by ethnomusicologist David Rycroft (in Wachsmann 1971: 213–242). The melody is sung in a call and response format, where the **phrases** of each section **overlap** with each other. The song is performed in **four-part harmony**—with one male soprano, a few altos and tenors, and everyone else on bass; and the chord progression references the ***marabi***[10] **harmonic cycle**: I-IV-I6/4-V7-I, a cycle that underpins much of South Africa's most enduring twentieth-century tunes (briefly discussed in Chapter 6). The performance occurs in a cyclical structure, with seemingly infinite cycles of repetition i.e., there is no obvious **cadence** or point of closure. The melodic phrases are **pentatonic**; and each melodic line joins the musical fabric in a **staggered** manner. Dance is an integral dimension of the song's execution in its original context of performance.

Even if no drums accompany "The Lion Sleeps Tonight," drums are not completely absent from Southern Africa, though they do not form the core of performance. In rural areas, and certain urban performances, one might instead witness a range of instrumental possibilities: xylophones, marimbas, ***mbiras***, whistles, flutes, harps, **musical bows**, **guitar-like instruments**, rattles. You may hear the far more pervasive electronic keyboard, drum machine, electric guitar, drum kit, bass guitar, and a wide assortment of brass and woodwind instruments. But mostly in Southern Africa, you will witness the power of the human voice in song, individually, accompanied by a solo instrument, or collectively. Sometimes the voices will sound **homophonically**—as in the Christian hymn; at others, voices will sound simultaneously but not in **unison**, each individual articulating his or her own space in a more **improvised** or **polyphonic** musical fabric. It is the richness of vocal utterance that has characterized the majority of music made over the last century in South Africa.

Representing South[ern] African Music

"Obviously," writes Kofi Agawu (2003: 31) "there is a place for studies committed to constructing African music as a unified cultural practice. And equally obviously, there is a place for studies that do not ride roughshod over the particularities of individual expressive forms. Finding imaginative ways of negotiating the continuing dialectic between the particular and the general ranks high among the challenges of representing African music." Agawu's invocation to consider both the particular and the general when we think about the music of Africa is an appropriate point of departure for this book, though I shall expand his binary frame to four levels of analysis: the national (South Africa), the regional (Southern Africa); the continental (Africa as a whole), and then the global, mostly in terms of South Africa's relationship to those who colonized the continent: Europe, Britain, and culturally, the United States, albeit from a distance.

The shift in viewpoint I am suggesting—of examining South African music as the music of a (unified) nation, inside a region, a continent, and in relationship to the world at large—is not completely new, though what we mean by "African" changes through the twentieth century. In the early twentieth century, conceptions of the "African" in "African music" referenced Black Africa in contrast to the "European" from Britain and Europe, and it was defined as such by those born outside the continent, or recently arrived from Europe. In post-apartheid South Africa, "African" is defined as a more unified vision in which all people born on the continent, regardless of racial or ethnic heritage, are identified as "African." In contrast, in the mid-twentieth century, it shifted again when musical research became more focused on individual nations, and nations-within-nations—Ndebele, Zulu, Sesotho, and so forth, as part of apartheid ideology in South Africa, and postcolonial recuperation in independent states like Ghana, Nigeria, and Tanzania.

Before proceeding with the musical issues, here are some basic facts about South Africa, Southern Africa, and the African continent as a whole.

South Africa (since 1994)

- Total population (2003) about 46.5 million people; racial breakdown: about 37 million (79.5 percent) Black, 4 million (8.6 percent) Coloured, 4 million (8.6 percent) White, and just over a million (2.3 percent) classifying themselves as "Indian" (of Indian descent)

- Eleven official languages since 1996: Afrikaans, English, isiNdebele, isiXhosa, isiZulu, Sepedi, Sesotho, Setswana, Siswati, Tshivenda, and Xitsonga. Zulu is the first language of about 24 percent of South Africans, Xhosa of about 18 percent, Afrikaans 13 percent, Sepedi 9 percent, English and Setswana about 8 percent each. IsiNdebele is the least spoken of the eleven official languages—by just over 1 percent
- Nine provinces: Western Cape, Eastern Cape, Northern Cape, Free State, KwaZulu Natal, North-West, Gauteng, Mpumalanga and Northern Province. Note: prior to 1994, in the apartheid years (1948–1990; transition years: 1990–1994) there were four provinces, and eleven homelands/*Bantustans*. This is discussed further in Chapter 2.
- Three capital cities: Cape Town as Legislative, Bloemfontein as Judicial, and Pretoria (Tswane) as Executive
- Geopolitical borders with Namibia, Lesotho, Swaziland, Zimbabwe, Mozambique, and Botswana
- Total size is equivalent to the size of the state of Texas (USA)
- South Africa has fossil evidence of humankind that dates back several million years—modern human beings have lived in South Africa for over 100,000 years

Southern Africa (for this book)

- Includes Lesotho, Botswana, Swaziland, Mozambique, Namibia, Angola, Zimbabwe, Zambia, Malawi, and Island of Madagascar[11]
- South Africa is the dominant nation-state in this region, with the largest economy, most active music and film industry (see Chapter 3)
- Total population: about 140 million people
- Wide range of European and African languages spoken e.g. French, Portuguese, German, Afrikaans, Shona, Ndebele, Siswati, Setswana, Sesotho
- Rich mineral resources
- Several types of terrain: coastal, mountainous, savannah, tropical, and desert

African Continent

- 10 percent of world's population, 25 percent of which lives in urban areas
- 3,000 ethnic groups
- 1,000 indigenous languages and thousands of dialects
- European languages: English, French, German, Portuguese, and Italian. Also Asian and Arabic dialects
- Development of languages forged from cultural contact—Afrikaans is one of these
- All major world religions represented and thousands of indigenous religious groups, Pentecostalism one of the fastest growing religious practices today
- New technologies, particularly Internet and cellular phone technologies, are revolutionizing life on the African continent
- Second largest continent in area covered in the world, with the most number of independent countries—fifty-four in total
- Home to the world's largest desert, the Sahara, and longest river, the Nile
- Generally agreed among scholars that Africa was home to the earliest origins of humankind

Imagining Africa Musically from a South African Perspective

Reestablishing political, economic, and cultural ties with the region and the continent as a whole has been one of the goals of the post-apartheid government in South Africa. Many of those formerly inaccessible places in the rest of Africa have opened up to South Africans over the last ten to fifteen years, and the **African National Congress**-led government has developed significant partnerships both with Southern Africa as a region and the rest of Africa—combining business, cultural, and technological goals, and increasing access with improved air travel and technological ties between South Africa and other parts of Africa. As a result, ten years after assembling the first iteration of materials that were transformed from course notes at the University of KwaZulu Natal in the mid-1990s into chapters in a book that would also address North American students, it is hard to think about South African music *without* being aware of the country's relationship to neighboring and more remote countries in Africa.

This is not a completely novel formulation, though its context of articulation has certainly shifted. In the early part of the twentieth century, African music collector and broadcaster Hugh Tracey, missionary the Rev. A. M. Jones, and anthropologist Alan P. Merriam were interested in "African Music" as a unified entity. But what constituted "African" in that era was implicitly a racial identification—people called "African" were those living in Africa, not of European, or Asian descent. In the early twentieth-century accounts of the work of these men, there is very little sense of the "voice" or "perspective" of the African musician. Everything was written in a more "scientific" and "objective" style, i.e., they were largely concerned with the positivism of early comparative musicology—measuring pitch, scales, intervals; examining instrument structure, discussing the relationship between one instrument type and another, and searching for origins. With a few exceptions, from the 1950s through the 1980s when books on "African popular music" began to be written, this approach differed from the more individualized studies of particular places, musicians, and cultures that started to be published in the late 1950s.[12]

It behooves us, then, to examine the recorded and written archive from the early part of the twentieth century, to reflect on how South Africa's musical relationship to the rest of the continent was institutionalized through the extraordinary travels of South African resident Hugh Tracey from the 1920s through the 1970s. Born in 1903 in Devonshire, England, instead of going to one of the British universities to be educated, he went to Zimbabwe with his brother, Leonard, to farm tobacco. While there Hugh Tracey learned a local language, Karanga, and began to sing and transcribe songs of Karanga farmworkers. This began a lifelong love affair with the traditional music of Africa, a passion begun in Zimbabwe, but which incorporated all of Southern Africa and much of sub-Saharan Africa. His first recordings of African music, some of the first of African music ever, were made of Zimbabwean men in Johannesburg in 1929. Columbia Records (based in London) made the recordings on a visit to South Africa. These recordings were then sent to jazz talent scout and record producer John Hammond who was working for CBS in New York City, and just beginning his concert series, "From Spirituals to Swing," in Carnegie Hall in 1938. It was Hugh Tracey's recording of African drumming that opened the first of these Carnegie Hall performances.[13] With these concerts Hammond was insisting on a clear place for jazz, and a distinctive African American presence, in

American history. Hugh Tracey's recordings suggested those ties ran all the way back to the African continent—several decades before the Civil Rights movement and the work of critics like Amiri Baraka and Franky Kofsky. Nevertheless, even if juxtaposing African drumming with a performance of spirituals, the blues, and swing was an inherently politicized gesture, the "African" in Tracey's conception of the music referenced the musical and cultural dimensions, rather than political and economic, because Africa in the early twentieth century was under European colonial rule.

The archive left by Hugh Tracey, his International Library of African Music (ILAM), the "Sound of Africa" series, the smaller "Music of Africa" series, the African Music Society, and *African Music*, the official journal of the Society all founded by Tracey, provide a rich starting point for reflecting on the twentieth-century archive of African music, the music of Southern Africa, and South Africa specifically. The life and work of this British-born man who came to love the music of Africa with a passion that divided him from most of his White peers in his lifetime touches all four levels of analysis: the national, regional, continental, and the world-at-large. Though his work and contribution continue to invoke criticism and debate in South Africa, there is no doubt that Tracey was a man of extraordinary vision, zeal, and sheer productivity.

A small digression before continuing: I recall sitting at the University of Zululand in the mid-1990s at the annual Symposium for South African Ethnomusicology, a symposium started by Hugh Tracey's son Andrew in 1981. We were fresh out of the apartheid era, an era in which much of the work of ethnomusicology in South Africa had been dominated by White South Africans, Europeans, and Americans. At that meeting, deep in the heart of many significant sites of Zulu cultural pride and history, the International Library of African Music came under heavy scrutiny from many of those attending the Symposium. Delegates wanted to know, for example, if ILAM was actually the personal property of the Tracey family, what the "African" in ILAM referred to, and why there wasn't better public access to the contents of the archive. There were several intense and awkward encounters in the course of the meeting that year. The outcome of the encounter, however, has been quite extraordinary, and its fruits are being made visible through the worldwide web. See the virtual site of the International Library of African Music for yourself at http://ilam.ru.ac.za. You might also visit the Smithsonian Institution's Global Sound site: http://www.smithsonianglobalsound.org, where you will find on that site close to 1000 tracks of African music recorded by Tracey, made available worldwide by ILAM. The Library is currently digitizing hundreds of photographs taken by Hugh and Andrew Tracey, putting the tables of content of *African Music* and the *Proceedings of the Symposiums on Ethnomusicology* online. Finally, ILAM has partnered with SWP Records in the Netherlands to reissue the "Music of Africa" recordings on CD, a collection I discuss further below.

In 1931, on a trip to London, Hugh Tracey met composers Gustav Holst and Ralph Vaughan Williams, both of whom encouraged him to just get the music of Africa recorded, and to worry about its use in transmission and cultural identity later. He followed their advice by prioritizing recording. He began securing Carnegie Foundation funding from the South African Director of Native Development, Harold Jowitt, that enabled him to undertake field research from June 1932 to July 1933 in Zimbabwe. He recorded 600 tracks on aluminum discs. Tracey made several more recordings of Zimbabwe traditional and town music in this period and, alongside Rev. A. M. Jones, who published the seminal text "African Music" in 1934, set in motion the recording of and research into Zimbabwean music, very soon to incorporate much of Central and Southern Africa as well.

Few Black Africans at the time were sufficiently interested in their own traditional music on record, perhaps because they were still performing much of this music on a regular basis, so the industry didn't see the production of thousands of copies as commercially viable. Tracey's solution: travel to South Africa and begin a broadcasting career. He used the microphone to spread his love for the music of Africa to South African radio audiences. Despite the sense that African music would not sell, Tracey's next financier was none other than Eric Gallo, the man who founded Gallo Records. Gallo agreed to press and release portions of Tracey's growing archive—some of which would become commercial hits for the company.

In 1948 Tracey and anthropologist Winifred Hoernle formed the African Music Society; in 1953 they created a headquarters for the organization in Roodepoort, South Africa, with Gallo underwriting the finances for the move. In 1953, while lecturing in Britain, Tracey was awarded a grant from the Nuffield Foundation, and further support from the mines in the Democratic Republic of Congo, Zimbabwe, and South Africa, to establish a non-profit organization, the International Library of African Music, which is now housed at Rhodes University in Grahamstown. From that library, and with support from the United States State Department and the Ford Foundation, Tracey was able to issue a "Sound of Africa Series"—an academic collection of 210 long playing disks—and a shorter "Music of Africa Series," both of which are currently being digitized and reissued by the International Library of African Music and the Smithsonian Global Sound digital archive.[14] An archive built prior to the "world music" marketing category invented in the mid-1980s, Tracey's collections were deposited in university libraries around the world.

There were many sides to the historical figure of Hugh Tracey. Clearly he was a man of his times who operated in a transnational, Anglo-American network of White men who did the work, and other White men who financed it. Though he was not trained in musicology as such, Hugh Tracey produced several books, which continue to be available through ILAM. One in particular provides an early model of African musical ethnography: *Chopi Musicians: Their Music, Poetry and Instruments* (1948).[15] Unlike many of his contemporaries, however, Tracey strongly believed that the European and American missions in Africa had been bad for Africa and her music. Tracey understood the artistic and humanistic value of contemporary forms of music-making, and viewed the increasingly audible sounds of the northern hemisphere, and of American popular music specifically, as a destructive presence for the continent.

In response to the rapid urbanization of African performance, Hugh Tracey, through his recording projects, broadcast activity, the African Music Society, and the journal, *African Music*, gathered a small group of like-minded men around him. His chief concerns were largely pragmatic and preservationist: to build an archive of the music of Africa—which he recognized as being under threat; to write textbooks on African Music for use in schools—as such he devised an "African Music Textbook Project" to encourage African universities to teach African music to their students (rarely done in Africa for most of the twentieth century, with notable exceptions); and to analyze the music.

When Hugh Tracey died in 1977, his son Andrew succeeded him as Director of the International Library of African Music. Andrew's real passion was the music of the *mbira*—in performance and history—particularly the diffusion of the instrument throughout the African continent and elsewhere in the world. He was a driving force behind the creation of the Symposiums on Ethnomusicology, the first of which was held in 1981 with a handful of interested people. ILAM took responsibility for publishing the proceedings of the Symposiums. Andrew Tracey linked ILAM to Rhodes University's Department of Music; he also collaborated with American ethnographic filmmaker Gei Zantzinger on several projects pertaining to Chopi xylophone musicians (from Mozambique and the mines of Johannesburg), and *mbira* performances in Zimbabwe specifically. Zantzinger later collaborated with Southern African music specialist David Coplan on a film about Basotho migrant workers' "auriture" i.e., oral performances, and made a film on Cape Verdean music prior to his death in 2006.

The work of Hugh Tracey remains the most comprehensive archive of sub-Saharan African music in the world. With the growing restrictions placed on the movement of people, both inside South Africa, and within Southern Africa by the apartheid regime (1948–1990), it became increasingly impossible to continue the kind of recording projects undertaken by Hugh Tracey, or to replicate his vision elsewhere. Those who continued researching the music of Africa increasingly located themselves in single sites, working in greater depth with individual communities. In the 1950s, John Blacking arrived in South Africa and began his work amongst the Venda peoples—though he was banned by the apartheid government because of his illegal relationship with his soon-to-be wife, a woman of Indian descent; David Rycroft spent many years working with Zulu language materials—from the bow songs of Princess Magogo to his work on the boundaries between speech and song in ***izibongo*** (Zulu praise poetry), to the formation of urban styles of traditional music in South Africa. Jacques Malan edited the multi-art *Encyclopedia of South African Music*, with a substantial entry on "**Bantu Composers**" by SABC employee Yvonne Huskisson, though the volume privileged European music-making and history in South Africa. As director of music programming at the SABC, Huskisson would update the entries on Black South African composers in several subsequent publications. Anthropologist Thomas Johnston and musicologist Christopher Ballantine conducted research on traditional instrumental genres in the 1970s; Jonathan Clegg on Zulu ***maskanda*** and ***isishameni*** dance styles; and Deborah James on the music of migrant women in Johannesburg. It was not until the early 1980s, with the arrival of German ethnomusicologist Veit Erlmann as the first ethnomusicologist to be hired at a South African university, that South African music research began to really flourish. From the 1980s on, universities like KwaZulu Natal, Cape Town, and Wits would become the centers of insider- and outsider-research into a whole range of South African music—much of it focused on the music of unwritten traditions, and of Black South Africans. **Afrikaans**-medium universities like the University of the Free State, Pretoria University, and the University of Port Elizabeth had tended to focus their research on White South African art and other music—mostly that of Afrikaans-speaking White South Africans—certainly through the early 1990s. For the most part, this work remained tied to particular genres, communities, or categories of performance: *maskanda*, *isicathamiya*, gumboot dance, *marabi*, ***kwela***, South African jazz, Indian popular music,

White folk song, Coloured working-class culture and so forth (see Parts II and III for select discussion of these styles). Writing comprehensive, dialogical narratives of South African music that truly represent all of its people has remained elusive for those of us working in the area, for a host of reasons discussed at the end of this chapter. None of our scholarship has yet reflected on South Africa's musical relationships to the rest of the African continent.

Imagining Southern African Music via South Africa

Reflecting on South African music in relationship to the Southern African region became possible in the 1990s, when the military offensive pursued by the South African Defense Force under the apartheid regime against neighboring countries was halted. Instead of viewing our neighbors as threatening hotbeds of resistance to the apartheid government, South Africans have experienced the in migration—legal and illegal—of citizens of these states into the country over the last decade. Legislation about languages that emerged in the early 1990s, when South Africa moved from having two official languages—English and Afrikaans—to eleven, enabled South Africans to begin to understand their deeper ties to the Southern African subcontinent. Of the eleven official African languages (amidst many more that are spoken in the country or represent the linguistic heritage of many of its citizens), at least five reference those spoken in neighboring nation-states: Ndebele (Zimbabwe), Siswati (Swaziland), Batswana (Botswana), Tsonga (Mozambique, whose speakers moved from present-day Zimbabwe), Sesotho (Lesotho), pointing to the historical ties between native speakers in South Africa and those living in the region. Furthermore, the assertion of the rights of the Khoisan/Bushmen in post-apartheid South Africa has reminded South Africans that the traditional music of these "Bushmen" is distributed across Namibia, Angola, South Africa, Botswana, and Lesotho. Similarly, studies of the musical bow incorporate every country I have included in defining Southern Africa; and each of these places has assimilated the guitar into its local repertory, indigenizing its sound and style according to local musical conventions. Though it is not my intention to expand the conversation on regionalism in this book, beyond drawing attention to its significance, there are many other musical connections that transcend contemporary political borders between states.[16]

Traces of these ties can be found in two volumes on South African traditional music, published seventy years apart, Percival Kirby's *Musical Instruments of the Native Races of South Africa* (1934) and Laurie Levine's *The Drumcafe's Traditional Music of South Africa* (2005). Both implicitly underscore the linguistic, musical, and historical connections between those currently living in South Africa, and their distant relatives residing elsewhere in the region. It is clear that an updated version of Kirby's research for the twenty-first century on the musical instruments of Southern Africa is needed, and could provide a stimulating comparative narrative to the seminal work of almost a century ago. Nevertheless, Kirby's volume is an important cornerstone in the constitution of a canon of works on Southern African music in the twentieth century, creating unity across the instrumental practices of the "native races" through the classification of instrument types. A work of its historical moment—the "native races" are juxtaposed with the "Europeans" in an us–them binary typical of its era—it is particularly important for three reasons: for the scope and depth of research into instrumental performance in a region that is clearly dominated by vocal music; for the pre-twentieth-century record of African performance Kirby cites in the course of his commentary; and finally, for the comprehensive treatment of musical genres by a single researcher. Almost a century later, the archive of information created by Kirby is unparalleled, and still widely referenced. Laurie Levine's recently published counterpart is a well intentioned but strange, even naïve, text. Levine creates the mirror image of Kirby's work: where Kirby organizes chapters by instrument category, Levine divides her material by "tribe"—she calls them ethnic or language groups, but in effect she might as well call her categories of people "tribes." As such, it is not clear why "South African" doesn't include those of Indian, Chinese, Coloured, or European descent—a surprising gesture in a post-apartheid context of publication. What of the music of Levine's own "tribe?" Whatever its weaknesses, the useful part of the book is the earlier history of each language group/tribe she discusses.[17]

In the mid-1950s a group of archeologists and other researchers at the University of the Witwatersrand in Johannesburg formed the Kalahari Research Committee, a study group funded by the British Nuffield Foundation. Chaired by Philip Tobias, the group ventured into the Kalahari Desert to study the "Bushmen" or Khoisan peoples. This work triggered interest in the United States and Britain, notably from the Harvard-based Marshall family in the United States, and several British scholars, all of whom began work in the Kalahari. Nicholas England was one of the first to write about Khoisan music (1995), though many others would extend this research on the music, dance, and healing practices of the Kalahari Bushmen. It was one of the few bodies of scholarship that cut across nation-states in Southern Africa at the time. Finally, we catch a glimpse of regional possibilities when we read about the formation of popular music styles, like *kwela* and ***mbaqanga*** (both discussed in Chapter 6), in neighboring states—Zimbabwe, Zambia, Mozambique—because of the dominance of South Africa's recording industry and radio transmission in the region.

Nevertheless, until very recently with the visions of the South African Music Project and the reconstituted Society for Research in South African Music, it was historians and literary critics rather than ethnomusicologists or African musicologists who most coherently conceived of Southern Africa as a conceptual and cultural entity. Historians Leroy Vail and Landeg White were the first to publish a volume (1991) that examined "Southern African voices in history," a book which purposefully considers the unifying aesthetic principles across the region. Vail and White argue for the importance of poetic license because the poetic is privileged as a mechanism for articulating the conventionally unsayable. "The advantages of this argument are that it establishes the continuity of a particular poetic tradition over a wide area of Southern Africa and over a long period of time, linking together types of poetic performance—praise songs, entertainments, satire, work songs, possession songs—that have hitherto been described separately" (Vail and White 1991: 319). The volume interrogates songs as "maps of experience": Ndebele and Swazi royal praises, song and history amongst Timbuka women in Malawi, and the oral history of Paiva, a Mozambiquan worker song.

Vail and White were followed by Liz Gunner's edited collection, *Politics and Performance: Theater, Poetry and Song in Southern Africa* (1994). Gunner doesn't specifically think through the unifying elements of Southern African performance, certainly not with the sense of purpose conveyed by Vail and White. She is quite loosely interested in a range of themes that emerge out of the individual contributions to the volume: performance and politics, identity, gender, the agency of audiences, scripted versus unscripted performance, and the question of state control. Each country remains a world unto itself contained "in Southern Africa"—there is little sense of overarching ties that bind individual states into regional unity.

Then came literary historian Michael Chapman's tome: *Southern African Literatures* (1996), a comprehensive and theoretically astute intervention. South Africa is clearly the dominant force for literary production in Chapman's account, but his coverage has historical depth and a certain largesse, even if the literature he writes about is all in the English language, either originally or in translation. The core idea that unites the region, according to Chapman, is that

> the texts of politics have wanted to overwhelm the texts of art: that public events have confirmed a history of domination and resistance, in which ancient charters have felt the intrusion of harsh, modernizing forces. This modern pattern begins with Bushmen hunter-gatherers and Khoi pastoralists—the earliest people of the region—having to defend themselves against expanding African groups (the descendants of iron-age Bantu-speaking people) and from the seventeenth century against encroaching Dutch trekboers . . . (Chapman 1996: 1)

Chapman ties "forms of literature" to particular social events in order to fully reflect the centuries of dominance, cultural encounters, voice-overs, and innovative responses to the often impossible circumstances. Finally, there is a volume edited by Duncan Brown (1999), *Oral Literature and Performance in Southern Africa*. Focused less on the political and more on the medium of transmission, Brown engages with the methodological and epistemological challenges in constituting a body of literature in South Africa that is both written and performed. There is little reference to historical specificity in his conceptualization of the region as a totality.

Imagining South Africa Musically

We are well into the second decade of a democratically elected government in a country whose constitution is one of the most progressive in the world: it is one that strives to represent and protect the linguistic, cultural, religious, economic, and legal rights and interests of all of its peoples. The last three decades, since 1980, have seen an exponential growth of research, recording, and publication on many of South Africa's most popular and enduring musical traditions and commercial genres.[18] This work, in partnership with the political transformation, and the pivotal place of the *Graceland* album in South African music history, the recent legal triumphs over the "Mbube"/"The Lion Sleeps Tonight" copyright issues have opened a place for South Africans in the "world music" industry abroad.

The question we need to ask at this point is whether we can forge a sense of a unified nation through an account of the music made by and in South Africa in the twentieth century? We are confronted with the extraordinary levels of diversity and difference—

linguistic, cultural, class, gendered, and religious—among those living in South Africa, as well as the fact that there has been significant movement of South African musicians from South Africa to elsewhere in the world. These factors pose, I believe, a significant challenge to those of us striving to write about South Africa's musical past. Can we create a cohesive canvas of the past, even though such cohesion was impossible to experience because of the divided way in which we lived? How might we construct a narrative about the twentieth century that is inclusive and fully representative?

The **Truth and Reconciliation Commission** was South Africa's attempt to move forward out of the atrocities of the apartheid era; one of the spin-offs was the restoration of narrative to the nation (see Ndebele 1998). Once the foundations of the apartheid regime had been dismantled, ordinary people were free to tell a story that wasn't just about apartheid; creative writers were free to let the imagination play in a world outside of apartheid; and ultimately, South Africans could begin to imagine what a collective memory of South Africa's very divided past might look and sound like. Providing access to education for all was a mechanism for righting the wrongs of **Bantu education** and the privileges of White education. Linguistic diversity has been accounted for by granting official status to nine more languages than previously represented South Africans. What of music? How do we recuperate a sense of a national past in the field of music, a field in which so many of its main creators, performers, producers, and distributors are no longer with us—either because they died destitute, often unrecorded, and certainly barely recognized for their creative contribution in South Africa, or because they left the country for greener pastures? How do we move forward with a vision for the future in music for all South Africans if we have not yet accounted for the full range of twentieth-century history: across more than eleven language groups, many genres—local, imported, and in hybrid forms; amongst the working class and the elite; through censorship and celebration; and even in the condition of exile? Voluntary and involuntary exile scattered South African music and musicians quite literally across the globe: into the African continent, particularly for the post-1976 Soweto generation who joined Umkhonto weSizwe—the armed wing of the African National Congress Youth League; into northern Europe—Sweden and Denmark in particular; and into other parts of Europe, the former Soviet Union, Cuba, and the United States. By what means do we begin to think about the complexity of South African music in the twentieth century when it presents such a dense and complicated terrain of investigation?

In the early 1990s, the White-controlled South African music industry imagined the concept of **cross-over**, an international industry term to talk about the movement across marketing categories, such as religious to popular, or rock to rap, being used to local ends. In an effort to forge the capacity for a kind of musical national unity they talked about the "cross-over" of a Black artist, for example, into the White marketplace in South Africa. Covering a similar time period, new technologies such as the Internet, the worldwide web, and even cellular telephones have enabled us to circumscribe common space in new ways. Imagining particular configurations of communities, places, and peoples gets easier and easier with the unifying capacities of these technologies. Southern Africans are using the worldwide web, for example, to constitute a musical nation through virtual means: one website on "Zambian music" lists all the people who were born in Zambia, who may or may not still be living in that country, but are making it musically in the world. A Zambian woman living in China, others living in Europe, and the United States are all inserted into the virtual constituency called "Zambian music." The amateur video site YouTube has opened up all kinds of possibilities for people who cannot travel to faraway places, to watch video clips of music happening on the streets, in tourist zones, and other out-of-the-way sites, now just a URL, a keyword, and a click away. While we certainly cannot capture any in-depth scholarly analysis of the music as we view it, we are presented with a snapshot and a sound bite of what is happening in the world of amateur music making. In the early twenty-first century, we have extraordinary capacity to "see" what is happening the world over, without having to move away from our computer screens. And the African continent is a key player in this process, even if most of the video clips are not yet being made and displayed by Africans.

Perhaps the new possibilities afforded by technological innovation offer a series of novel modes of representing the musical past. Surely, the democratic imperative at this historical juncture in South African musical scholarship is to revisit the past we have created so far, from Kirby and Tracey through to the newest research embodied in recently conceived journals of African music—the *Journal of the Musical Arts of Africa*, *Muziki*, *South African Music Scholarship*, and the revived *African Music*—and to give equal voice and representative space to all of the music made in and by South Africans in the twentieth century. We need to gather the stories, recordings, and images of all, both inside and well beyond the geopolitical borders of the nation. To capture an image of how this might be produced, we might visualize a map of the world created in HTML. The map would highlight a range of places in South Africa, tracing the travels of South African musicians and styles between towns and countryside, in the Republic, neighboring countries in Southern Africa, through the continent, and out into the world at large. We could focus on particular sites—the communities, recording studios, and performance venues that have historical significance—enabling a kind of virtual tour around the country. As the virtual visitor stops at each site they might hear clips of people reminiscing, even bootleg copies of live performances. We might think too, about the sites of radio, television, and film transmission in neighboring states—like **LM Radio** beamed out of what was then Lourenco Marques (now Maputo) in Mozambique, or the sounds of the **Voice of America radio** so popular in post-World War II South Africa. The technology of the worldwide web provides a user-friendly mechanism for tracking the routes of those who went into exile. Through the web, consumers will be able to listen to their stories, read the reviews of their performances, and hear their music in ways it was impossible to do in lived experience.

Ultimately, we are not as concerned about these pasts for the sake of history, but more as mechanisms for recognizing the richness of that past, the funny stories about what made it and what didn't, the tragedies of life as a musician, and indeed of some of the roaring successes of musicians, producers, and distributors who left South Africa but have made it big in other parts of the world. We will never really have viable visions for the future in South African music until we have a rich and textured, full-bodied understanding of how we have come to the place we presently inhabit in the early twenty-first century.

Keywords (words that appear in boldface in the body of the text)

African National Congress majority political party in South Africa

Afrikaans a language that developed out of the encounter between European colonists and Arabic-speaking slaves and exiles from Indonesia

arrangements newly conceived versions of a musical piece or performance

Bantu composers the term used to describe Black South African composers (largely of choral music) in the apartheid era

Bantu education describes the kind of inferior education provided for Black South Africans under apartheid

***Billboard* Top 100** used as a measure of a song's popularity and commercial value; *Billboard* has been the central trade publication of the music industry in the twentieth century

cadence the sequence of pitches and chords that signal the end of a passage of music

call and response musical structure in which a leader sings a melodic phrase (the call) and a group of singers repeats the call as response. Often the line sung by the group starts before the line sung by the leader is complete, resulting in overlapping musical phrases—see below

close-harmony singers a popular music style in which single-sex voices harmonize their parts in four or more parts; barbershop quartets are a good example of this style

copies are commonly generated when individuals and communities of people want to learn how to perform popular music. Typically a musician or singer will try to emulate the original, either heard live or more commonly through repeated listening to the radio or a recording

covers are versions of popular songs that are sung in imitation of a song already popularized by a better-known group

cross-over is a term used by the music industry to talk about a song or recording originally classified in one marketing category—classical music, for example—that unexpectedly or intentionally sells large quantities in another category—like "world" or "popular." It takes on a particular meaning in South Africa—when it is used in racial terms—where a Black singer, like Margaret Singana for example, sells high numbers of recordings to White consumers

cyclical structure a musical form that repeats endlessly, without clearly articulated structural points of beginning and ending. It is a form that doesn't move from point A to point B, but seems to continuously return and start over again

doo-wop 1950s street-singing in which a rhythm and blues melody is harmonized with nonsense syllables

four-part harmony a style emerging out of the Bach Chorale tradition, where voices are divided by function and register in soprano, alto, tenor, and bass, a structure modified and indigenized in twentieth-century South Africa, e.g., in *isicathamiya* performance

Gallo until 2006 when Warner International bought the company and its archives, Gallo Music was the most important recording enterprise in South Africa.

global economy refers to the interconnected nature of the marketplace into which

South African music has been inserted, and through which South Africans have consumed music from elsewhere in the world

guitar-like instruments in Southern Africa, guitars have been copied in a variety of materials and configurations, particularly by those who could not afford to purchase their own instruments. Many musicians start their musical careers on cheap replicas of the original instruments

harmonic cycle a chord structure that repeats over and over

homophonically the musical texture that best describes singing in four-part harmony—there is a dominant melodic line in the soprano, with the other three voices singing in harmonic support of the melody

improvised often used in contrast to music that has been pre-composed, improvised music is that which is played in the moment, where musicians draw on previously rehearsed musical materials. Improvised music often indicates that there are no two performances that are ever exactly the same (other than those which have been recorded)

isicathamiya also called *mbube* after the "Mbube"/"Wimoweh" hit of the mid-1930s in South Africa, is the close-harmony a cappella male singing made famous by Ladysmith Black Mambazo

isishameni a song and dance style from the Midlands of KwaZulu Natal, a style valued by Ladysmith Black Mambazo leader Joseph Shabalala

izibongo a Zulu word referring to praise poetry

kwela pennywhistle music of 1940s and 1950s South Africa

LM Radio a commercial radio station beamed out of Maputo/Lourenco Marques, Mozambique in the mid-twentieth century

marabi working-class music created and performed in illegal drinking establishments or shebeens in 1920s and 1930s South Africa

maskanda a Zulu musician, usually a guitarist, musical bow, or violin player; also refers to the style of music played by such a musician

mbaqanga originally referenced African/township jazz, increasingly came to mean the studio produced, government controlled sounds of 1960s Zulu pop

mbiras lamellophones commonly found in Africa, consisting of a wooden sounding board with several iron tongues arranged on the sounding board, often enhanced by rattling bottle tops, and inserted into a gourd amplifier

migrant worker a person who moves from rural to urban areas, or from one country to another, in search of work, and who returns home on occasion

musical bows derived from hunting bows, these instruments can be bowed, plucked, or struck with a bow. They are typically solo instruments, on which a solo singer accompanies him/herself

Nguni the collective word that includes Zulu, Xhosa, Sotho, and Tswana speaking peoples of Southern Africa

pentatonic the five-toned scale used for song composition

phrase overlap often in a call and response and cyclical musical structure, phrases that overlap are those that start before the preceding phrase has come to an end

polyphonic literally means more than one voice, typically a polyphonic texture is one in which several parts (voices) of sounds interact independently of each other

royalties the money paid to composers for the sale of their works

South African Broadcast Corporation (SABC) the government controlled and publicly funded (through taxes) media corporation, that continues under new leadership in contemporary South Africa

staggered entries a musical texture where one voice starts, and others enter later: they do not begin simultaneously

Tracey, Hugh African music collector, record producer, and founder of the International Library of African Music (ILAM)

transnational a process which extends over several nations, states or corporations

Truth and Reconciliation Commission a commission of inquiry established between 1990 and 1994 to investigate crimes against humanity committed under the apartheid government (1948–1990)

unison musical parts functioning as one voice i.e., all singing/playing the same pitch simultaneously

Voice of America radio radio programming aired in many countries around the world to spread ideas of American democratic culture around the world

world music a marketing category created by the music industry in the mid-1980s to sell music that was not part of the popular music mainstream.

CHAPTER 2
Twentieth-Century Political History

The year 1994 must surely stand as a momentous year in South African and, indeed, in global history, for it was the year that South Africa finally moved towards a fully **democratic dispensation** for all her people. With this date in mind, I begin this chapter by referring you to figure 2.1. It is a picture of a group of Black South African women singing, their hands extended in the air. The singers are dressed in brightly colored robes. The choir uniforms are not just arbitrary colors, however. These women have wrapped their bodies in the design and colors of the South African flag, the symbol of the birth of a new nation in 1994. This newly designed flag is also a reminder of the new South African Constitution, which was hammered out in the 1990s to protect men, women, and children of all races and creeds from violation by other citizens and by the state itself. Both the constitution and the flag are signs of newfound rights and freedoms, mostly achieved at great cost: many people were injured, abused, or destroyed in the fight for a new political order in South Africa. Wrapping their bodies in the design and colors of the flag symbolizes the protection that the women hope will be guaranteed by the new flag. Both the flag and the constitution are now held to be sacred by all South Africans.

In this particular context, I am told, the women in the photograph were singing South Africa's newly composed national anthem, an anthem forged out of two separate anthems sung previously by groups in a divided South Africa. The first is **"Nkosi sikelel'iAfrika,"** the official national anthem of the African National Congress and several other countries in Africa. It is a song sung in at least two languages: typically Zulu or Xhosa and Sesotho. That anthem was skillfully combined with the apartheid regime's national anthem, **"Die Stem" (The Call)**, also regularly sung in two languages—English and Afrikaans. In other words, much like the newly formed democratic nation in South Africa, while the constituent parts of the anthem are not new, the manner in which each part has been woven together to create a single anthem is what has changed. The women in the photograph performed on the steps in front of the Union Buildings, the legislative seat of government in Pretoria. The Union Buildings were initially built to celebrate the unity of English- and

Figure 2.1 South African women sing their national anthem, wearing robes printed with the South African flag. Photo © David Turnley/CORBIS

Afrikaans-speaking peoples of European descent in the early twentieth century. They have become something different as they have been covered afresh with the memories of the inauguration of the first Black South African president, Nelson Mandela, on May 10, 1994, an event mass-mediated to the wider world through the channels of Cable News Network (CNN) and the South African Broadcast Corporation (SABC).

South African Music and Apartheid

Segregation under British rule in South Africa, and then apartheid, profoundly impacted on all South Africans, and certainly on all musical traditions and production from the late nineteenth century through to the present. **Apartheid**, legalized racial discrimination, was established by a body of laws made by a minority of people of European and British descent in response to their fears of living in a country where the majority of the people were of Black African descent. The White minority was largely educated, while most Black South Africans had had very little exposure to European forms of education. British mining interests controlled a large portion of the economy, and from 1948 through 1990, those of European—Dutch, German, French, and Portuguese—descent, called Afrikaners, ran the government. In other words, if you are to come to an understanding of musical performance in the twentieth century you will have to have some knowledge of the making and dismantling of the apartheid system of government. This chapter provides an overview of the twentieth-century legislation that both brought the apartheid government into being and kept it in place, and then it tells of the laws that brought democracy to all South Africans in 1994, and the subsequent actions that have helped to build South Africa's presence in Southern Africa, the African continent, and the world at large.

Apartheid legislation

The year 1948 marked the coming to power of a group of Europeans whose ancestors had begun to settle in South Africa from the mid-seventeenth century. This period of settlement and colonization in South Africa is considerably earlier than in many other parts of Africa, an important point if you are to gain some sense of the depth of "Europeanization" of the region on one hand, but also in some ways for the degree of "Africanization" of parts of its settler communities on the other. By extension, it means that African musical traditions are often deeply imbued with European musical instruments or forms, even though these traditions are now viewed after centuries of practice as more African than European. Noteworthy too is the fact that while it is often assumed that apartheid has defined South Africa for its entire history (it was first settled by the Dutch in 1652), it did not become state policy until 1948 and began to be officially dismantled in the late 1980s. Certainly, racial segregation was common practice and sometimes legislated between 1652 and 1948, but the move towards a deeply oppressive system of governance began in 1948 when White South Africans voted the Afrikaner Nationalists into power. The political environment in South Africa, like that of the United States, underwent continuous transformation in the course of the twentieth century. Musical performance often reflected, resisted, or predicted these changes in remarkable ways. It is true, nonetheless, that ideas about linguistic, cultural, and racial difference, and frequently extremely racist sensibilities, characterized the colonization by Europeans of various parts of Africa, Asia, and the Americas, mostly in the nineteenth century.

While the new rulers in 1948 called themselves the Afrikaner Nationalist Party, their goal was *not* to forge a single nation out of the enormous diversity of South Africa's

Several films and recordings were issued in the 1990s and early 2000s that tell the story of the apartheid years, largely through the spoken word and through musical performance, particularly, though not exclusively, from the perspective of Black South Africans—those who were arguably the most affected by the system of government. The South African Broadcast Corporation (SABC) issued a single CD titled: *The Voice of Nelson Mandela: Extras from Famous Speeches* (1999). A two CD package, *Long Walk to Freedom* (2002; the same title as Mandela's autobiography), provides a representative sample of South African music from the 1960s to the 1990s—the era of "Grand Apartheid" when the worst effects of apartheid were felt by South Africans. Finally, American filmmaker Lee Hirsch directed a powerful film about the central place of music in the anti-apartheid struggle, titled *Amandla! Revolution in Four-Part Harmony* (2002). The soundtrack to the film is also available on CD, though the film is the more powerful document.

inhabitants. Even though White South Africans had fought a bloody conflict with each other in the Anglo-Boer War (1899–1902), where the English had confined many Boer (meaning "farmer")/Afrikaans women and children in concentration camps, killing thousands, the two groups created the Union of South Africa in 1910. In 1948 the Nationalist government sought to build a nation for "White" people only on this union of people of British and European descent. Building on earlier legislation made by the English-dominated South African government, the Nationalist plan for Bantu-speaking peoples, the numerical majority in South Africa, was to use them as labor in a rapidly growing modern economy based on agriculture and industry, but not to allow them permanent residence in White urban areas. This was modernity without its accompanying practice of democracy. While they might spend most of their lives working in the urban areas, the status of the Bantu-speaking people was always "temporary" and even that was permitted only with the correct documentation: all non-Europeans were required to carry the infamous **pass** (also called ***dompas***) on their person at all times or face jail time or deportation back to their **"homeland."**

The policy of apartheid has been called a kind of social engineering because what the Nationalist government increasingly forced on South Africa was the opposite of the more natural processes of social practice, of people engaging with each other despite racial, cultural, and linguistic differences. Where early South African history is characterized by far more racial and cultural mixing or **creolization**, particularly after the arrival of Europeans in what became the city of Cape Town, the Nationalist government in the mid-twentieth century stressed racial purity and separation in order to divide South Africans. It drew on ideas that had been prevalent in Germany under Adolf Hitler: national socialism, racial purity, and White superiority. To expedite the creation of a society that conformed to these ideals, the Nationalist government introduced a series of laws starting in 1950 that tightened restrictions on non-Europeans and established strict geographical boundaries between people of different racial backgrounds, languages, and cultures. By 1960, the framework of the apartheid regime was in place, even though apartheid was not comprehensively enforced until March of that year when state forces massacred more than sixty Black South Africans protesting against the pass laws, in what is now remembered as the Sharpeville Massacre.

So under the apartheid plan, the "real" homes of people of African descent were found in one of the nine *Bantustans* or "homelands" created by the Nationalist government on a small portion of the total landmass of the country: at one point, 80 percent of the population inhabited only 13 percent of the land. Those employed in urban areas entered the city and its surroundings under a series of laws aimed at "influx control," which at the very least, required all Black South Africans to carry "passbooks" on their person at all times. (The nearest parallel in the United States is the use of one's driver's license as a form of identification that one carries around but "non-Europeans" in South Africa were constantly asked for their documentation and immediately punished by police if they failed to produce it.) Black South Africans were allowed to stay in the urban areas only if they had had ten years of permanent employment with a single employer, had lived in the area for fifteen years (and could prove it), or had been born there. If they fulfilled none of these requirements, they were not permitted to stay longer than seventy-two hours, after which they would be "deported" back to the "homeland."

Apartheid Legislation, Made and Unmade (1948–2007)

1948 English-dominated United Party loses election and Afrikaner Nationalists come to power.

1949 Prohibition of Mixed Marriages Act is passed; mission schools for Black South Africans come under scrutiny of Nationalist Party government.

1950 Immorality Act forbids sexual relations between Whites and any people of color; Population Registration Act introduces legalized racial classification—White, Coloured, Native, and Asiatic;[1] Group Areas Act divides the country into residential areas based on racial classification; Suppression of Communism Act defines "communist" as anyone hostile to the government; South African Communist Party dissolves; many join the African National Congress.

1951 Government legislation removes Coloureds from voters' roll; Bantu Authorities Act creates tribal and territorial authorities, re-tribalizing the African/Bantu population, i.e., making those living in urban areas return "home" to the rural areas where they were to take up their "tribal" ways.

1952 Native Laws Amendment Act extends **influx control** to all urban areas, meaning all non-Europeans are required to carry a reference book (called the pass or *dompass*—stupid pass) of ninety-six pages detailing work and residence rights; the Defiance Campaign, in which women protest the pass laws, begins.

1953 Public Safety Act enables Governor General to declare states of emergency and rule by decree.

1954 Native Resettlement Act allows for **forced removal** of Black residents from Sophiatown, Johannesburg, over five years. Bantu education legislation removes Black education from the control of the missions and places it in the hands of the apartheid government.

1955 African National Congress draws up Freedom Charter.

1956 Industrial Coalition Act reserves certain skilled jobs for Whites; government tries 156 ANC activists for treason in what becomes known as the Treason Trial.

1957 Union Jack—the flag of Britain—is removed as dual official flag of South Africa.

1958 National Party wins large majority in first all-White election; Black women and some White women protest the pass laws, and about 2,000 are arrested.

1959 South African **Prime Minister Hendrik Verwoerd** launches the "independent homelands" project, creating separate areas for each tribal/cultural group: for example, Transkei for Xhosa, Zululand for Zulus; Extension of University Education Bill excludes all non-Whites from White universities and creates separate universities for Blacks, Indians, and "Coloureds"—those of mixed racial heritage or married to someone of such mixing; Pan Africanist Congress (PAC) is formed with strong Black-consciousness focus.

1960 Police fire on PAC-inspired march against pass laws (Sharpeville Massacre), killing 60, wounding 178; Bantu Radio is established; United Nations Security Council calls on South African government to end apartheid.

1961 South Africa is proclaimed a Republic; Albert Luthuli, ANC President (1952–1967) receives **Nobel Peace Prize**; Treason Trial ends after four years, with all 156 ANC members found guilty.

1963 General Law Amendment Act allows police to arrest and detain suspects for ninety days without trial; police capture ANC underground leadership, including Nelson Mandela, Govan Mbeki, Walter Sizulu, and all are charged with sabotage (punishable by death without appeal); Transkei becomes self-governing.

1964 Mandela and others are sentenced to life in prison; South Africa is banned from participation at Olympic Games because of apartheid.

1965 Bantu Laws Amendment Act denies 7 million Black people the right to live inside South Africa except as temporary dwellers.

1967 Defence Amendment Act requires White South African men to undertake military service; Terrorism Act defines terrorism as anything that threatens law and order, and gives government unlimited power to arrest, detain, and try without jury.

1968 Black Consciousness Movement is constituted with Steve Biko as its first president.

1969 Bureau of State Security is established with wide investigative powers; newspapers are prohibited from reporting on Bureau activities.

1970 Bantu Homelands Citizenship Act makes all Black South Africans citizens of a tribal homeland, regardless of their place of birth.

1972 Bophutatswana, Ciskei, and Lebowa become independent homelands, with the KwaZulu part of present-day KwaZulu Natal as semi-autonomous.

1976 Television comes to South Africa; Soweto school children protest Afrikaans as medium of instruction (Soweto Uprising) and police fire on them, killing many and sparking months of protest countrywide.

1977 Steve Biko is detained under Terrorism Act and dies in jail of brain injuries.

1970–1980s Trade union and anti-apartheid activity; South African Defense Force activity in surrounding countries.

1983 United Democratic Front (UDF) is formed to coordinate resistance inside South Africa; United Nations resolves to blacklist foreign entertainers traveling to South Africa and Sun City.

1984 Archbishop Desmond Tutu, first Black leader of the Anglican Church in South Africa and an outspoken leader of the UDF (1931–present) is awarded Nobel Peace Prize; Tutu and others renew call for economic sanctions against South Africa.

1985 Political protesters are fired on; indefinite state of emergency declared; Congress of South African Trade Unions (COSATU) is formed; Paul Simon (American folk rock singer) travels in secret to South Africa to record with South African musicians.

1986 Pass laws, Prohibition of Mixed Marriages, and Prohibition of Political Interference acts all abolished; US Congress resolves to declare blanket **economic sanctions** against South Africa; Simon's collaborative *Graceland* album released.

1987 Political turbulence in KwaZulu Natal intensifies.

1988 Church leaders begin to assume role as spokesmen for political organizations.

1989 Frederik Willem de Klerk elected State President of South Africa (in a Whites only vote).

1990 State president F. W. de Klerk unbans political organizations, including ANC and PAC, announces release of Mandela and other political prisoners from prison; Separate Amenities Act repealed; state of emergency lifted.

1991–1992 CODESA I and II (Convention for a Democratic South Africa), vehicles to guide South Africa towards a democratic dispensation, are succeeded by the Negotiating Council, the council that will draft the new constitution.

1993	With old government still in power, Transitional Executive Council is formed to oversee transition to democracy. Nelson Mandela and President F. W. de Klerk jointly awarded the Nobel Peace Prize for their leadership in ending apartheid.
1994	First free democratic elections held April 27–29; Nelson Mandela is elected first Black president of South Africa, inaugurated May 10.
1995	Truth and Reconciliation Commission is called for by Mandela and legislated by South African Government of National Unity with the Promotion of National Unity and Reconciliation Act, No. 24, 1995.
1996	The new South African Constitution is ratified.
1998	Thabo Mbeki (b. 1942) is elected second Black South African president. A Presidential Job Summit is held in South Africa.
2002	Launch of the African Union, hosted by South Africa.
2003	Development Summit held in South Africa.
2004	South Africa hosts the Pan-African Parliament, and the third national elections retain Thabo Mbeki as President.

The rhetoric used by the Afrikaner Nationalists was one of "separate development": each cultural group would develop along its own lines and on its own terms in its separate areas. Each "homeland" was identified by language and culture: Zululand was for Zulu people, who must speak Zulu as their mother tongue and practice Zulu customs and traditions; Pondoland for the amaMpondo people; Transkei for the amaXhosa people; Bophutatswana for the baTswana. To this end, the government appointed "tribal" chiefs and administrators of these "homelands." They were paid by the Nationalist government and were largely puppets of the White government. At times, their political power was reinforced with the military power of the Nationalist government, though this was not acknowledged publicly.

By law, European South Africans owned most of the land in South Africa, in both rural and urban areas. Since agricultural production constituted a core piece of the South African economy, farms required Black labor to function efficiently. So the apartheid government created a set of laws that enabled White farmers to employ Black laborers while monitoring and controlling their movement. A Black South African could stay on a White farm (that is, a farm located in areas designated for Whites only) if employed by a farmer, but there was a quota system to control the numbers of Black workers on farms. It was on these farms that many of the more traditional Zulu-speaking men first heard the sounds of the banjo, ukelele, guitar, concertina, and violin. Typically, they heard European folk music on these instruments; some might even have learned to play this music for the Europeans. Ultimately, it was this encounter between the Afrikaans farmer, or "*boer*," and his Black laborers (often house servants), which came to constitute one strand of the history of *maskanda*, a genre of migrant performance discussed in Chapter 8.

Even those considered racially and culturally closer to Whites—officially labeled "Coloured" and "Asiatic" by the government—were separated from their White neighbors in urban areas by Group Areas legislation. Coloured people were primarily those of mixed racial heritage: many had come as slaves or political exiles from Central Africa and Asia; some were born out of interracial relationships between Black Africans and European settlers in South Africa. The Asiatic group was largely comprised of Indians who had initially arrived from India in the nineteenth century, either as indentured laborers or as free passengers. The Group Areas legislation allowed them to reside and work in urban areas, but they lived largely in racially segregated residential spaces.

To effect these new social divisions, millions of South Africans were forcibly moved from racially integrated into segregated areas. By 1972, 1.8 million people of African descent, 600,000 categorized as Coloured, Indian, and Chinese, and 40,000 Whites had been removed to facilitate the Group Areas Act. The government had brought into being about twenty separate laws that enabled forced removals, the harshest of which prevented Black South Africans from requesting a court interdict to prevent their removal. Sophiatown (Johannesburg), District Six (Cape Town), and Cato Manor (Durban) are perhaps the best-known communities destroyed through these processes. Composers have inscribed the memory of all three places in musicals written about the three areas.[2]

As you can imagine, this kind of rule of law impinged on the lives of every South African. South Africa is now in what State President Thabo Mbeki calls the "second decade of freedom." What confronts South Africa in the contemporary moment is not just ensuring the fundamental human rights of all its peoples in the political sense: there are further enormous challenges that confront all South Africans. Globalization impacts on the lives of all in South Africa, as does the HIV/AIDS epidemic, the digital divide, poverty, rampant crime in certain parts of the country, and the need to create an environment of sustainable development, of peace and greater stability for all its citizens.

Keywords

apartheid system of laws that forced people of different cultural and language backgrounds to live in separate places, and be treated unequally and often unjustly before the law in South Africa (1948–1990)

creolization often what happened in the early years of South African colonial occupation—a blending together of different cultural ways to create forms that were peculiar to the local environment

democratic dispensation though South Africa had held elections before, on April 27, 1994 the first democratic elections were held in which all South Africans over the age of 18 who had registered were eligible to cast their vote. This ended White rule in South Africa

"Die Stem" (The Call) the bilingual (English and Afrikaans) national anthem of apartheid South Africa

economic sanctions were applied against South Africa in an effort to cripple the economy and bring about political change during apartheid

forced removal many communities were destroyed by government decreed forced removals, sometimes to clear racially mixed slum areas, and other times to purge White neighborhoods of "other" racial groups

homeland in an attempt to keep all "non-Europeans" out of White space—83 percent of the total land mass of South Africa—the apartheid government created a series of

"Independent Homelands" also called "*Bantustans*," which were intended to be the "homes" of all Black South Africans according to language, culture, and so forth. This included those who had lived in White urban areas, who were then forced to return to their "home" lands if they lost their jobs, or didn't have written proof of employment. These "homelands" were not recognized by any significant world organization, like the United Nations

influx control a set of apartheid laws put in place to control the movement of Black South Africans in and out of White space, and urban areas in particular. These were repealed in the early 1990s

"Nkosi sikelel'iAfrika" meaning "God Bless Africa," is a hymn composed by Enoch Sontonga in several South African languages, used as an anthem of the liberation struggle in South Africa and elsewhere in Africa in the twentieth century. It has now been recomposed to incorporate "Die Stem" as a gesture of musical reconciliation in forging a democratic nation

Nobel Peace Prize has been awarded to four South Africans—Albert Luthuli, Archbishop Desmond Tutu, Nelson Mandela, and F. W. de Klerk. Each award has served to highlight the problems of apartheid and exert pressure from the international community on South Africa to change its policies

pass/*dompas* the documents required of all non-European South Africans when they traveled in South Africa under apartheid. Failure to produce the document for police resulted in jail time and/or deportation to one's "homeland."

Prime Minister Hendrik Verwoerd the architect of the apartheid regime

segregation racial discrimination prior to the apartheid era

CHAPTER 3
Twentieth-Century Entertainment History
Live and Mediated

State Broadcasting

In his much-cited book *Imagined Communities: On the Origins and Spread of Nationalism* (1983), Benedict Anderson argues that because of the size of the average **nation-state**, the sense of being a part of a nation is something that people imagine rather than really experience. Anderson argues that the citizens of the nation experience the sense of nationhood through the common experience engendered by the mass media—he focuses specifically on newspapers. No one can actually know everyone in the country, and there is little face-to-face interaction between citizens. Instead, those living inside a nation-state imagine connections through participating in collective rituals at the same time of day, albeit not in the same place. So, for example, many in the nation read the same news in the daily newspapers on the same day. Alternatively, millions listen to the six o'clock news simultaneously, each in their own spaces. Everyone consumes the same news and shapes their understanding of the world based on the same information. The knowledge garnered through citizens' habitual, common activities enables members of the collectivity to imagine themselves part of something larger, something we might call a "nation."

In the twentieth century, Anderson's theory worked selectively for the apartheid government's idea of the nation, insofar as "nationalism" was an idea promulgated by the media. But instead of newspapers (most South Africans were illiterate in the twentieth century), radio was the medium that the apartheid government used to engineer a new kind of social order. Rather than articulating national unity, however, radio was used to separate out on the basis of difference between groups of people, largely determined by language use. It was a remarkably expensive policy, because so many languages are spoken in South Africa (recall that the new political dispensation lists eleven official languages and many more unofficial ones). By the early 1960s, the state introduced **"Bantu**

Radio" in which each of the major languages spoken by South Africans had its own radio station and program content. In the apartheid context, people of British/European descent were the only people who qualified for "South African" citizenship; everyone else belonged to the "nation" of their language and cultural group, and lived or belonged to separate "homelands." All Zulu speakers, for example, were thought to practice the same traditions and were targeted as a single radio audience on what eventually became Radio Zulu; this was similarly the case for those from the Eastern Cape who spoke the Xhosa language and by apartheid reckoning, engaged in traditional rituals of the ama-Xhosa people. National boundaries so-defined might be likened to that of the present day European community: German-speaking people live in Germany, Italian speakers in Italy, French speakers in France, English speakers in England.

These ideas about nations and national identity extended into radio broadcast: Zulu-speaking announcers were used on Zulu language programs, reinforcing the sense that the news, music, and ideas were truly "Zulu" rather than "European." Listeners fostered ties to radio announcers, not necessarily because they knew them personally, but because they identified more generally with the sound of the voice and the language of the message. Strict rules governed performers' behavior, program content, and mode of presentation; government censors scrutinized every item publicly disseminated before it was presented for the first time. There was a hierarchy of value attached to whiteness over blackness, and much greater economic support provided for the media and cultural interests of Whites than for the "traditional practices" of Black South Africans. Although not every Black South African bought into the ideologies of apartheid expounded on Bantu Radio, it is not difficult to understand why a significant proportion did.

Radio Music and Apartheid

There were two distinctive agendas for European and "non-European" radio programing as set out by the South African Broadcast Corporation (SABC). Using the British Broadcast Corporation's (BBC) class-based model for radio, the SABC sought to educate and enlighten its audiences, to maintain social control by not engaging with any political troublemakers, and to program according to Christian values and morals. In addition, all events in South Africa were portrayed positively, and programs were developed that celebrated the excellent heritage and culture of Europeans. Any negative event in South Africa was blamed on outside forces, especially the infiltration of communists and their ideology into the country. This was the **Cold War** period, the era of McCarthyism and the fear of communism in the United States. The parallels between the rhetoric of the South African and US governments in this historical moment are quite striking.

In the Cold War period, music comprised a fair proportion of radio programing for all constituencies in South Africa. For those of European descent (English- and Afrikaans-speaking) it consisted of religious and European classical music, along with some American and British popular music. In the 1950s, rock'n'roll was considered morally unacceptable, so it was not permitted on radio. Instead, light music from the pre-rock times was regularly played. Program titles from the period focused on beautiful melodies, particularly those from the swing dance era. Only the more commercial Springbok Radio, which broadcast in English and Afrikaans, aired contemporary South African

Outline of Radio Broadcasting History in South Africa[1]

1923 On December 18, first **public broadcast** as transmission by South African Railways at British Empire Exhibition in Johannesburg.

1924 **Commercial radio** begins with three independent agencies (Johannesburg, Durban, Cape Town) broadcasting over a 200-mile radius.

1927 African Broadcasting Company (ABC), a private corporation, takes control of the three agencies, offers programs in English initially, then one short program in Afrikaans in 1931.

1936 Broadcasting Act establishes a single state-run radio service, the **South African Broadcast Corporation (SABC)**, and control passes from a commercial enterprise to the state. The SABC program content is modeled on the British Broadcasting Corporation (BBC), whose goal is to educate and uplift. Music is largely European classical and religious, with occasional "light" music: semi-classical and social dance music of the educated.

1936–1947 Hugh Tracey, director of Natal Studios of SABC, records traditional "native" music for broadcast in the 1950s. The SABC manufactures its own tape recorders for use in field recordings.

1937 Two language programs: the A program in English, and the B program in Afrikaans.

1940 SABC radio broadcasts to "natives" in **townships** or **"locations"** near cities, initially as an emergency wartime measure.

1945 SABC proposes greater radio programing for Black South Africans to be presented by Black South Africans. These include programs of lectures, drama, and music, in the vernacular but interpolated in English and Afrikaans programs. Music includes light versions of African American music, Black choral, and traditional music.

1950 Radio is increasingly used to control Black South Africans; Springbok Radio is created, offering commercial radio in English and Afrikaans; programing for Black South Africans is expanded; European classical music is introduced to African listeners.

1952 **Rediffusion service** for elite Black South Africans, to "provide the native with entertainment in his own home . . . to contribute to prevention of crime . . . and towards the education of the Bantu" (Hamm 1995: 215). Traditional music is used to keep a record of dying traditions and maintain pride in culture. No Black working-class popular music is aired until 1960. Initially, 4,300 homes subscribe to the Rediffusion service; by 1956, 14,000 homes subscribe.

1959 Promotion of Bantu Self-Government Act, with radio integral to this process. Radio viewed as "constant companion of man in modern times in all his activities, moulds his intellect and his way of life." Radio broadcasting to express "unique South African way of life" (*SABC Annual Report* 1959: 4).

1960 Bantu Radio established with revised Broadcast Act. Creation of Bantu Program Control Board expands Zulu and Xhosa services; new services to Sotho, Tswana, Venda, and Tsonga listeners; increased reception areas for all services.

1962 Black South Africans own 103,000 radio receivers; by 1968, 2 million own sets.

1966 Among White high school seniors, 45 percent listen to LM Radio broadcast out of Lourenco Marques in Mozambique, circumventing the controls of SABC, which refused to play British and American rock and pop music as LM Radio did. A further 20 percent listen to Springbok Radio, 19 percent to Afrikaans Radio, and 4 percent to English radio stations.

Late 1960s Bantu Radio broadcasts in seven African languages, twenty-four hours a day.

1972 SABC takes control of LM Radio and renames it Radio 5.

1976 Television comes to South Africa with two hours of evening programing, English- and Afrikaans-language programing on alternate evenings (7–9 p.m.). No significant television music programing at this stage.

Late 1970s Bantu Radio's audience is 5 million listeners.

1980s SABC plan to completely dominate the airwaves is fully functional, molding the intellectual and daily life of South Africans. But, **independent radio stations** begin to broadcast from so-called independent states, or *Bantustans*, including Capital Radio (1979) from Transkei, Music Radio 702 from Bophutatswana, numerous Christian radio services, the BBC, and Voice of America on short wave (which seems to have broadcast to South Africans since the 1950s).

1990s A complete turnaround for the SABC, which now airs previously silenced voices of musicians and political figures from liberation movements on SABC radio.

1994 Creation of Independent Broadcast Authority (IBA), established to work through the transition to democracy.

1995 Proposed legislation for introduction of local music quotas by Independent Broadcast Authority to promote the local music industry in South Africa and ward off the re-colonization of the airwaves by foreign music and companies.

2000 ICASA Act, brings together the IBA and South African Telecommunications Regulatory Authority to form sole telecommunications regulatory body.

2004 In February the SABC creates X-Kfm, a **community radio station** using the San languages of Xu and Khwe.[2]

2005 Amongst the South African population, 92 percent listen to radio, 88 percent of households own a radio. There are 122 licensed radio stations in South Africa. African languages are the dominant medium of communication. A further 16 international and African radio stations also available through DStv satellite audio channel including BBC Radio, Voice of America, World Radio Network and Radio Nederland. African stations: Radio Wave and Energy (Namibia), Christian stations: TransWorld Radio and Radio Veritas. Community radio on the increase in terms of availability and listener attention.

and international popular music, though it also steered away from rock'n'roll. Jazz occupied a complex position on European radio in South Africa. The traditional Dixieland and swing eras were adequately represented, but with the arrival of bebop, the more experimental "Black" form from the United States, jazz vacillated in popularity with radio producers and the team of censors working behind the scenes.

In devising radio programs for Black South Africans, the SABC promoted differences between Black and White South Africa. These distinctions carried economic and political benefits. Politically, Bantu Radio was of strategic importance to Prime Minister Hendrik Verwoerd's plans for implementing what has come to be known as **Grand Apartheid**, beginning in the late 1950s. Radio's purpose was to make Black South Africans concede to their place in the *Bantustans*, where they should relish their traditions and not create political havoc. Radio was also used as a medium to increase the sale of commodities to a growing number of Black consumers. However, radio was a new technology to Black South Africans, and listening habits were completely foreign. To draw Black listeners to the radio, the SABC, with loans from the government, installed high-quality, good-reception radio technology in the mid-1960s to expand the reach of the radio propaganda. And they did so using the newer FM transmission, because it allowed a number of radio frequencies to be used simultaneously.

Music on Bantu Radio stations differed in purpose and style from that played on European stations. Like the European programing, Black radio had to adhere to Christian ideals and not undermine "national"—meaning White—interests. Music played on Radio Zulu should be culturally consistent with a reified idea of Zulu tradition and culture. So, too, for Sotho and Tswana music. Only Zulu-language song texts were used for Radio Zulu, Xhosa for Transkei Radio, and so forth. All song texts were subject to scrutiny from a control/censorship board before being aired. The goal was to make the music appealing to listeners so that Black South Africans would tune in, digest the messages about traditional culture and homelands, and buy the products advertised.

The 1962 *SABC Annual Report* summarizes the musical content of Bantu Radio programs in three categories: popular, traditional, and choral music. As Charles Hamm (1995) remarks, enormous amounts of airtime were given to **traditional music**, the perfect music to articulate one's **"tribal" identity**. The SABC invested significant resources recording and broadcasting the traditional music of groups represented by its stations. The idea was to capture the ears of traditionalists in rural areas or migrant workers moving between rural and urban areas. Urbanized Black South Africans had largely rejected their traditional pasts as a result of the mission influence. They were fed two kinds of more Westernized music: choral performances in the vernacular and popular music. The most important South African genres aired on Bantu Radio from the early 1960s were: *isicathamiya*, albeit without any political references in the lyrics (see Chapter 7); African jazz, and the more commercial sounds of American swing jazz and film music (often translated into the vernacular); *kwela* music, the hugely popular pennywhistle music developed in the streets of Johannesburg that became popular in Britain and the United States in the 1960s; and finally, the studio-produced sounds of South African "jive" (later known as *mbaqanga*).[3] This is the music that best served the needs of Bantu Radio: the textless instrumental music was without political inference, and the vocal jive drew on the traditional images and language of a particular group to reinforce "tribal" identity.

Though ethnomusicologists have not specifically addressed the manner in which Bantu Radio shaped the lives of the thousands of migrant workers, particularly from the 1960s, there can be no doubt that with the availability of personal transistor radio, radio created vital connections between urban and rural homes. This continues to be the case for migrant workers—evidenced by the significant growth of radio consumers in the last five years in the country (see outline above for the year 2005). Black South African migrant workers moved between rural and urban areas, never really belonging in the place where they spent most of their lives. They owned no property and often had no place of residence. The place where they were supposed to belong, the "homeland," they only visited for a maximum sustained period of one month a year. Longing for home is a common theme in the lyrics of the primary musical genres of migrant workers: *isicathamiya*, gumboot dance, and *maskanda*.[4] Radio united the two social spaces. Migrant men and women heard the same radio programs at home in the city and at home in the reserve. The presence of **Radio Zulu/Ukhozi Radio** in the living and workspaces of people I have worked with in my research suggests that radio is central to everyday life in both town and countryside. I remember hoping, when I spent time with Shembe girls in *ibandla lamaNazaretha* (see Chapters 13 and 14) that I might hear them singing together as they went about their daily tasks. But the only voices I heard in song through much of the time I spent with them in July 1991 were those streaming from Radio Zulu!

In post-apartheid South Africa, the number of avenues for radio broadcast has increased, particularly in terms of community radio. In addition to continued programing in English and Afrikaans, nine African-language radio stations were designated by the Independent Broadcast Authority (IBA) in 1994. This meant that stations like Radio Zulu continued to operate using Zulu as the primary medium of communication, but in an attempt to distance the stations from the prior associations with language, culture, and "national" identity, the stations changed their names. So Radio Zulu became Ukhozi Radio, the station of the Black Mountain Eagle. These radio stations are now programed to reflect greater cultural diversity (Radio Zulu began producing programs that dealt with African indigenous religion, Christianity, and Islam, ending the exclusive focus on a narrowly defined Christianity under apartheid). The continued focus on African languages reflects a concern for the nurturing of linguistic diversity and development.

A major challenge in post-apartheid South Africa has been to generate **local music** products that can compete with, and perhaps be sold to, international markets (Abrahams 2003 and Baines 1998). Musically, the IBA recommended in 1994 that the nascent music and television production industries be protected from foreign competition with the introduction of local music quotas required of public and commercial radio and television stations. The problem with much English-language radio broadcasting of popular music has been its dependence on foreign music imports for local music consumption. One of the problems in the growth of a specifically South African music scene, as we will explore below, has been the lack of music industry support for local musical creativity, particularly from Gallo Records, the recording company with the longest history in South African musical production and consumption. ***Kwaito***, the South African creation of a kind of post-apartheid, first-decade-of-freedom styled hip hop, is certainly the musical form that has created a distinctively South African sound and filled the air with its messages.

Imported Musical Entertainment

South Africa is a country whose population has felt rupture and division as a consequence of segregationist and apartheid legislation and the movement of peoples, either locally through labor migration or transnationally through immigration. Even if it was not the intention of those who controlled the mass media in South Africa, one of the outcomes of its availability was that it provided people on the move with a mechanism for fostering connections between places. Purchasing products from the global centers of entertainment enabled South Africans to imagine alternatives to what increasingly became a politically oppressive and controlled social environment. As long as these media continued to be imported, South Africans still had a sense that they had some freedom of choice in the music they consumed and in the cultural milieu they participated in.

Nevertheless, South Africans responded in two ways to the impact of foreign music and media on the local scene: with celebration, and with anxiety (Feld 2000). On the celebratory side, the importation of foreign recordings and movies by the dominant recording interest, Gallo (Africa), and African Consolidated Theaters in the mid-twentieth century, for example, meant that South Africans could connect to the world outside. Local performers imitated the recordings and cultural models seen in Hollywood movies shown around Cape Town or Johannesburg, and these communities prided themselves on having their own Nat King Cole, Frank Sinatra, or Elvis Presley. American jazz, available for decades on local radio and on recordings, developed multiple layers of meaning in South Africa. For liberal, English-speaking veterans of the World War II Entertainment Corps, jazz signified membership in an enlightened international community. For South African Indians, jazz connoted Anglicization and modernity. For those who knew of its ties to racial struggles in the United States, jazz spoke to **diasporic** forms of suffering, and for Afrikaner nationalists it embodied the devil—too much freedom in the sounds of Black performance. Knowledge of the jazz repertory gleaned from recordings also enabled South African musicians to connect with the international jazz world when they went into political exile in the late 1950s and early 1960s. Finally, jazz represented a force with the potential for integration of all race and language groups, a vision of the possibilities of a "rainbow nation" in both the middle and later years of the twentieth century. Indeed, what defines "jazz" even in the contemporary marketplace, in South Africa and elsewhere, is itself a mix of genres and styles—one just needs to take a look at the programs of jazz festivals and the mix is self-evident. On the darker, more anxious side, the mass media and recording industry were manipulated in very particular ways by the apartheid government, in order to limit South Africans' access to information and the outside world, to selectively record musicians, and to silence noncompliant voices. We now take a closer look at how commercial forms of sound recording and film worked in twentieth-century South Africa.

Sound Recordings

In his landmark study on Black South African urban performing arts, *In Township Tonight!* (1985), David Coplan suggests that from the earliest days, the transnational entertainment corporations realized the commercial potential of the urbanizing Black workforce. On one hand, British and especially American films became a core part of the working-class experience among urban dwellers, across racial groups, from the 1920s. On the other, record companies like Pathe, HMV, Columbia, Decca, Brunswick, and Polydor all established subsidiaries or marketing channels in South Africa as early as the 1920s. Though there was only minimal recording of African traditional music in the early twentieth century, scholarly interest was sparked by the work of Hugh Tracey, as outlined in Chapter 1. The South African Broadcast Corporation (SABC) also played a central role in recording local traditional music through their **Transcription Series**, geared toward radio audiences rather than the sale of recordings—spearheaded by

Hugh Tracey. Consistent with the ideology of apartheid, the SABC focused its efforts on Afrikaans folk music and ***boeremusiek*** (local Afrikaans-language music for romantic crooning and social dancing), European classical music, and the folk music of "tribal" peoples. English-language popular music was typically recorded **under license** from England or the United States, i.e., there was minimal support for new composition in the English language.

We catch a glimpse of the attitude of SABC employees toward the traditional music of Black South Africa when a writer for the SABC reports in 1952 on a recording trip made into the rural areas of present-day Northern Province. The ideas then current about "native tradition" are illustrated in the following excerpt—that the African and his singing were "tribal" and "pre-modern," while the European and his technology were modern and sophisticated. Reading between the lines, one can nonetheless capture the sense of wonder felt by the writer at the magic of sound recording technology, a technology that enables the capture of live performance, and its capacity for playback far from the site of the original performance. Sound recording in this context provides a critical intervention in African history—it allows for the creation of a text/transcription against which future performances can be measured and history written. The excerpt reads:

> The South African Native has a song for everything . . . and every day of the sun-baked year these melodies echo and re-echo through our hills and fade-away into the distance of the plains . . . To do this [recording of traditional native music] successfully, we traveled in the giant recording van of the SABC to where the various tribes of the Bapedi nation have their towns . . . Only when one sees it personally can one appreciate the extent to which singing plays a part in the native national life . . . We captured on magnetic tape about a dozen songs . . . Chief Maserumuli called his singers together with the aid of the microphone in the recording van. We came back laden with treasure for we had captured in that area of great scenic beauty something even greater. Contained in a dozen rolls of magnetic tape we had something [that] was far more dear to the Native heart than anything a camera could possibly produce. (*SABC Magazine*, September 26, 1952)

The mainstay of the local music recording and publishing activity in South Africa in the twentieth century was Gallo (Africa).[5] Eric Gallo began Gallo Records in 1932 when his father purchased the Gauteng agency of Brunswick Records (USA) in Johannesburg. Because the White, English-speaking purchasing community has always been quite small and closely allied with its "home" culture in Britain, Gallo rarely recorded original music in the English language, preferring to either import superior British recordings or, at most, to use South African voices singing British and American hits under license from the parent companies in Britain and the United States. Because of the relatively small consumer base, it simply was not profitable for Gallo to record English-language performance in South Africa. This is not to say that White South Africans did not use music as a vehicle for social and political protest. But those who did were never given recording contracts by Gallo, because the market for this music was too small to make a profit, and when performers did articulate any kind of criticism of the apartheid government, the music was immediately either censored or banned outright, foreclosing potential markets for this music.

Foreign recordings were first advertised in South Africa in 1912. These included several English-language titles and one Afrikaans-language song, "Vat Jou Goed en Trek, Ferreira/Pack Your Bags and Leave, Ferreira" (Trewhela 1980: 44). Although Gallo began experimenting with record pressing in the mid-1930s, all local recordings continued to be pressed in Britain and shipped to the port city of Cape Town, where they were distributed across the country by land or later by air. During World War II however, it was almost impossible to import any foreign musical products. In 1949, Gallo opened its first pressing plant. In the first two months of production, Gallo manufactured 500,000 records (Trewhela 1980: 45). From the early 1950s, local production of foreign music, much of it translated into Afrikaans, created a vibrant market for sale to White Afrikaners in particular. In 1953 African Consolidated Sound Industries near Johannesburg opened a new high fidelity record-production plant. This meant that by the early 1950s, the local market was shaped by both South African and imported products. There were advertisements in the local press for the international corporations including Columbia, Decca, EMI, His Masters Voice, Capitol Records, and South Africa's Gallo Records.[6]

Independent labels, archival reissues

Independent labels began to play a critical role in expanding the possibilities for recorded music in South Africa in the 1980s. Perhaps the most important label at this time was Shifty Records, but there were numerous others. David Marks is an independent recording artist and producer in Durban. He has been involved in the recording of South African artists since the 1960s and now has an expansive archive of South African performance that was not aired nationally in the dark days of apartheid. This archive has begun to be digitized and made publicly accessible through the Internet, in a project funded by international organizations, and more recently by the Human Sciences Research Council in South Africa (see www.3rdearmusic.com).

In post-apartheid South Africa, multinational entertainment corporations like Sony (Japan), BMG, and EMI Records, who withdrew during the **cultural boycott** and economic sanctions imposed in the 1980s by many countries, including the United States, returned to South Africa. (See Chapter 4 for further discussion of the boycott.) In addition, Black South Africans entered the marketplace through musical creativity and ownership, as exemplified by *kwaito*, a musical form created, produced, distributed, and owned by Black South Africans. Furthermore, numerous independent and locally owned labels emerged in the 1990s, and the Internet and worldwide web are used by those who have the computer and financial resources for advertising their groups, narrating histories and biographies, and selling their products. This book would have been a very different book if it had been written in the pre-worldwide web days.

One of the really interesting projects of Gallo Records in the 1980s and 1990s was the series of reissues the company created as a means of recuperating the lost voices of South Africa's musical past—voices lost both directly, through the harsh years of censorship and silencing of much musical performance by the apartheid government (see Allen 1996), and indirectly, when much of South Africa's rich musical heritage and abundant talent disappeared from public hearing with the move into exile of many South African musicians from the late 1950s through the early 1990s. The archivist at Gallo, American

Rob Allingham, has made a significant contribution to the recuperation and revision of South African music history with his liner notes, often written in collaboration with musicians or those who participated in the musical culture, enclosed in CD-format reissues of the surviving highlights of South Africa's musical heritage. With the 2006 creation of Warner Music Gallo Africa, the entire Gallo catalog became **digitally available**. This meant that the eighty-year-old catalog could be distributed worldwide in almost any format, fundamentally altering the value of the idea of archival "reissues." The African market became a primary target of South African music recorded by Gallo.[7]

Film[8]

South Africa made no real contribution to the early inventions of global motion picture history but it certainly participated in the excitement and intrigue invoked by the novelty of moving images in the late 1890s. Thomas Edison's name was held in awe by South Africans bewildered by his invention of electricity, the gramophone or "talking machine," the kinetescope (a peep-show of moving pictures), and the kinetophone, which simultaneously transmitted moving pictures and accompanying sound. This kinetophone was first exhibited in Durban in August 1895. "The effect of 'talkie' films was achieved by looking through the slot at the pictures while applying the tube of the phonograph contained in the same box to the ear" (Gutsche 1972: 10). This mechanical marvel drew a crowd of 2,000 people on the night it first appeared in Cape Town in January 1896.

A wide range of mechanical novelties was brought to South Africa where they were typically introduced to the public as acts in the context of **vaudeville** and **variety** shows, i.e., juxtaposed with live entertainment. Women were rarely in the audience at these performances, i.e., there were clear class and gender distinctions in the consumption of this culture in late nineteenth- and early twentieth-century South Africa. Mechanical novelties were either imported by South Africans who traveled to England and Europe to purchase the machines and bring them back for commercial purposes, or they were introduced to audiences by itinerant showmen and women who traveled the world as magicians.

It was not until the late 1920s, however, that the first "talkies" were introduced to the world at large, and to South Africa specifically. By this time, numerous permanent cinemas had been constructed throughout the country, and movie-going had lost much of the social stigma that surrounded its initial introduction in debased musical halls and seedy entertainment sites in South Africa's rapidly growing urban centers. The first "talkie," a British production called *Mr. Smith Wakes Up*, was shown in Johannesburg on July 6, 1929, and was enthusiastically received. *Syncopation*, first run in Johannesburg on September 13, 1929, was the first full-length "talkie" to appear in South Africa. Ten weeks later, Al Jolson's *The Singing Fool* followed. *The Singing Fool* provided Cape Town audiences with its first taste of a feature-length movie with synchronized sound in one of the earliest **atmospheric theaters** in the country. *Syncopation* arrived in Cape Town on December 16, 1929.

Rio Rita (1930) was the film that made a lasting impression on South African audiences, many of whom had been skeptical of the durability of "talkies" over the excellence

> A quick note on terminology used to describe this emerging form, as outlined by Gustche (1972). Gutsche writes that a certain Mrs. James popularized the term "bioscope" when she traveled around South Africa in 1898 with Edison's "American Bioscope." At the time the term referred to "anything to do with moving pictures." Gutsche suggests that the word was popular in the USA for a short time. In England, people preferred to use "cinematograph," shortened to cinema; and Europeans (from the Continent) used the word, "kinematograph," shortened to kino. Ultimately in the USA the term "moving" or "motion pictures" was preferred because it dignified the rather vulgar entertainment milieu, the result being that "movies" was the most durable word used for motion pictures. "Bioscope" was commonly used in South Africa to refer to the cinema until the 1960s.

of a thirty-year tradition of silent film. "Produced entirely in Technicolor and combining attractive music with comic dialogue . . . *Rio Rita* captivated its audiences. People who had been to the 'bioscope' only once or twice in their lives, journeyed to the Astoria [Theater] at Woodstock, Cape Town to see it during a season of several weeks" (Gutsche 1972: 220). These early films exploited old variety and vaudeville music and comic turns, while exploring new performance possibilities.

In South Africa, the Disney cartoons, animated with sound and music, suggested new levels of artistry and attraction for the public. *The King of Jazz*, starring Paul Whiteman and his orchestra (1930), through the conventions of "trick photography," in this case, showing Whiteman holding the entire orchestra in the palm of his hand, moved Hollywood movies onto a new level for South African audiences. *Snow White and the Seven Dwarves* was one of the first cartoon character films shown in the country.

In the 1950s a handful of films about Black South African experience and culture were made in South Africa. Three in particular have recently been reissued by Villon Films in Canada: *Zonk!*, *African Jim*, and *Song of Africa*. *Zonk!* is perhaps the most interesting film because it represents the kinds of live variety show performances common in Black and Coloured theaters in the period, and so provides a remarkable historical document for those of us not alive or present at the performances in South Africa to catch a glimpse of how deeply American performance culture had embedded itself in South Africa.

In a review in the largely White Cape newspaper, *The Argus*, in December 1944, the journalist writes about *Zonk!* He describes it as a nationally celebrated African revue that performed in the Cape Town City Hall. He praises the show for its originality, applauding the performers for their talent and versatility, and for being "better than their American prototypes." *Zonk!* contains many good things. "There is some excellent tap dancing, a first rate band, some Negro spirituals; in short, almost a surfeit of good things. The performers, without a single exception, have amazing stage presence and present their various turns with verve and evident enjoyment."

Zonk! is typical of the kind of variety shows common in South Africa between the world wars and in the post-World War II era. Called "African" entertainment, you might be surprised as viewers at the amount of seemingly "non-African" material presented. You may be a little uncomfortable with the pervasive shadow of minstrelsy that characterizes the show. But it is important in watching performances that originate in one place and travel elsewhere not to read the same contexts and messages into the texts.

Zonk!

Zonk! the film consists of fifteen individual acts introduced by an emcee. The actors participate in both working-class and elite Black and Coloured culture. The emcee and actors perform in several South African languages including Zulu, English, Afrikaans, and Sotho. This emcee occasionally reflects on the specific nature of the performances, and on their relationship to images and sounds that South Africans have borrowed from.

If you are able to locate and watch the video, make a list of the range of performances included in the film. How many languages are used? Where do the different items derive from? What makes them feel decidedly South African? What were your expectations of the video before you watched? What surprised you? Disappointed you? Offended you? What are possible reasons for your responses?

The *Zonk*! program reads much like a typical variety show with South African content. The film program runs as follows:

1 *Zonk!* opens with a jazz singer backed by a close-harmony male vocal group and jazz ensemble. They are singing a song of praise to the makers of the film, and indeed, to *Zonk! The African People's Magazine*, the sponsor of the film. This opening cut reveals the profound influence of nineteenth-century minstrelsy on Black South African performance culture. References are made, again, near the end of the film, to the culture in which a Black man sings the music of a White man who in turn is singing the music of a Black man.
2 This item is the song made famous by African American Paul Robeson, but performed here by South Africa's own version of Paul Robeson (Robeson visited South Africa in 1936 to star in the film *King Solomon's Mines*). The stage setting in *Zonk!* could easily have drawn its model from the very popular ***Cabin in the Sky*** (aired in South Africa in the late 1940s, see Chapter 11).
3 A male vocal trio sings in English and Zulu with a jazz lineup behind them. The song is about the "Copper Coloured Girl" in a "Happy Days are Here Again" styled rendition. The singing is accompanied on piano and bass. The singers perform a tap routine in the middle of the song.
4 It is not just jazz, but the European classical vocal repertory that Black South Africans have come to perform. In this scene, a Black woman rocks her baby to sleep while singing Brahms' lullaby. The emcee introduces the song with a narrative about composers of beautiful music better known to some than to others. The singer is accompanied on an organ (not seen on stage).
5 The emcee signals a change in performance culture by switching into Afrikaans as he introduces the Cape "Coons" from Hanover Street in District Six (see Chapters 6 and 11). Notice the white soft shoes, and the dandy style of body movement, tying this genre to *isicathamiya* and the larger history of minstrelsy in South Africa. These twelve men sing in a mix of English and Afrikaans. They represent the Coloured working class from the Cape.
6 Abafana Kumnandi, a group who sing in the "Manhattan Style," are a close-harmony vocal quartet (see Ballantine 1999). This tune sounds remarkably like a Glenn Miller styled "In the Mood" performance, with the song text in Zulu, focused on the theme of *istimela*, the train.
7 Representing the traditional migrant worker longing for his rural home, which is

painted in the backdrop to this act, we see a Sotho man singing a very slow ballad about traditional life. Once again the voice uses a deep, Robeson-like timbre. (See Part II, discussion of music in migration.)

8 The Zulu Melodians sing a moral ditty about the vices of alcohol, with an eleven-piece jazz band backing them up. They are introduced in Zulu by the emcee. He tells a story to contextualize the song.

9 Here we have a wonderful example of early gumboot dance called *isicathulo.* The dance is performed in the staged context of a "ritzy" restaurant, and watched by the woman (a man dressed as a woman) who runs the restaurant. The dancers are accompanied by Zulu *maskanda* guitar playing, in the ***ukuvamba*** style of performance. The dancers are given cornmeal for lunch, suggesting the real migrant worker image typical of *amaBhaca*, the men who created gumboot dance from southern KwaZulu Natal (see Chapters 8 and 9 for further discussion.)

10 Richard Majola, a South African tap dancer, sings and dances with jazz ensemble accompaniment. Note the reference to "Harlem" in the song he sings. Tap dancing was the elite dance style, and gumboot the style of migrant workers.

11 In Part III, Chapter 11, there is reference to **"*langarm*" dance band** performance in Cape Town. Here we see a *langarm* band, singing in Afrikaans. Note the predominance of saxophones in the band.

12 The girl on the cover of *Zonk!* the magazine is a beautiful blues/jazz singer who only sings the melody—no scatting for her. In this track we see the two venues representing two sides of jazz performance: the elite ballroom dance context, and the more rowdy working-class environment. As is evident in my discussion of Cape jazz performance in the 1950s, singers and instrumentalists frequent both sites.

13 Here we return to the reflections on **minstrel history**. The emcee tells us that Black singer Skip Mphahlane sings the song "September in the Rain," made famous by a White man imitating the Black man. "September in the Rain" is sung with a jazz lineup.

14 In the grand finale, the *Zonk!* girl singer is joined by the jazz band, and the entire cast enters and performs together.

15 With visual flashes to all kinds of rural images of African life, the cast sings "Nkosi Sikelel'iAfrika" (see discussion in Chapter 2), the anthem of the African National Congress which was banned by the government in the apartheid era, but became an integral part of the new national anthem in the 1990s.

Minstrelsy and its impact on Black performance culture is a complex historical and political issue. In other words, as we think about the ways in which music and culture from one place travel elsewhere, we should be careful not to simply assume that the meanings of performances translate exactly from one place to the next. We need to remain open to other readings of the images and sounds that streamed in from the outside and rooted themselves locally in new and different ways, and to ask why practices that had seemed so demeaning in one place continue elsewhere with similar or different values attached to their articulation.

The post-World War II period was a period of enormous optimism, exuberance, and remarkable achievement for Black South Africans. Many people of color had undertaken military service, traveling north into various parts of Africa to serve on the side of the Allies. They were optimistic that the freedoms they had witnessed in other parts of the world would soon be theirs. Several had participated in the Entertainment Corps and returned brimming with enthusiasm about the exciting music they had played and the skills they had acquired in the process. Many South Africans think of the 1950s as the pinnacle of artistic, literary, and cultural development of the country as a whole. It was the decade of growing collaboration musically between people of different racial groups. Few believed that the government would actually enforce the new apartheid legislation. After all, even political marches and rallies that called for equality and fairness for all South Africans were tolerated by the government in the 1950s.

Though they lacked formal institutions for music and dance training, South Africans' ears were finely tuned from generations of aural transmission, they listened closely to the records available for purchase, and they watched the gestures and costuming of American performers on the silver screen. These foreign models of performance were re-enacted live in South Africa's communities, often translated into vernacular performance aesthetics and languages. South African jazz was one genre initially formed through regular visits to local movie theaters to see American-made musicals and Westerns (see Chapter 11 for further discussion).

White South Africans sought to harness this talent and enthusiasm on film and to export it to Britain in the postwar era in three films: *Jim Comes to Joburg/African Jim* (the Zulu man migrates from the rural to urban areas, encounters African Jazz and the commodities of recorded music, and becomes a performance star); *Song of Africa*, showcasing the "Zulu jazz" performance of a man who migrates from the rural areas to the urban, learns jazz, and teaches it, via the purchase of a gramophone and disks, to his rural people; and *Zonk!*, a film showcasing African variety and jazz performances typical of the 1940s and 1950s. These films are treasured witnesses to a remarkable era in South African performance history that was soon to be brutally silenced by the apartheid government. They were, nevertheless, profoundly shaped by Hollywood versions of Black performance culture. Ideas about "Africanness" in the modern world that traveled to the United States from West Africa were transformed through a period of 200 years, then taken up by White performers, and finally returned to South Africa in a highly mediated version.

In post-apartheid South Africa the local film industry has taken enormous leaps forward. The National Film and Video Foundation and the Independent Development Corporation are the two major sources of financial support for full-length feature and documentary films in South Africa. Several films made about South Africa, in South Africa, or by South Africans have won awards at film festivals, and have featured in the Emmy and Oscar Award Ceremonies in the United States. Many of these films have highlighted South African music in their soundtracks. These include the Academy award-winning *Tsotsi* (2006), *Mandela* (1996), *Yesterday* (Academy Award nomination, 2004), and Golden Bear award-winning *uCarmen eKhayelitsha* (2005). The last film was directed in the Xhosa language, though it featured the music of European composer Georges Bizet.

Foreign Music Live and Mediated

In the twentieth century, imported and locally produced recordings and the fairly regular visits of foreign musicians worked together to shape local culture in quite profound ways. I provide two examples here to illustrate the appeal to some South Africans of live performances "from overseas" on the one hand, and of new forms conveyed by sound-recording technologies on the other. They illustrate audience responses in two decades: the live performance in the 1930s and the recorded performance in the mid-1950s, though until the mid-twentieth century, both forms of imported performance intermingled in South Africa, especially for those in the growing urban centers. In Part III we discuss further the different ways in which various modes of performance shaped the musical experiences of musicians in 1950s Cape Town. In the two excerpts here we are given a rare glimpse into audience/consumer responses to both live and mediated musical cultures, and ways in which the individual imagination worked in the process of listening to the music.

The first account is derived from the memories of White South African Percy Tucker on the visit of British film and **music hall** star Gracie Fields (1898–1979) to the country in the 1930s (Tucker 1997: 10). Percy Tucker was one of the central figures in shaping White South African entertainment in the twentieth century. He was involved in the world of local and international show business through most of that century, and in 1997 he published a thick book of his memories of his life. At the beginning of the book is a moving account of his first encounter with a living performer from Britain, Gracie Fields. Fields came to Tucker's hometown, Benoni, situated just outside of Johannesburg. Fields sang in the local movie theater, a common practice of the period.

Tucker recalls the palpable excitement he and his peers felt at the prospect of a live performance by Gracie Fields, of the absolutely transformative moment in his life when Fields entered the cinema stage.

> The lights dimmed, and the orchestra struck up. I don't remember what they actually played, but the entrance of Gracie Fields is as vivid in my mind as if it were yesterday. Tall, fair-haired and wearing a long blue dress, which sparkled under the spotlight, she seemed to me, aged seven, the most glamorous of creatures. (In reality, she was quite a plain woman, but with a very strong and inviting personality.)
>
> I suppose Gracie Fields was the first person to win my heart. As her clear and resonant voice soared over that **cinema** auditorium, my love of vocal music, which was to expand and embrace the whole spectrum of music over the years, was born, and my young soul was filled with total happiness. There was no holding me back after that. (Tucker 1997: 10)

The second is an account by Black South African journalist Gideon Jay writing in *Zonk! The African People's Magazine* in the 1950s about how he listens to his recordings.

> Is there anything so wonderful as a **gramophone** record? That hard, flat circular piece of inert material that comes to life when you spin it and put the point of the needle in the groove. It comes to life and plays on your emotions, bringing joy

> or sorrow: you tap your feet or you shed a tear . . . How do you listen to YOUR records? In my case, I sit alone and spin the discs (usually in the small hours of the morning). I get the feeling that the artists come to me through the loudspeaker of my radiogram. They step out, take a bow and sing or play, and then step back through the speaker and the curtain comes down as the automatic switch clicks the turntable to a standstill. And I am left again with a cold disc. (*Zonk!*, December 1952, 45)

Gideon Jay's evocative description of his relationship to sound recordings gives us a wonderful sense of how Black South Africans were listening to recorded music in this period—as if it were the real live performance.

Television

Television was not introduced into South Africa until the end of 1975 for White South Africans; a Black television channel began broadcasting in 1982. Numerous explanations have been suggested for the absence of television. These include the views that the apartheid government did not want Black South Africans to see any interracial relationships on television, that they did not believe that television was necessary in a country where people spend large amounts of time outdoors (the climate is conducive to outdoor activity almost year round), and that there was not a large enough consumer base (of White people only) to pay for the cost of introducing television and sustaining programing.

But the question of television for South Africans had been debated ever since it was first introduced in the United States. There is, for example, a lovely description of a television screen in a White South African entertainment magazine in 1954. Take note of the awareness the writer displays of what is happening in the English-speaking world beyond South Africa, i.e., having a television would be a sign of participation in a transnational English-speaking world.

> In the homes of millions of Americans, Canadians, and Britishers, particularly in the living room, there rests an innovation that has become an integral part of their mode of living—the television set . . . As you approach the receiver there is found a large grey area, round on some sets and rectangular on others. This area is framed by a light colored border and then a metallic frame. Commonly called the TV screen, this area is the face of a cathoid ray tube. It is covered by a plate of glass that extends to the metallic frame that is set into the cabinet. Below, or beside, the tube there are two dials. (*Bandstand Magazine*, April 1954, p. 16)

When television did finally come to South Africa in 1975–1976, the SABC-TV offered two hours of programing each evening between 7 and 9 p.m. The programs alternated between English-language shows and Afrikaans-language material. There was no significant music programing at that time, other than the national anthem at the end of the transmission. It was more cost-effective to import American shows and dub them into local languages; initially this was only into Afrikaans, but when Zulu-language programing was introduced in the 1980s, it was not uncommon to see a show like "Love Boat" dubbed into Zulu—that is, a pleasure boat filled with White people all talking to each other in Zulu! Standard television channels continue to be controlled by the SABC—South Africans are expected to pay for these services by purchasing television licenses each year. There has been a significant growth in the availability of cable and digital television programs from around the world, in many non-South African languages. Music Television (MTV) beamed out of Europe, and more recently a channel aimed at promoting African music, are now available in South Africa as cable channels. Since 1994, television in South Africa has been profoundly reshaped by the Independent Broadcast Authority's concern for the nurturing and protection of African languages, and the use of television as an educational tool for language development. The most popular television programs include local music programing, soap operas (foreign and local), game shows, and talk shows.

In the 1980s, the only music aired on television was found in imported films of European and American symphony orchestras and local Afrikaans *boeremusiek*—piano accordion music with a drum kit, bass, guitar, and singer, strongly influenced by the sounds of east European folk music translated into local idiom and language. In the last decade, local music has found its way into the channels of the national network. Sunday morning television features religious music of local and African American gospel performers, along with popular music of the African and Asian diaspora. Several nights a week South African traditional music, including choral performances, *maskanda*, *mbaqanga*, other local–global fusions, and a wide selection of current, imported acts from Europe and the United States are made available to local viewers. Post-apartheid South Africa has seen the airwaves open to a greater diversity of music, dance, and language, with a significant growth in local representation.[9]

Keywords

atmospheric theaters movie theaters that created their own "atmosphere," e.g., they had stars in the ceilings to evoke a feeling of being in a magical space in order to watch the latest film

"Bantu Radio" the 1960s name for apartheid radio programs for Black South Africans

boeremusiek traditional music of the "farmers" or Afrikaans conservatives, mostly but not exclusively White, that derives from European folk/dance traditions—schottishe, the waltz, the two-step—often tied to social dancing, though it also developed as a form of music for television

Cabin in the Sky a popular film with Black entertainers in a variety style performance

cinema/bioscope two terms used in South Africa to refer to movie theaters

Cold War the post-World War II era where the threat of a "communist" takeover of the world was accompanied by the fear of an arms buildup. The two superpowers were the former Soviet Union and the United States

commercial radio radio sponsored by commercial activity

community radio station a radio station that broadcasts to, and represents the interests of the local community

cultural boycott a ban imposed on South Africa by several countries, whereby their citizens were forbidden to travel to, or sell their performance in or to South Africa

diaspora the dispersion of communities of people, languages, and cultures that were previously located in a single place; there is often a narrative of suffering and dislocation that accompanies the process of dispersion

digitally available creating digital versions of analog recordings enables them to be loaded onto electronic distribution sites, like iTunes, Napster, and other file sharing programs

gramophone the machine that played records (33, 45, and 78 rpm discs)

Grand Apartheid period from the 1960s, when the laws established in the 1950s began to be enforced in South Africa

independent labels record companies run independently of the major recording corporations, which often use the majors for distribution

independent radio stations radio stations established to run independently of the state and often of commercial support

kwaito South African hip hop for a post-apartheid era

"*langarm*" dance band the name for a Coloured dance band in Cape Town

local music music made locally for local consumption, in contrast to the norm of broadcasting music produced elsewhere in the world, the USA and Britain, for example

minstrel history a globally disseminated history about performers who wore blackface and entertained in variety shows

music hall the British name for vaudeville

nation-state independent state recognized internationally as sovereign, typically of a homogeneous national identity, and able to interact with the world at large as such

public broadcast radio and television broadcast funded and shaped by national or regional government

Radio Zulu/Ukhozi Radio until the early 1990s, the regional radio station run by the SABC with the largest number of listeners in South Africa (about 5 million)

rediffusion service the name of the system that distributes radio programs

townships or "locations" the peri-urban areas in which Black South Africans, both migrants and permanent urban dwellers, lived under apartheid, and where many continue to live, though there is more mixing happening along class lines

South African Broadcast Corporation (SABC) the government controlled and publicly funded (through taxes) media corporation, that continues under new leadership in contemporary South Africa

traditional music a very complicated label in South African history, because of the ways in which "traditional" music underpinned the apartheid plan; but today traditions are valued by even the most progressive citizens

Transcription Series the service the SABC created to record most of the local music they broadcast. Very little of this music from the early decades of the twentieth century exists today because tape was reused and the state didn't see the archival potential in retaining the recordings

"tribal" identity like "tradition" tribe is a complicated term—much scorned during the apartheid era because of its association with primitiveness and backwardness, "tribalism" has been given new value in the tourism industry in contemporary South Africa

under license the system in the music industry in which songs recorded in the United States, Britain, and Europe would be covered "under license" in South Africa, i.e., local singers would sing the songs of the Beatles, or Abba, or the Rolling Stones, and sell records legally

ukuvamba vamping, or strumming chords on guitar

variety theatrical show consisting of a program of short acts of different kinds, including song, comedy sketches, dance, and magic acts

vaudeville late nineteenth and twentieth-century entertainment comprising song, dance, and comedy acts

CHAPTER 4
Graceland (1986)
World Music Collaboration

Introduction

In the minds of many involved in the production of South African music in the late twentieth century, longtime American **popular musician Paul Simon's *Graceland*** album (1986) was a turning point in South African music history. A collaborative recording project between South Africans and the American singer-songwriter, the *Graceland* album **showcased** South African music to a worldwide popular music market at a critical moment. The (mostly Black) South Africans included in the project were **Joseph Shabalala** and his unaccompanied ***isicathamiya*** group **Ladysmith Black Mambazo**, guitarist **Ray Phiri**, bass player Bakhiti Khumalo, drummer Vusi Khumalo, percussionist Makhaya Mahlangu, singers General MD Shirinda and the Gaza Sisters, piano accordionist Forere Motloheloa, and the township group, Boyoyo Boys. White South African pennywhistle player Morris Goldberg appeared on a couple of tracks, and exiled South African musicians Miriam Makeba and Hugh Masekela joined *Graceland* for the African Tour. There is no doubt that for Black South African music in particular, the *Graceland* album opened the doors to the world and popular music marketplaces in ways few other recordings have.

And yet, despite the positive outcomes of collaborative effort between these two constituencies of musicians—African and American—the *Graceland* album incited outrage from many around the world, particularly those who were aware of the struggles of Black South Africans against the apartheid regime.

In this chapter we take a closer look at both the political context in which this collaborative project was produced and released to the world—a political context shaped in part by another recording that urged foreign musicians *not* to work in South Africa; we examine the ways in which different musical ideas and traditions were used in composing the songs that constitute the *Graceland* album; how the re-release of the album ten years later changed its tone; and finally, we take a brief look at some of the responses from musicians to the album and the spirit of the project itself.

1980s Politics: "Rhythms of Resistance"

The mid-1980s in South Africa were the most repressive years in apartheid history, a period in which the government expelled foreign journalists and declared numerous "states of emergency" because political resistance to apartheid, inside and outside of the country, was at an all-time high. As a result, state security forces were ever-present in Black townships and White urban areas, and thousands of mostly Black South Africans, including hundreds of children, were arrested and detained without access to legal representation, let alone a free and fair trial. It was also the era of the mega "**charity rock**" concerts like Live Aid, Farm Aid, and We Are the World,[1] which were beamed by satellite to the world from London and the United States. In these events the stars of the entertainment world presented themselves, and were marketed as, socially conscious musicians. This was the moment in which American rock musician and producer **Little Steven** released the collaboratively created ***Sun City: Artists United Against Apartheid*** video, album, and book package.[2] The music video had been made with MTV audiences in mind and aired on that channel (the American Public Broadcasting Services, PBS, had refused to air the video for fear of alienating its largely White viewers, and there was no Black Entertainment Television [BET] at the time). *Sun City* was not just a moneymaking event; it was designed to raise people's consciousness and to get them to think about South African policies of apartheid and reflect on parallel experiences of racism in their own countries.

To comprehend the controversy generated by *Graceland*, we must consider four points: (1) the international cultural boycott that had been called for by South Africans in exile in Europe and the United States and applied against South Africa—its government and its people; (2) **"Sun City,"** the entertainment center in South Africa that symbolized the evil of the apartheid regime; (3) ***Rhythm of Resistance***, a video documentary on Black South African music directed by British filmmaker Jeremy Marre in 1979 and aired publicly in many live and mediated places; and (4) the musical **collaborations** across racial divides that had begun to form inside South Africa in the 1980s.

Cultural boycott

The history of **cultural boycotts** against South Africa reaches back beyond apartheid to the 1940s. As early as 1946 the American Actor's Equity resolved to discourage its members from working in South Africa because of racial discrimination. India initiated the first boycott in 1947. It was an Anglican priest, Father Trevor Huddleston, who had worked in Sophiatown, Johannesburg, a community destroyed by the government, who called for a boycott against South Africa that achieved international media attention in the 1950s. The poignancy of his message was reinforced with the Sharpeville Massacre in March 1960. In response, Equity, the British Actors' Union, and the British Musicians' Union refused to allow their members to perform in South Africa from the late 1950s. Nobel Peace Prize winner (1960) Albert Luthuli invoked **United Nations Organization** principles to call for an even larger boycott in the 1960s. In 1965, sixty-five performers and actors pledged to refuse to perform in apartheid South Africa (1948–1990), including Harry Belafonte, Sammy Davis, Jr, and Nina Simone.

In 1969, the United Nations resolved to encourage member states to suspend all ties with the South African government: political, sporting, and cultural. When television was introduced to South Africa, no British shows were aired because of the boycott. By the 1980s, South Africa had become quite isolated from the international cultural and sporting arenas.[3] In the early 1980s the United Nations declared that it would blacklist any performer who traveled to South Africa. Essentially, the United Nations cultural boycott meant that there would be no exchange of performers or performances between that country and the rest of the world. (Nevertheless, since the boycott could only be policed in terms of entertainers traveling in person, recordings of many famous artists continued to be sold in South Africa through the 1980s.)

By traveling to South Africa in 1985, at the height of public awareness of the evils of apartheid, Paul Simon broke the terms of the cultural boycott, which was supported not only by the United Nations, but also by numerous arts organizations the world over. Simon had not acquired permission to travel to South Africa from either the United Nations or the African National Congress, the two organizations at the forefront of the boycott. The international anti-apartheid community feared that if someone as powerful as Paul Simon did not abide by the principles, the struggle against the South African government would crumble. It was a struggle that had gained momentum with the political messages of another group of British and American musicians—the musicians who called themselves **Artists United Against Apartheid**, led by rock guitarist Little Steven (Steven van Zandt) who a year earlier had released a song about boycotting South Africa.[4]

Sun City: Artists United Against Apartheid

Sun City is the Las Vegas-style casino and entertainment center created by Sol Kerzner, funded in part by the South African government. South Africa's equivalent to Donald Trump, Kerzner built the casino in what was then the "independent" homeland of **Bophutatswana**,[5] north of Johannesburg. It was opened in 1979. There was no international political acknowledgment of these homelands. Nevertheless, overseas entertainers were lured to the site with offers of significant financial packages and the assurance that Bophutatswana was not part of South Africa, but rather, an independent state. The problem was that Bophutatswana was just one of the official ***Bantustans*** into which Black South Africans had been relegated, so most of the Black residents of the homeland lived in dire poverty, in contrast to the significant resources the South African government covertly poured into the entertainment oasis.

In 1985 American and British musicians worked together to create the MTV-targeted music video ***Sun City: Artists United Against Apartheid***, and a series of other recordings made in the spirit of the international anti-apartheid movement. Recordings included the song "Biko" by Peter Gabriel, "Apartheid is Wrong" by Stevie Wonder, "Nelson Mandela" by Youssou N'Dour, "Tutu" by Miles Davis, and "No Easy Walk to Freedom" by Peter, Paul, and Mary.[6] The music video, book, and record package articulated the collective resolve of musicians not to be coerced into playing at Sun City. *Sun City* was issued in 1985, the same year that Paul Simon quietly traveled to South Africa to record tracks with three groups he had heard on a cassette titled *Gumboots: Accordion **Jive** Hits Vol. II*, given to him by a friend. Many considered Simon's project to be a blatant disregard for the cultural boycott, action interpreted as a lack of concern for the suffering and plight of the same Black South African musicians and their communities. The negative media attention did not hinder record sales—*Graceland* has sold millions of copies the world over. South African guitarist Ray Phiri claimed in 1998 that 13 million copies had already been sold.[7] As I comment at the end of this chapter, in retrospect, there have been many positive outcomes for the project.

Rhythm of Resistance

In an effort to build sympathy for Black South African performers abroad, British filmmaker Jeremy Marre traveled to South Africa in the late 1970s to make a documentary film for the BBC titled *Rhythm of Resistance: Black South African Performance.* Produced before the cultural boycott, Marre's documentary fleshed out the politics of musical performance and production in the apartheid period. Ladysmith Black Mambazo was one of the groups featured on this documentary, a film frequently shown at anti-apartheid gatherings especially on college campuses in Britain and the United States in the 1980s.

Marre's agenda in *Rhythm of Resistance* was clearly to expose the hidden forms of street and studio performance of Black South Africa, labeled "tribal" music, that were used by performers and their audiences as acts of resistance to apartheid (see Chapters 4–6 for deeper discussion of these genres). Marre later produced the video/DVD documentary (discussed below) about the *Graceland* album as a collaborative project, in which clips from *Rhythm of Resistance* were inserted, visually connecting the two documents and the stories behind the music in each. Paul Simon claims that it was this documentary that inspired him to travel to South Africa and record with local musicians.

Documenting South African Music

The thirteen-part video series *African Wave: South African Music and Its Influences* (see Bowey 1998 in DVD/video list, Appendix 3) tells the stories of thirteen South African musicians/groups whose lives intertwine in the aftermath of the *Graceland* album. Countering the separate development/apartheid images of South African performances under apartheid, this series stresses the "multicultural music of South Africa, its major musicians, and the traditional and contemporary influences that color their work" (see video cover for Bowey 1998). Included in the series are those who have recorded with Gallo Records: township pop singer Brenda Fassie; the contemporary queen of popular music in Africa Yvonne Chaka Chaka; African Jazz Pioneers leader Ntemi Piliso; Ladysmith Black Mambazo; Ray Phiri, Sipho Hotstix Mabuse (the latter three all participants in the *Graceland* recording); White rock copies Little Sister; South African reggaeman Lucky Dube; Mango Groove; hybrid Soweto duo Marcalex; hip hop artists Prophets of da City, and the late great Zulu dancer and growler Mahlathini. The most pervasive themes in the series are (1) market cross-over, which in South Africa means racial and genre cross-over—that is, groups that sell to more than one group of consumers defined by race/culture and language; (2) covering and borrowing sounds and styles from abroad; and (3) the significance of *Graceland* to their music.

Collaborations across the racial divide

Rhythm of Resistance provides the first glimpses of the kinds of musical collaborations that South Africans themselves had begun to form anew in the late 1970s, such as that of the singer-songwriter duo of White South African Johnny Clegg and Black migrant worker Sipho Mchunu. I remember discovering the music of the duo, called Juluka, and the band they subsequently formed—and dancing the night away with my friends to recordings of this music in the mid-1980s. But I also recall attending one of their performances in the Durban City Hall at about the same time—the sheer presence of Black and White men performing together in public was reason for the stage to be guarded by South African police, who stood in the wings the entire performance to quell any public unrest that might be generated by the interracial group. Fortunately, the only thing generated by the performance was huge enthusiasm for the sounds streaming from the stage.

Soon other groups also began to transgress the racial ideologies of apartheid. Later in the 1980s, Mango Groove, an interracial ensemble, recorded and performed South African popular music, integrating the sounds of *kwela* and *marabi*, sounds that evoked a deep nostalgia for a bygone, pre-Grand Apartheid era (see *African Wave, Part Seven: Mango Groove*). The African Jazz Pioneers was another popular group, made up largely of Black South African musicians who had played jazz in the 1950s but who re-formed as an interracial group. They included a White trombonist in their group in the 1980s (see *African Wave, Part Ten on African Jazz Pioneer Ntemi Piliso*).

The *Graceland* Album

A great deal has been written about the *Graceland* album since its release in 1986—much of it in response to the controversy itself.[8] But since the recording and the controversy were recorded more than two decades ago, my purpose here is to use *Graceland* to flesh out the many meanings and interpretations that are generated by a single musical recording. The *Graceland* case study should enable you to reflect on the relationship between South African music history and that of the United States, on one hand, and more generally on some of the issues raised by the *Graceland* collaboration and the production of "world music," on the other.

At its core, *Graceland* is a musical collaboration between Paul Simon and a host of other musicians. These included Cajun zydeco music of Rockin' Dopsie and the Twisters, the Chicano Rock of Los Lobos, the Everly Brothers in the United States, as well as a large contingent of South Africans, with Joseph Shabalala and Ladysmith Black Mambazo, and Ray Phiri and Stimela in the foreground. The *Graceland* album included a different set of musicians than did *Graceland: The African Concert* (presumably for logistical reasons, but the changing personnel and the difference between studio production and live performance are important in coming to terms with the ownership of *Graceland*).

Like so many recordings, including *Sun City*, the *Graceland* album was the result of numerous studio recordings creating multiple tracks of sound that were then combined to create the single texture we now hear as the final *Graceland* product. And these recordings occurred in Johannesburg, London, Los Angeles, and New York City. One of the criticisms of the album is that even though Simon was showcasing musicians to the world, they were not properly credited for their creative contribution. By all accounts they were well paid as studio musicians but were not compensated as artists. Responding to this accusation in Marre's video, Paul Simon talks not so much as a musician but as a producer, shifting the idea of musical collaboration to one where he and his engineer collected raw materials in South Africa that required the vision of the producer to bring it all together and "refine" it for the popular market.

There are eleven tracks on the CD, to a greater and lesser degree incorporating or shaped by South African vocal and/or instrumental performances. Excluding the Zulu texts of Joseph Shabalala, the words of all the songs are attributed to Paul Simon. A number of tracks are discussed in detail on the Marre DVD (1998), *Paul Simon's Graceland: Recounting the Journey of a Legendary Music Recording*. These are: track 1, "Boy in the Bubble"; the least South African in sound of all tracks, track 2, "Graceland"; track 8, "Homeless," which is the most easily identifiable as a South African sound; four more tracks discussed and showcased are track 9, "Crazy Love Vol. II," track 7, "Under African Skies," track 6, "You Can Call Me Al," and track 5, "Diamonds on the Soles of her Shoes." Five of the eleven tracks are analyzed to varying degrees below.

Marked differences are contained in the liner notes inside the 1986 original and 1996 reissue. The 1996 notes are considerably expanded. They are written by *Billboard* magazine's editor-in-chief, Timothy White, who discusses how the album was produced and the shifting political context of its production and reception since 1985. The photographic image of Paul Simon leaning against a wall, alone, which was originally on the front of the album, is moved to the back in 1996; the "more African" image, the Ethiopian print of King George on a horse, has moved from back to front. All the musicians who contributed in some way to *Graceland*, and their record companies, are carefully listed and acknowledged in the same way in both sets of notes. What has changed significantly is the discussion of the political significance of *Graceland* in light of the new South African democracy, a change few in the 1980s had imagined would be possible just a few years later. In short, a recording made and distributed globally in 1986 primarily as an American masterpiece written in the first person by Paul Simon, with a brief personal narrative of how it all came about, is completely reframed in 1996. The emphasis on a personal journey is gone. In its place is a politically informed story that relates the *Graceland* album and its production more intimately to South African music and political history, and places Paul Simon firmly into that archive, along with the South Africans who worked with him. Even if our response two decades later is to shrug our shoulders and say "So what?" to 1980s racial politics, it is clear that the controversy generated by *Graceland* in 1986 forced Paul Simon and Warner Brothers to reevaluate and reconfigure the presentation of the product for the global marketplace.

The Paul Simon Video: Making *Graceland*

Unlike the *Graceland* album, which was made in the apartheid era, Jeremy Marre's video, *Paul Simon's Graceland: Recounting the Journey of a Legendary Music Recording* (1998), was released well into the post-apartheid era. Its contents, like the liner notes of the 1996 *Graceland* release, are far more politically engaged. In this environment musicians like

Paul Simon—those Western popular musicians who have collaborated with those from less powerful places in the global economy—have become far more aware of relationships of power, the need for mutual respect between all musicians, appropriate payment and accreditation for multiple layers of musical sound that collectively constitute the final product, and the proper acknowledgment of musical collaboration. Since the mid-1980s, the view of third-world musicians as sources of inspiration has shifted to viewing them as co-creators. One might argue that the *Graceland* controversy not only raised awareness of the political plight of Black South Africans, but also highlighted issues of African creativity and the need for proper compensation. Although some cynically call it an atmosphere of political correctness, the present era is at least characterized by a heightened sensitivity to the politics of musical production, especially those between so-called first- and third-world musicians.

The brief recording chronology runs like this. Paul Simon spent several weeks listening to a cassette, a copy of *Gumboots: Accordion Jive Hits, II*, given to him by a friend, Heidi Berg, in the summer of 1984. Simon, then in something of a creative slump, was looking for personal and compositional renewal. He heard in this music a certain kind of familiarity, a resonance with popular music of the 1950s—hearing the familiar in the different would in fact come to be a defining characteristic of 1990s world music consumption (Taylor 1997). Simon asked Warner Brothers to track down the source of the cassette. They made contact with record producer Hilton Rosenthal in Johannesburg, who sent about twenty recordings of the gamut of contemporary Black South African performance. Simon listened closely and repeatedly to these recordings, allowing them to shape his musical thinking. Producer Hilton Rosenthal set up a recording date with Paul Simon and three groups that performed on Simon's cassette: Tao Ea Matsekha, General MD Shirinda and the Gaza Sisters, and the Boyoyo Boys bands. (Clips from these recording sessions are included in the Marre video.) Paul Simon and his engineer, **Roy Halee**, quietly traveled to South Africa in February 1985.

Soon after the Johannesburg recording session Paul Simon sent a letter and tape to Joseph Shabalala with some compositional ideas drawn from previous Mambazo recordings, to shape what became Simon's contribution to "Homeless." Then Shabalala and Ladysmith Black Mambazo traveled to London to record with Simon. Simon returned to New York and over the next few months invited several other musicians, including Nigerian pedal steel guitarist Demola Adepoju and Senegalese singer Youssou N'Dour, to record rhythmic and vocal tracks that would be dubbed into the recording mix. Some of this recording took place in Los Angeles. Although the album was scheduled for release in the summer of 1986, Warner Brothers delayed until the fall. South African musicians were in New York City because Ladysmith Black Mambazo and the Soweto Rhythm Section were to appear on *Saturday Night Live*. The South Africans went into the studio with Paul Simon in New York City and recorded in a few takes "Diamonds on the Soles of her Shoes," which was never intended to be on the original album.

Two ideas form the core of Marre's video on the making of *Graceland*: **collaboration** (see Meintjes 1990 for a thoughtful exploration of this idea in *Graceland*) and **composition** in the artistic sense. These two concepts work in tension with each other because a truly collaborative project would have required Simon to give artistic (and royalty) credit to the other artists, whereas the composition of a work of art by an individual composer enabled Simon to take the credit and royalty checks. Like the montage of musical traditions that defines the *Graceland* project, Marre integrates video footage from a range of sources: live interviews with musicians and technicians; footage from his own archive as used in *Rhythm of Resistance*; excerpts of *Graceland: The African Concert* (filmed in Zimbabwe in the late 1980s); news footage of political turbulence under apartheid; still images of 1950s Black South African performance, particularly of pennywhistle *kwela*; studio footage from Johannesburg, London, and New York; footage taken from *Saturday Night Live*; and several music video clips that both illustrate the words of the songs and present a single track ("You Can Call Me Al") with Chevy Chase lip-synching the words in a humorous rendition of the song.

Analyzing *Graceland*

There is a pervasive sense in Marre's documentary on *Graceland* that when Paul Simon initiated contacts with and traveled to South Africa in 1985, he was on a personal journey as an artist out to expand his creative resources, and as such, was largely concerned with essentially musical and creative processes. Paul Simon's travel to record in South Africa does not appear to have been a journey with a political motivation, as Marre's *Rhythm of Resistance* video so clearly was. His was a musical journey, a singularly artistic process—initially, anyway—one in which art/music and politics did not have to mix. Simon's position is not that unusual amongst creative people—who often argue that they simply want their music to speak for them, that politics is not their mode of engagement. What Paul Simon would quickly discover is that it was impossible for him to separate the musical, political, and even the personal because in the South Africa of the late twentieth century, the personal, political, economic, and even musical were inextricably intertwined.

In addition to telling of the politicized character of the "journey of a legendary music recording," Marre's video contributes to an understanding of South African music in the global economy in ways that are important to ethnomusicologists. First, it provides rare footage of the inside of a recording studio, and not just one but several studios. Second, the video reveals the complex layers of compositional process, from Paul Simon's jotting of words onto paper, to the "jam" sessions held with South Africans, to the careful crafting of the final mix. Third, we witness some of the interaction between Paul Simon and the South African musicians as the tracks are laid. The voices of the musicians are woven into a narrative that provides different perspectives on a single process and portrays the complex negotiation that occurred as *Graceland* came together. Finally, the footage of engineer Roy Halee provides a rarely heard voice from inside the industry itself. Both men, Simon and Halee, are presented as thoughtful and frank in their discussion of the musical and traveling experiences that ultimately resulted in the *Graceland* recording.

Simon's narrative of how he came to make *Graceland* and the processes by which he selected and multi-tracked the final product are key organizational nodes in the film. About halfway through the video an educational segment on South African music deconstructs the layers of South African sounds in the musical product. Perhaps the most useful information we glean from the video is how specific musical tracks were created, what parts were specifically South African, and what parts came directly from Paul Simon. Let us take a more in-depth look at three of these.

"The Boy in the Bubble"

The opening measures of the album not only introduce to the audience strands of the familiar-but-strange sounds of Southern African migrant worker performance; they also represent the whole concept of *Graceland* sonically. It was a social and musical experiment, collaborative to its very core, inspired by the sounds of **accordion**, guitar, drums, and bass on the *Gumboots: Accordion Jive Hits, II.* The song starts out with several measures of solo piano accordion playing, and the powerful beats of the drum enter to place the beat firmly in its 4/4 frame. For almost eight measures these two instruments establish the groove that carries Paul Simon's voice and lyrics through the remainder of the track.

"I think we always knew that this would be the start of the album. It began so unusually, and the sound of those drums sounded so 'African.' It was really an announcement that said you haven't heard this before . . ." Simon says. For engineer Roy Halee the song suggested the uncertainty of the moment, musically and politically. "It represents that whole experience: a very dark, very brooding quality about it. It most represents the whole trip, the whole concept, the recording in that studio" (Marre DVD 1998).

The song text, particularly in its refrain, explains the recording project as a connection created between the center and its "distant constellation," a "long distance call," urging its mainstream audience to think globally, to extend their listening ears to the place of "lasers in the jungle" (even though there is no "jungle" in South Africa). Retrospectively, the stress upon "miracles and wonder" has an eerie prophetic sense to it. But as Paul Simon remarks on the video, he knew that political change would eventually come to South Africa, but it seemed, in the mid-1980s, a very remote possibility. It is significant that the narrative about the radical political transformation of South Africa in the 1990s also used words like "miracles" and "wonders."

"Homeless"

The most removed in sound and musical arrangement from the experience of mainstream popular music audiences is the eighth track of the *Graceland* album, "Homeless." This is the track that most powerfully demonstrates the possibilities of musical collaboration between South African musicians and Paul Simon, even though they come from extremely different musical traditions. This track is also the most authentically "South African" in its sound—dear to many South Africans, but certainly the most remote to cultural outsiders because of its Zulu language text, which is not translated for the listener, and the sound of the Zulu language (and its clicks).

The song begins with Joseph Shabalala intoning the "call" and Mambazo men "responding" in traditional African style. They sing Simon's original ideas in Zulu but do not directly translate his words. Of all the South African musical traditions represented on *Graceland*, the unaccompanied four-part harmony vocal arrangements of *isicathamiya* is the one most flexible in meeting the requirements of the recording while remaining faithful to the tradition. *Isicathamiya*, which means "to walk stealthily, like a cat," or "to walk on tiptoes," traces its roots to mission hymnody (the four-part—soprano, alto, tenor, bass or **SATB format**) and the visit of African American performer Orpheus McAdoo and the Virginia Jubilee Singers to South Africa in the 1890s.[9] As the performance aesthetics of *isicathamiya* shifted in the twentieth century, so has its name. From *mbube* (discussed in Chapter 1) it was subsequently called *ibombing* because of the loud, near shouting style of its performance. Under Joseph Shabalala it has assumed a softer, sweeter, more harmonious sensibility, and is now performed with *isteps*: soft, stealthy dance routines reminiscent of nineteenth-century minstrel performances that took place all around South Africa.[10] Joseph Shabalala has frequently explained that performers learned to step lightly to avoid drawing police attention to their song and dance activities at night in the townships.[11]

As you listen to "Homeless," try to separate the distinctly "African/South African" aspects and those that are more familiar, more "mainstream" in American popular music. In thinking about the idea of familiar but different, an idea that characterizes the music on this album, and indeed the central characteristic of the success of "world music," think first about language (Taylor 1997). While Mambazo and Simon both sing in English, listen to the intonation of Black South African English. How does it differ from the American accent? The structure of the piece is largely sung in a call and response format—sometimes Joseph Shabalala is the leader, calling for a response; at other times Paul Simon assumes leadership, and Shabalala's voice is subsumed into the larger choral response.

Isicathamiya, as we have seen, is about four voices—soprano, alto, tenor, and bass—in harmony. Is this texture African or Western? This is an important question. Because of the long history of European, and more recently American, colonization of South Africa (largely through the missions and more recently through the entertainment industry), the musical texture of the mission hymn has become so much a part of Black South African performance practices, not only in *isicathamiya* but also in other styles of choral music, that it is now considered African. Clearly, **borrowing**, **assimilating**, even **appropriating** musical styles and ideas across the oceans has not been a one way process—Africans of European traditions, White Americans of Black African styles, for example—but is indeed an ongoing feature of the musical exchange between the two continents throughout the twentieth century, and in some cases, even earlier.

But as it has been indigenized, the SATB texture has taken on its own peculiarities. In the *isicathamiya* context, the soprano and alto voices usually sung by women are missing—the women are back at home in the rural areas, left behind by men who migrated to the cities for work. When migrant men began to form vocal groups and sing in the mission style, they adjusted the sound to a bass-heavy texture. In *isicathamiya* most voices sing bass, then tenor. Typically only one or two higher male voices sing alto, and the leader sings the soprano line. This is what you hear in Ladysmith Black Mambazo's singing both on *Graceland* and numerous other recordings they have made over the last four decades.

Finally, notice the creative, perhaps unusual use of the human voice on this track. Near the beginning of the song, we suddenly hear something that sounds like "rrrrrp rrrrp shek shek" in one of the voices. These are vocal imitations of sounds Joseph Shabalala recalls hearing in his childhood on his family farm. A little later one of the men, perhaps Shabalala, ululates—a high-pitched articulation typically done by women to express approval and joy in performance. Near the end of the song, the English phrase "Somebody say" is juxtaposed with alternating English words and syllables that are purely rhythmic in function: "ih hih hih ih." In all of these instances the human voice is used both melodically and rhythmically—a key feature of much vocal performance in South Africa. These are the familiar but different elements of *isicathamiya* performance that Tim Taylor, author of *Global Pop: World Music, World Markets*, argues appeal to world music consumers (1997). If you listen carefully to the Zulu lyrics near the end of the song you will hear a "click" sound in the middle of the word "*omanqoba*." (The letter "q" represents the click.) The Zulu language actually uses three different click sounds, the letter "c" is a soft click; "q" is a harder click, almost like the sound of horses galloping one can make with the mouth; and the letter "x" represents a click created at the back of the cheeks. South African singer Miriam Makeba popularized the Xhosa-language "Click Song" in the late 1950s and early 1960s when she sang with Harry Belafonte in New York City. The clicks clearly represent the exotic for those of us who speak English.

When listening to the "Homeless" track we might be tempted to presume that the marriage of cultures, languages, and voices was a happy one from the beginning, because its final product works so beautifully. But in the Marre video, Joseph Shabalala comments on the struggles that Ladysmith Black Mambazo had working with Paul Simon's initial ideas for the song. Simon sent his ideas to Shabalala before they met together to work out the song more fully. Shabalala recalls that he liked Simon's lyrics very much, but making the music work was far more of a challenge.

> It's a little bit difficult to blend the voices, the American voice, the African voice. The first day we were just touching, many people were trying to help us, and I just said, OK. Even the producer . . . was there, trying to teach us. That was confusing me, it was his first time to teach us: we didn't know him. We are used to working together alone, and come with something solid and good. (Shabalala in Marre DVD 1988)

There may have been some misgivings among the group, too, because Shabalala remembers having reassured the group that Simon was a good and a polite man. Roy Halee agreed. "At the beginning it felt a little strange, [Ladysmith Black Mambazo] are tricky to record because they don't produce a lot of sound, those bass voices are very soft" (Halee in Marre DVD 1988).

When the group returned to their hotel, they prayed. They decided that they would just give Paul Simon what they knew and not try to do what he wanted. Mambazo would give what they knew, and Paul Simon would give what he had. The plan worked, and the next day the "Homeless" musical collaboration began to take shape.

"Gumboots"

This track on *Graceland* is composed using the music on the cassette that Simon first listened to in 1984. The original tracks were performed by a South African band, the Boyoyo Boys, now overlaid with the wailing saxophone sounds of South African jazz performed principally by Barney Rachabane. These saxophone sounds are clear signifiers of the sounds of South African jazz, harking back to the excitement that African jazz produced for South Africans in the 1940s and 1950s—sounds that were silenced by the apartheid regime, particularly if they brought people of all races together in a single place.

Missing from the recording, but included in Marre's *Graceland* video, are the actual sounds of **gumboot** dancing, the boot dance of migrant workers from southern KwaZulu Natal who worked both in the port city of Durban and on the mines in Johannesburg. I have a peculiar attachment to gumboot dancing: I learned to perform the dance in 1985, trained by a migrant worker, Blanket Mkhize, and his team. When I visited the United States in early 1986 and told people that I gumboot danced, I would regularly be confronted with blank stares. "You mean Gumby?" people would laugh. But by 1987, *Graceland* had been released to the world, and far more people signaled recognition when I mentioned that I was a gumboot dancer—oh, from the *Graceland* album, people would inevitably remark. (See Chapter 9 for discussion of gumboot dance and its globalization.)

South African Responses to the *Graceland* Recording

Several musical responses to the plight of Black South Africans in the mid to late 1980s were generated both inside and outside of South Africa by the publicity associated with *Sun City: Artists Against Apartheid*, and the *Graceland* project.

Sarafina

Out of the workshop-style theater training identified with protest-theater in the 1970s and 1980s, South African playwright Mbongeni Ngema created a Broadway musical, ***Sarafina! The Music of Liberation***. It tells the story of Sarafina, a woman who teaches history at a school for Black South Africans in the township of Soweto. Sarafina seeks to teach history in a way that the South African government disapproves of, so she is arrested and put in prison. In the stage production, Sarafina symbolically represents Mandela—a man emasculated and feminized by his imprisonment. At the end of the production, Sarafina returns from her imprisonment as a man—the male figure of an imagined Nelson Mandela (he was still in prison at the time, and all visual representation of his face was banned in South Africa until his release in 1990). The Broadway production of *Sarafina* was subsequently produced for a popular audience in Hollywood, starring Whoopi Goldberg as Sarafina (Singh n.d.). A documentary film on the making of *Sarafina* from the perspective of its performers/co-creators was also made in the late 1980s (Noble 1988). There are several aural connections created between *Graceland* and *Sarafina* in the video made about the production of *Sarafina*. It opens with the South African performers standing close to one of Manhattan's famous bridges singing "Homeless." And *mbaqanga*, the popular musical style used in *Sarafina*, was introduced to the world by the *Graceland* album.

Field recording, March 1988, AmaOti, KwaZulu Natal

One of the first local responses to the *Graceland* recording I heard in South Africa was in an informal township school in AmaOti, in the Durban Metropolitan Region, in March 1988. (This is close to where the Shembe community, discussed in Chapters 13 and 14, has its headquarters.) My husband, a US citizen, was teaching in the school and had been called to an all-day parents' meeting. At the time, Inanda, the area in which the AmaOti school was located, was a hotbed of student protest against the apartheid government, school boycotts, and political instability. Partway through the performance, the choir suddenly moved from a series of religious and gospel style songs to a version of "Diamonds on the Soles of Her Shoes." I recall the sense of amazement I felt at the relative speed with which the *Graceland* album had rooted itself in this community. Even more amazing was that these students were clearly politically aware—and yet they sought to emulate the music of the recording that had generated so much heated debate elsewhere in the world. They could have refused to sing the song because of its use of South African musicians despite the cultural boycott. Instead, they sang the song with enormous pride and satisfaction on that Sunday morning in 1988. In a recent documentary titled *On Tip Toe* (2002), Joseph Shabalala claims that he had not even heard about the United Nations cultural boycott when Paul Simon invited him to collaborate on the *Graceland* project. Clearly, Radio Zulu was effectively screening out international concerns about apartheid.

Soweto String Quartet, Zebra Crossing (1994)

This album features the *Graceland*-inspired track "The Paul Simon *Graceland* Collection" which includes excerpts from four songs, "Homeless," "Diamonds on the Soles of Her Shoes," "Graceland," and "You Can Call Me Al" arranged to sound like a single piece.

The **Soweto String Quartet** hails from Johannesburg's largest and best-known Black urban township, Soweto. It has clearly established itself in an attempt to give respectability to the traditional and contemporary music of Black South Africans—to "classicize" the music. This is a recording made by Gallo (Africa) Records, the White-controlled commercial record company that is the dominant force in the South African recording industry. There is a dual signification in the title, "Zebra Crossing." On the one hand, the black and white of the zebra represent a kind of racial mixing, the zebra symbolizes Africanness, and the unity of Black and White in a single space; but the Zebra Crossing also resonates with global popular culture, referencing the Beatles' *Abbey Road* cover imagery from three decades earlier!

Distancing the group from the cloud of controversy that hung over the release of the recording, the author of the liner notes for this recording celebrates Paul Simon's intervention in South African music history by showcasing South African music and musicians. The collaborative project is justified by the already hybridized nature of *mbaqanga* music—adding a little more to the *mbaqanga* pot where "the rich flavors of South African black music culture simmer" (Soweto String Quartet 1994, liner notes). The notes convey appreciation to Paul Simon and the *Graceland* project for opening the ears of the world to South African music, and for "stirring up" the *mbaqanga* pot once more.

David Kramer (1996), Klassic Kramer

David Kramer is a South African singer and writer of protest song and theater. Born in England, he immigrated to South Africa many years ago and now lives in Cape Town. He is well known in the Cape for his depictions of the Afrikaans poor and working class (largely White) in the Western Cape. On his CD *Klassic Kramer*, he tells a story to a live audience about the time he met Paul Simon in 1985 when Simon visited South Africa to record what became the *Graceland* album. The story he told in 1991 at the Dock Road

Theater in Cape Town, South Africa begins with a song he calls "Weskusklong," sung in Afrikaans that I have translated into English here.

The earth is large and the stars are small
Only lizards in the desert
Deer and thorn and the bitter aloe
I know the "East Coast," but its not the same
Biscuits and biltong, I am a West Coast Khoi

Give me a whip, give me a stick
Give me a wife in a red floral dress
Give me the open veld where the deer pasture
You'll find me there between the stones
Biscuits and biltong, I am a West Coast Khoi.

Kramer's narrative is significant for the way in which he positions himself in the relationship between the powerful American music industry, represented by Paul Simon, and South African musicians. It revolves around being invited to the studios in Johannesburg (Marre's documentary provides a series of clips of these recording sessions, though none has Kramer in the frame) to witness Paul Simon and the South African musicians collaborating. Though Kramer is himself a popular musician in South Africa, he is not asked to collaborate with Paul Simon. Instead, at the studio in Johannesburg he invites Paul Simon and Roy Halee to visit him in Cape Town, a place many in South Africa consider the treasure of the country. He never thought Paul Simon would actually come, but it turns out he decided to after all.

So Kramer took the popular American musician to the Cape Point, the place where one can see both the Indian and Atlantic Oceans simultaneously, a place of great beauty and a popular tourist destination for foreign and local visitors. While they were there, Kramer was standing next to Paul Simon when a busload of tourists arrived and disembarked from the bus. When the tourists saw the two men, they came rushing towards them, asking Kramer for his signature. Nobody seemed to recognize Paul Simon, though they probably knew his voice and his music. So there Kramer stood, signing autographs, while Paul Simon, the powerful international star, stood to the side. It was an extraordinary example of the power of being known in the local context, over being the more widely known, but less recognized international name.

That night Paul Simon and David Kramer shared songs and stories at Kramer's home. Simon sang for Kramer, and then asked Kramer to sing for him. And the song he sang was "Weskusklong." As Kramer tells the story, Paul Simon took a copy of Kramer's song back to New York with him, and a little while later he had a call from Bob Dylan asking permission to do a cover version of the song. Kramer asks Bob Dylan to send him a cassette of the cover version. And he ends his story by imitating Bob Dylan's distinctive voice singing "Weskusklong."

David Kramer's spoken narrative is remarkable for the way in which it generates ideas about how the margins and centers operate, not from the perspective of global centers, but indeed, from the margins. In this narrative, the focus has shifted from the global star to the local: rather than the unknown international star, at least a star known only in voice and not in body, the tourists flock to the person they know from live performance and television commercials (Kramer did a commercial for Volkswagen on national television). Then of course, there is the lovely idea of a famous musician like Bob Dylan not being able to sound like anything other than his own voice, not being able to cover the music of others, even though they have been covering his songs for decades. Finally, Paul Simon, the famous musician, is unable to categorize David Kramer's music because he doesn't recognize it. The joke is on him, because it derives from the singer-songwriter tradition shaped by Paul Simon himself, just in another language. Ultimately Kramer's narrative is a discourse about shifts in the balance of power: who holds the power depends on what your perspective is.

Leeukop Prisoners' Choir (c. 1996) "Homeless"

The recording of "Homeless" by the inmates of a Pretoria prison provides a poignant example of the way in which the words represent the real experience of not having a home for many South Africans. In this context, however, "Homeless" comes to mean something very particular: men in a high security prison, trained by two White choral directors, express anxiety about the possibility of having no home when they are released from prison. Once again, a close copy of the original version, but without the White voice of Paul Simon, the **Leeukop Prisoners' Choir** extends the *Graceland* archive deeper into South African musical history and experience.

Khayelitsha United Mambazo

Geared toward the tourist market, **Khayelitsha United Mambazo** is a look-alike and sound-alike group modeled on Ladysmith Black Mambazo. They were selling this CD at the edges of their performance space while they sang at the Victoria and Albert Waterfront, a popular tourist destination in Cape Town's harbor, in July 2002. The disc has two songs sung in *isicathamiya* style. This group has clearly identified themselves as part of the larger Mambazo musical network, hoping to sell copies of their CDs to tourists for whom the name "Mambazo" and the sounds of the group will probably ring a bell. Copies and imitations are the ways in which South Africans have learned the repertories of the global entertainment industry. These actions foster a sense of connection to the centers of power. Imitation has long been a tradition in South African performance. In the past African people copied the sounds and gestures of animals and birds to harness their power; in the nineteenth and twentieth centuries, the model shifted to recorded objects and radio programing when the performances originated elsewhere in the world, though they relished imitations of local acts as well.

Inspiration's "Homeless"

Established in 1989 at the University of Pennsylvania, **Inspiration** is a student a cappella group that celebrates the power of Black music, by singing the music written and performed by people of the African diaspora.

Conclusion

Part I begins and ends with discussion about two important moments in twentieth-century South African music history that involve the recording and global travel of South African music: the "Mbube"/"Wimoweh"/"Lion Sleeps Tonight" recording and the *Graceland* collaboration. In between, we examined in some detail twentieth-century South Africa's political and media history. We began with the story of "Mbube," because in many ways, it bookends two very different political contexts, particularly for Black South Africans. In the first, the late 1930s, the years of segregation and before the extreme years of apartheid (1948–1990), Black South Africans were not considered citizens of what was then the Union of South Africa. They were simply uneducated "natives" with no rights in a nation-state. So, Solomon Linda, "Mbube's" composer, ceded his composer rights time and again, because in reality, he didn't really have any. He was not considered part of the modern South African nation—a nation conceived under apartheid, as including only people of European descent. By the early 2000s, when the Linda family came to a legal agreement with George Weiss's Abilene Music Company, about royalty payments for the melody of "The Lion Sleeps Tonight," South Africa had been radically transformed: in 1994 it had become a democratic nation—all South Africans over the age of eighteen were entitled to vote for the people they wished to govern them. Along with the right to vote came a range of constitutional, economic, and human rights. Righting the wrongs of the past included fighting for royalty payments denied in an unjust social system.

We ended this section with a discussion of *Graceland*, the collaborative musical project produced by American Paul Simon with among others, several South African musicians in the mid-1980s. Once again, we examined political contexts and transformations, but this time in a very particular historical moment—the mid-1980s when political oppression of Black South Africans by the apartheid government was at its peak, and resistance (both internally and internationally) to apartheid was mounting. We have seen that the *Graceland* recording, while extremely contentious at the time, in retrospect played a key part in putting South African music into the hearts and minds of consumers around the world. It put South African music on the popular music map. But, *Graceland* also conveyed to South Africans in a slightly more symbolic way, that it was possible to work together, to create something new, across racial and cultural divides. The musical experiment that *Graceland* represents could become a model for wider social, political, and cultural experiments. *Graceland* as a project also outlines an important process in the creation of "world music"—ultimately, it is a highly successful story about the capacity of very different musical practices to find a way to blend, harmonize, to become palatable to a wide range of musical tastes both in South Africa and the world at large. Ultimately, the *Graceland* project put on display through musical composition and collaboration a range of traditional South African genres, many formed through internal musical migrations in the twentieth century. In Part II we will take a closer look at several of these, most especially gumboot dance, *maskanda* guitar traditions, and the globally renowned *isicathamiya* styles popularized by Joseph Shabalala and his Ladysmith Black Mambazo.

Keywords

accordion musical instrument played in many parts of the world, with keyboard/buttons for pitch played on the right and left sides, and a middle that expands and contracts to create the air on metal reeds that produces the sound
appropriate an important concept in the study of world music—pronounced in one way and used as an adjective, it means something done in accordance with expectation; used as a verb it means almost the opposite—something taken without permission
Artists United Against Apartheid a 1980s political group formed around Little Steven, the rock musician, who urged musicians and entertainers to refuse to play in South Africa until apartheid was dismantled
assimilation to take on the ways of others in order to fit in
Bantustan homeland created by apartheid government, not recognized internationally
borrowing a process in which one musician uses the materials of another, but with permission
Bophutatswana the independent homeland where Sun City, the casino and entertainment complex, was located
charity rock rock concerts and musicians who perform at specific venues and events to raise money and awareness about poverty, starvation, and other humanitarian causes
collaboration the word used to describe the process of song-creation on *Graceland*, whereby musicians work together to create new music
composition the creative process involved in producing new songs
cultural boycott a movement in which musicians and artists refused to send their work or travel themselves to South Africa while apartheid was in place
David Kramer a British-born South African singer-songwriter who met Paul Simon when he was in South Africa recording tracks for *Graceland*
Graceland even if this was not Paul Simon's explicit intention, *Graceland* refers to both his collaborative album with South Africans and other musicians, and the home of rock'n'roll star Elvis Presley (who was strongly criticized for appropriating and profiting off Black American music)
Gumboots the name of the recording that inspired Paul Simon to record with South African musicians, but also a category of migrant worker boot performance (discussed in Chapter 9)
isicathamiya means to walk on tip toe, or stealthily like a cat; is the quieter version of "mbube" styled close-harmony singing from South Africa, made famous by Joseph Shabalala and Ladysmith Black Mambazo
Inspiration the student ensemble at the University of Pennsylvania that recorded a version of "Homeless" from the *Graceland* album
jive lively dancing between a man and a woman, with the man "swinging" the woman, accompanied both by jazz and then rock music; very popular in Black communities in the 1940s and 1950s in South Africa; often called "Zulu jive" or "sax jive" for example.
Joseph Shabalala leader of Ladysmith Black Mambazo
Khayelitsha United Mambazo copycat group of *isicathamiya* singers who perform for tourists at the Victoria and Albert Waterfront in Cape Town, South Africa
Ladysmith Black Mambazo the *isicathamiya* group who performed on *Graceland*,

literally means the "black axe from Ladysmith" (KwaZulu Natal), so-named because they won all the choir competitions

Leeukop Prisoners' Choir a South African choir formed in the Leeukop prison, and who performed the song "Homeless" in reference to those who would be homeless when released from prison

Little Steven rock musician who created the *Sun City: Artists Against Apartheid* film and song collaboration

Paul Simon American folk rock singer-songwriter who collaborated with South Africans on the *Graceland* album

popular musician a musician who is recorded, marketed, and distributed by the global entertainment industry and sells thousands of records

Ray Phiri South African guitarist and leader of Stimela, a popular South African band

Rhythm of Resistance the film produced by British filmmaker Jeremy Marre for the BBC that inspired Paul Simon's project

Roy Halee Paul Simon's recording engineer, who traveled with Simon to South Africa in 1984

Sarafina! The Music of Liberation a Broadway production of South African protest musical theater written and directed by Mbongeni Ngema in the late 1980s

SATB format four-part harmonizing

showcased *Graceland* put on display, through the compositional and collaborative processes, the sounds of South African music for popular music consumers. This becomes an important mechanism of musical display for those who might not have access or typically choose to listen to "world" music

Soweto String Quartet an important post-apartheid string quartet that has "classicized" much South African music by arranging and performing it in a quartet environment

Sun City the casino opened by South African developer Sol Kerzner that continued to host foreign entertainers when the United Nations Organization had called for a boycott of such activity while the apartheid government stayed in power

Sun City: Artists United Against Apartheid the documentary video made for MTV urging American and British artists to boycott South Africa

United Nations Organization a transnational organization headquartered in New York City that works to protect people or countries under siege, and to act on behalf of those whose human rights are violated by states or parastatal organizations

PART II

Twentieth-Century Musical Styles: Music in Migration

Introduction to Part II

Part II begins the telescoping effect: we move from the general information on South Africa, to more focused discussion on the music itself. In Chapter 5 we pick up the conversation begun in Chapter 1 where we began to think about ways in which we might represent the past in South African music by taking advantage of the new possibilities enabled by the worldwide web. In Chapter 5 we extend that conversation by creating five **historical periods** beginning in the early twentieth century and moving into the contemporary era. Chapter 6 outlines a handful of key **musical styles** you might encounter either as a **world music consumer**, i.e., those styles that have traveled outside of South Africa in the twentieth century, or those you might see or hear if you travel yourself to that country as a tourist or student in a study abroad program. Chapters 7 through 9 focus on three musical styles that have traveled in the last three decades: ***isicathamiya*** (made globally famous by Ladysmith Black Mambazo with the *Graceland* album); ***maskanda*** (related to ***mbaqanga***, township pop of the 1960s–1980s and ***mqashiyo***, the vocal genre popularized globally by Mahlathini and the Mahotella Queens); and gumboot dance (performed the world over, keyword "gumboot dance" in YouTube for a variety of examples). I have studied all three styles in greater detail than I have the styles presented in earlier chapters.

You might find interesting the high levels of **musical dialog** that happen between South Africans in the twentieth century, and European, British, and American music. This interaction happens largely through the **mass media**—through sound recordings, radio, to a lesser extent television, and now through the Internet, satellite broadcast, and so forth. In other words, it was South Africans consuming foreign music, copying it, expanding on it, making it their own, and then creating very local sounds and musical stars out of this process. But South Africans were also involved in internal **musical migrations**, moving from rural areas, around Southern Africa, largely into South African industrial and urban areas, in search of work, and bringing their musical traditions with them. In other words, musical migration, which characterizes much of twentieth-century music making in South Africa, happens at many levels in generating what has become a peculiarly South African music heritage and spectrum of sounds. By the end of this section you should have a fairly comprehensive understanding of the South African musical landscape.

Keywords

historical periods classifying significant historical events/developments in specific time periods. In European music history, for example, we talk about the "Baroque" or "Medieval" or "Viennese Classical" periods

isicathamiya the close-harmony vocal music of groups like Ladysmith Black Mambazo

maskanda Zulu version of the Afrikaans word "*musikant*" which translates into English as "musician," i.e., it is a musical form forged in contact with English, Afrikaans, and Zulu communities and individuals. Primarily a musical bow or guitar with singer tradition

mass media the technologies and institutions that convey information—radio, television, sound recordings, and now computers and the Internet

mbaqanga originally a word referencing African jazz, it came to mean studio produced, largely Zulu-language music in the 1960s, and has subsequently come to stand for the anti-apartheid liberation music produced abroad, e.g., in the musical theater of Mbongeni Ngema. It involves guitar, drum, bass

mqashiyo the vocal counterpart of *mbaqanga*, that entered the world music marketplace via the performances of growler Mahlathini and his Mahotella Queens

musical dialog conversations between individuals, groups, even nations that take place through musical means

musical migration the movement of music through physical travel of musicians, or more virtual travel via sound recordings, radio, and television

musical styles music of clearly identifiable sound that is identified by genre or community

world music consumer those who listen to and buy the category the industry calls "world music," i.e., songs not sung in English, music often produced collaboratively between "first" and "third" world musicians; or music that just sounds different from the popular music mainstream produced in the United States or UK

CHAPTER 5

Representing the Past in South African Music

At the end of Chapter 1 we began to reflect on processes by which we might create a comprehensive account of South African music in the twentieth century. The challenge, I suggested there, was to create a mechanism for representing a past that no one person actually experienced in his/her lifetime. In other words, we have to think about forms that are able to fairly represent a very divided past—first through the years of segregation, then through the divide-and-rule policies of the apartheid era, and finally, in the post-apartheid era, when we are still working out what it means to be South African, to belong to a democratic nation that, in a relatively small space, contains enormous levels of diversity. These differences are not just between those who listen to hip hop and those who prefer ska, reggae, global pop, or alternative rock. These are real differences of race, social class, language, culture, education, and so forth. As a result South Africans are asking who would be sufficiently qualified to create such an historical narrative?

Several people have tried. Yvonne Huskisson (briefly mentioned in Chapter 1) worked for many years for the South African Broadcast Corporation (SABC). A White woman who was involved in broadcasting the music of many Black South African musicians, she contributed to a four-volume *Encyclopedia of South African Music*, and has subsequently published books on "Bantu Composers." Her perspective was shaped by her position inside the government-controlled environment of apartheid broadcasting. In the early 1980s, when the apartheid government was at its most brutal and oppressive, South African journalist Muff Andersson wrote a coffee table style account of South African popular music, she called it *Music in the Mix* (1981). (The book provides a useful companion narrative to Jeremy Marre's later *Rhythm of Resistance*.) It was the first significant account that sought to incorporate the full spectrum of South Africans—it deals with popular music in a "**non-racial**" manner, i.e., she is racially inclusive in her approach. Though she focuses on "popular" music—we would expect a story about music produced by the music industry—Andersson captures the complexity of what popular meant in the apartheid era. She talks about the music producers and their stars, but she also provides extensive commentary on those who have tried to sing, but have been censored, harassed, or silenced and arrested by the apartheid government. And it is not only Black South Africans this happened to—Andersson writes about the largely White folk music movement, about those who strove to mount non-racial music festivals, about others who sought to create non-racial musical ensembles but were arrested, policed, and sometimes just gave up the fight, other times left the country in order to survive as musicians. There are some radical gestures in her book: she names musicians banned by the apartheid government from having their music broadcast or performed live in South Africa. Just to name people who were banned was to break the law—Andersson took it one step further by publishing their names. And her book was sold almost exclusively in South Africa, not in the international markets of products "banned in South Africa."

Then Rob Allingham, the American archivist at Gallo Music, the most significant record company in twentieth-century South Africa, provides a useful account of twentieth-century South African music in the *World Music: The Rough Guide* book. Once again, his perspective is shaped by his position in the industry—he tells the story from the recordings that are available. American anthropologist David Coplan and musicologist Charles Hamm have written extensively on South African music, but done so largely from the perspective of Black South African history. Recently, British journalist Gwen Ansell has written about South African jazz and popular music, but once again, it focuses on Black traditions (meaning all those who identify as Black—Coloured and Indians as well).[1]

In Chapter 1, I suggested that we might use the new possibilities of **worldwide web and internet technology** to map the quite literally global spread of South African music and musicians in the twentieth century. That is one point of departure that I will discuss further below, but we have to ask, just how will we tell the story of that past? What will the narrative strategy look or sound like? How do we represent the past in South African music? What are models elsewhere in the world that have outlined a nation's music history that might work for the South African case study? Perhaps we should look to the ways in which jazz in the United States has been written about: starting in the early years of the twentieth century, jazz history has been organized into a pattern of one style, one decade, up through the late 1960s/early 1970s, when it mutated into a variety of styles and personalities. What about the European classical tradition—starting in the ninth century, we have historical periods that initially span two or three centuries, and as we get closer to the present, the archives are larger and the stylistic periods become more compressed in time.

Following this model, of a confined period of time in which musical creativity and innovation amongst a select group of musicians follows a particular path, and then it changes significantly into a new period of musical innovation in a different style, which then changes . . . and so on through to the contemporary period, I have suggested elsewhere, that we might construct **historical periods** for South African jazz in a similar manner. It is possible that the model for jazz would work for the rest of South Africa's twentieth-century musical past.

The model is as follows:

(a) *Prehistory—through World War I.* The prehistory begins with the earliest archeological evidence of human presence in South Africa—and many believe that South Africa has some of the oldest evidence anywhere in the world. It would have to begin with a discussion of those who are called Khoisan, relying mostly on evidence created by European explorers, missionaries, and administrators, some of which is referenced by Percival Kirby in his 1930s work on musical instruments (1934). This earlier period would include discussion of the arrivals of European and American missionaries in South Africa from the eighteenth century through to the present, and the impact of mission culture on South Africa. It would also discuss other forms of traditional music; the music of slavery and those exiled in South Africa sent from Indonesia, India, the Philippines, and China in particular. This would include music of a range of religious practices—Hindu, Muslim, Christian, Jewish, and the hybrid forms that emerged out of the South African mix. Next, we would have to write about the cultures of seafaring peoples, and others who traveled the world, Christy minstrels, African American jubilee singers, and so forth; and finally about the early years of the worldwide music recording industry—the arrival of the first recordings in South Africa, and the first forms of radio broadcast.

(b) *World War I through 1940.* In this period, the migration of Black men in search of work in the newly emerging urban centers, begun in the late nineteenth and early twentieth century, intensifies. Eric Gallo starts his music business, the SABC begins serious recording of local—Black and Afrikaans—music; one or two Black South African groups travel to London to record—notably the **Reuben Caluza Double Quartet**; Hugh Tracey begins his work. This is the era of South African "blues"/*marabi* culture. Jazz and other popular music is imported on record; there is the growth of local religious music, the development of SA classical music centers in the cities; university music departments are formed; there are lively cultures of social dancing, entertainment for charity purposes, and working-class moviegoing communities. Traditional music in rural areas starts to feel the impact of urbanization and mission culture. The first mention of "jazz" as a "craze" and "frenzy" is mentioned in South African newspapers in 1913, and heated debates ensue in local newspapers about the value of American culture. These continue through to the present.

(c) *World War II through the end of the 1950s.* Black, White, and Coloured men enlisted for the war effort, many joined to entertain the troops and raise funds to support those fighting in North Africa and Europe on the side of the Allies—though there was division amongst White South Africans, between the English- and Afrikaans-speaking, about whether they should support Hitler or the Allies. Nevertheless, the wartime musical experiences proved critical in terms of training musicians, especially Black and Coloured musicians who had few other venues for this kind of musical education. Swing was in!

The 1950s is still singled out nostalgically as the decade of political optimism for a non-racial future for all South Africans; it was a period of the "**Americanization**" of South African performing arts, but also of **pennywhistle *kwela*** (see Chapter 6), and ultimately the era that would enable Black South Africans to travel locally and abroad, as entertainers in shows with South Africanized content. Many decided not to return to the country when they went abroad because it eventually became impossible to survive as artists and entertainers of color inside South Africa. **Sophiatown**, an interracial community of the working class and the poor embodies the optimism and escapism of the era—it is razed to the ground in the 1950s. Nevertheless, jazz in its commercial, swing, bebop, and traditional forms is consumed by a wide range of South Africans—a point not yet fully recognized in any of the current accounts of this era.

The postwar era was the time of avid movie attendance with films like ***Cabin in the Sky* and *Stormy Weather*** providing models for Black urban performance. As suggested in Chapter 3, this was also the period of the growth of local variety shows, of White people producing Black performance in shows like **African Jazz and Variety**, the **Golden City Dixies**, **Township Jazz**, and most notably ***King Kong: An African Jazz Opera***. These shows traveled, and they were filmed for the overseas market. ***Zonk!*** and ***Song of Africa*** were two of these films. All this activity was enthusiastically celebrated by Black journalists in the White-owned Black press—to such an extent that the 1950s is fondly remembered as the "Drum Decade," after *Drum Magazine*, which was perhaps the most famous of these publications.

(d) *1960–1980s*. If you think back to the political history in Chapter 2, you will remember that the era of **Grand Apartheid** began with the **Sharpeville Massacre** in March 1960. It was the period in which a variety of apartheid laws were introduced, including those that denied a place in the cities for all who were not White/European. Through **"influx" control** and the **Group Areas legislation**, all "non-Whites" were sent "home" to the rural areas called homelands or *Bantustans* if they were not carrying their passbooks, or they were forcibly removed as entire communities. Musicians who stayed in the country, both Black and White, often stopped performing, some drank themselves to death, others continued but with a much depleted sense of musical community. Muff Andersson's book *Music in the Mix* (discussed above) provides a tangible reminder of those difficult days in South African history, and musical past.

In the late 1980s, musicians in South Africa who recalled the "glorious decade" of the 1950s began to re-form their bands—most notably the African Jazz Pioneers and Mango Groove—both interracial groups. They both brought the sounds of 1950s pennywhistle *kwela* and African jazz to the ears of all South Africans. The University of Natal (now KwaZulu Natal) hired the first ethnomusicologist in 1981, and the first jazz educator, Darius Brubeck (son of Dave Brubeck of "Take Five" fame) in 1983. Both established innovative programs that would begin to expand the research and performance possibilities for South African music, and integrate the university on racial lines. The University of Cape Town followed suit. South African musicians living abroad began to be recorded on major and independent labels, though little of this music was aired in South Africa—most of these musicians were banned, i.e., their passports had been revoked. Many began to speak out about the atrocities of apartheid while living abroad; building the international anti-apartheid movement that would push for the United Nations boycott against South Africa. Paul Simon traveled to South Africa to record with South African musicians in 1985, and released the *Graceland* album in 1986.

(e) *1990s to the present.* The February 1990 release of Nelson Mandela and a host of other political (not criminal) prisoners by the apartheid regime, and the move toward a fully democratic dispensation, mark this era. Many of those musicians who had left the country were now permitted to return, and they did so. A handful of South Africans began to be recorded locally by the transnational corporations like Sony (South Africa) and BMG International, who re-entered the South African record scene once the international community stopped the cultural boycott and removed the economic sanctions against South Africa. There has been a significant growth in festivals of South African music, of a variety of styles and genres, often with local and global musicians performing side by side. There has also been a significant surge in local interest in documenting South Africa's media and musical past, amongst musicologists, cultural theorists, journalists, and community members. South African music is certainly coming into its own, both inside the country, and in the world at large.

Three points emerged in constructing this kind of model. First, each period is defined not just by musical transformations of style, but also by wider sociopolitical events. In twentieth-century South Africa everything was infused with the political. Second, much of that history pertained to wars fought both in other parts of the world and on South African soil (colonialism, the liberation war against apartheid, and South Africa's own wars against neighboring states out of fear of both the "Black danger," i.e., a White numerical minority living in a region far outnumbered by Black Africans, and the "red danger"—the fear of communist-inspired rebellion and ideology). Often those conscripted worked as entertainers, or in the international anti-apartheid movement, or they sang themselves through the political turmoil. Third, different media—radio, television, and recordings—shaped the particular ways in which South Africans consumed, responded to, and defined the music they listened to, and its value to them as South Africans.

The next possible form of representation of South Africa's musical past follows on what began in the late 1950s, individual scholars writing about individual musical cultures, either ethnographically or historically, or some combination of the two. Sometimes these musical cultures are defined by language and culture, i.e., Venda- or Zulu-speaking peoples, or by genre, *marabi*, *kwela*, or *mbaqanga*. For example, anthropologist John Blacking worked with the Venda people, as does Jaco Kruger; Veit Erlmann with *isiZulu* music, and eventually *isicathamiya*; David Dargie with the amaXhosa, and specifically women throat-singers and musical bow players. But these kinds of divisions reinforce the idea of self-containment, of styles out of contact with others. The question is how to put them all in conversation with each other. Should we allow separate narratives to co-exist, without putting them in dialog with each other to constitute a sense of their coevality?

The quintessentially hybrid quality of many identifiably South African musical genres and styles means that the "history" or "past" or at least ancestry or musical DNA of a style is often exactly what defines the style itself. Perhaps the most obvious example, itself made possible by new recording technologies of sampling, overdubbing, and scratching, is the post-apartheid youth genre: *kwaito*, a music so hybrid everyone who wants to could probably find a piece of themselves or their past in its sound and make-up (see Chapter 6).

Alternatively, should we move away from the idea of narrative, of a beginning, middle, and an end, of moving from point A (on the left) to point B (in the middle) to point C (on the right), of one moment in time and place becoming another significant point-in-time. Perhaps we have to think about the mode of representation as less linearly progressive, and conceive of a new kind of spatial and temporal configuration. Instead of the narrative ordering of the past we might re-conceive of the past in terms of the **palimpsest**. A palimpsest is an artifact created when a scribe uses an old manuscript to write something new, in other words traces of the past remain visible in the present. This is much like Bushmen paintings where one painter painted over the prior work of another painter. The result is that the painter never completely erased the past, but allowed its traces to seep through into the new image. There is a spectral quality to such kinds of representation, allowing for the presence of one's ancestors in contemporary forms of representation, which is not that far from traditional belief systems in much of the African continent.

Three key concerns characterize this project, regardless of how we decide to represent South Africa's musical past. The first is the nature of the **archive** and its capacity for recovering any kind of past—so much of what happened, particularly under apartheid, was never recorded. The only way to begin to recover that activity is through oral history, photographic archives, and so forth. Second, in a country so influenced by northern hemisphere music and culture, a key problem pertains to ideas about **originality in a mass-mediated world** of copies and covers—at what point does something that sounds like something else come to be defined as distinctive? And third, we will have to reflect on how we measure and **value** ideas about music itself—is art music more important than popular or township music? How do we think about the operatic tradition in South Africa, a tradition now completely inhabited by Black performers whose first language is a tonal language, and whose ideas about tonality are simply not the same as the standardized European ideals? They clearly belong to the world of opera, but then how do we rethink Georges Bizet's *Carmen* when it has been translated into Xhosa and its story recontextualized? To whom does Bizet "belong"? Finally, the challenge, as I suggested in Chapter 1, in constructing a viable account of the past for South African music is to examine that account in relationship to Southern Africa, sub-Saharan Africa, and the world at large as we move toward quite literally a whole world of music in the present, with a future, and without question a series of possible pasts.

Keywords

African Jazz and Variety traveling show for Black and Coloured South Africans in 1950s, run by Alfred Herbert

"Americanization" the post-World War II period in South Africa was a time in which South African culture was strongly shaped by American music, film, and other forms of entertainment, spread largely through the mass media

archive the resources used to constitute a past for South African music

Cabin in the Sky* and *Stormy Weather two American films featuring African American performers that had a significant influence on shaping urban culture in the postwar era in South Africa

Golden City Dixies the first traveling group of Black performers to travel abroad in the 1950s

Grand Apartheid from 1960 to 1990 when the laws of apartheid were implemented

Group Areas legislation the laws of apartheid that forced people of different racial, language, and cultural groups to live in places defined by those differences

historical periods five in all for twentieth-century South African music: through World War I; WWI through 1940; WWII through end of 1950s; 1960–1990; 1990 to the present. These are musical eras clearly defined by the changing political landscape

Influx control apartheid laws that prohibited the movement of Black South Africans in and out of urban areas

King Kong: An African Jazz Opera an interracial collaboration that traveled to England in the late 1950s, launching the international careers of several Black South African performers, most notably Miriam Makeba

non-racial while in the United States for example, diversity usually means multi-racial, South Africans have stressed the significance of a non-racial society, i.e., a society that doesn't define itself in racial terms (see ANC Freedom Charter for an early example of such thinking)

originality in a mass-mediated world there is always a question of what is "original" and "new" in a world that sells music as commodity, i.e., by definition commodification creates products that are exactly the same as the original

palimpsest a form of representation in which traces of prior inscriptions remain visible to the eye, even when new layers are inscribed, e.g., Bushmen paintings

pennywhistle *kwela* a township music that preceded the development of a distinctive South African clarinet and saxophone sound in jazz

Reuben Caluza Double Quartet one of the earliest recordings of Black middle class choral music, made in London when Black South African composer and educator Caluza traveled with his ensemble to record in London

Sharpeville Massacre a turning point in apartheid history, when the apartheid government fired on those protesting the pass laws in Sharpeville, Johannesburg in March 1960

Song of Africa a film very much shaped by Afrikaans ideology, but describing the formation of "Zulu jazz" as part of the rural to urban cycles of migration in the 1950s

Sophiatown one of the interracial areas in Johannesburg destroyed by the apartheid government

Township Jazz a live musical performance, recorded and reissued by Gallo, that celebrated Black South African jazz in the 1950s

value is the question addressed when we strive to create fair historical narratives of all of South Africa's music

worldwide web and internet technology we ask how the possibilities of these technologies might inform how we think about and represent the past in South African music

Zonk! both a live stage production created at the end of World War II in South Africa, and the film made in the 1950s that illustrates the content of South African variety shows of the same period

CHAPTER **6**

South African Music: Brief Definitions

By this stage in the book, you will be quite aware of the complex landscape of South African music in the twentieth century. In this chapter, I have selected a few key genres of this music, those you are most likely to encounter through the global circuits of the world music marketplace or if you travel to the country yourself. I provide short definitions of each, and refer you to one or two key recordings that are commercially available that should enrich your understanding of each category. Where available, I also point you to further literature on the subject. All recordings alluded to here are listed in a more comprehensive discography in Appendix 3.

Marabi, *Kwela*, Township Jazz

Listening to the CD, *Township Jazz and Jive, 18 South African Urban Swing Classics from the Jivin' '50s*, a compilation of reissues from 1950s South Africa, one is tempted to dismiss South African jazz as simply the improvised popular music of Black South Africans derived from American big band swing. Certainly, this is the music that was popular in that decade of South African music that was filled with optimism both for the present and the future of all South Africans. The early history of this "township" ***marabi***-based style of performance has been carefully researched and written about principally by South African jazz scholars Christopher Ballantine (1993), David Coplan (1985), and Lara Allen on pennywhistle ***kwela*** (1999). The basic structure of *marabi*-styled jazz is explained by Ballantine:

> It was primarily a keyboard, banjo or guitar style based on a cyclic harmonic pattern, much as the blues was: the basic marabi cycle, however, may be said to have stretched over four measures, with one measure for each of the following chords: I-IV-I6/4-V. The cyclical nature of this style clearly derives from traditional sources . . . This then was the manner: cyclical repetitions of one melody or melodic fragment

> yielding eventually, perhaps, to a similar treatment of another melody or fragment, and perhaps then still others, each melody possibly from a different source ... Throughout, rhythmic accompaniment would be provided by a player shaking a tin filled with small stones. (Ballantine 1993: 26–28)

Historically, this performance was accompanied by huge amounts of alcohol consumption and exuberant dancing throughout the night. Ballantine's 1993 book, *Marabi Nights* was published with an accompanying cassette of a representative sample of what remained of *marabi* in the archives of Gallo Records in the early 1990s.

Kwela is the quintessential sound of South African pennywhistle music that came to the world's attention in the 1950s. It was one of the direct relatives of *marabi*. Initially, young boys stood on street corners playing the music they heard on record and performed live by older musicians, on cheap pennywhistles. The instruments could be played solo or in groups, and they continued a longer tradition of pipe and flute playing characteristic of the rural areas of the northern parts of South Africa. The word "*kwela*" derives from the word used to warn township people that the police were coming: "*kwela kwela*" would sound out when the police vans were heard approaching, and all music would stop. Three of the most famous pennywhistle performers and recording artists were **Lemmy "Special" Mabaso**, **Spokes Mashiyane**, and **Elias Lerole**. Lerole had an international hit with his 1959 recording "Tom Hark," which was arranged by famous British bandleader Ted Heath for his dance band in England. *King Kwela, featuring Spokes Mashiyane* is perhaps the best example of this music currently available on CD. Many who began playing pennywhistles moved on to clarinet and saxophone and into South African jazz performance.

South African township jazz was borrowed from foreign recordings but infused with fragments and memories of the traditional musics that migrants carried to urban areas, the principal sites of music-making in African jazz in this period. To unpack these strands of tradition requires a deep understanding of the diversity of musical traditions in South Africa, something not really possible to find in a single musician—these traditions were divided by different linguistic configurations (remember South Africa now has eleven official and many more unofficial languages). Listen, for example, to track 5 on the *Township Jazz and Jive* CD. The sound of the repeating high notes on the banjo is similar to those in musical bow playing. In a different context, guitarist Blanket Mkhize translated bow playing onto guitar using a hair "comb" bow (see track 3 of the CD in the back of this book). This is **township jazz**, in contrast to the **jazz as art or freedom** ultimately developed by **Chris McGregor**, **Abdullah Ibrahim**, **Sathima Bea Benjamin**, **Dudu Pukwana**, **Kippie Moeketsi**, **Johnny Dyani**, and others.

What we hear on this CD, nonetheless, are the core features of South African jazz that people like Moeketsi, Ibrahim, Benjamin, and McGregor would expand and develop into a more sophisticated, and yes, elite and international-sounding South African jazz. They were strongly influenced by a range of American jazz musicians, most notably Duke Ellington, Billie Holiday, and Thelonious Monk but also the "free jazz" musicians like John Coltrane, Albert Ayler, and Ornette Coleman, many of whom they would meet when they traveled to Europe and the United States in the 1960s. The core musical elements of these musicians have been described to some extent in Maxine McGregor's book about her late husband and his ensembles in *Chris McGregor and the Brotherhood of Breath* (1995) by Michael Rossi (2001), Ansell (2004), and in Lars Rasmussen's quite extraordinary publications (2003a, 2003b, 2002a, 2002b, 2000a, and 2000b).

Making the style distinctively South African were elements that reflected the strong connection between instrumental performance and vocal style. As Rossi comments, in South Africa the saxophone is the primary instrument in jazz ensembles, and at times, is quite dominant, with up to ten saxophones in a jazz band lineup on some occasions. The sound of the saxophone is likened to the cry of the human voice in these contexts. At times it is completely faithful to the melody, sounding out each original note. The play with timbre and pitch is a space where South Africans explore their own distinctive sound—often accused of playing "out of tune," they bend, expand, and push the limits of tone color. At times performers sound as if they are going to blow their instruments to pieces because they are blowing so hard and so loud. But they also incorporate grunts, growls, smears, and pitch fall-offs, scooping and gliding with pitch. There is extensive use of repetition, either exact or slightly varied, to increase the intensity of a performance. South Africans can also refuse to swing the eighth note, instead playing right on the beat. Each of these musical qualities have contributed to creating a distinctive musical vocabulary for South African jazz musicians in forging a place for themselves in the transnational world of jazz over the last fifty years.

Abdullah Ibrahim (previously Dollar Brand) is the most prolific South African musician in the world. He has been recording his own music since the early 1960s, with a comprehensive discography compiled by Danish fan and used-book dealer Lars Rasmussen (first and second editions, 2000, 2002). Abdullah's music is widely available in Europe, Asia, the United States, and South Africa. There are at least two full-length documentary films focused on Ibrahim—*Brother with Perfect Timing* (1988) and *The Struggle for Love*; and Ibrahim is a key character in Lee Hirsch's documentary, *Amandla! Revolution in Four-Part Harmony* (2002). Sathima Bea Benjamin, discussed at length in Part III, is the most recorded jazz singer in South Africa—she has ten CDs to her name, all self-produced and recorded in Europe, the United States, and South Africa. Three of her CDs are available on iTunes. Miriam Makeba covers more genres than Benjamin, and has also been recording since the late 1950s, with a range of musicians from South Africa and the African diaspora. Hugh Masekela, who is of the same era as Makeba, Ibrahim, and Benjamin, covers a wide range of African jazz, pop, and world music categories, and has also recorded widely since the late 1950s. Both Makeba and Masekela have written autobiographies. Other useful compilations or reissues of the early years of South African jazz include *Township Jazz* (volumes 1 and 2), *From Marabi to Disco*, *The Elite Swingsters*, and several *kwela* compilations, published by Gallo Records, with much of it now available through iTunes.

Mbaqanga and *Maskanda*—1960s Onwards

Originally "*mbaqanga*" was the word used to describe the next stage of the *marabi*-swing style of the 1930s and 1940s, in developing a distinctive African jazz sound. In the 1960s, when most of the jazz community either left the country, or stopped playing, ***mbaqanga***, sometimes called ***msakazo*** (broadcast music) became a largely studio generated, more popular township sound. *Mbaqanga* has become an umbrella term used to describe the music made by small bands playing the music popular in Black communities from the 1930s to the present. It is the style featured in much of the protest music-theater of the 1980s and early 1990s, in the productions of Mbongeni Ngema specifically. This includes *Sarafina!* (the musical and the movie starring Whoopi Goldberg with an appearance by Miriam Makeba).

Finding ***maskanda*** in the United States is not difficult. It has been well documented and available in "world music" bins and online archives for the last two decades. One of the first compilations made available was Shanachie Records' *Indestructible Beat of Soweto* (43033). The Earthworks label in Britain has issued a four-volume compilation under the same title, but the album I refer to is the one originally released by Shanachie Records (USA).

Recorded prior to *Graceland*, this CD represents some of the traditions in transformation pertaining to indigenous guitar styles in South Africa. Though it claims on the liner notes that the music is all *mbaqanga*—basically the studio-produced sounds popular in Black South African townships around Johannesburg and Durban (that is, largely Zulu-language, guitar-based popular bands)—this recording actually includes four popular styles: *maskanda*, *mbaqanga*, ***mqashiyo***, and ***isicathamiya***. *Mbaqanga* and *mqashiyo* are the least traditional-sounding of the four, with *maskanda* and *isicathamiya* situated between rural traditions and urban styles. The most strongly *maskanda* in style are tracks 1 and 6 by Udokotela Shange Namajaha. Tracks 2, 3, 4, 7, 8, and 11 are clearly in the *mbaqanga* range, though the use of concertina hearkens back to *maskanda*, perhaps of the *isishameni* style (one of the less traditional-sounding *maskanda* styles). Track 8 is more specifically in the *mbaqanga* style used in the *Sarafina!* film and musical of the 1980s discussed briefly at the end of Chapter 4. Tracks 5 and 10, performed by Mahlathini and his group, are in *mqashiyo* style. Track 9 by Nganeziyamfisa no Khambolomvaleliso presents a style somewhere between *maskanda* and *mbaqanga*—it is in the format of a *maskanda* band, with bass guitar, concertina, and drum kit. Finally, track 12 presents Ladysmith Black Mambazo in a typical *isicathamiya* performance of the early 1980s. There are three distinctive sections to their piece. The introduction is sung standing still. Then the words "*halalala*" repeated over and over signal a new rhythm, the point at which *isicathamiya* groups begin their synchronized dance movements. The concluding part of the song is marked with a deliberate slowing in tempo and an increased sense of musical and textual closure.

There are two important female *maskandi* in the contemporary scene in KwaZulu Natal: Tu Nokwe and, perhaps better known internationally, Busi Mhlongo. Busi has three CDs that are commercially available, and individual tracks of her music can be found on iTunes. In addition, world music labels have made several compilations of *maskanda*, *mqashiyo*, and *mbaqanga* music—the quintessential sounds of the South African townships in the apartheid era.

1950s Traveling Shows

I talk about the **traveling shows** of African jazz and township performance in several places in this book. In the next few pages I have provided extended descriptions of three of these shows, as written about by journalists at the time (1950s and early 1960s) and in personal memoirs since then. The first is from Johannesburg in the 1950s, and it describes the show called African Jazz and Variety (which was later changed to the African Follies). Jairus Serongoane writes in *Zonk!* in November 1962:

> In 1954, a new young theater, the Windmill in Bree Street (Johannesburg) was struggling to keep its doors open. Some shows staged there were good, some plain lousy, and the customers stayed away. What to do to keep the queues at the box office? Alfred Herbert, who had been approached for suggestions, came across with the idea of staging a Variety Show featuring African talent. Some of those connected with the theater were dead against the idea—after all, they said, Africans lacked the know how of entertainment, and could never put up a decent performance. Herbert persisted . . . The word went out that auditions were being held on a Saturday afternoon, for a show to open on the next Monday night—from those auditions and from that show, was born "African Jazz and Variety" which after eight years shows no sign of ever folding up.
>
> In that first performance, Dolly Rathebe, Isaac "Zakes" Nkosi, leading the Hot Shots Band, and others drew applause from world-famous film star, Danny Kaye, who was in Johannesburg, and attended the opening performance. African Jazz and Variety with Alfred Herbert . . . and a cast of approximately forty, has played in every city, and most towns in the Republic [of South Africa], the Federation [Zimbabwe and Zambia], Mozambique, and the Congo. Over the years the pattern of the show has hardly changed, yet its appeal never misses.

Serongoane includes in his article a list of African performers whose careers were launched by their performances in African Jazz and Variety, a large number of whom, by 1962 were pursuing their careers abroad. These include names like: Miriam Makeba, Hugh Masakela, and Sonny Pillay in the United States, Gene Williams who traveled to Britain to work with bandleader Jack Parnell, and Jeff Hujah and Gambi George in Sweden. Some, like Abigail Kubeka and Dolly Rathebe stayed in South Africa, to pursue solid careers as singers in that country. Following the success of "AJ and V," the newly formed Union of Southern African Artists organized the now well-known "Township Jazz" concerts in White areas (recordings of these sessions have been reissued by Gallo Records (South Africa).

The next description is of the Golden City Dixies, the first performing ensemble to travel abroad. In April 1959, *Zonk! The African People's Magazine* reported on their impending trip.

> At last, after many years of having farewell concerts and publicity about going overseas, a show is really going overseas, and our congratulations and good-luck wishes go with the Gold Dixies, a live vital coon show which has left by air for a tour of Britain and the Continent, the first entertainment group from the Union [of South Africa] to tour overseas. They will give concerts and have been booked to appear on television . . . Corrine Harris and Elizabeth Julius, both polished performers, are the female contingent of the show. Arthur Gillies, the wizard of the keys, is on the piano. Gambi George, South Africa's king of the drums, handles the

percussion; Shimmy Peter Radise, tenor sax master; Graham Tainton is show compere and other famous artists such as Jusuf Williams and Brian Isaacs go to make up a very competent group of performers.

And the most internationally famous and nostalgically remembered show of all is the first African musical opera called *King Kong*—not the *King Kong* of Hollywood fame, but rather, *a King Kong* that tells a very South African story. Harry Bloom wrote the book, Todd Matshikiza composed the music, and Pat Williams created the lyrics. (A recording of the original production was reissued by Gallo Music Productions in Johannesburg in 1996.) It toured South Africa and ultimately went to London for a good run. A trip had also been planned for New York City, but characteristic of these productions, they ran out of money, and so disbanded in London. These are the contents of a program from the performance in London.

King Kong: The jazz musical opera

The synopsis of scenes from the program for the Prince's Theatre in London, February 1961. (CD of *King Kong: The Musical* is available from Gallo Records, through www.oneworld.co.za.)

ACT I

Scene 1	Early morning in the yard of a Johannesburg township. The present
Scene 2	Midday in a township street, 1954
Scene 3	Same as Scene 1
Scene 4	Back of the Moon, a shebeen on a night when business is good, 1954
Scene 5	A summer night in the streets of the township, 1954
Scene 6	The township yard, the present and the past
Scene 7	A Sunday in the township, about 1956

ACT II

Scene 1	A corner of the township, about four months later
Scene 2	A road in the township
Scene 3	Jack's boxing gym, two months later
Scene 4	Early morning at the bus terminus, a week later
Scene 5	Jack's boxing gym
Scene 6	(a) The township yard, the present
	(b) In court, February 25, 1957
	(c) The township yard, the present

MUSICAL NUMBERS

ACT I

Sad Times, Bad Times	CHORUS
Marvelous Muscles	KING KONG and CHORUS
King Kong	KING KONG and CHORUS
Kwela Kong	CHORUS

Back of the Moon	JOYCE, LUCKY, and CHORUS
The Earth Turns Over	PETAL and FRIENDS
Gangsters Dance	LUCKY and GANGSTERS
Damn Him!	LUCKY
Party Tonight	KING KONG SMALL GROUP
King Kong	CHORUS

ACT II

Be Smart, Be Wise	POPCORN and CREW
Tshotsholosa-Road song	MALE CHORUS
Quickly in Love	JOYCE and CREW
In the Queue	CHORUS
It's a Wedding	CHORUS
Wedding Hymn	CHORUS
Death Song	KING KONG and MALE CHORUS
Sad Times, Bad Times	CHORUS

The various types of South African song and dance in the production were explained in the 1961 program notes for the London audience. They read as follows:

> The Gangsters' Dance
> This dance is largely based on the steps of a Sotho war-dance. The weaving action of arms, the whirling and stamping of legs has its origins in ancient tribal dancing lore. The dance here, however, has been adapted to its modern context, knives and broken bottles taking the place of stabbing spears and knobkerries (fighting sticks).
>
> Kwela and Patha Patha
> Are the most popular forms of dancing among the urban African youth. They resemble jive in their absence of formal steps, but the sinuous hip movements, the seductive torso weaving of the women, and in the Patha Patha (touch touch) the intimate play of hands on the partner's body are pure "township." The dancers perform with great abandon—to wild almost barbaric music, with interjections of whistling and shouting.
>
> Road Gang Song
> African laborers always work to chants and songs which bring a mass rhythm into their actions and so lighten the work. Tshotsholosa, the chant sung by the road-workers in King Kong was actually taken from a gang of laborers working in the street. The song originated among railway gangers—the words suggest the sound and heavy effort of a train, as also the rhythm of its piston driven wheels—but has become popular among all forms of work parties and for some reason not discovered, especially among hard labor convicts. (Refer to discussion in *Gumboots!* Video about hard labor and gumboot dance.)

Religious groups
There are a large number of Evangelist groups in the African townships. Their adherents wear special uniform—in King Kong red and white blouses—and on Sundays they parade through the townships behind banners and drums, very much as the Salvation Army does in other countries.

Penny whistle troupes
Johannesburg is one of the few cities that still has street minstrels—ragged urchins from the townships who perform on the pavements for coppers tossed to them by passers-by. The lively, simple, yet poignant flute music of these groups is heard all over the town and adds a flavor all its own to the life of Johannesburg. The music is improvised—none of these urchin musicians have ever learnt a note of music—and the playing is usually accompanied by exuberant dancing and acrobatics. LEMMY SPECIAL has been playing the penny whistle since the age of seven when he collected together and led a group of street performers twice his age, supporting his family of nine out of the proceeds. One day an official of the Union of Artists saw him in action on his favorite pavement pitch, bundled the whole troupe into a car and took them to a rehearsal for a concert. Lemmy and his group stopped the show and since then his rise to fame and success has been swift. He is a great radio favorite and his records are best sellers. Now, a self-assured young man of fourteen, he brings the quaint child-art of the penny whistle to the London audiences, and seems certain of stardom.

Gum Boot Dance
Originally a Zulu [actually amaBhaca] tribal dance, it was practiced in secret by pupils of a mission school near Durban during a time when local tribal dances were forbidden. Eventually it found its way into Durban and became a favorite among the dock laborers who performed it in the rubber boots supplied them as protection when handling chemical cargoes. The new effects obtained by the slapping and pounding of rubber boots made it a popular dance with laborers everywhere, especially on the Witwatersrand where it has been developed to a high degree of perfection in the compounds of the gold mines and municipalities. The dance divides into a number of separate routines, each with a name such as "Salute," "Horse Ride," "Shoot." It is accompanied by a loosely improvised guitar melody and the convention today is to use it as a means for all varieties of comic and satiric expression.

Finally, there is a remarkable piece written about *King Kong: The African Jazz Opera* by a White South African, Percy Tucker (1997), whose experience watching Gracie Fields perform live in South Africa was cited in Chapter 2. Mr. Tucker was the man who invented computerized ticket sales for entertainment events in South Africa in a system he called "Computicket." I am citing quite lengthy excerpts from Tucker's memoir because it provides information, first, about the creation and production of *King Kong*; second, about the interaction between people of different racial groups; and third it lends itself to an understanding of the problems of cultural (and language) translation that surfaced when *King Kong* traveled to London in 1961. In Chapter 4 a similar issue emerged in the production of the *Graceland* album, and in Chapter 9 we talk about it once more in regard to the globalization of gumboot dance.

> In the 1930s African jazz had flowered in the township to become an important feature in the lives of urban Africans. Some remarkable talents emerged, acquiring a huge following among their own people, but remaining largely unknown to whites.
>
> When (Englishman) Father Trevor Huddleston was seeking to raise funds to build an Olympic sized swimming pool for his flock in Orlando [township] in 1953, he enlisted the help of John Bolon. The outcome was the staging of a concert at the Bantu Men's Social Center, given by black entertainers. Names well-known in the townships—Dolly Rathebe, the Manhattan Brothers [see Ballantine 1999] and others—featured in the program, and an unknown young composer named Todd Matshikiza wrote a choral overture dedicated to Father Huddleston.
>
> The handful of whites in the packed hall, an influential group, responded strongly to the event and voiced the feeling that these gifted performers should be more widely seen and heard . . . Bolon called a meeting of black entertainers to which some three hundred people came, and the Union of Southern African Artists was born, with Bernhardt soon leaving the commercial world to run it full time.
>
> The Union functioned as educator, promoter, and protector of black artists, and in 1956 the indefatigable Alfred Herbert launched the first of his "Township Jazz" concerts at the City Hall, familiarizing ecstatic white audiences with the Manhattan Brothers, Sonny Pillay, Lemmy Special, Kiepie Moeketsi, and a host of other gifted musicians. ["Township Jazz" concerts were recorded by Gallo Records and were reissued as part of the Gallo archival series in the 1990s. They are available for purchase through www.oneworld.co.za.]
>
> In 1958 lawyer and writer Harry Bloom accompanied Ian Bernhardt one evening to listen to some new black singing groups at the Salvation Army school in the Eastern townships [of Johannesburg]. Harry Bloom was enthralled by these young performers. Like Bernhardt he felt the time was ripe to develop black potential in vehicles more substantial than concerts. He conceived the idea of developing a jazz opera and set about looking for a suitable story that would embody the unique flavor of township life through music and drama. When he read reports of the death of Ezekiel Dhlamini he knew he had found his subject.
>
> Dhlamini was a champion boxer, a township hero with gangland associations,who lost his grip and became a fallen idol. Having killed a gang leader with his bare fists, he subsequently murdered his girlfriend in a fit of jealous rage and was sentenced to twelve years' hard labor. Shortly afterwards, he committed suicide, drowning himself in the dam near the Leeuwkop Prison.
>
> The life and death of Ezekiel Dhlamini had everything that Harry was looking for: the vibrancy of township life, its glamour and its squalor, laughter and tears, and the dark underside of tragedy. He discussed the idea with Ian who suggested Todd Matshikiza as a possible composer. Matshikiza accepted . . .
>
> In due course the government would crush the principles of academic freedom

> in its ever-tightening vice, but at the time of King Kong the [University of the Witswatersrand] Great Hall was still protected by its charter and was open to non-segregated audiences. Union Artists secured a booking at the Great Hall for February 1959, and Leon held auditions to select his massive cast of sixty-three singing actors [and a fourteen piece jazz orchestra] . . .
>
> Most of the cast had to work at their jobs by day and rehearse at night. Transport was difficult and many of the company had no concept of timekeeping or the necessity for it. Each night a specially hired bus carried home those who lived in the Western townships, while a roster of volunteer drivers (of whom I was one) took back others who lived in the suburbs. It was a bizarre situation: cooks, nannies, gardeners, messengers and delivery "boys" by day became equals of the white production team at night and were then delivered back to servants' quarters. I was much affected by this anomaly and could only guess how the people concerned coped with their schizophrenic existence.
>
> After three months of exhaustive, and exhausting, preparation, King Kong opened on 2 February 1959, to a packed house at the University Great Hall . . . To describe the evening as a sensation is totally inadequate. Music, sets, lights, costumes and performances—all were of the highest order. The stage of the Great Hall exploded into life. Arthur Goldreich's designs, simple, linear, and brightly colored, immediately captured the atmosphere of the township. The energy of the cast was electric, the music alternately seductive, exhilarating, and haunting. The final curtain fell to an ovation rarely heard at a Johannesburg first night for a locally produced show, and I lost count of the curtain calls. The roars grew louder as Leon Gluckman finally appeared on the stage. Obviously exhausted, he stood for a moment then, turning his back to the audience, bowed low to his sixty-three actors. It was one of the great and memorable nights in the history of South African theater, and all those who had made it possible were rewarded with a monumental hit . . .
>
> Word on King Kong had traveled. For the first time ever, American and British producers flew out to take a look at a South African show, rather than the other way round . . . On 23 February, 1961, two years and three weeks to the day since its momentous first night, King Kong opened at the Princes Theater, London, having played a special Royal Command Performance for Princess Margaret the previous night.
>
> The London reviews were favorable and a few were glowing, but ecstatic raves were missing. The public loved it, but only until September, and—a major disappointment to all concerned—the proposed Broadway season fell through and the company left for home on 7 December. I had attended the gala performance and have to admit that the original impact was missing. Certainly, I thought the theater far too big and barn-like, and I have always suspected that the tampering to cater for English tastes watered down the magic. (Tucker 1997: 127–133)

South African Mike Phahlane provides another reading of *King Kong* in *Zonk! The African People's Magazine* in March 1959. Excerpts of the article are as follows:

> The days of imitating (often poor imitations) American artists have passed. This era of show business certainly served its purpose, it spotlighted the latent talent possessed by our African artists, it also went to show that we were capable of great things, but let's face it, it was not our own—there was nothing African about our theatre . . . Now after hard work and plenty of courage, the "King Kong" team has come up with something that is really our own, really African and above all real theatre . . .
>
> There are many bouquets to be handed out—the whole conception of the show is remarkable and what "Porgy and Bess" means to the Negro of America, "King Kong" will mean to us. Todd Matshikiza's compositions, Spike Glazer's direction of the band, Harry Bloom's scripting, Leon Gluckman's production and the cast itself all deserve the highest praise!

It is important to note that the victories won with *King Kong* were bittersweet: with travel overseas came the opportunity for several of *King Kong*'s performers to remain abroad.

You might be wondering how Black South Africans came to perform in these kinds of shows. Where were they trained? Johannesburg-based singer Miriam Makeba (who would leave for Europe and the United States a few years later) recalls singing with the "Cuban Brothers" in Johannesburg in the late 1950s. This excerpt is taken from her autobiography, *Makeba: My Story* (1987: 44–50). As you read this excerpt take note of how American and Latin American culture had saturated South African jazz and dance band performance in the 1950s to the point of being completely "natural" to those who participated in its local culture; take note also of the contexts of performance; and reflect on Makeba's experiences as a woman performer, on the obstacles she had to overcome in order to make it in the world of music.

> One day Zweli [MM's cousin] asks me to the rehearsal of his new band, which he calls the Cuban Brothers. The name is a fantasy, because no one is from Cuba/none of us have even met a Cuban. From the movies, though, we know they look like Cesar Romero and Carmen Miranda. Also none of the Cuban Brothers are real brothers with anyone else in the band. This doesn't bother Zweli. He is full of plans . . .
>
> Zweli doesn't have to ask me twice. Before, I never wanted to sing around my in-laws' house. I was too sad. But now I want to sing my lungs out, and forget all my troubles. The Cuban Brothers have practiced several Big Band hit songs. I get to know these, and soon I join the rehearsals. Zweli has a spunky little group: a drummer, a piano player, some brass and some boys, who back me up when I sing. We have fun together. Soon we will be performing before the public. Nobody knows what is in store for us. Certainly I do not.
>
> We are happy amateurs. Whenever there is a community sing, or a fund-raising activity for the church, or an amateur contest, the Cuban Brothers are there. I am the band's female vocalist. Like the others, I do not get paid. It's just fun for me. I like my friends in the group, these young boys . . . Of course, I am only twenty years old. I am very shy too . . . except when I sing. Then, watch out! "Come on-a my house I give you candy!" The hit songs from America make their way over to us. We include some in the Cuban Brothers' performances, along with ballads and

> dance tunes in all the tribal languages. We are getting to be known in our township of Orlando East. People come to the Donaldson Community Center to hear us. They dance. We have a good time.
>
> But it is difficult for a young woman to be on stage. Many people in our society look at it as something bad. The old thing that women are not supposed to go on stage and show themselves takes some time to die. I have heard the neighbors gossip: "So-and-so's daughter is a whore because she is on stage." I can imagine what they are saying about me: "She left her husband to show herself on stage! Why isn't she at home raising her child, instead of having her mother do it so she can sing?"
>
> . . . But I am not a female Cuban Brother for long. Some men show up at the Donaldson Center during one of our shows . . . one of them is a singer named Nathan Mdhledhle. Mr Mdhledhle is the leader of one of the country's most popular bands: the Manhattan Brothers.
>
> Everyone has heard of the Manhattan Brothers. WE listen to them on the radio. They put out records, and they tour all over the country. When I finish singing with the band and Mr Mdhledhle comes up to introduce himself, I can't believe it . . . "You have a lovely voice, it's the voice of a nightingale . . . I want you to come audition for us. The Manhattan Brothers need a female vocalist."
>
> Rehearsals begin at Nathan's house. I learn right away that with four men singing behind me—Nathan Mdhledhle, Ronnie Majola, Joe Mogotsi, and Rufus Khoza—I have to be loud. There will be times when I won't have a microphone to help me. On their own, the men sing American songs by the Ink Spots and the Mills Brothers. When we are together we sing native African tunes as well as popular songs in English. Because we are black, however, we are not permitted to record songs in the English language. Six musicians make up the band: a sax, a trumpet, straight-up bass, piano and the drummers . . .
>
> I am to be paid five pounds per show . . . The shows, held in concert halls in the black townships, are long. We sing for four hours, from eight in the evening until midnight. The audience sits in chairs, which are removed for dancing afterward. The musicians then play until five in the morning . . . In South Africa there is a new dance every week. The couples like to show off before the bandstand. But they are not the only ones who are showing off. Gangsters come to the clubs. I have been warned they can be rough places . . . Some of our shows end in riots . . . They are like actors, these gangsters, although they do not play. In South Africa, movies are taken very seriously, and there is a movie in the cinemas now in which Richard Widmark plays a hoodlum. They call him Styles, and he dresses up in a hat, a belted jacket, and those Florsheim shoes . . .
>
> The Manhattan Brothers are recording stars for Gallotone records. I join them in the studio many times to make 78 rpm recordings. [For further information on the Manhattan Brothers and other close-harmony vocal groups in Johannesburg, see Ballantine 1999: 2 and 7.]

Miriam Makeba would go on to assume a place of enormous significance abroad, both musically and in terms of her increasingly outspoken position about the apartheid government—she was banned from returning to South Africa after she went before the

United Nations Organization and testified against the apartheid government. She was only allowed to return to the country in the early 1990s, as South Africa transitioned from apartheid to Black majority rule. In the interim, the singer created an extraordinary recording and live performance archive, now available in CD and online formats.

Cape Town's "Coon Carnival"

In Chapter 11 we talk more about an annual festival in the port city of Cape Town, the "**Coon Carnival**"—a festival of Cape Town's working-class minstrelsy—that looks and sounds quite a lot like Philadelphia's **New Year's Mummers Parade**. French jazz critic and fan of South African music Denis-Constant Martin conducted some important research on the Carnival, its music, costumes, and rituals, which he published in 1999. What follows is an excerpt from that book, describing the festival as he witnessed it in the 1990s in Cape Town. The Carnival itself began in the early years of the twentieth century, and has taken place most years when the troupes were given permission to march through the streets of Cape Town. Such permission was withheld in the extreme years of the apartheid government.

> Christmas and New Year Celebrations in Cape Town
>
> It's midnight on New Year's Eve in the Bo-Kaap, at the foot of Signal Hill. People flock to the pavements [sidewalks] lining the narrow streets. Whole families . . . arrive with folding chairs, picnic baskets, thermos bottles, and blankets to keep warm in the cool summer night. Here and there small stalls have been erected where *boerewors*, *samoosas*, or *koeksisters* can be bought . . . There is an atmosphere of tranquil gaiety and friendliness, but there is nevertheless, a sense of expectation . . .
>
> At first it's like a rumor. One can hear "they're coming" whispered by hundreds of mouths. After a little while, a steady beat and a solid melody drift up from the direction of Wale Street . . . A *voorloper*, a drum major, appears and capers wearing his peculiar high hat adorned with ostrich feathers, followed by a group of men dressed in track suits and caps and carrying sticks. They walk a sort of dancing step until they stop in front of the Star Club. All along they have been singing, and as they come nearer, the words become clearer. It's a ***moppie***, a comic, upbeat song, making light of events that are a source of worry. The group, a ***nagtroep***, on other occasions also called a *Hollandse* team, *sangkoor* or Malay choir, stops at the foot of the stairs leading to the Club. Its members assemble in a half-circle, with guitars, cello, and the ghoema drum at one end. A singer stands in the middle and starts a beautifully ornate tune in a high yet sweet voice. It is a love song, praising the faithfulness of a lovely sixteen-year old girl. The choir answers quite squarely and on certain sentences the fusion of the soloist's melody and the chords sung by the group creates a unique, almost magic sound.
>
> When they are finished, the choir climbs the steps to the Star Club and are congratulated by listeners massed on the *stoep* [porch]. Inside the club they are offered a *tafel* (literally a table) of drinks, snacks, biscuits and sweets. They do not stay long for there are many other places to visit where the same ritual will be repeated.

> At about the same time, another episode of the New Year festivals is being prepared. Women, men, girls, and boys gather at a *klopskamer*, that is the headquarters of a carnival group known as a *klops* (club) or a Coon troupe . . . The costume of a troupe must differ from year to year, and was originally inspired by the stage attire of nineteenth-century blackface minstrels: the same comedians who introduced the word "coon" in Cape Town. The costume has evolved over the years . . . Before leaving the *klopskamer*, members apply make-up to their faces. Some stick to the old minstrel pattern: black with white circles around the eyes and the mouth, or a variation on it where half the face is painted black while the other half white. Many now prefer to use bright colors and a sprinkle of glitter, while others do not put on make-up at all . . . Outside the stadium, the troupe gets into formation. Two drum majors lead the way, sometimes followed by a *moffie*, a transvestite character. Then comes the board bearer, followed by the musicians, the "juveniles," and the rank and file kept in good marching order by "committees" who assist the captain. They enter the stadium and parade on the track. The competitions [between troupes] are about to begin.
>
> On 2 January, the traditional *Tweede Nuwe Jaar* (the second New Year) is celebrated. On this day the Coons take to the streets of central Cape Town for the road march, one of the most important events of the New Year's Festivals.
>
> New Year is first celebrated by the *nagtroepe* or Malay Choirs. Some Malay Choir singers do not like to be confused with Coons because they consider the latter as unruly, low-class people, bunches of gangsters, a far cry from the respectability and honesty they embody. (Martin 1999: excerpts from 7–24)

Carnival rhythms and musical terminology don't stay enclosed in the routines of minstrelsy. Many of the musicians who have performed in the carnival over the last century have also played in local jazz and dance bands, in a style unique to the Cape called *langarm* (literally long arm, like the arms in the tango!). As the musicians shift musical gears, so the language of one genre crosses over into the talk of another. Cape Town dance band musicians use the language of festival marching to describe what happens when playing in the dance bands!

Cape Town librarian and jazz musician Vincent Kolbe recalls:

> When the carnival troupes marched from the center of the city they had to walk directly uphill to Schotsche's Kloof, the band leader would cry "Heuwel op!' (Go up the hill!)
>
> It can mean "heavy" or, musically, it means you've got to really pump now because you're going uphill now [. . .] but I know the old band leaders on the dance floor would now shout to the band, "Heuwel op!" Which means, you know, the drummer does something to the beat, you know. Or the after-beat is either sooner, or the after-beat is delayed. And that actually was reflected in the dance halls as well, in the movements [. . .] And this must affect the way you create your rhythm and the way you create your melodies, you create your accompaniment and you arrange your instrumentation and things like that. (Kolbe in Nixon 1997)

The group that best represents the Cape Town dance band tradition is the Philadelphia Rhythms (they have been around, with changing personnel, since the 1950s). They recorded a CD called *Philadelphia Rhythms, Live at the Goldfinger*. Cape Town minstrel music is available on a CD titled *Cape Culture Band*.

There are several other genres of South African music not discussed in this book, but that may be of interest to you, many of which have familiar labels but, you will find, have very different words and musical styles than what you might have expected from your own experience of these categories. Several that I list below have in industry terms "crossed over," i.e., from one marketing category to the next. Even in South Africa (as it did in years past in the United States) cross-over has political overtones—it may mean playing or consuming the music of another racial group than "your own" and profiting from that process! ***Kwaito*** is the most recently forged youth music—there are many, many websites and recordings of *kwaito* currently available—it is really South Africa's own style of hip hop/rap in a post-apartheid youth culture; then there is South African opera, other art music, a long history of White rock, punk, and folk music that continues today; and of course, the ever present and highly adaptable strands of musical and religious tradition present in all kinds of places, both rural and urban, in contemporary South Africa. (See the list of recordings in Appendix 3 for examples of this music.)

Keywords

Chris McGregor, Abdullah Ibrahim, Sathima Bea Benjamin, Dudu Pukwana, Kippie Moeketsi, Johnny Dyani names of some of the experimental and truly innovative jazz musicians of the late 1950s and early 1960s, all of whom left South Africa in the early 1960s (see Ansell 2004; Muller with Benjamin forthcoming)

Coon Carnival the New Year's Festival held annually by the working-class Coloured community in Cape Town

isicathamiya close-harmony singing modeled by Ladysmith Black Mambazo

jazz as art or freedom in contrast to the repeating cycles of township jazz (see below), a small group of musicians began to experiment with local sounds and the international sounds of jazz, to invoke the freedom of expression that jazz performance implied, and to work towards a specifically South African, but also free, sound in their music

kwaito popular music of the new South Africa, that plays with transatlantic Black genres like rap, reggae, and hip hop

kwela pennywhistle music of 1940s and 1950s South Africa

Lemmy "Special" Mabaso, Spokes Mashiyane, and **Elias Lerole** the three most important *kwela* performers

marabi the shebeen-generated music of the 1920s and 1930s, largely a keyboard style, a truly hybrid musical form

maskanda Zulu migrant musical forms, largely of musical bow and guitar/concertina

mbaqanga originally referenced African/township jazz, increasingly came to mean the studio produced, government controlled sounds of 1960s Zulu pop

moppie upbeat comic song sung by working-class Coloured people from Cape Town, often in New Years festivities

mqashiyo style of popular music in Johannesburg townships and on radio

msakazo literally meant broadcast music
nagtroepe night troupes who entertain communities in Cape Town at New Year
New Year's Mummers Parade Philadelphia, USA's annual mummer's parade, which resonates with Cape Town's Coon Carnival in significant ways
township jazz the popular, lighter forms of African jazz commonly performed in South Africa's Black townships in the postwar era
traveling shows several of these emerged in the 1950s

CHAPTER 7

Labor Migration: *Isicathamiya*

(to walk stealthily, like a cat, on tip toes)

Labor migration, the movement of Black South Africans from the rural regions of South Africa into urban areas in search of work, is one of the most powerful forces shaping Black South African life, music, and performance in the twentieth century. A substantial literature exists on labor migration and its musical consequences. But for our purposes we can simply note that for centuries, people from the present province of **KwaZulu Natal** migrated from the northern, southern, and interior parts of the province to the ever-growing cities of **Durban**, **Johannesburg**, **and Kimberley**. Beginning in the latter part of the nineteenth century, those who migrated to Johannesburg and Kimberley went in search of work in the mines. (Johannesburg is known in Zulu as **eGoli**, "the place or city of gold," and Kimberley, the city where the first diamonds were mined, as **eDiamane**, "the place or city of diamonds.") Others found work and housing in Durban in the harbor or as house servants or gardeners for White and, increasingly, for Asian families. The early migrants were predominantly men, though women began to enter the urban areas by the mid-twentieth century.

Three performance cultures are discussed in this and the next two chapters: ***isicathamiya***, ***maskanda***, and **gumboot dance**. Although I have participated as a researcher in all three musical cultures to a greater or lesser degree, I have been more deeply engaged with *maskanda* and gumboot dance, but it is certainly *isicathamiya* that is more known in the world music circuits. We have Paul Simon and the *Graceland* recording to thank for that! All three traditions moved during the twentieth century from being performances of largely illiterate, Zulu-speaking migrant men from KwaZulu Natal into genres of performance that are now available in the United States through world music labels and sources. This remarkable transformation of very local traditions has been accompanied by significant shifts in who performs, the sound of *maskanda*, what audiences have come to expect, and the standardization of all three genres.

Migrant Music on Video

In Chapter 4 I mentioned that in 1979, British documentary filmmaker Jeremy Marre produced a video titled ***Rhythm of Resistance*** in his series *Beats of the Heart.* Shot on location in Johannesburg, it features the music and larger sociopolitical context of Black South African musical production in the late 1970s, a period in which the Afrikaner Nationalist government's policy of apartheid was fully entrenched and enforced. Marre's book, also called *Beats of the Heart*, provides an expanded version of the narrative used in the video. The book gives the reader a powerful sense of the obstacles a foreign, White filmmaker faced in trying to make a movie on Black South African life and music in the 1970s. First, Marre was required to have a permit from the South African government because, like all White South Africans, he was prohibited from entering Black residential areas, either in the rural parts of South Africa or in the townships. Second, he was only permitted to film in White cities, and because he chose not to abide by the restrictions, the police constantly followed his vehicle and harassed him and his crew. Third, he describes the anxiety Black South Africans experienced in relationship with Whites, even those who live in the rural regions of KwaZulu Natal that seem, from the outside, idyllic.

In many ways *Rhythm of Resistance* is a useful audiovisual documentary source for these three chapters because, though it was filmed in Johannesburg and rural KwaZulu Natal, it is quintessentially a film about music and migration. All three of the performance styles discussed in this chapter are addressed in the *Beats of the Heart* book, though gumboot dance is only mentioned and then dismissed by Marre at the end, a point I return to below.

The video begins with the all-night male choir competitions of *isicathamiya* held in both Johannesburg and Durban. The next important group in the video is the singer-songwriter duo that Marre simply calls "the Johnny and Sipho group." In South Africa, Johnny and Sipho are more lovingly known as founding members of the group Juluka. They are significant not only because they represent a much larger and older tradition of Zulu guitar-accompanied singing called *maskanda*, but also for the politically transgressive performances they created in the 1980s simply by appearing on stage together, a Black and a White South African.

The *Rhythm of Resistance* video focuses on the sacred dimension of the group **Ladysmith Black Mambazo** in its pre-*Graceland* days, performing inside a Black church. Between segments on several traditional musicians, the video zooms in on the studio production of Black, KwaZulu Natal-derived popular music, *mbaqanga.* Although they are not a part of my discussion in this book, the spirited performances of the Zulu war dancers, the very lively Mahotella Queens (who continue to perform though they are all in their sixties now), and Abafana Baseqhudeni provide energetic interludes.

Should you have the opportunity to view *Rhythm of Resistance*, which I strongly urge you to do, you should bear in mind the particular "voice" or position of the filmmaker. When I first viewed the film in the mid 1980s, it seemed to me to convey a message of political urgency, a need for social and political transformation and reform in South Africa. I sympathized at the time with Marre's project. In the post-apartheid era, I watched the video again, and this time I was acutely aware of its strong political message, a message that suddenly turned the video into a historical document for me. It was clearly a document from and about the past. In the mid-1990s, as I re-viewed the video in writing this chapter, it took on another new tone, and in the post-apartheid era the director's view of Black resistance politics seems to me to be quite romanticized.

Without doubt, the laws and realities of apartheid impacted all South Africans. To claim, however, that all Black South African performance was resistance against White domination, and that no Whites (besides the White filmmakers) knew about Black performance, is to present a crude image of both Black and White South Africans, even for that period. If you look, for example, at www.3rdearmusic.com and find the reminiscences of White South African Dave Marks, who did the sound for numerous events involving Black musicians in the 1970s and 1980s, you will realize that racial divisions were not as clear-cut as Marre claims they were. Furthermore, to convey the idea that all Black South Africans are the same, with the same agenda, is to deny to millions of people with diverse experiences, education, language, and family backgrounds the individual intelligence and ability to act upon the world on their own terms. While reducing all political struggle to a single issue might assist sloganeers and political campaigners, it does not allow for a more insightful and nuanced reading of a political moment or the value and meanings of its music and dance performances.

The absence of gumboot dance footage in the video provides a case in point. At the end of his chapter on *Rhythm of Resistance*, Marre suggests that in the twentieth century,

> white colonizers have imposed their own cultural forms on blacks as a means of domination. And the black people of South Africa have taken up those forms and transposed them into their own rhythms of resistance . . . Most publicized of all the tourist traps are the so-called miners' gumboot dances which we were asked to film one day. Nattily dressed miners in polished gumboots performed in a sort of circus for the avid, chattering tourists who photographed the show to take back as a "real slice of black South African life." It was, in fact, funded by the mining authorities. (Marre 1986: 50).

Marre closes by contrasting his unwillingness to film the "contrived event" of gumboot dancing with the

> real Ngoma [dance] in a workers' hostel inside Johannesburg . . . Amongst the milling, tired workers marches a procession of Zulu workers beneath the harsh glow of a setting sun. They were naked, except for loincloths, wrist and ankle decorations and the spears they brandished . . . Every week they danced and sang their message of defiance—towards the enemy from within. (Marre 1986: 50)

Marre seems to want to keep Zulu men pre-modern and untainted by commercial interests—naked except for their loincloths rather than clothed in the Western dress and footgear worn by the gumboot dancers. And the distinction he draws between the Zulu gumboot dancer as co-opted by White rule and the defiant and implicitly free Zulu in his loincloth is flawed. Jeff Thomas, Zulu linguist and social anthropologist turned *ngoma* dancer, has argued convincingly (1988) that even the "traditional Zulu war dancers" adapted their attire to meet the criteria of White management and their dance judges. Changing traditions to meet the requirements of the judges was, after all, a strategy for winning. Certainly, the recently produced video titled *Gumboots* (2000, discussed at the end of this chapter) presents a different perspective on gumboot dance in contemporary South Africa and its place in twentieth-century Black South African performance history. Finally, my own video footage of male union members performing gumboot dance at labor rallies in 1985 provides evidence that gumboot dance has long been a sign of worker solidarity and obvious political consciousness.

Isicathamiya

We began this book with a discussion of the triple-titled song "Wimoweh" or "Mbube," which begins with the words "In the jungle, the mighty jungle, the lion sleeps tonight," the song that figures in the early history of *isicathamiya* in South Africa. The song was originally composed by a Zulu-speaking man, Solomon Linda, and recorded in 1939 in South Africa for Gallo Records. Gallo and ethnomusicologist Veit Erlmann have both reissued that original recording. The tune itself is believed to have been adapted from a traditional wedding song. The story is that in the 1950s White South African record producers sent a version of that song along with others to the United States to showcase local talent and songwriting skills. Several folk groups covered the Zulu melody with English lyrics and new musical arrangements.

The contemporary manifestation of *mbube*-style performance or *isicathamiya* is found in the weekly **all-night choir competitions** held from late Saturday evening through Sunday morning in the cities of Durban and Johannesburg. I was first exposed to these all-night competitions as an undergraduate student at the University of what is now called KwaZulu Natal in 1984. My fellow student Janet Topp Fargion and I had been asked by our teacher, Veit Erlmann, if we would like to judge one of these competitions, which were held regularly in the Glebeland hostel for male migrant workers in Umlazi, one of the townships on the fringes of Durban. Janet and I had no idea what was in store for us on that night in 1984. All we knew was that a man in a van would meet us on the steps of Memorial Tower Building at the University of Natal in Durban at 2 a.m. on a Sunday morning. When the driver arrived, Janet and I scrambled into the front seat of the little van and were taken to the performance site. We were instructed not to talk to anyone, and we were told which groups had won several times in the recent past and encouraged to let others take home the prizes.

By the time we were seated at our table, with our backs to the audience so that we could not be influenced by any of the supporters, about eight or nine groups had already registered. That seemed like a reasonable number of choirs. We did not realize at the time that nine or ten more would still arrive and expect to perform. An event that was already in full swing with the ***praktisa*** (rehearsal) session would clearly continue long after the sun rose on Sunday morning. Several of the supporters were napping in their seats, waiting for the actual competition to begin. We had no guidelines about what should be the winning qualities of a choir; it was presumed that because we were music students we would know.

I still have a vivid sense of the moment the first choir began to sing. Impeccably

Figure 7.1 Group leaders sign up for an all-night *isicathamiya* choir competition and pay an entrance fee, the proceeds of which contribute to the monetary prize at the end of the evening. Beatrice Street YMCA, Durban, September 1996, taken by Carol Muller.

dressed in suits, with white gloves, sparkling white shirts, shiny black shoes, and red socks, the group processed into the humble hall. Deep, rich strains of men singing Zulu words in close harmony resonated throughout the building. I recall the chill that ran up my spine, because I had never before heard a sound as powerful as the voices of those men. The leader, dressed in opposite colors to his team, led his group in a solo call and choral response. As they moved in single file down the middle of the hall between two groups of enthusiastic supporters, the men raised their legs together, and then released, their shoes brushing the concrete floor. Walking stealthily, like cats. Moving, but not stepping. In Zulu, *ukucathama* means "to walk stealthily, like a cat," and *isicathamiya* is the name of the music and dance style.

The men proceeded up the steps and on to the stage, singing in four-part harmony as they went, with the leader singing soprano, two voices on alto, a couple on tenor, and everyone else in the bass (the mixed-voice choral **SATB format** was sung here by men only). Their bodies bent, their legs moved smoothly, voices and bodies in harmony. The first part of the performance was in the old ***makwaya*** (choral) format: the choir sang with their bodies still, as in the old mission style. In the second part, the men began to dance, the rhythm of their bodies in sync with the rhythm of the song. At this point, the participants' girlfriends or wives came up individually to show their support for the men they were involved with. One woman took the necklace from around her neck and placed it over the head of her lover. As she left the stage she gestured to the audience that the man was taken—not available. Another came up and put her wallet inside the pocket

Figure 7.2 Men heating up in the circle at the back of the hall before parading down to the front to perform in front of the judge. Beatrice Street YMCA, Durban, September 1996, taken by Carol Muller.

Figure 7.3 Women supporters standing on the sideline, showing their admiration for the group of male *isicathamiya* performers, and staking claim to their lovers! Beatrice Street YMCA, Durban, September 1996, taken by Carol Muller.

Figure 7.4 Same group doing "*isteps*" this time joined by one of the female supporters, who lays claim to her male partner in the group. This takes place in the *praktisa* part of the evening. Beatrice Street YMCA, Durban, September 1996, taken by Carol Muller.

Figure 7.5 Same group parades around in front of the judge and back onto the small stage in front of the hall, still accompanied by their female supporters. Beatrice Street YMCA, Durban, September 1996, taken by Carol Muller.

of one of the other performers. The group's **followers applauded**. (Clapping from the audience is not generalized but limited to one's own supporters.) Having completed their two songs, the choir left the stage, winding their way back through the audience to the back door as the next choir prepared to make their entrance.

In the mid-1990s I returned to *isicathamiya* competitions, not as a judge this time (White judges are no longer used for these events), but as the ethnomusicologist from the music department at the University of Natal. Since I had first heard *isicathamiya*, Bongani Mthethwa, Paulos Msimango (both now deceased), and Grammy award-winner **Joseph Shabalala** had formed an organization called the South African Traditional Music Association. It was instrumental in rethinking the rules of *isicathamiya* performance to eliminate the White influence that had been so pervasive when filmmaker Jerry Marre had been on site in Johannesburg in the 1970s and to reclaim *isicathamiya* as a form of traditional music. Competitions were no longer held in the Glebeland hostel but at the YMCA in Beatrice Street in the center of the city of Durban. (See CD track 2 for an example of *isicathamiya* performed at this venue.)

Though the format of *isicathamiya* competitions remained the same, the YMCA competition introduced some variations on the basic theme. Between the rehearsal and the formal competition, a competition for the best-dressed man was regularly held, with the winner decided by the music judge. On occasion, a similar competition for the best-dressed women would take place. All who registered to enter the competition now paid a voluntary amount to the event's conveners, and the contribution of each group was announced as they entered the hall to perform. But the most profound change to *isicathamiya* performance in the last two decades of the century was the fact that Joseph Shabalala and his Ladysmith Black Mambazo group had achieved worldwide recognition. To give back to the community that supported *isicathamiya* in South Africa, Shabalala and his group regularly conducted workshops for aspiring *isicathamiya* singers. The effect of Shabalala's workshops could be heard in the more polished tone and overall quality of performance of those groups taking part.

The leader of an *isicathamiya* group is usually its founder and composer. However, a composer among migrant workers is not someone who writes down songs in musical notation but rather someone who creates new songs in a variety of ways. Social historian and musicologist Chris Ballantine (1996) interviewed Joseph Shabalala in the 1990s about his compositional process. Shabalala composes at night, he told Ballantine, when his body is sleeping and his spirit is at work. New songs come to him in different ways, he says, but often in response to songs he has heard or things he has seen that trouble him. He strives to address the troubling situation by composing a new song. Since he does not read or write music, he either takes the song directly to his group to begin working on it in performance or tapes portions of it until the song is more complete.

Shabalala also explained to Ballantine how he came to **compose** in the particular style of *isicathamiya*.[1] For a period of about six months in the early 1960s, Shabalala says, he was visited by voices in his dreams. These were the spiritual elders who were singing in a new style. Night after night, they taught him this style. It was like attending school in his sleep, he recalls. Later on, after the voices had visited for several months, Shabalala was given a kind of final examination in which spiritual elders tested his musical knowledge in his dreams. Each of the twenty-four elders asked a question of the student musician,

Figure 7.6 The *isicathimiya* group that has prayed and warmed up at the back of the hall in a circle now proceeds down alongside the audience members to the front where they will perform in front of the judge. Beatrice Street YMCA, Durban, September 1996, taken by Carol Muller.

and Shabalala achieved a perfect score. Then they asked one more question, which he struggled to answer. Ultimately, he achieved his goal of satisfying these elders. Since then Joseph Shabalala has composed hundreds of new songs and has had a group singing in the style of Ladysmith Black Mambazo for four decades.

A good performance of *isicathamiya* includes a call and response, multi-layered vocal polyphony. For the most part, an *isicathamiya* song sung at a competition starts off with the group standing in a semicircle with the leader in front of the group; all are facing the judges and the audience. Although some of the earliest recordings of *isicathamiya* have piano or banjo accompaniment, because the record producers thought the instruments would appeal to the Black elite, *isicathimiya* is typically performed **a cappella**.

Ladysmith Black Mambazo in concert

On February 15, 2003, Ladysmith Black Mambazo (LBM) were scheduled to perform at the Annenberg Center at the University of Pennsylvania in Philadelphia. It had been more than a decade since I had seen them perform live in a theater in Stamford, Connecticut. At that earlier event, just a few years after the *Graceland* recording release, their onstage performance paralleled what one might have expected of an *isicathamiya* group singing at one of the all-night competitions in Durban or Johannesburg. Their music was sung exclusively in Zulu, but their performance style was in the historical tradition of European choral styles, though there were a few differences. Each song began with bodies still,

Figure 7.7 *Isicathamiya* group enters the stage in the competition, Beatrice Street YMCA, Durban, September 1996, taken by Carol Muller.

Figure 7.8 *Isicathamiya* group stand in a line ready to start singing. They will later do the lifted leg dancing or *isteps*. Two women supporters make themselves known to the audience. Beatrice Street YMCA, Durban, September 1996, taken by Carol Muller.

Figure 7.9 *Isicathamiya* group doing "*isteps*" for the competition at Beatrice Street YMCA, Durban, September 1996, taken by Carol Muller.

Figure 7.10 Same group "gets down" as the singing and dancing intensify. They make clear eye contact with the judge of the competition as they do so. Beatrice Street YMCA, Durban, September 1996, taken by Carol Muller.

but the singers gradually began to move and, through dance movements, illustrate what the songs were about. Shabalala "conducted" his group while facing the audience rather than the group. But like more classical choirs, LBM engaged the audience minimally.

The evening at the Annenberg Center fifteen years later was a different kind of performance. It was clear that Ladysmith Black Mambazo had become accustomed to performing the same songs concert after concert, city after city, because one moment in the live performance that night strongly resembled a track on the *Ladysmith Black Mambazo Live at the Royal Albert Hall* DVD. In the Philadelphia concert, one Mambazo member remarked to the audience that because they had traveled far and wide, north, south, east, and west, they no longer had any sense of where they were. "What is the name of this place?" he asked the group. "Ah, something beginning with P." Then Shabalala proceeded to teach the audience the words of "Homeless," the most South African-sounding track from the *Graceland* album. As we saw in Chapter 4, this song begins in Zulu, but the English text that comes in later is not merely a translation of what LBM sings in Zulu at the beginning. In a call and response form, Shabalala proceeded to teach the Philadelphia audience the Zulu words.

Ladysmith Black Mambazo's performance had changed in other ways as well. First, it was clear that numerous social and political issues pertaining to life for Black South Africans in KwaZulu Natal weighed heavily on the minds and hearts of Shabalala and his group. A large hand-painted backdrop covering the entire stage portrayed contemporary issues, such as HIV/AIDS, crime, violence, and rape, along with the heroes of South African society, including Nelson Mandela and Archbishop Desmond Tutu. The group used the performance to educate the audience. One of Shabalala's wives had recently been murdered—Shabalala had been beside her in the car when it happened. So the group opened the performance with a song about heaven, the place they would go after they all died. They sang about the deep sense of separation from their homes and families that accompanied global travel and performance. But there were also several humorous moments in the performance, where members of Mambazo played out the tensions between the older and younger generations.

Second, the level of interaction between Shabalala and the audience had increased markedly. When I first heard LBM in Connecticut, they filed on to the stage and began to sing to the audience with Shabalala conducting. At the Annenberg Center, Shabalala and Mambazo communicated with the audience at several levels, not just in the harmonious strands of mostly Zulu-language *isicathamiya*. The audience members laughed as Mambazo acted out a series of scenes that they could identify with in their own lives, there was less sense of distance between audience members and performers, and everyone went home to listen to the *Graceland* album's version of "Homeless" knowing now how to sing the opening lines of the song.

The third significant change occurred in the opening moments of the show. Instead of Ladysmith Black Mambazo walking on to the stage to start the performance, two Zulu *maskanda* (traditional musicians playing on European instruments, guitar and concertina) appeared on stage to perform. These two musicians from South Africa were being used to "open" for the bigger act. It struck me then that Joseph Shabalala had taken on the same role Paul Simon played in the mid-1980s. It was now Shabalala and not Simon who was using his powerful place in the global networks of the entertainment industry to showcase South African music. The difference was that it was live performance, without the intervention of high-tech music producers reshaping the act and the sound to suit the needs of a mainstream popular music audience. The *maskanda* performance came across as unmediated tradition, quite unlike the "cleaned up" sounds of Mambazo that one hears on the *Graceland* album. Joseph Shabalala was not "producing" *maskanda* performance, as Paul Simon had done at the mixing board in the recording studio in New York City by manipulating many tracks of sound recorded in South Africa. Shabalala was simply showcasing the musicians in their own traditions.

Back in South Africa it is quite striking the extent to which being musically successful overseas impacts the local environment, even among those who might appear quite cut off from the wider world. Musicians in South Africa now dream of international success in a way that is quite startling and, in my experience, less common in the United States. Even the partially literate or non-English-speaking South African carries inside him or herself images of the world "out there." This was driven home to me one day while I was studying at New York University in 1988. I received a package in the mail containing a cassette made for me by my gumboot dance teacher and his team. On the cassette, Blanket Mkhize played his Zulu guitar and sang a song he composed in which he asked me to "Open the gates of New York City for gumboot performance!" Clearly, Joseph Shabalala was opening the gates to world performance for these two street musicians as Paul Simon had done for Ladysmith Black Mambazo two decades earlier, and as Blanket Mkhize hoped I would do for him in New York City.

Finally, several documentary films and live concert DVDs have been released that have Joseph Shabalala and Ladysmith Black Mambazo as their central characters. These include the live recording of Ladysmith Black Mambazo at the Royal Albert Hall in London in 1999; a documentary made in the 1990s in South Africa as part of the African Wave series; and another wonderfully rich documentary about the group called *On Tip Toe* (2002). In addition, over the last decade the musicians in Ladysmith Black Mambazo have engaged in other kinds of musical collaborations. Ladysmith Black Mambazo's audio recording *Long Walk to Freedom* (2006) is a particularly powerful musical dialog between *isicathamiya* and a host of "world" and "popular" musicians: Lucky Dube, Melissa Etheridge, Taj Mahal, Sarah McLachlan, Emmylou Harris, and Joe McBride. They have also recently performed with the English Chamber Orchestra on a recording titled *No Boundaries* (2006). Each of these recordings takes the idea of *isicathamiya* into new acoustical spaces, and global relationships that not even a dreamer like Joseph Shabalala could ever have imagined possible growing up on a farm close to the rural town of Ladysmith in KwaZulu Natal.

Keywords

a cappella sung without instrumental accompaniment

all-night choir competitions the most common site of *isicathamiya* performance in KwaZulu Natal and Johannesburg remains the weekly competition

compose Shabalala is the composer of all of LBM's new repertory. He was given the style in a dream in the 1960s, and continues to write in response to dreams, doing much of his song writing at night

Durban, Johannesburg, and Kimberley the three major sites of Zulu migrant worker performance
eDiamane the Zulu name for the diamond mining town of Kimberley
eGoli the Zulu name for the gold mining region of Johannesburg
gumboot dance boot dance discussed in Chapter 9
followers applauded applause in competitions is only provided by a team's immediate supporters for fear of influencing the final outcome of the competition
isicathamiya the name of a music and dance style, meaning "to walk stealthily, like a cat," a clue to how the dance is performed and the kinds of sounds produced by these performers
Joseph Shabalala leader of Ladysmith Black Mambazo
KwaZulu Natal the province where the majority of *isicathamiya* performers live
Ladysmith Black Mambazo the world-famous *isicathamiya* group
makwaya Black South African choral tradition
maskanda Zulu migrant worker guitar/concertina/musical bow traditional music
praktisa the rehearsals before an *isicathamiya* competition
Rhythm of Resistance film about migrant musical performance produced by Jeremy Marre in 1979
SATB format four-part harmonizing

CHAPTER 8
Labor Migration: *Maskanda*

Maskanda Migrant Performance

Older South Africans in Johannesburg and Durban might recall seeing **domestic workers** and gardeners strolling the then White neighborhoods playing guitars and singing softly to themselves on Thursday afternoon, the scheduled "afternoon off." This was the time when guitarists, collectively called ***maskanda***, walked the street singing songs of migrant experience in a style that reminded them of their rural homes. Davies (1994) suggests that the *maskanda* musical style emerged either in the early decades of the twentieth century or in the late nineteenth century, when guitars were first made available in KwaZulu Natal. She cites Johnny Clegg, who dates the Portuguese introduction of the guitar into the region to about 1880. An old Zulu–English dictionary completed in 1894 by a missionary named A. Bryant includes an entry for "guitar": *into e-shaywayo nezimTambo* ("the thing that is struck or sounded by means of strings or with a bone"). It is quite possible that rural Zulu speakers who had never heard an English or Afrikaans word for guitar used this unwieldy description. This suggests that the first encounter with the guitar by rural Zulu in the late nineteenth century was in the rural rather than urban areas of South Africa. Those who first saw it simply described it without having a word for the object.

The word *maskanda*, however, suggests a different kind of encounter. *Maskanda* is a Zulu version of the Afrikaans word for musician, ***musikant***. In KwaZulu Natal what Europeans called "music" was called *imusic*. All other forms of Zulu traditional performance were called ***ngoma*** (song-dance-drumming-healing complex). Clearly *maskanda* was associated with music made by Afrikaans-speaking people, in this case, White farmers who played their music for relaxation on the farms where Zulu men worked in the nineteenth and early twentieth centuries. The word *maskanda* then suggests three levels of musical and cultural encounter in the shaping of twentieth-century Zulu guitar performance: (1) European music, (2) translated into **Afrikaans** cultural practices, (3) borrowed and

Figure 8.1 Zulu mouth bow, drawn by Daphne Maree.

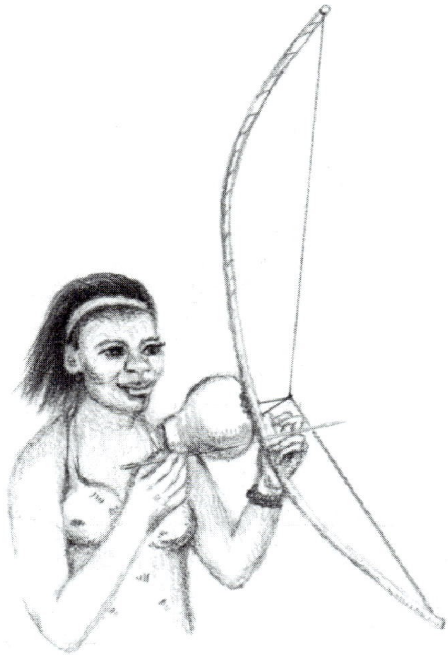

Figure 8.2 Zulu *umakweyana* bow, drawn by Daphne Maree.

transformed by Zulu-speaking musicians into a musical language more consistent with their own aesthetics but played on European instruments like violin, concertina, piano accordion, and most important, the steel-string guitar.

From musical bow to guitar

Although the **musical bow** is not played much any longer, Zulu guitarists have borrowed and transformed principles of Zulu traditional musical bow performances for guitar performance (much as Thomas Mapfumo did with *mbira* music in Zimbabwe in the 1980s, and as Salif Keita and others have done with *kora* music in Senegal and the Gambia). The musical bow is a technologically simple instrument with several features that vary from one bow to the next. Like the hunting bow, all musical bows consist of a sturdy piece of branch trimmed and bent into a semi-circle, with the ends of the branch held together by a piece of wire. Some bows are **braced**, others are not; some use the mouth as the **resonator**, others a gourd; some are struck with a wooden stick; others are bowed more like a violin. The idea of the braced bow transfers into the use of a **capodastra** on the guitar to raise the register of sound produced while keeping the same finger positions for the chords.

Though the instrument may seem simple, the acoustical principles it is based on are more sophisticated. The pitch material for the musical bow is a single wire, string, or gut. When the wire is plucked, it creates a low-sounding tone we call, in the conventional language of acoustics, the **fundamental tone**. If the wire is pinched (or braced) and then struck, plucked, or bowed, it creates another fundamental tone that is higher than the fundamental of the un-pinched string. The exact pitch of the fundamental depends on where exactly the string is pinched or braced. The point is that on an un-braced musical bow the player can produce two fundamental pitches by striking the string stopped or unstopped. Each time a musician creates a fundamental tone, however, he also sets in motion a series of **overtones.** But most people's ears are not sensitive to hearing these higher and softer pitches unless a musician or instrument has a mechanism for amplifying these sounds.

These overtones are produced in a particular order. Typically one hears the third, fourth, and fifth partials or overtones above the fundamental, and they sound two octaves above the lowest tone. This means that by setting the fundamental pitch D in motion, we can hear the third and fifth pitches above D as well: D F# and A, plus the D two octaves above the fundamental. Similarly, if the musician produces as his second fundamental tone an E, the performer can produce the E G# and B. This gives the performer a fair range of pitches for melodic use. The scale produced with two roots and three overtones with each is D E F# G# A B and D'.

Most Nguni musical bows operate using either two or three fundamental pitches or roots. These fundamentals resonate in two kinds of chambers, either a gourd attached to the frame of the bow, which is moved back and forth from the musician's body, or the performer's mouth where the bow rests on the lips of the performer and is constantly reshaped to selectively amplify harmonics. (This process parallels the way in which we produce vowel sounds. As you say the vowel sounds, you reshape the resonating chamber—your mouth—to selectively amplify certain harmonics that result in different vowel sounds.) Quite often, three fundamentals, D E and G, are played to produce only the fifth above the fundamental tone, that is, a D and an A, an E and a B, a G and a D. The result is a **pentatonic scale**—D E G A B D'—the basis of much traditional music in South Africa. From here we can see it is an easy jump to the common chords of much mainstream popular music and the harmonic progression of the Christian hymn—I IV V I, or I IV I6/4 V I, or I ii V I. Chord I is D A (without a third), chord ii is E B, chord IV is G D, I6/4 is A D, chord V is A E. All are missing the third of the chord.

The transition from the traditional root progressions of the musical bow to the common chord progressions of the Christian hymn and more mainstream popular music is embodied in the traditional performances of *maskanda* guitarists, who structure their music by using two or three root progressions, the first two a whole tone apart, such as C and D, and the third root, the interval of a fifth above the C. The oscillation between the two root pitches is commonly heard in the more traditional sounds of Shembe singing discussed in Chapters 13 and 14 but is also heard on the 1979 commercial recording by **Johnny Clegg and Sipho Mchunu**, *Universal Men.*

Track 9 of *Universal Men* demonstrates the relationship between musical bow performance and *maskanda* guitar styles, because it freezes in performance the transition between the musical bow and *maskanda* guitar playing. (An audiovisual clip of the track is also available on the *Rhythm of Resistance* DVD at the end of track 3, leading into track 4, titled "Zululand Roots.") In this example, Johnny Clegg plays a traditional mouth bow with the two fundamentals, a C and a D, created with the cane or wooden stick scraping first the lower fundamental and then the higher fundamental. Quickly one hears the overtones

Figure 8.3 A group of Basotho men living in the mountains of Lesotho gather together on a misty morning to listen to the sound of the *lesiba* mouth bow and homemade guitar, or *ramkie*. June 1994, taken by Carol Muller.

in the melody produced two octaves above. The melody of the bow repeats several times until a clear rhythmic and melodic groove is established. These overtones are amplified both in the mouth and electronically in this recording.

At this point Sipho Mchunu joins in the performance on guitar, sounding out three interweaving and **contrapuntal** melodies, a bass line, a line in the middle that keeps the rhythm steady, and the melody. Mchunu sings the words of the song using the same melody Clegg introduced on the bow and also sounds out the melody in the upper register of the guitar. Clegg and Mchunu start to sing in call and response between the two voices, with their melodic phrases overlapping each other. Sipho sings in a higher range than does Clegg, but both voices seem to blend in with the tone color of the stick scraping against the gut of the bow.

It is clear that there are eight pulses per measure, grouped into two beats of four pulses each. But this does not induce the same 4/4 feel one might have listening to marching band music, for example. Rather, the strong and weak beats, or the stressed and unstressed beats, continually pull against each other. The tempo is steady, and the melody Mchunu produces on the guitar repeats in numerous cycles through the course of the performance. About two-thirds of the way into the piece, Clegg improvises in the higher ranges of the mouth bow, producing a whistle-like sound with the overtones. The pitches he uses include C D E G and A, a pentatonic scale that fluctuates between the C root and the D root. Clegg and Mchunu harmonize their melodic lines in intervals of parallel fourths and thirds.

Figure 8.4 Basotho shepherds entertained by a *ramkie* player, early morning in the mountains of Lesotho, June 1994. Blankets are commonly used for warmth in the winter months in this region. Photo taken by Carol Muller.

Listening to the combined performance of Clegg on mouth bow and Mchunu on *maskanda* guitar in this example helps one understand the transition from mouth bow to guitar in Zulu *maskanda* performance. Clegg starts the performance on the mouth bow, the instrument that preceded Zulu music on guitar. Mchunu enters playing the same music but on guitar. The traditional musical principles of the musical bow then seamlessly transfer onto the guitar. The same song and its accompaniment can be performed on either instrument. Here the historical relationship between the two instruments is clearly illustrated.

Maskanda technique

Gumboot dance teacher Blanket Mkhize observes that the guitar is like a band—it can play all the parts. It can produce rhythm, melody, and harmony, and can sound like an entire choir of voices. The guitar is also relatively inexpensive and easy to buy. Because of the central importance of the guitarist in *maskanda*, it is usually the guitarist who is the composer and leader of a group. The capacity to play up to three separate melodic lines on the guitar while rapidly declaiming self-praise is a skill admired in *maskanda* performance.

Guitars used in *maskanda* have six steel strings, which produce a more percussive timbre than do strings made of nylon. The guitar is played with plectrums, which are called *ikati* because they resemble a cat walking on the floor.

In *maskanda* performance there are two styles of guitar playing: ***ukuvamba***, strumming chords percussively in the tradition of township *marabi* from the 1920s and 1930s, and ***ukupika***, finger-picking styles from north of South Africa. Typically, *ukupika* is the more desired style, because it usually demonstrates greater skill and complexity on the part of the performer and is thought to adhere to the laws of the Zulu, *umthetho womZulu*. There are numerous kinds of ***chuning***, that is, ways in which the strings of the guitar are tuned in terms of both register (how high or low the overall sound is) and pitches used. Some styles, such as ***isiZulu*** from northern KwaZulu Natal, use only five of the six strings, while those of ***umzansi*** from the southern coastal area use all six in performance. A typical tuning draws on the Western system but starts on the D rather than the E above middle C. So the common pitches tuned to in *maskanda* guitar are (from the D above middle C descending down two octaves) D B G D A E. This pitch pattern suggests a structure based on intervals rather than absolute pitch—usually a *maskanda* tunes his or her instrument to match the register of the singing voice. In other words, the starting pitch is relative while the intervals between pitches remain constant.

Many *maskanda* guitarists learned musical technique by first playing on a homemade guitar or violin. According to Nollene Davies (1994), a boy would start off on an instrument with one or two strings—a "toy instrument." The one-stringed instrument was called *udloko*, *ubhek'indlela*, or *ikopi*. If the boy proved to be talented, he would gradually add to the number of strings and the complexity of his musical performance. It was usually when a man began "courting" that he would finally purchase a guitar to woo his lover. Although these musicians are usually self-taught, a more experienced player will often guide the novice in learning the basic principles, even if these sessions are not regarded as formal lessons. The young student is taught the tuning of the instrument, various styles of *maskanda* music, and compositional techniques.

As with the leader of an *isicathamiya* group, the *maskanda* must be a skilled composer who can create original songs and lyrics, including the three kinds of texts produced in a good *maskanda* rendition: the choral part, the narrative part, and the self-praises. Davies tells the story of one *maskanda* who said that he did not care about politics, but because his audiences wanted to hear what he had to say about such things, he composed songs that addressed political matters. The *maskanda* has a powerful pulpit, as audience members are painfully aware. One audience member warned Davies that anyone who knows

African Guitar Styles

Ethnomusicologist Gerhard Kubik's video *African Guitar* shows the finger-picking style of guitarists filmed and recorded by Kubik over almost three decades (1966–1983). The video has a detailed set of liner notes, telling of the lives of musicians and of their style of guitar performance. It is a wonderful audio-visual document on African guitar styles generally, and it also suggests the kinds of musical exchanges that might have taken place between Black South Africans and other Africans who migrated into the country from the north in search of work. *Graceland* guitarist Ray Phiri traces his gentler style of guitar playing to the influence of his father, a migrant worker and musician who came to South Africa from Malawi in central Africa.

a *maskanda* should guard his actions because the *maskanda* might write a song to shame that individual in public.

Although the principles of *maskanda* musical performance are integrally linked to Zulu tradition, the social position of these traditional urban musicians was often contested. There is a Zulu saying about *maskanda* performers: ***isiginci asak'umuzi*** (a guitar doesn't build a homestead). The guitar was viewed negatively because it was associated with the values of ***isidolopho***, "the urban or township life," and the concertina was thought to be the "instrument of Satan." There were several reasons for this perception among rural people. *Maskanda* used to wander from homestead to homestead in the rural areas, which created the impression that they were vagabonds. They smoked wild hemp or marijuana, locally called *isangu*. Furthermore, the *maskanda* was thought to be popular with young women and to use his musical and verbal skills to lure them away from their homes and good living. Finally, they were usually migrant workers and away for a long time. When they returned to their rural homes, they brought new instruments, sounds, and ideas to the more traditionally minded communities. And if a *maskanda* successfully recorded his music in the studios in town, his success was likely to lure him away from his rural home forever.

Maskanda: tradition in transformation

In August 1993, just after a large gathering of ethnomusicologists at the South African Symposium on Ethnomusicology at the University of Natal in Durban, the music department hosted another of its annual *maskanda* competitions for migrant worker performers. My colleague Bongani Mthethwa initiated this competition in 1988 out of his and Joseph Shabalala's growing concern for the demise of traditional music in KwaZulu Natal. While Shabalala dreamed about starting a music school for traditional performance, Mthethwa decided that a competition organized by the University of Natal, with its attendant prestige as an educational institution, would help rejuvenate passion for the intricacies and beauty of *maskanda* performance in the region. Initially the competition was quite small, but within a few years the first rounds of the competition were held in six separate regions, with the final showdown on the university campus. By this stage, the competition was funded by National Sorghum Breweries, a locally owned brewer of traditional sorghum beer, also known as *iJuba*.

The final round of the 1993 ***maskanda* competition** was held in the sports hall at the University of Natal in Durban. The audience, judges, and emcee were seated on the spectator stands around the central performance space. Six microphones were set up to accommodate singers and instrumentalists in larger groups. The emcee for the competition was the ever-popular "Bodloza" Nzimande, local radio personality from Radio Zulu (now Ukhozi Radio); the primary judge was *maskanda* expert Sipho Mchunu, who performs with Johnny Clegg as part of Juluka.

There were three broad categories of *maskanda* competition: for guitarists as soloists or leaders of *maskanda* groups; for musical bow players; and for those who played the jaws harp, the accordion or concertina, violin, and the mouth organ, or homemade versions of these instruments. While there were not separate categories for men and women, women tended to play the musical bow, mouth organ, and jaws harp, and men the concertinas, violins, accordions, and guitars. Because of the large number of participants in the competition, each individual/group entry was allowed to perform only two songs. Typically, a song would begin, and once the judges were satisfied that they had heard enough, the emcee cut the musician off, and the second song began. In this context, musicians rarely completed an entire song/story performance before being told to stop.

The body has long been central to effective *maskanda* performance. Unlike *isicathamiya* and gumboot dance performances, however, there were no guidelines or rules about what *maskanda* competitors should wear. At this event, there was a wide range of costumes, from the humble to the extremely elaborate. Some were quite traditional—using animal skins and ankle rattles; others were more familiar, with small modifications, such as trousers with Zulu traditional designs sewn into the pockets or around the edges. These *maskanda* used a range of materials in creating the densely layered costumes: animal skins, beads, rattles, layers of pleated fabrics, plenty of elaborate and colorful trim on trousers, skirts, and shirts. The instruments themselves were often decorated with rich colors, textures, and designs embodying the character and spirit of the performer.

The more ambitious groups in the competition typically included a troupe of *ngoma* dancers performing on the side of the stage. Attired in animal skins—from deer, to goats, and sheep—they kicked their legs up and dropped them hard on to the floor, their legs reinforcing the rhythms created by the guitarist and his rhythm section.

Several individuals and groups incorporated a humorous element in their performances. Either they sang songs that made the audience laugh, or they included one or two performers in the front of the group who gestured and danced in ways that elicited much laughter from the audience. One group had a young man breakdancing on the floor, while a second performer gestured in comical ways. Laughter makes for a memorable performance, and with so many competing to win, it was important to leave a strong impression on the judges.

The 1993 competition was the last held at the University of Natal, and 1994 was the final year of the event. In the space of just six years, the competition had served its purpose. *Maskanda* had reasserted its popular presence on radio and national television; it had even become a force in the dissemination of South African music abroad. But at the same time, the competition had contributed to the growing commercialization and standardization of *maskanda* musical performance in KwaZulu Natal.

Guitarist John Bengu began the commercialization of *maskanda* in the 1950s and began recording in the 1960s. In the process he changed his name to **Phuzushukela** (Sugar Drinker), and formed a *maskanda* band with bass guitar, drums, electric guitar, *ngoma* dancers, and backup singers. He was so successful in the 1960s that he helped create the 1970s performance category called "Zulu-Trad" on the radio and in the local recording industry. This kind of performance became standard recording and radio fare, with numerous bands playing a *maskanda/mbaqanga* mix of music on Radio Zulu and other stations. As *maskanda* became more of a mediated than live sound, Sipho Mchunu recalls that women listeners often chose the recorded version, with its booming volumes, over the softer voices of live performance. The mediation of *maskanda* began to transform traditional notions of masculinity and courtship between young men and women in rural areas of KwaZulu Natal. To appeal to women, musicians now needed a recording contract, and they preferred *maskanda* music loud, and accompanied on bass drums.

The standardization of *maskanda* through competition occurred because of the privileging of one or two regional guitar styles over others: *isiZulu* from northern KwaZulu Natal (including the region you see in *Rhythm of Resistance*, where Sipho Mchunu grew up) and *Umzansi* (the style developed in the coastal region south of the city of Durban). To win an award at the *maskanda* competition, the musician had to display technical virtuosity and be a showman. He or she also had to compose their own words and music, words that would speak to the experiences of the audiences and about current events, some political, others more social. The song was divided into four sections: the *intela* or improvised introductory instrumental section; the chorus part, where the musician's voice sang in harmony with the guitar voices; the narrative part, where the *maskanda* told his or her story; and the ***izibongo*** part, where the musician sang his/her own praises as a musician. Musicians who could do these praises while accompanying themselves on the guitar were considered to be outstanding *maskanda*. (This musical structure is further discussed in the section on Thami Vilakazi and can be heard on the Vilakazi tracks of the accompanying CD.)

Guitarists personalized their instruments by decorating, painting, and putting stickers on them so that they expressed something of the player's own character and place of origin. Each guitar part had two or three voices that intertwined with the melody sung by the *maskanda*. The middle voices had to keep a steady beat, the beat that implied certain dance steps to the musician and the audience. The thumb played the lower voices of the guitar, called *amadoda* (the men). The upper voices, which represented young girls (*amantombazane*), usually copied the melody of the singer, both while he or she sang and in the instrumental interludes. Ultimately the guitar and the voice had to sound in sync with each other, without any sense of conflict between the parts, and each of the voices of the guitar had to be so clear that they could separately communicate their musical messages to the audience.

The contexts of performance have also begun to shift in the last two decades. Earlier, in the rural areas, a *maskanda* wandered from one homestead to the next. Today, in the urban areas, musicians may play when requested by their immediate community, but more frequently they seek out a deal to be recorded and mass-mediated. As a result, record producers play a pivotal role in reshaping *maskanda* performance to suit the perceived tastes of the listening public. Thus the extremely fluid maskanda tradition is constantly manipulated to reflect on and critique the social reality of audiences in the rural and urban environments of KwaZulu Natal.

More recently the texts have been adapted to cohere with the contemporary issues surrounding love. *Maskanda* now sing about women who love men but who also break community taboos, carry venereal diseases, drink excessively, and smoke. More recently, mass-mediated *maskanda* musicians like **Vusi Ximba, Phuzekhemisi, and Kethani** have become popular because of their biting social and political satire. One of the most profound changes to the urban *maskanda* practices in the 1990s, however, was the way in which women musicians began to assert themselves as guitarists and recording artists. The musical bow was traditionally the instrument of women in the rural areas of KwaZulu Natal, and when migrant men began to play guitars, they drew heavily on the musical practices of rural women in the cities. More recently, however, several women have reclaimed a musical space for their own compositions and performances. Three of the best-known female artists are **Tu Nokwe**, **Busi Mhlongo**, and a woman mouth organ player, **Five Roses**, who won the *maskanda* competition at the University of Natal in 1992.

Maskanda guitarist Thami Vilakazi

When I first interviewed *maskanda* guitarist Thami Vilakazi in 1994 he was a migrant worker, often unemployed, who lived in Cato Crest, Durban. He learned to play the *maskanda* guitar style while he was growing up in Eshowe, in northern KwaZulu Natal. As a young boy in Zululand, Vilakazi made his first *igogogo* (guitar) from an oil can and a plank, using fishing line for the strings. He played alone but learned the sounds and style of *maskanda* performance by following young men in his district who went off to court young women with their songs and guitar sounds. (This was the primary activity of a Zulu guitarist, who would progress onto the concertina once he was married.) Vilakazi recalled that he would hide away so that the courting couple could not see him and listen as the man played for his lover (personal communication, June 1995). He would then go home and work out the tuning system for the guitar, and gradually he began to compose his own songs.

Vilakazi's community has acknowledged his special talent as a guitarist and songwriter with the name they have given him: **Chakide**. The name derives from the Zulu root form *chaka*, which means "to blurt out a secret, publish openly a secret affair; betray a person's identity; give away; tell on; report" (Doke et al. 1990: 108). *Chakide* also refers to a mongoose or weasel, and Chakijana is the proper name for a cunning little mythical being in Zulu folklore (Doke et al. 1990: 108). Vilakazi explains that like the Zulu trickster, the subject of many folktales, he is called Chakide because he is "clever, very, very clever" (personal communication, 1994). He portrays the image of Chakide in the section of self-praises he inserts into the majority of his compositions. Thus Vilakazi brings to the urban space a strategy for self-definition that draws on a belief system far removed from the everyday struggles of life in the city. Similarly, he gives textual form to these experiences in a performance that uses traditional Zulu musical principles to groove on the instrument of the city, the instrument of the devil: the guitar. These sounds performed by the Zulu *maskanda* underpin the creation and reenactment of the urban stories, myths, and legends.

The twenty songs of Thami Vilakazi that I have recorded draw on his experience as a migrant worker in the city of Durban in the early 1980s. From his experience as a restaurant cook, a painter, a gardener, and an unemployed worker living in one of the squatter settlements in Durban, Vilakazi constructs in performance a vision of the urban environment that contrasts sharply with his "home" in Zululand. To construct his vision of urban life, he walks through the city. The physical act of walking, combined with thinking, is his method of composition.

> I am not talking to anybody. I am just thinking, just thinking. And touching here and touching this side [of the guitar], then you get what you like. If you get what you like, you have to think now again, what [are] you going to say with your mouth?

> That means composition. Sometimes, if I walk, I am thinking, I am thinking, I am always singing. I am singing, singing, singing. If I get something I can sing about, then I take it . . . It's easy. No problem. If you are thinking, you must get what you want. (Personal communication, December 1996)

Each of the pieces Vilakazi performs is an original composition. Through the total musical package of text, guitar sound, and song structure, he articulates his own moral and geographical vision of the urban experience—a vision that exists in tension with his vision and memory of the rural Zululand of his childhood.

What does he sing about? He remembers the stories that people have told him, and these become the substance of his performance. When the song is complete, he takes it to the person who told him the story and sings it for him or her. People are almost always happy that he composed a song about them, Vilakazi says (personal communication, December 1994).

Most of Vilakazi's songs consist of three kinds of verbal text that differ in content, presentation, and audience addressed, each framed by instrumental sections. Vilakazi himself assumes a different performance persona in each. The performance begins with an introduction called ***intela***, ***izihlabo***, **or** ***isawundi***, in which the tuning is tested and skillfully executed melodies are presented. The introduction is followed by an instrumental section consisting of several interweaving lines, a sung section that is fairly repetitive in text and sound, the self-praises, and sometimes an additional narrative (the song section is often repeated), and finally, an instrumental conclusion with a gradual fading out of sound. There is some flexibility in the ordering of the verbal sections, so Chakide's praises may be heard more than once, or the song section might return, possibly with the lines of text presented in a new sequence.

Although the practice of praise singing or praise naming is not new, it has generally focused on praising others rather than self-commendation. The self-praises of a *maskanda* might be understood as a specifically spatial practice, de Certeau (1988 [1984]) argues, a strategy for delimiting one's own place and for inscribing the individual into the moral and cultural topography of strangers that characterizes the urban environment. It is through his self-praises that Thami is able to articulate the superiority of his performance when compared with that of other *maskanda* guitarists, and it is through these words that he becomes known and remembered in his community.

The contents of Thami's self-praises illustrate the mongoose/weasel image of *chakide*. Although the details may vary from one context to the next, the central ideas become the "signature tune" in each of his performances. Every repetition creates continuity from one song to the next within a single performance, and from performance to performance (CD track 8 has one version).

Zasha phela madoda kuChakide	Men, its burning for Chakide
uPhumekanje bathi bamkakile	He went like this when they surrounded him
Wabaphosela uhlamvu	He threw them a kernel of grain
Bathi bayalunqaka	When they caught it
Kanti bathinta isitingi senkhukhu	They touched chicken shit
UChakide waphuma kanje	Chakide comes out the other side

This text suggests a scene in which the weasel or mongoose (*chakide*) is stealing chickens. In an attempt to catch him out or trick him, the people surround him. But he tricks them by throwing some grain at them. Instead of catching hold of the weasel, however, they grasp in their hands nothing but chicken shit. The weasel disappears around the corner. His wit and guile can clearly not be matched by anybody around him.

Vilakazi's representation of himself as *chakide*, the clever one, refers to both his guitar skills and the manner in which he creates his texts. As Chakide (the man transformed into animal/musician), the quick-witted, sharp, guileful guitarist and storyteller, he is able to beat any who dare challenge him. Such a transformation of self through performance is crucial if Vilakazi is to be the metaphorical *chakide*—the reporter, the teller of people's secrets and affairs. The attribution embodies a particular tension between Chakide and his community, for in telling others' tales, regardless of the artistic expertise with which he does so, he risks community retribution. The potential conflict is conveyed in another section of his self-praises (CD track 7):

Usehleli phezulu-ke manje	Now he is right on top
UChakide ukhanda kulendoda	Chakide is on top of this man's head
Ilibele ukuvimba ubala	He tries in vain to stop [Chakide]
Abangani bayo	[The man's] friends
Bayayibuza ukuthi	Are asking
Ubani lapho wemfowethu	"Who is that there, my brother?"
Hayi!	"Hey!"
Kululekani nina	"You relax
Khohlwani yimina	And forget about me.
Khon'uChakide la.	It is Chakide here."

Vilakazi explains this section in the context of competition between musicians:

> You see, I say to other *maskanda*, I say, "You are not very good for playing, you *maskanda*. So, if you want to come to me and hear what, how I am playing here, you can't see me. Even if I am in front of you, you can't see . . . No, no, you can't see me. You are looking at me, you ask other people, you ask other people, "Where is this Thami?" You can't see me because now I look like a *chakide*.
>
> And what else? Even if you sit like that, I can stay on your head. You ask "Where is Chakide?" The people they are going to tell you, "There is the *chakide*, on your head." You say, "No, it's not Chakide, it's my hair. My hair is very big." The people say, "Oh, you are very stupid man. There's the *chakide*." You say, "No, it's not Chakide, it's my hair." (Personal communication, February 1995)

In the context of Vilakazi's performance the trickster is praised for his adeptness at guitar playing, though his relationship to his community is considered with some ambivalence in terms of the stories that he sings about. Such ambiguity is embodied in the uncertainty in his friends' identification of him as either hair or *chakide*.

In the sung sections of his performance, Vilakazi criticizes the morals of the members of the urban community in which he stays. This is the "poetic license" that Vail and White (1991) suggest is a central aesthetic principle in Southern African performance. However, the subjects of Vilakazi's songs are not those distant from daily life, such as government officials or religious leaders, but the people with whom he interacts on a daily basis. In Vilakazi's view, their moral fiber is inferior to that of the people of his home in Zululand, to whom he appears to address his critique. The songs are simple in text and structure. They usually consist of four or five lines that are repeated several times.

Akuyiwo naw'amanga kulelizwe (9x)	There are so many lies in this world (9x)
Kukhona abathi sebazi	There are some who say that
uNkulunkulu emafini	They know God in the clouds
Kukhona abathi sebebuya	There are some who say they have come
KuNkulunkulu emafini	From God in the clouds
Akuyiwo naw'amanga kulelizwe	There are so many lies in this world
Ngikhonz'idlozi	"I honor the ancestors
Mina Baba ngixolele (3x)	Father, forgive me"(3x)
Tathi sembato sakho	"Take your church attire
Sihambe sontweni (3x)	We are going to church"(3x)
Ngikhonz'idlozi	"I honor the ancestors
Mina Baba ngixolele	Father, forgive me"
Akuyiwo naw'amanga kulelizwe	There are so many lies in this world.

Vilakazi's song texts are remarkable for their embedded conflicts. In this song, there is a contest over belief systems—Christianity versus Zulu traditional religious practice (the ancestors); implicit in the text is a generational difference—Vilakazi addresses his "father" and asks forgiveness for the discrepancy between his own and his father's worldviews. There is also a dissonance over domains of truth and deception, of what people say versus how they act. Each of these contradictions is framed by Vilakazi's urgent desire for truth: "There are so many lies in this world." With the repetition of sections of this song at the end of the performance, Vilakazi sings that line no less than sixteen times!

Both the self-praising and the personal narratives inserted into Vilakazi's performances are delivered very rapidly and with minimal repetition, following the style of the conventional *imbongi*—somewhere between sung and spoken poetry (Rycroft 1984). The delivery is rapid, with minimal repetition of complete lines or blocks of text. The crucial differences between the traditional *imbongi* and the *maskanda* are the musician's guitar accompaniment to his praises and the narrative style of the *maskanda*'s performed texts.

In the narratives, where he exposes the untruths and deceptions that he senses characterize his urban environment, Vilakazi articulates the moral disconnection he senses between rural and urban spaces. He suggests, for example, that the *sangoma* (traditional healer) is not a real healer but someone interested only in the money. He sings of a man who steals everything he sees, of young men and women who transgress traditional moral boundaries by sitting and kissing in the park in front of young children, of the impossibility of marriage, of a young woman who ran off with all his money.

The following narrative is taken from a song addressed to his father: (CD track 8)

Akenithulenini phela kenginixoxele	Be quiet while I tell you a story
Ngitholiphepha lapha incwadi	I received a paper, a short letter
Libhalwe usisi obath'ufun'umendo	From a sister seeking marriage
Ngisukenaye lomuntu la eThekweni	I left Durban with this person
Ngimuse ekhaya afik'agilimkhuba	I took her home, only for her to break taboos
Aqomabafana lababelusa izinkomo	She fell in love with the herdboys
Ngitheng'isidwaba	I bought her the skirt for marriage
Athi isidwaba siyamusinda	She said "The skirt is heavy"
Ngeke asifake	She won't wear it
Usekhohliwe ukuthi ifun'umendo	She has forgotten that she seeks marriage
Ucabang'ukweqa manje ashon'eGoli	She is now thinking of running off to Jo'burg
Thenengakeqi nje wabanjwa ubaba	Before she could do so, my father caught her
Eshuk'igudu la emva kwendlu ngenhla	Rolling a joint behind the house
Wakhuz'ibhadi ubab'ebon'imikhuba	My father was appalled at the behavior, a spectacle
Abizumama ukuba azombukisa	He called my mother to see for herself
Kuthe kunjalo-ke washaya wachitha	She ran away immediately
Umakhoti wami lona esebhek'eGoli	My bride, to Johannesburg
Uma ngithi ngiyabuza ukuthi	When I asked her,
Kwenzenjani	"What is wrong?"
Ahleke kancane nje athi gwegwegwe	She just laughs a little, gwegwegwe
Unginika malini njengoba	"What do you give me for
Wangithat'ethekweni	taking me from Durban
Wathi uyongithengel'inyama	Saying you are going to buy me meat
Kanti uyongidlis'imfino	But giving me only greens"
Awukahle phela khoti ukutheth'	"Hold on a little, my bride, lower your voice
Ekhaya	At home
Ubab'uzothini ngoba usafika emzini	What will father say? You are new in the family"
Anginamsebenzi mina, ngizobuyel' Ekhaya.	"I don't care, I will go back home"
Yeyeni webantu kanti eThekweni Kunjani.	Oh my, my, such are the people of Durban.

Vilakazi closes his song addressed to his "father" in Zululand with a rueful lament over the kinds of people he knows in the city of Durban. In conversation, Vilakazi insisted that, even though he sings in the first person, the song is not about himself. It is a story about the experiences of one of his friends from Eshowe, which he then transformed into song performance. Vilakazi suggests that the conclusion to be drawn is that you cannot marry "a woman of loose morals."

The distaste that Vilakazi articulates toward lax moral practices in the urban areas is contrasted with the image he projects in his self-praises, where Vilakazi constructs for himself the role of a teller of the truth through the sounds of his guitar and the words of his songs and stories. In the song "*Akuyiwo naw'amanga kulelizwe*" ("There are so many lies in this world") cited above, Vilakazi adds to his self-praises a conversation he has with a brother, the chief from Eshowe, in which he tells him that this Chakide is the same Vilakazi that he knows.

Kuseyiyo leyondoda wethu	It's the same man, brother
Hlala phanzi uthule uthi du	Sit down and be quiet
Uzwekahle intambo	And listen carefully to the strings
Ngizibambe zonke wethu	I am holding all of them
Angikulobhi	I am not cheating you
Yathula inkosi	The chief Mkhathini is quiet
UMkhathini lapha phezulu eNgogo	Up there at Ngogo
Awunikeze umfowethu uMashokani	Please pour my brother Mashokani
Injongo ibeyinye isiqatha	A tin of the brew [*skokiaan*—a powerful homebrew]
Athi ukushaya kancane khona	So he can drink a little and
Ezozwa ukuthi ngenzejani la.	Hear what I do here.
Hop!	Hop!
Ngikhathele!	I am so fed up!

At another moment in his self-praising, Chakide tells us that we must watch the various voices in his guitar strings so that none of them falls down. He monitors individual guitar voices carefully, in a manner that parallels his moral surveillance. Chakide can tell others' secrets because he presents himself as the bearer of moral right, of cultural truth.

Keywords

Afrikaans South African language created from a mix of Arabic, Dutch, French, and English

braced bow a musical bow whose single wire is captured at ninety degrees by a second wire to create two separate sections and two distinct fundamental pitches

capodastra a brace used on guitars to tighten the strings and raise the fundamental pitches of each string

Chakide a trickster figure, and the performance name of Thami Vilakazi, a South African *maskanda* guitarist and composer

chuning the Zulu version of "tuning" used on guitar

contrapuntal two or more independent melodic lines that sound out against each other in a single musical texture, common to Baroque keyboard styles for example

domestic workers initially Black men and later women who worked in mostly White households as servants. They historically had very little free time, though this has changed significantly since 1994

fundamental tone the loudest and lowest sound produced in overtone singing and musical bow playing

intela, izihlabo,* or *isawundi the opening section of maskanda performance, where the tuning of the instrument is explored
isidolopho the urban or township life and values, set in contrast to rural values in KwaZulu Natal
isiginci asak'umuzi a rural belief about professional musicians: "a guitar doesn't build a homestead"
isiZulu the music from northern KwaZulu Natal
izibongo praises sung usually to a person in power, but in *maskanda* they become self-praises, telling of the skills of the musician
Johnny Clegg and Sipho Mchunu perhaps the two most important *maskandii* in South African recording history—they were the first interracial duo to record *maskanda* music, truly crossing over in the marketplace in the late 1970s. Their music can be found in iTunes
maskanda Zulu musician who uses traditional musical principles on new instruments like guitar and concertina
***maskanda* competition** a competition for *maskanda* was hosted by the University of KwaZulu Natal for a brief period in the late 1980s and early 1990s, to reinvigorate interest in the traditional music of KwaZulu Natal
musical bow a traditional hunting bow used for musical purposes
musikant Afrikaans word meaning musician
ngoma a dance, song, healing, drumming complex, also refers to particular style of song and dance among Zulu-speaking men
overtones also known as partials, the high-pitched tones produced by a musical fundamental
pentatonic scale a scale of five distinct pitches
Phuzushukela also known as John Bhengu, one of the earliest artists to record *maskanda* music on Zulu radio
resonator the mouth or gourd used to amplify the soft sounds of musical bow playing
Tu Nokwe, Busi Mhlongo, Five Roses three of the most important women *maskandii* (see iTunes for Nokwe and Mhlongo)
umzansi music from southern KwaZulu Natal
ukupika finger picking guitar style of *maskanda*
ukuvamba chord-strumming style
Vusi Ximba, Phuzekhemisi, and Kethani three of the most important male *maskandii* played on radio (see iTunes)

CHAPTER 9

Labor Migration: Gumboot Dance

Gumboot Dance

For some time after the historic 1976 Soweto uprising, schools in South Africa's Black townships were in chaos. So a local community organizer in Soweto, as happened in other parts of the country as well, decided to create a community center for Black youth. She raised funds to build a structure where she taught a group of young men traditional and contemporary dance—the cha cha, gumboot dance, traditional Zulu dance, and a host of others. Ultimately, this group went on to busk on the streets of Johannesburg and perform in a community arts festival. After their director, Zenzi Mbuli, transformed their busking into a theatrical production, they became known around South Africa. British film director Wayne Harrison, from Back Row Productions in London, traveled to South Africa and decided to film the production. *Gumboots: An Explosion of Spirit and Song* (2000) is a commercially produced video of their show.

The video is divided into two sections. The first shows the production that has traveled internationally to festivals and music theater stages in Europe, the United States, and Asia. Here gumboot dance as a cultural practice of migrant workers has been transformed into a stage production about being gold miners in South Africa in the twentieth century. It is a moving production that combines narrative, gumboot dance, drumming, and singing. The performers use a mix of English and Zulu, and the instrumental accompaniment has been worked into a musical language palatable to an international audience.

The second section of the video is a fifty-three-minute commentary on the performance. It provides insider perspectives on gold mining, language use, and the creation of the *Gumboots* production itself. Rare and old footage of the early days of labor migration and migrants in the gold mines as well as old dance performances are interwoven with the documentary narrative. Excerpts from the stage performance are also inserted into the documentary as the narrator explains the larger meaning or history of a specific sequence. In addition to what it tells us about gumboot dance, this documentary provides a lens through which we can see how local performance is remade for a transnational audience. In the spirit of the documentary portion of the gumboots video, I have inserted segments of information from the video into my own ethnographic and historical narrative on gumboot dance as I learned about it from my teacher Blanket Mkhize over a period of almost two decades.

Entering the world of gumboot dance

My entry into the world of gumboot dance came quite unexpectedly in 1984, when Blanket Mkhize invited me and fellow ethnomusicology student Janet Topp Fargion to learn to gumboot dance. For our initial meeting we were instructed to travel to the same place that *isicathamiya* competitions were held, the Glebeland migrant worker hostels. Neither Janet nor I spoke any Zulu at the time, and Mkhize and his fellow dancers spoke almost no English. Initially we agreed to meet on Saturdays and Sundays at the Glebeland hostel community hall for lessons, although Mkhize had asked us to come every day for long periods of time, which was more in line with how migrant workers themselves taught each other and rehearsed their routines. But we couldn't afford the cost in time and expense of traveling to and from Umlazi so frequently. Furthermore, the townships were dangerous for both Black and White South Africans, because migrant worker hostels only housed men. Women stayed out of the townships, not only out of fear but also because it was illegal to enter without special permits. We were also meeting Mkhize at the migrant worker hostels, large barracks for single men. No women were allowed to live in these buildings, so the few women there tended to be either family members on brief visits or prostitutes.

We met in the Glebeland hostel for several weeks, but ultimately our lessons became more complicated to negotiate. In 1985 the apartheid government declared at least two states of emergency, clamping down on what it called "political unrest" by putting a curfew on travel in Black residential areas and increasing security force surveillance, particularly in a township like Umlazi, because of the migrant worker hostels at the entrance to the township. These were the sites of politically motivated violence and killings in the 1980s and early 1990s. Mkhize became concerned for our safety at the hostel, so we agreed to rehearse at the University of Natal. This meant that Janet and I had to pick up and drop off the gumboot dancers every time we met.

The classes consisted of a couple of dancers simply going through their dance routines at speed, over and over, and expecting us to pick up the moves somehow. It was hard. Slowly we began to work out a way that might work better for us. It was clear that Janet and I needed to have the steps broken down into smaller units, even though the dancers themselves had learned them in much larger segments. At one point we asked Mkhize if he would mind if we videotaped the moves so that we could learn them at home. He agreed.

Our first public performance with the team of Blanket Mkhize was at the University of Natal's Music and Dance Jamboree held at the South African Music Educator's Conference in August 1985. We performed alongside a variety of musical groups, including an *isicathamiya* ensemble from Umlazi. The audiences were amazed that women—White women, at that—could do the dance. Although Janet and I both left South Africa at the end of 1985 to study abroad, we were able to perform together with Blanket's team at several other events later in the year. I maintained contact with Mkhize over the years, and when I returned to South Africa in the early 1990s, we reestablished our performing relationship. I danced with Mkhize several times until I again left South Africa in September 1996.

On January 6, 1996, when both Janet and I were back in the country, Blanket threw a party at his homestead in the southern part of the province of KwaZulu Natal. Blanket told his chief that he and his neighbors would be welcoming to his homestead the two White women he had taught to gumboot dance in Durban in 1985. As with all traditional Zulu celebrations, an animal (a sheep, in this case) was slaughtered and its meat shared with the community and guests, *utshwala* (traditional sorghum beer) was brewed beforehand, and competitive song and dance took place.

Two teams of dancers prepared to perform. Mkhize's sons and their friends, who lived in Jolivet (near Ixopo) in the interior part of southern KwaZulu Natal, the area known as Umzansi (below the Tugela River), had been rehearsing their own gumboot dance team, and a second team arrived in a mini-bus taxi from Creighton, the Bhaca area in southern KwaZulu Natal. Most of the members of that team were migrant workers employed by the parastatal company called Spoornet, formerly the state-controlled South African Railways. The Railways had been active sponsors of gumboot dance until the mid-1980s, when political violence disrupted urban life in South Africa, destroying much of the vibrancy of the Black urban culture that existed.

Late on the morning of January 6, 1996, as is typical of gumboot dance, a visiting team of dancers arrived with a guitarist and concertina player playing a cyclical riff that moved between the tonic, subdominant, and dominant chords. The leader of the team walked ahead of the dance team, who moved into the performance space with a stylized walk, their arms outstretched at the sides of their bodies. Occasionally, the dancers punctuated this movement by hitting their boots together at the ankles in a quick rhythmic pattern. They circled around the open space in the homestead, and then moved into a stationary straight-line formation, with the leader and musicians standing apart from the rest of the team.

The leader was dressed slightly differently from the others, but all had on the traditional black Wellington boots, baseball caps, black trousers tied at the knee with a white handkerchief, and "cowboy" shirts. One or two of the dancers had tied pieces of wire with bottle tops strung on them around the lower part of their boots, to create the sound of rattles.

The dancers claim that the bottle top rattles remind them of the history of gumboot dancers' experiences in the mines. The sounds, they say, resonate with the sound of chains around the ankles of miners in the early years of mining history, a claim that corresponds to reports that prisoners were often supplied as cheap labor to the mines and may well have been chained together. However, since the ankle rattles in traditional Zulu dance were made from dried pea pods, it may be that the natural materials from rural environments were simply replaced with new materials available in the urban context.

Blanket Mkhize had a different version of ankle rattles. These rattles, called ***amakhehlezi* or *amaspeaker***, were round shoe polish tins with small stones inside. The lid of the tin had been pierced with multiple holes to make it look like a speaker. The speakers were attached to large strands of rubber that were pulled over the boot and placed at the ankle. Mkhize told us that it was an honor to wear these speakers because only those who had mastered the movements were allowed to put them on.

While the dancers waited for the leader's call, they marked time with a quick marching movement in place. The leader paced up and down in front of the team, checking the attire and making sure that everyone was standing in the correct position. The stronger dancers usually stand at the outer ends of the line, with the weaker ones in the middle. "Lef-light" called the leader, and the team responded with a quick hitting of the boots together as they continued to march on the spot. He began to call out a series of commands more aggressively. The team of dancers responded with precision and power. **"Attention!" "Attention!" " Two-Attention!" "*Nasisalutho*!"** ("***Salutho***" is one of the first dance sequences performed on *Gumboots*, the video.) The leader continued to randomly shout out a series of commands. Each of these called for a fixed pattern of steps that had been composed by individual dancers and learned by team members over time in many rehearsals.

The gumboot style of dance draws on a variety of sources: Bhaca tradition; the various missionary heritages, such as that of the German missionaries; dances of sailors who visited the port city of Durban, such as Russian folk dance; the popular social dances that accompanied jazz music in the 1930s and 1940s, such as the jitterbug; and most clearly, **tap dance**, as performed by the visiting minstrel groups of the nineteenth century and popularized through the films of **Fred Astaire and Gene Kelly** in the mid-twentieth century. The aesthetic of gumboot performance also embodies the regimentation of military marching and the discipline required of mine laborers working underground. The dancers are expected to respond quickly, without hesitation, regardless of what the leader commands. Precision of movement—starting and ending on the same beat—is crucial to effective and powerful performance.

The community of people that had gathered at Blanket's homestead that day stood in a circle around the dancers. Those watching the gumboot dancing hardly noticed the dust kicked up by the fast-moving footwork, boot slapping, and thumping on the ground as the group performance intensified. Women ululated and danced in front of the dancers, men whistled, and everybody cheered at the sharpness and discipline of this team of dancers in peak condition. The leader paced back and forth across the line of dancers, occasionally blowing on his police whistle to keep his team alert and responsive. **"*Abelungu!*" (White People—Watch Out!) "*Amaphoyisa!*" (Police!) "*GwazamaZulu!*" (Stab the Zulu!) "*Germiston*!" (name of a mining town) "*Jowanisberg!*" (Johannesburg!)**

Sometime in the middle of the collective performance of ***amadoubles***, the leader called for singles. These are highly competitive solo performances by individual team members where each dancer demonstrates his improvisatory skills. It is in these singles that the links with the tap dancing of Hollywood film stars such as Fred Astaire and Gene Kelly are particularly evident. With each new improvised sequence, the power of the performance increases.

There are several moments in the *Gumboots* video performance where singles are danced. (See especially the item "I'm too sexy for my body" where the man proves his manliness by displaying his improvisational skills in gumboot dance.) Such display reminds us of the *isoka* qualities of the *maskanda*—the physical and musical display of

Figure 9.1 Blanket Mkhize (guitarist on right), and his 1985 team, including Janet Topp Fargion (on left) and Carol Muller (to the right), perform at a school function in KwaZulu Natal, taken by Douglas Muller.

Figure 9.2 Blanket Mkhize (guitar) and his sons gumboot dance at a community celebration in rural KwaZulu Natal, September 1996, taken by Carol Muller.

attributes of a man that would make him a good lover. After all, successfully courting a young woman was the goal of being a skilled singer and Zulu guitarist.

Selected members of the community began to throw small coins at the performers, to communicate to the dancers and the rest of the onlookers which of the soloists they favored. The more coins thrown, the better the spectacle. The practice of throwing money has a long tradition in Black performance culture. Coplan (1985: 76) describes the auctioneering and bidding on performance that characterized shebeen culture in the slumyards of South African cities in the 1930s and 1940s. Similarly, Hugh Tracey describes these practices in urban townships in the 1940s: "In many concerts, members of the audience show their appreciation by showering pennies upon the stage, or by walking up and putting silver in a saucer. The 'Turn' will oblige just so long as the pennies fall. It is an infallible indication of the degree of popularity" (1948: xi).

Finally, the leader called "*Shiyalekhaya.*" All the dancers re-formed the straight line to "leave behind at home," as the leader had instructed. They danced a few more patterns, and finally the performance ended, as freshly slaughtered and grilled meat was passed around to all in attendance.

Although the dancers did not mention it that day, their party coincided with the centenary of gumboot dance performance, which had emerged a century earlier among Bhaca migrant workers from KwaZulu Natal as a Black, predominantly male genre. Beginning in the late 1890s, these men migrated, sometimes on foot and often by train, to and from both the gold mines in Johannesburg and harbor and railway work in the port city of Durban. Gumboot straddles the rural and urban spaces within which migrant workers from southern KwaZulu Natal have operated for the last 100 years. Though there are traditional characteristics embedded in the performance, as the video *Gumboots* demonstrates so powerfully, the gold mines in and around the city of Johannesburg were the environment most critical to the development of gumboot style. For most Bhaca migrants to eGoli, the City of Gold, work and leisure were continually controlled by structures of authority and surveillance in the form of mine bosses, managers, and police. Gumboot dance was forged out of migrant worker experience: it is a style that reflects on that experience, commenting with humor and at times with biting satire on its brutality.

This genre embodies what Hannerz (1997) calls the "global ecumene"—the simultaneous presence in a single performance of ancestral beliefs and dance style, Hollywood cowboy and tap dance films, nineteenth-century Anglo-American minstrel performance, industrial labor relations, European folk music, mission Christianity, and ethnic tensions. In this sense, gumboot dance is neither essentially African nor Western, neither Christian nor ancestral, neither traditional nor modern. Much like its migrant practitioners, who are neither fully urban nor fully rural, gumboot dance has long existed in the interstices of South African society.

Early history of gumboot dance

Several elements of gumboot dance are characteristic of **pre-colonial Nguni musical practices**: the call and response interaction between dance leader and the rest of the team; the competitive element, both between dance teams and within the teams; the importance

Figure 9.3 Blanket Mkhize (guitarist on the right side) plays for his team who arrive to perform at the community celebration in rural KwaZulu Natal, September 1996.

Figure 9.4 Gumboot team of Steven Shelembe competes against the team brought by Blanket Mkhize to celebrate the visit of researchers Janet Topp Fargion and Carol Muller, Creighton, KwaZulu Natal, January 1995, taken by Carol Muller.

of audience/community support during the performance; the comical element, drawn from both traditional and minstrel performance; and the manner in which gumboot dance engages with and is constituted from the substance of everyday life and experience.

What clearly distinguishes gumboot dance from earlier rural dances is the use of footgear for its performance. The differences in footgear and style distinguish two different kinds of gumboot dance performance. The first, ***igumboots* dance**, is deeply connected to the heavy stamping of the traditional dance of Zulu men. It is also clearly associated with the working class—with those who labored in the mines, in the Durban harbor, and perhaps even on White farms. The second is more directly connected to the civilizing project of the mission station. It is the lighter style, one more clearly tied to light stepping or tapping—what Mkhize's dancers call the style for girls. This is ***isicathulo***, the style developed with shoes and performed by the likes of Reuben Caluza (see Erlmann 1992) and other members of the mission-educated elite of KwaZulu Natal.

Pre-colonial dance forms were generally performed barefoot. The Zulu name given to gumboot dance—*isicathulo*—provides the first indication of innovation. Initially, the word referred to the leather shoes worn by warriors who had to travel long distances. In the nineteenth century, it also began to refer to other types of shoe and rubber Wellington boots, both of which were crucial apparel when an African came into contact with Europeans and Americans on mission stations and farms and, later, in the urban areas. In all cases, *isicathulo* constituted signs of contact with the Western or non-African world. The root of the word *cathama* means to walk softly, quietly, and stealthily. It has been incorporated into two kinds of Black performance culture in South Africa: *isicathulo* and *isicathamiya* . The first is the gumboot dance style described above. The second is the style of music and dance performance recently made famous by Joseph Shabalala and Ladysmith Black Mambazo (see Chapter 7). In this context it means to walk softly like a cat.

The earliest evidence of the new dance styles that emerged with the introduction of shoes and boots appeared at the mission stations. Besides *isicathulo*, several terms associated with gumboot dancing point to the Western influence on its development: *thamba*, *boloha*, *isicathulo* and *umqhumqhumbelo* (Cockrell 1987: 422). The first, *thamba* (discussed below), refers to dancing in a straight line with uniform movement controlled by a conductor who usually plays a concertina. Such movement is typical of gumboot dance performance as we learned it from Blanket Mkhize. *Boloha* is possibly an Afrikaans or Xhosa derivative of the word "polka." It is defined as a boot dance (and cross-referenced with *isicathulo*), a rough concert, or an all-night carnival party. *Umqhumqhumbelo* is perhaps the most intriguing in terms of the development of gumboot dance. It is defined as "a modern rhythmic dance adopted by certain Christian natives, in which dancing is both individual and in groups" (Cockrell 1987: 422). *Umqhumqhumbelo* is also related to the word *umqhuqho.* This translates into the onomatopoeic sound of the trotting of a horse and the clopping of its heels. A reference to the sound of horses ties in with the word used in competitions to indicate poor performance: ***ihashi*** or horse. According to Jonney Hadebe, *ihashi* is what is called out when a team makes two or more mistakes and is disqualified from the competition.

In addition to the linguistic evidence pointing to the missions as the points of origin for gumboot dance, Hugh Tracey (1952: 7) suggests that the origins of the dance itself are to be found in step dances developed in a mission station where traditional Nguni dancing was banned. Several Catholic missions are located in the Bhaca region, which suggests the impact of mission culture on local Bhaca communities from the nineteenth century. In the documentary *Gumboots*, the director Aubrey Powell suggests that the German missionaries forbade traditional dance and replaced it with their own folk dancing. However, the film footage from earlier in the century also shows Russian sailors who visited the city of Durban and demonstrated their dancing to local workers in the harbor.

The following primary source material suggests that mission culture had an additional influence on the shape of gumboot dance because of its stress upon marching and musical drills, elements common to the older style of gumboot dance that we learned from Blanket Mkhize in the 1980s.

> MUSICAL DRILL, 1st Exercise.
>
> Marking Time
>
> When the children have marched to their places they should be made to "Mark Time!" This is done by alternately raising the left foot and knee and setting it on the ground again, then raising the right foot and knee and setting it on the ground again, always stepping in the same place and keeping time to the music.
>
> The children should be instructed to place their feet on the ground very softly each time, not to stamp, and not to move from their places. This marking time should be done with the hands in the attitude of "Attention," but, to prevent any tendency to swing the arms about, they may be folded behind the back, or with the right hand grasping the left arm behind the back, and vice versa.
>
> (Mariannhill Monastery, Catholic Mission Archives)

It is clear from Hugh Tracey's photographic essay *African Dances of the Witwatersrand Gold Mines* (1952), as well as the archival film footage on the *Gumboots* video, that the mines were central sites in the shaping of gumboot dance style. (Mkhize's father participated in the dance at the mines.) Tracey locates the next development of the genre in the Durban harbor, where migrant workers were issued gumboots when they began to handle chemical fertilizers. Performing outside at both mining and municipal compounds (where migrants were housed) would have required more sound, so boots would have become preferable to the shoes of the mission station.

The influence of the minstrel show

The other cultural force that shaped gumboot dance was the minstrel show, performed in Durban by American and English troupes beginning in the nineteenth century. Jonney Hadebe, one of the members of Blanket Mkhize's team, explains the early history of gumboot dance in a program note written for the South African Railway's gumboot dancers:

> In 1896, subsequent to watching white men tap dancing and clapping their hands, the amaBaca decided to make a dance of their own. They called it the gumboots

> dance. The dance was a rhythmically performed act of dancing, clapping hands and slapping the calves—the calf muscles being protected by the rubber gumboots.
>
> In the year 1896, the group consisted of eight members in all, six dancers and two playing musical instruments. In those days, the soles of the gumboots were cut off and the dancers wore shoes.
>
> With the passage of time, the group became more sophisticated in their dancing performances. They started playing a guitar, concertina, violin and a piano accordion all at the same time. The group presently consists of from twelve to twenty persons. After performing all over the country, where they did their duty towards the younger generation, the group changed their base from Johannesburg to Durban.
>
> The amaBacas dance in the SATS [South African Transport Services] tournament and have danced in Johannesburg, Bloemfontein and Durban. I have been a gumboots dancer for the past twenty-three years. (Jonney Hadebe c. 1978)

Both Cockrell (1987) and Erlmann (1991) provide evidence for the tours of mostly White minstrels from America (such as the famous Christy Minstrels) and England who entertained South Africans with the painted black faces in the nineteenth century, although the African American troupe of Orpheus McAdoo also visited South Africa several times in the 1890s. Cockrell highlights the outstanding features of the minstrel show, many of which became central to the shaping not only of *isicathamiya* performance (as embodied in Joseph Shabalala and Ladysmith Black Mambazo) but also of *isicathulo* and gumboot dance.

> Perhaps the most striking feature of a typical [American] minstrel show was the makeup used by the performers. In the early years all the entertainers were whites in blackface, who wore additional makeup to exaggerate their lips and eyes. Their dress was of two sorts: shabby, ragged, and grotesque to depict southern rural slaves, or fanciful and dandified—replete with tails, white ties, and white gloves, all in excruciatingly bad taste . . . The troupe was arrayed in a semicircle. The interlocutor was usually named Mr. Johnson and sat in the center. He served as the butt of jokes that streamed forth from the end men, typically called after the instruments they played: Mr. Bones and Mr. Tambo. Other minstrels formed the chorus and played banjos, guitars, fiddles, concertinas, triangles, or other instruments. The entertainment took the form of derisive mimicking of the black man. (Cockrell 1987: 419)

Several of these elements transferred into gumboot dance performance: the exaggerated makeup (still used by Black school children in Durban in the mid 1980s, often to make their audiences laugh at the exaggerated images); the shabby dress for the leader (the dance leader, Mkhize typically wore such attire) and dandy dress for the chorus (smart attire for the team could make or break the group in competition); the leader in the center (Mkhize typically paced up and down in front of the group); satire and humor in the performance (Mkhize frequently deliberately fell over in performance to make the audience laugh); and finally, musical accompaniment in the form of guitar, violin, and concertina.

Hadebe's narrative of gumboot dance links its early history to these minstrel performances in several ways. The first is with his reference to "white men tap dancing and clapping their hands." It is quite feasible that the amaBhaca saw minstrel shows by White blackface minstrels in the year 1896. It is not clear, however, if it is tap dancing or simply the complex footwork of minstrel performance that impacted upon these men in that year. It seems more likely that Hadebe is recalling two distinct processes in the development of gumboot dance style: what was recounted to him by older gumboot dancers with regard to minstrel performances in the 1890s and what he may have seen himself in mining compounds in Johannesburg in the 1950s—films of tap dancing by Fred Astaire and Gene Kelly. Tap dancing is also reported to have been extremely popular at the Bantu Men's Social Center in Johannesburg in the 1930s (Phillips 1938: 297). This would have been the more sophisticated gumboot dancing that Hadebe subsequently discusses.

Hadebe's description of the early troupe as a group of eight with six dancers and two instrumentalists also points to the influence of the minstrel shows. Cockrell (1987: 420) quotes an article called "Kafir Christy Minstrels" from the local Durban newspaper, *The Natal Mercury*, that describes a Black minstrel troupe: "A novelty this Christmas, is a troupe of eight genuine natives, *bones and all*, complete who really get through their songs very well" (my emphasis).

The two instruments mentioned may well have been the bones and *tambo*. Cockrell suggests that the bones played by White minstrels were similar to indigenous instruments played by Black South Africans in the early twentieth century. Perhaps the reason the bones of the minstrel show are replaced with the guitar in gumboot dance performance is that the guitar is viewed as a percussive instrument as well as a melodic and harmonic one.

Mining culture and gumboot performance

No one needs to be reminded that mining is hard labor. But perhaps we do need to be reminded, as social historian Dunbar Moodie observes, that mining is a particular kind of hard labor. As a form of production, he writes, mining is hard labor undertaken under conditions of extreme discomfort, exacerbated by tension stemming from the need to watch constantly for signs of potential hazard. "Whenever you go down into a shaft," says a Sotho miner quoted by Moodie, "you are not sure that you will come out alive. You don't want to think about it . . . Death is so real you keep on praying and thanking God each time you come out alive" (Moodie 1983: 180).

The *Gumboots* video shows mine experience as the narrative into which gumboot sequences are inserted and reshaped. Similarly, the peculiarities of mine experience, or **mine culture**, have been indelibly imprinted into popular consciousness through the very substance of the older style of gumboot dance performance. Although gumboot dance has clear precedents in the radical shifts away from pre-colonial performance cultures as they were repressed by the mission and re-modeled on nineteenth-century Euro-American popular culture, I argue that it was the experience of migrant labor in the gold mines of South Africa that most powerfully shaped the distinctive features of what is now called gumboot dance. Gumboot dance engages and comments on the exigencies of everyday experience in mine culture. Perhaps the most revealing source of information on the development of the dance style and on the mine culture itself is the dance as practiced by the older dancers and transmitted to their sons in KwaZulu Natal.

Men who entered into the culture of the mines in South Africa walked into an environment quite alien from their prior rural experience. This was particularly true for those who went underground. One captures a glimpse of the differences, of the harshness of this culture, from the documentary section of the *Gumboots* video. Two miners explained it to Moodie: "One man told me that when he goes to work underground he is not a full person. Another said: 'When I am underground I do not think of anything else except coming out of the mine'" (Moodie 1983: 183).

The mine culture worldwide is characterized by emotions of both pride in the courage to go underground and fear of doing so. The ambivalence the miners feel about mine labor is articulated in the *Gumboots* video where the miner begs the owners not to shut down the mine because he has a family to support. Without the mine, he has no hope of subsistence, yet the mine is a dangerous place. In South Africa, this ambivalence was intensified, because South African mining culture differed in two ways from that in other parts of the world: first, racially structured authoritarianism defined the local culture and second, labor migration for mine employment involved only the men, not their families. As we are told in the "Jo'burg" segment of the *Gumboots* video, a man's family remained a thousand miles away, and he might see them only once in a period of six to eighteen months. He ate, slept, and worked within the confines of the mine and the compound—the cramped, sometimes prison-like buildings where miners lived year round.

The mine compounds were highly controlled residential dormitories in which workers resided for the length of their contract. They were convenient and efficient for mine owners: "The compounds were located close to mineshafts, making rapid and efficient mobilization of labor for work possible. Furthermore, they provided a fit workforce, absenteeism would easily be policed, and strikes could be broken with a minimum of effort" (James 1999: 3). But for the miners, life in the compound was difficult. They were crowded into rooms that might house from sixteen to eighty men at a time, and there was little possibility of private space or time—even during their time off from work.

Nevertheless, the men found means to relieve the stress of their jobs inside the compound, through both officially sanctioned activities and those they organized themselves. The official channels were films shown in compounds and competitions in sport and traditional dance organized by the Chamber of Mines from at least the 1940s. This was one of the spaces in which Bhaca migrants from southern KwaZulu Natal gumboot danced, certainly in the 1940s (James 1999: 3) and, according to oral history, much earlier. The unofficial activities, which the *Gumboots* video alluded to, included alcohol, drugs, and sex, either in the compounds or in nearby urban townships, such as Sophiatown and Vrededorp.

Miners underground

Hugh Tracey (1952) provides visual documentation of a wide range of dances performed by migrant workers at the gold mines in the Johannesburg area in the early decades of this century, including the gumboot dance of the amaBhaca. Though several of the teams of dancers in Tracey's book are wearing shoes, the amaBhaca are the only ones wearing the boots that typify mine labor. This dance attire suggests the close relationship between the content of the dance and mine experience, which is articulated in contemporary gumboot performance. I argue that the tensions associated with the underground experience of Bhaca miners provide the material for the formation of a worker-style dance performance. More than simply reflecting mine experience, it constitutes a satire on labor discipline and interaction as shaped by the experiences of mining and living in a compound. This is manifest at several levels.

Early groups of miners were organized into gangs or teams of workers, each with a Black "boss-boy" who was answerable to the White miner. The boss-boy's relationship with the White boss frequently conflicted with his loyalties to his Black subordinates, fostering considerable tension between teams, the boss-boys, and White management. This gang structure of early mining operations is reflected in the outstanding feature of gumboot dance performance: the team.

The nature of the relationship between ordinary workers and the boss-boy is embodied in the call and response interaction between the dance team leader and the team. In the dance structure, however, the boss-boy (dance leader) holds total control. Whenever he calls and whatever he requires, his team has to respond with rigor and precision. He often blows on a police whistle to keep his team in tow—a standard of discipline and teamwork that was also important in the mines. In the mines, Moodie points out, any worker who did not cooperate put his own life and that of his teammates on the line:

> According to an observer who worked underground, Black miners "are keen that every one of them should do a perfect job . . . else they all face the risk of danger from falling rocks. They try hard to prevent or minimize accidents at work places by giving advice and helping one another." Despite ethnic tensions in the compound, Black underground workers in South Africa "regard themselves as members of their work team first and foremost and do not appear to have any interest in ethnic composition" (Moodie 1983: 180–181)

Because of the danger intrinsic to underground mine labor and the racially loaded authority structure, the interaction between supervisor and workers was authoritarian. Immediate response to commands was demanded on at least two levels: between the boss-boy and his team and between Black laborers and White superiors. This style of interaction was entrenched in the racially constituted labor relations of South African mines from the earliest days and is indelibly imprinted in gumboot dance performance itself.

As the *Gumboots* documentary video corroborates, the linguistic manifestation of this unequal pattern of communication became known as ***fanakalo***. *Fanakalo*, which means "do it like this," is defined as a "pidgin language used and sometimes taught as lingua franca on the mines." It was embodied in a series of booklets issued by the Chamber of Mines from the 1920s through the 1970s under various titles, such as the *1920 Miner's Companion in Zulu, for the Use of Miners on the Witwatersrand Gold Mines (Issued by the Prevention of Accidents Committee)*, the *1938 Miner's Companion in English, Afrikaans, Sesotho and Mine Kaffir*, and the 1970s version of *The Miner's Dictionary in English, Afrikaans and Fanakalo*. The preface to the most recent version, *The Miner's Dictionary*, explains that the language originated with Indian workers in KwaZulu Natal in the nineteenth century. They developed the language while trying to learn English and Zulu simultaneously. The Chamber of Mines explains that it is a language that developed between Black and White miners for effective communication in a context of linguistic diversity.

Fanakalo has been generally regarded with contempt by Black South Africans, who view it not only as the defilement of languages such as Zulu and Xhosa but also as a language of subservience. *Fanakalo* consists of a set of instructions issued by the White miner to the Black laborers. The majority of words in the dictionary are commands with exclamation marks. Examples of the *fanakalo* for miners include:

Qala!	Begin!
Bulala!	Destroy!
Penduka!	Go Back!
Suka!	Go Away!
Pas Op!	Look Out! ("Pas op" was also the name given to the supervisor, presumably because that was all he ever said to the miners.)

This dictionary, compiled by White miners and their boss-boys, had a specific goal: to give workers enough language to keep them safe in an extremely dangerous situation but not enough to enable them to talk back to their supervisors. It also set the precedent for race relations in South Africa for many decades. The only common language for some Black and White South Africans continues to be one symbolized by *fanakalo*, that of master and servant.

The pattern of interaction established by *fanakalo* constitutes the core of gumboot dance performance, which does not simply reflect the timeworn tradition of a respectful call and response. Rather, it is deeply loaded with mine labor tensions and frequently caught up in racist patterns of social relationships. These commands became the titles of specific dance sequences: *Bulala!* (Destroy, Murder!), *Dayinja!* (Danger!), *Attention!* (Attention!), *Gobek!* (Go back!), *GwazamaZulu!* (Stab the Zulu!). Just as a team member underground in the mines never knew what command would be issued next, a gumboot dancer cannot predict which dance sequence the leader will order next. He has to be ready at all times to obey the command or he will put his team at the risk of loss—of life when underground, or of losing the dance competition.

Miners in the compounds

A constant feature of a miner's life in the compound was the presence of police, both mine police around the compounds and state police monitoring the movement of Black South Africans in the urban areas. Mining police enforced particular modes of behavior among migrants by frequent patrolling and checks for drugs and alcohol in the compounds. Jonney Hadebe attributed the two names of a single dance routine, *AmaPhoyisa!* and *AmaBlekjek!*, to the presence of both kinds of police in Johannesburg. The commands represented the warnings miners issued to each other when the police were coming. Dancer and team leader Steven Shelembe commented that another routine, *Isihamba nodali* ("to go with your darling"), was the way around police harassment. If a man walked alone in the urban areas, the police would often harass or arrest him. If he walked along with a woman, the couple would be warned but seldom arrested.

A less stringent type of worker control took the form of films that were regularly shown in the compounds, both to educate largely illiterate workers and to keep them

Collage of Thoughts on Performing Race and Gender in Gumboot Dance

Carol Muller

gumboot dance
the boot performance of zulu-speaking male migrant workers in south africa
believed to be the creative form of amabhaca men
who migrated from southern kwazulu natal to egoli, the place of gold
the witwatersrand
where black men went to mine gold and diamonds for de beers and
    anglo-american corporation
black men, white diamonds, yellow gold, white capital

gumboot dance
forged from the fear of going underground
lef-lite
(i.e. right-left)
right (234)
right (234)
attention!
attention!
Two-attention!
kaps! (234)
off! (234)
kaps! (234)
off! (234)

gumboot dance
call and response resignifies as
fanakalo!
literally do it like this!
white miners' pidgin for commanding multilingual black miners
nasisalutho! dayinja!

gumboot dance
the dance of amabhaca men
despised by other black men
amabhaca
bucket people
who clean toilets in the middle of the night
gwazamazulu!
watch out for the zulus who stab

gumboot dance
black male bodies in cowboy shirts

shirts with tassels cover the backs of white cowboys in movies from hollywood
white cowboys from hollywood control black workers in johannesburg

gumboot dance
black men tap with heavy boots
black men tap like white men from hollywood
white men from hollywood tap like black men from harlem
fancy footwork of black men from harlem looks like fancy footwork of black men from africa
fancy footwork of black men from harlem looks like fancy footwork of white irish cloggers
(or germans or russians)

gumboot dance
in the 1870s
black men saw white men from england and america
make their faces look black like theirs
white men called christy minstrels
on stage performing in south africa in the 1890s
with faces painted black with white around the eyes and lips
ragged shirts and full of laughter
the "kaffir christy minstrels"
took the stage
in durban

gumboot dance
1959
king kong the african musical opera with gumboot dancers
miriam makeba and dorothy masuka
black women with black boots on stage
perform for black and white audiences
though never together

gumboot dance
1960s
wait a minim
white African music specialist andrew tracey
Spreading the message of african music
dancing in black boots for white liberal audiences
in johannesburg, durban, london, and new york
an eerie sense of twentieth-century minstrelsy?

gumboot dance
1987
white woman in white wedding dress
hitched up with black belt
white hosed legs inside black boots
gumboot dancer?

gumboot dancer
march 1985
white woman invited to learn to gumboot dance
by a black man named blanket
a bhaca man living between creighton and durban, kwazulu natal south africa
a migrant now for almost thirty years

blanket
black male gumboot dancer
works for defy
defy
in addition to political rhetoric
is blanket's place of work
defy corporation
assembles electrical appliances, washing machines, stoves, dishwashers
blanket offered the white woman learning to gumboot dance
a good deal on a stove
blanket's home has no electricity
white woman with a stove, ok
but white woman to gumboot dance?
white english-speaking woman at university living in a house with a "defy" stove
to perform
black male migrant worker dance from the gold mines of johannesburg?

gumboot dance
abelungu! white people! (watch out!)
black leader with his team
team with musicians
musicians play white man's guitar and concertina
with black man's *chuning*
black man's *chuning* from black woman's musical bow and white man's mandolin

gumboot dance
learned by all in zulu migrant worker hostels in black townships
white women don't go to black townships
nice black women and nice white women don't go to male migrant worker hostels
basopha! watch out!
1985 declaration of state of emergency
townships manned by white south african defense force
white women breaking the law going into the townships
stopped by white soldiers
amaphoyisa! amablekjek!

gumboot dance
durban, south africa, 1996
gumboot dance for reconstruction and development

london england 1996
the state president nelson mandela's award gumboot dancers perform in london's music village
winston salem usa 1997
white woman gumboot dancer sees african american steppin'
surmises some global connection
tappin' steppin' cloggin'

gumboot dancing

busy in their time off. Phillips (1938) provides a list of some of the films shown in the compounds in the 1930s, which included both Hollywood-style entertainment and educational materials developed by the Chamber of Mines. Considering the lists of films starring Charlie Chaplin, Fred Astaire, and Gene Kelly, as well as Jonney Hadebe's account of the early history of gumboot dance, some music historians have suggested that later gumboot dance style may have been modeled on the humor and the tap dance steps in these films (specific examples of the links are detailed in Muller and Topp Fargion 1985: n.p.). Certainly, the cowboy movies powerfully influenced the kinds of attire worn by dancers—such as the handkerchiefs tied around their legs, the cowboy shirts, and the Stetson hats typical of movies in the 1950s and later.

A third connection between gumboot dance performance and the mining compounds was the institutionalization of competitive dance between mining teams by the Reef Consolidated Mines in the 1940s. As the *Gumboots* documentary suggests, it has been reported that dance competitions at the mines were open to the public earlier in the century. In 1943, this mine dancing was institutionalized as a tourist activity with the construction of a semicircular stadium or amphitheater at one of the mine compounds. The money set aside for dance attire and the criteria by which teams were judged (usually by White adjudicators) profoundly shaped the emergence of gumboot dance as a genre peculiar to mining experience.

A final though less obvious link between miners and the compounds is embodied in the commands "*Skhula numtwana!*" ("The child is still growing!"), "*Shiyalekhaya*"*!* ("Abandoned at home!"), and "*Germiston!*" (Germiston is the name of a mining town where Hadebe first worked, and he composed the Germiston sequence in memory of that experience.) Each of these commands refers to the rural home (a homestead or *fum*—farm) a miner leaves behind and sometimes never returns to when he goes off to find work in the urban areas.

Maskanda musical accompaniment

Though gumboot dance performance almost certainly originated with Bhaca migrants from southern KwaZulu Natal, the musical accompaniment is more clearly associated with **Zulu *maskanda***. Nevertheless, the particular style of Zulu guitar that accompanies gumboot dance is an older one from the Umzansi region that is distinct from *isisha-*

meni and *isizulu*. Furthermore, the *isicathulo* style of gumboot dance in Inanda, north of Durban, for example, does not use guitar accompaniment, while the *igumboots* dance from southern KwaZulu Natal does. The instrumentation is typically guitar, concertina and/or piano accordion, and occasionally violin, though each of these instruments is re-tuned to suit a more traditional Zulu ear. The style of playing for gumboot accompaniment is *ukuvamba* (percussive chord strumming) rather than the finger picking *ukupika*.

According to Jonney Hadebe, there are two styles of tuning—the ***isiflench*** (French in F) and the ***isimondolini*** (in C). The French tuning is used if there is only a single guitar accompanying the dance, and mandolin if there are other instruments. The *isimondolini* is a style of Zulu guitar developed around 1940; it is the transitional style between traditional bow playing and urban sounds of *mbaqanga*. *Isimondolini* is similar to another style called double *ifesi* (double first string). It tends to stress the upper range of pitches; to accommodate the higher range, Blanket Mkhize would use a capodastro (or bridge) to raise the pitch. The tuning is as follows: from the top (that is, from the thumb position of the right hand or the lowest pitch) E A G D D G, or C F E♭ B♭ B♭ E♭. Hadebe explained that *isimondolini* is a C and D together, that is, in these two examples, a mixture of G and A or E♭ and F together. The strings are divided into two sets, with the thinnest strings in the middle to protect them from breaking under the pressure of the aggressive strumming. Jonney describes the arrangement of strings: "There are the small strings, the one in the middle, and the two basses; so to make it half and half." His description shows how traditional bow music has been adapted on the guitar: the two fundamentals a whole tone apart and the interval of a fifth above each fundamental form the basis for Zulu guitar *chuning*.

IsiMondolini Chuning

5	E♭
4	B♭
1	B♭
3	E♭
2	F
2	C

The *maskanda* re-tunes the concertina by opening up the inside and making the necessary adjustments. The concertina plays a harmonic ostinato on a four-chord riff in a thirty-two pulse cycle, typical of the early *marabi* style (as is the three-chord *ukuvamba* cycle). The concertina player may improvise melodically at will and frequently does so, shifting register and chord inversions. The violinist improvises melodically, filling in the pitches of the vamping chords (CD tracks 8–10).

The aesthetics of gumboot performance

The history of gumboot dance outlined above suggests multiple influences on the formation of this dance style. Each of these—pre-colonial performance, minstrel shows, mission culture, industrial labor, and migrant experience—has contributed to the development of a gumboot dance aesthetic, that is, a sense of what makes for good and powerful performance. According to this aesthetic, the best gumboot dance:

- engages with everyday realities, and it does so in a humorous and frequently satirical manner;
- includes performers that are highly skilled, both as individuals (soloists) and as a team;
- is deeply competitive, which is evident in the performances of both individuals and the group as a whole;
- is performed by a team that is together and "tight," and there is "power" in the resonant sound of their boots.

Jonney Hadebe describes the competitive dimension of gumboot dance, a dimension also common to other migrant genres, *maskanda* and *isicathamiya*, in particular.

> [Competitions] have changed. Now we go for money. Before, they were winning cups, and the compound manager was giving them food and beer. Now we want money . . . A team is supposed to be 12 [men] including the leader. Not the musicians, that means 14 . . . The best team [has] the leader [who] must shout nicely, and the players must know what they are doing. Then the uniform must be very nice, very smart. The steps must [be done] as one. They must all be the same . . . When you play it wrong, we call it *ihashi* (horse). When a team plays wrong, the people just hit their boots and tell [the others] to come out [stop performing]. The whole team must come out because they are doing it wrong. Then the other team goes in and if they do it wrong, we do *ihashi*, and they must come out. When all the teams have gone, we can start again. If you do one *ihashi*, you [lose] one point, if you do two, you lose two points . . . If you've done one *ihashi* then you are better than a team which has done two. (Quoted in Muller and Topp Fargion 1985: ch. 7)

When Janet and I learned to dance in 1985, Blanket Mkhize encouraged us not to watch the fast footwork so much as to hear its rhythms. He urged us to "fight" the boots, that is, to hit them hard, and the sounds of the boots were reinforced with the timbral qualities of the rattles or "speakers." Once a dance team achieves precision sounding together, the leader will pay attention to the details of performance, like whether you should be using the left or right arm. In contrast with the tightness of the sound, the body is expected to be flexible, creating a sense of fluid, relaxed motion.

Perhaps the definitive feature of this collective experience, however, is the manner in which this dance performance is shaped by a series of commands. Each member of the team looks and sounds the same in collective performance. It is only in the solos, which occur in the middle of the performance, that individuality is catered to. It is at this point that an individual man emerges from the anonymity of the team or the gang and is valued for his skill in improvisation—his capacity to take the patterns he knows and to transform them into a strategy for self-expression.

Contemporary gumboot performance

Unlike contemporary *isicathamiya*, which is strongly supported by the South African Traditional Music Association, gumboot dance had no centralized models or organizational structure until the creation of the theater production *Gumboots.* The rampant violence that began in the late 1980s continued to plague communities in KwaZulu Natal through the mid-1990s, effectively silencing cultural production such as gumboot dance performance. Community venues were often burned down or came under attack; schools stopped holding end-of-year celebrations where gumboot dance normally would have been performed; and the national sponsor, Spoornet, halted its involvement with gumboot dance in the late 1980s because of political violence between team members who represented opposing political groups.

The old spaces of performance disappeared, but gradually new pockets of gumboot dance performance began to emerge in the late 1990s in schools and dance companies. Gumboot dance is currently performed by a diversity of school and university students, and by labor unions and other worker groups. Since 1990, it has been featured in television commercials, by local performing arts groups, and at cultural events. In each of these new contexts, it is being imaginatively recreated to coalesce with the particular vision and daily experiences of each group of performers.

Blanket Mkhize and Steven Shelembe, Jonney Hadebe's brother-in-law and a leader of the Creighton gumboot team, have three goals for gumboot dance: to pass on the dance skills to the next generation (Blanket's sons are all superb performers); to boost their sons' chances of catching the eye of industry managers, who would then be more likely to hire them over some of the thousands of unemployed men desperate for work; and finally, to keep party politics out of gumboot dance performance. Currently anyone may join their team as long as they have no political affiliation. In their experience, party politics divides rather than unites its adherents. Gumboot dance is now viewed within the broader aims of programs for social uplift: it must keep young people busy so they do not become involved with drugs, alcohol, or criminal activity.

The local goes global

What does it mean for a South African genre of performance to be part of a global ecumene, a global community? How could these partially literate, frequently non-English-speaking migrant workers really articulate a relationship to the wider world through gumboot dance performance?

In the late 1950s, gumboot dancing was featured in a range of African stage productions. *King Kong: An African Musical Opera* traveled to England in 1961. In 1962 Leon Gluckman, an English theater director, Andrew Tracey, ex-director of the International Library of African Music, and a group of other White English-speaking South Africans produced a show titled *Wait a Minim!*, which featured gumboot dancing. *Wait a Minim!* traveled to London in 1964, where it played for two years, went on to the Golden Theater in New York for a year, and then proceeded into other parts of the United States, Australia, and New Zealand. *King Kong* was revived in 1979 with gumboot dancing in its opening scenes, but the show was not well received in South Africa. Finally, as we suggested in

Chapter 4, *Graceland*, Paul Simon's collaborative musical project with South Africans, features one track titled "Gumboots." The basic riff in the drums, bass, and guitar parts could be used to accompany contemporary gumboot dance.

Without doubt, in the twenty-first century, the production that has engendered the most interest in gumboot dance is the staged production represented in the video *Gumboots*. If you are able to view this video, I urge you to consider the way in which gumboot dance as a genre of music and dance from South Africa is reconstituted both by South Africans and those from abroad to meet a global audience and to make the show commercially viable—that is, to translate culturally for those who can neither speak Zulu nor perform the complex steps that make up the dance. Our musical and entertainment worlds are filled with world music and dance collaborative performance. Few projects, however, provide the kind of step-by-step discussion that the *Gumboots* project does on how the cultural form of unemployed young men was transformed into a worldwide music and dance phenomenon through their creativity and their openness to working together across national, cultural, language, and geographical distances. Note, too, the differences in the reception of gumboot dancing in 2002 versus 1986, and between the *Gumboots* collaboration and commodities produced and that of the controversial *Graceland* project. Lastly, ask yourselves just which dimensions in the music and dance in *Gumboots*, or indeed in the *Graceland* project, might be considered local and which are global. Is gumboots a universal music and dance language? Can audiences around the world really understand gumboots? What, if any, are the limits of thinking about music and dance as a universal language?

Keywords

"*Abelungu!*" (White People—Watch Out!) "*Amaphoyisa!*" (Police!) "*Gwazama-Zulu!*" (Stab the Zulu!) "*Germiston!*" (name of a mining town) "*Jowanisberg!*" (Johannesburg!) instructions for dance routines

amadoubles gumboot dancing as a team/group

amakhehlezi* or *amaspeaker the homemade rattles worn around the ankles over the boot

amasingles gumboot dancing in solos

"Attention!" "Attention!" "Two-Attention!" "*Nasisalutho*!" "*Salutho*" examples of some of the dance routines that make up an older style of gumboot dance, which are still evident in some contemporary dance teams

fanakalo the language developed in the multilingual mining compounds, as a master–servant form of communication, spoken in commands

Fred Astaire and Gene Kelly two important White American tap dancers who performed in many films shown in South African mining compounds

***igumboots* dance** working-class gumboot dance

ihashi literally means horse, signals the loss of a point in a gumboot dance competition

isicathulo elite gumboot dance, performed at schools

isiflench style of guitar tuning for *maskanda* accompaniment of gumboot dance

isimondolini style of guitar tuning for *maskanda* accompaniment of gumboot dance

mine culture gumboot dance is structured around mine culture and experience

pre-colonial Nguni musical practices what existed prior to colonial contact in KwaZulu Natal
tap dance dancing with tap shoes, action seen mostly on Hollywood films shown in mining compounds, or in live stage performances by local dancers
Zulu *maskanda* Zulu musicians who accompany gumboot dance in KwaZulu Natal (a rare sight these days)

PART III

Focusing In: Two Case Studies

Introduction to Part III

Part III is the place where the materials are presented in a more focused manner than in Parts I and II. As per the goals of this book series, Part III provides more in-depth discussion of the long-term research projects I have undertaken over the last two decades. Two distinct musical cultures are presented here. The first is jazz and popular music performance in the port city of Cape Town in the period after World War II, from the perspective of one woman, a singer. The second is located in the area around Durban, another port city further up the coast alongside the Indian Ocean in the province of KwaZulu Natal. Here we move from the English and Afrikaans-speaking "Coloured" community of the Cape to the Zulu-language peoples who are followers of Black prophet Isaiah Shembe and his successors. I have published numerous articles and three books on these two communities, and with the availability of music on commercial archives like iTunes, and video on sites like YouTube, it is possible for you as readers to expand your listening well beyond the single CD contained in this book. And I urge you to venture out and listen to the growing collection of South African jazz, gospel, and other kinds of religious music currently available worldwide through the internet sites and markets.

I have divided Part III into two sections, one of three and one of two chapters: the first three chapters focus on jazz singer Sathima Bea Benjamin and the musical environment that nurtured her as a child and young woman in Cape Town, South Africa; and the final two examine the ritual practices and song repertories of the followers of Shembe in KwaZulu Natal. We take a close look at the composition and performance of the Shembe hymns, a repertory that has been cherished by Shembe followers for almost a century, and we reflect on changes to that repertory from the late 1980s through to the present. This is the section in the book where those of you with knowledge of religious practices in the southern United States, and American popular music and jazz, might find the strongest resonances between the South African story and what happened elsewhere in the world in the twentieth century. It might be useful to have a discussion in your class and with your peers about such connections in the course of learning about the South African case studies.

Chapter 10 provides a context for Sathima Bea Benjamin's early life in Cape Town (1936–1962) by placing her voice musically. It moves on to a brief overview of Cape Town's cultural history and the racial politics of a community forced by the apartheid government to identify itself as "Cape Coloured." Chapter 11 tells the story of Sathima, postwar popular culture, and the community that nurtured her in Cape Town, preparing her for what would eventually become her life as a jazz singer. In Chapter 12, I focus on Sathima's move into jazz, and describe how she met American bandleader and composer Duke Ellington and his musical partner Billy Strayhorn in Europe in the early 1960s. She moves into being a composer and producer of her own recordings in New York City from the mid-1970s. In this period, Sathima strives to connect to the African American jazz community. I conclude the section with brief reflection on the ways in which Sathima and I relate to Cape Town, the mother city; and indeed, to her struggles to find a new place for herself in post-apartheid South Africa as a woman and as a singer of jazz.

No doubt it is in this section that you will recognize the most obvious parallels to the African American experience in twentieth-century music. It is important, nonetheless, to keep track of the contours of the South African jazz story from Benjamin's perspective. It is a story about a singer—not perhaps as unusual in South Africa as it is in the United States—the most recent iteration of the Cape Town International Jazz festival (2007) had almost as many singers featured as instrumentalists, and most of the singers were women. While the path may be a little easier now for jazz singers in South Africa, it was not that way in the mid-twentieth century. So, as you reflect on the story of Sathima Bea Benjamin and the path she created for herself as a singer of jazz, remember to think about the related factors of race—Coloured versus Black South African; class—she was really from the working class, but was slowly climbing the social ladder by becoming a teacher—spoilt by the disreputable profession of jazz singing; the problem of gender—how we value what men and women do in society according to their sex. Think too about the matter of "borrowed" music and culture—and ask yourselves, at what point does jazz become the musical language that feels like home to this singer? Is jazz a diasporic, cosmopolitan, national, or just personal musical language? Finally, why does Sathima embrace a language of "nature" when she talks about singing—what opportunities were available to her for professional training, how did she learn the repertory? Does it advance or inhibit her cause by using this kind of language to describe what it is that she does in jazz? And think about the place of personal memory in creating this story about the "history" of jazz in Cape Town, South Africa. Does it work for you? Are there other ways of recuperating this kind of history when the archival issues are so problematic?

First Case Study: Cape Jazz

CHAPTER 10
Post-World War II Cape Town

Before you begin reading this chapter, it would be instructive if you listened to tracks 11–15 on the CD in the back of the book. There are five songs: one traditional, one conventionally called a "jazz standard," and three original compositions. They are all excerpts of longer performances. To begin your listening to these I suggest you play them straight through. As you hear the music for the first time, imagine possible contexts of performance by listening to the words and musical arrangement of these words. Think of who might be hearing the music, what they are doing while the music is performed. Is this a seated audience, a community singing along, or a dancehall? What might some of the responses to both the words and the music be? What are the original sources of these songs?

As you listen a second time, try to separate out some of the layers of sound. For example, think about what elements of the music sound like standard American jazz singing in the style of Ella Fitzgerald or Billie Holiday. What in the music sounds a little different, perhaps more distinctively "African" or just "unusual." Try to identify these features sonically. You do not necessarily have to have deep understanding of European music theory to talk about what you are hearing—you may use ordinary spoken language to talk about the sound.

The third time round you might try to characterize the singer's style. If you have the musical knowledge, identify style in terms of melody, tone color, timbre, phrasing, pitch, tempo, pacing, and texture. What is the relationship between the voice and the instruments, the interaction between parts, and the use of instruments in unusual ways? Some of this section might best be made sense of by using analogy and metaphor: "the bass line sounds like a wailing human voice!" Discuss the text and its relationship to other kinds of jazz singing you might be familiar with. Finally, I have provided points of comparison for some of the textual and audio examples. One of the easiest means of solidifying your knowledge of a piece of music or performance is by comparing it with another, related piece or performance.

If you hadn't heard this music in the context of a book on South African music, you might have begun to wonder about the origins of this singer. What might make you think she was American? What suggests she comes from somewhere else? Are the words of her texts typical of the jazz vocal repertory?

In this chapter and the next two, we consider the life experiences and musical production of this South African-born woman of mixed race, originally named Beatrice, lovingly remembered in Cape Town as Beatty, and now known internationally as Sathima Bea Benjamin. Sathima spent the first twenty-six years of her life in Cape Town, briefly traveling around South Africa and its neighboring states. In 1962 she and her husband Abdullah left South Africa because it became impossible to perform jazz. Having returned to the country several times, they departed for good after the 1976 Soweto uprising. At this point they openly declared their opposition to the apartheid government. They came to live in New York City's famous Chelsea Hotel on West 23rd Street. This time they were unable to return to South Africa because the government withdrew their passports. New York was intended as a strategic retreat until such time as they would be able to return home. Since the lifting of the ban on the liberation organizations and the release of Mandela from prison in 1990, both Abdullah and Sathima have been free to go back to their place of birth. Abdullah has returned, Sathima has re-entered several times. The couple now keeps two places of residence: one in New York City and the other in Cape Town.

For those of you familiar with the conventional narratives of jazz history like Ken Burns' PBS series called *Jazz* (2001), which states that jazz is America's classical music, it might be surprising to learn of the many sites of vibrant jazz performance existing elsewhere in the world in the twentieth century. The cities of Cape Town, Port Elizabeth, Durban, and Johannesburg were four cities in South Africa that hosted such performance. But you might be a little surprised that there is not more attention paid to male jazz musicians, and instrumentalists in particular. To focus attention on a single musician is quite consistent with the ways in which the history of the European classical repertory has been written about in the twentieth century: just think of the great names in European music history, Beethoven, Mozart, Chopin, and Bach. Nevertheless, my purpose in highlighting the life and works of one musician is not necessarily to prove his or her greatness or genius, as has been the case with European music history, but rather to use her story as a lens through which to gain an understanding of larger musical, political, and cultural practices.

Sathima Bea Benjamin learned her art form at the southernmost point of the African continent, in the port city of Cape Town. We capture a sense of her early performances in a rare review reported in a local South African newspaper:

> There is no doubt about it, Beatrice Benjamin is the mostest, the greatest and the most appealing girl singer in the Cape, whispers Howard Lawrence. What she did to the audience at Post's show, "Just Jazz Meets the Ballet" was wow. I got it bad

> when she sang "I Got It Bad." Everybody else got it bad too and they kept shouting for more of that *feeling*. Most promising singer for 1959. Agreed.

This short review appeared on January 25, 1959 in *The Golden City Post*, one of a few South African newspapers that targeted a "non-White" audience and published in the English language. "I Got It Bad and That Ain't Good" is one of African American jazz composer Duke Ellington's songs. It was the song that Sathima Bea Benjamin recalls created an immediate and steadfast bond between herself and probably the most internationally recognized South African musician Abdullah Ibrahim (aka. Dollar Brand), the man she subsequently married. Benjamin and Ibrahim were each working on the Ellington tune when they first met at a jazz fundraiser in Cape Town in 1959.

What about the jazz critics in the United States, how do they respond to her music? We have had a couple of glimpses of the reception of her singing in Cape Town in the late 1950s; but what have the critics in her adopted home town, New York City, and those in Europe written? The Philadelphia civil rights lawyer and jazz critic for the *Philadelphia Tribune*, Jules Epstein, told her he thought her music sounded like the piano music of jazz pianist Thelonius Monk; he referred in particular to a recently reissued recording titled *Solo Monk* (recorded in 1964–1965, re-released in 1992 and again in 2003). Certainly, if you listen to that CD there are hints of the importance of the melody embedded in a beautifully emerging sonic tapestry of instrumental voices weaving in and out of each other as each "song without words" is spun out by Monk. And the album foregrounds the rhythmic complexity of ragtime piano that one hears in Monk, but that also rings in Sathima's own musical memory, as the sounds her own mother played. There are further similarities: as critic Lee Jeske says of the Monk reissue, here Monk is the link between past and present, between old and new. "It's a twentieth century time capsule," writes Jeske, a statement we might just as easily write about Sathima Bea Benjamin's style of song performance. It is both "complex and simple, sophisticated and naïve, dense and spare" (Jeske 1992).

Crowther and Anderson describe the singer in this way:

> When it comes to the moment of performance, an overriding quality comes into effect. Every song that she sings, from Victorian ballads to Ellington, the songs from the great musicals to her own musings upon life, is performed with impeccable taste. She treats each individual lyric with respect and with regard to the sentiment intended by the writer and in some cases finds therein more than perhaps the writer intended. (in Rasmussen 2000b: 62)

In a 1983 review of a New York recital, *New York Times* critic Jon Parales wrote:

> That voice is throaty and ethereal with just a hint of smokiness. Ms. Benjamin glides into a song, turning a melody into a series of smooth arcs and gracefully tapering off the ends of phrases. She favors slow tempos and even when her arrangements used a Latin or African groove—like the ingenious version of "I Let a Song Go Out of My Heart," her vocal lines took their time. She and the trio move in and out of time while maintaining a subliminal pulse, she could make a word cry out with just a flicker of vibrato. (*New York Times*, April 3, 1983)

At about the same time in *Downbeat* (1982), critic Fred Bouchard wrote glowingly of her performance in the Carnegie Recital Hall:

> Sathima's concert in the dim, cosy [Carnegie] recital hall was sheer autobiography in song. She began her smooth unhurried way by exhorting the music with free associative poetry: "Sing naturally, like a bird . . ." She soared through two more orienting originals, "Music" and "Africa," backed nicely by a quartet led by pianist Onaje Allen Gumbs. Her African grandmother reared her on pop ballads not jazz, so she sang oldies like "Just a Song at Twilight" and "When We Were Very Young," with tinges of Holiday tone and intensity and a beautifully relaxed phrasing all her own. Teenage nightclub days had her dust off "Embraceable You," "You Do Something To Me," and "Someone to Watch Over Me" (with a fine Gumbs chorus) that she built strong as pyramids, and creamy as kefir. Sathima developed the set with more standards, capped with a unique version of "Say It Isn't So" (in a Cape Town rhythm, a hair's breath from calypso, where she squeezed out languorous quarter tones) and "A Nightingale Sang in Berkeley Square," decidedly un-British with parts of phrases repeated with great warmth and feeling.

Bouchard relishes the individuality of Benjamin's style, while referencing the vocal timbre of early blues and jazz performer "Lady Day" or Billie Holiday. In fact, Sathima pays tribute to Billie Holiday with a song titled "Lady Day" on her album *Windsong* (recorded in 1985, the tune is reissued in Rasmussen 2000b). A close listening to Billie Holiday singing "Yesterdays," "Strange Fruit," or "You've Changed" (on vol. 3 of *The Jazz Singers. A Smithsonian Collection of Jazz Vocals from 1919–1994,* Washington DC: The Smithsonian Institution, 1998) suggests the parallels in sound that Sathima acknowledges, and Bouchard suggests, are present in the voices of both Holiday and Benjamin. Both have limited vocal technique relative to other jazz singers like Sarah Vaughan and Ella Fitzgerald; rather they stress the importance of the words, emotional depth, the tone quality and intensity of the voice, all of which arise out of life experience. Both Benjamin and Holiday claim to have considered their voices as horns (saxophones in particular) rather than just instruments for melodic singing. Bouchard's review of Benjamin's Carnegie Hall recital provides the connection you may be looking for as you read through the following materials on Sathima's life and music-making, wondering how the narrative and the music are related. In Bouchard's words the performance he heard in 1982 was "sheer autobiography in song."

In telling the story of Sathima's early life and musical experiences in Cape Town, her travels around Southern Africa, to Europe and the United States, and ultimately back to South Africa, I hope to provide possible answers to two kinds of questions. The first relates to general questions about South African jazz in relation to American jazz. For example, how did musicians so far from the United States come to know about jazz and American jazz musicians? How did they learn the style and repertory of jazz? What happened when South African musicians began to travel abroad in the 1960s—did they meet up with the "real" American musicians? How was their music received locally and abroad? Have South African musicians attempted to put their own musical stamp on to jazz history, i.e., have they made jazz from and in South Africa sound different to jazz elsewhere? Finally, how is South African jazz, particularly that made by those who went into exile, now viewed in South Africa? What are the similarities and differences in the history of jazz in the United States and that in South Africa? These questions are answered through the experiences of Sathima and her wider community. It is not a complete history of South African jazz. Such a narrative is only possible with wider reading and listening. The second set of questions relates to how Sathima operates as an artist, a poet, performer, and composer. For example, how does she "compose" her music? Where did she acquire her skills if not through conventional institutions of music education? How do we listen to her kind of jazz? What do we learn about artistic processes from reading about this remarkable woman and listening to excerpts of her music?

To help you to identify what is peculiar about Sathima's style as a singer and the leader of a jazz trio, take a look back at the characteristics of South African jazz briefly described in Chapter 6 and compare them with what you hear in her singing. In the earlier description I talked only about how South African jazz instrumentalists performed. There I stressed the importance of the sound and numbers of saxophones in articulating a specifically South African sound in jazz. Now listen for some of these elements in Sathima's voice. They include: "scooping" instead of hitting the pitch; playing with the pitch (especially on "Windsong"); the use of smooth vocal lines with small catches at the end of some words; a use of ornamentation (tied to Cape Town styles), including slides, slurs, microtonal movements, large glissandos, variations of intensity coupled with the introduction of some hoarseness, and discreet vibrato. Sathima plays with timbre, always in a subtle way. Like the saxophones, Sathima occasionally growls a little, she includes the sound of breath in her singing (Martin 1999: 41). Then listen closely to her phrasing of words and melody, to the melodic contour itself, at times quite awkward, at other times, quite gentle.

As for the musical arrangement, listen for moments in which you can hear what Sathima calls the "Cape Town rhythm" in drummer Basil Moses' percussive style on "I Only Have Eyes For You." Think also about the relationship between the instruments and the voice: this is not the usual scenario of the singer up front and the instruments just accompanying; rather, all four parts interweave in an equal way. Then think about the very relaxed tempo of the singer's performances. You might feel it is a little too slow, but it is quite consistent with the tempo of ballad singers from the mid-twentieth century, consistent with the relaxed pace required for slow dances after the more up-tempo numbers in Saturday night social dancing. Finally, Sathima's singing demonstrates several traditional sounds of African-ness in the use of call and response, bending of pitch, range of vocal utterances, grunts, growls, and shrieks, and the overall soft percussive quality she draws out of the drummer in particular.

Ultimately, Sathima Bea Benjamin's musical creation and re-creation of jazz standards is complex and deep. She adheres to no prescribed formulae—she makes complex musical phrases and never hits a pitch "in tune." Rather, she explores the full capacity of color and tone with every sound. The drummers all know that with Sathima they need to bring brushes. Musicians do not accompany her in the conventional sense, but weave together a musical fabric, which allows each voice to find a place and to be heard. Sathima suggested to me one day that what drew her to Duke Ellington's music was the way in which he wrote for horns: she always imagines herself as a saxophone. She has no concept of frontline musicians typical of big band jazz lineups. Everyone in Sathima's ensemble has an equal role in the making of the music. In a very real way, she creates a metaphorical community in the way in which she allows for jazz sound to emerge in performance.

South African Jazz?

Even if you are not surprised about jazz coming out of South Africa, you might be wondering just how I came to knowledge of South African jazz history. Much of it has to do with the progressive thinking of a small group of musicologists at the University of Natal in Durban, South Africa in the 1980s. This group was led by the work of South African jazz scholar Christopher Ballantine, but came to include the first ethnomusicologist hired at a South African university, Veit Erlmann, the South African born composer Kevin Volans, and ultimately included the American jazz musician, Darius Brubeck, son of Dave Brubeck who came to the University of Natal in the early 1980s while I was an undergraduate student there. Ethnomusicologist Veit Erlmann conducted pioneering work in Black South African music history, particularly in KwaZulu Natal. Kevin Volans was experimenting compositionally with African musical materials, Darius Brubeck established the Center for Jazz and Popular Music studies, and Ballantine was teaching upper-level undergraduate seminars on South African and American jazz. It was in these seminars that I first heard about the likes of Miriam Makeba, Hugh Masakela, Kippie Moketsi, Johnny Dyani, and Dollar Brand (who had by then changed his name to Abdullah Ibrahim) on one hand, but also of Duke Ellington, Charlie Parker, Dave Brubeck, on the other. At the time we could learn about the Americans but the South Africans were officially banned in South Africa—learning about them bordered on illegal action! Perhaps significantly, I did not hear of Sathima Bea Benjamin in that seminar in 1984. At the time, Ballantine had conducted numerous interviews with South African musicians in exile, and worked with local archives, in an attempt to reconstruct the early history of jazz in that country. Ballantine was conducting his interviews while Sathima was home looking after her children. And most jazz scholars at that time defined jazz worth writing about as instrumental music made by male musicians—this has begun to change in the last decade or so.

There are two messages I took from that seminar on South African jazz in the mid-1980s. The first was that the South African Broadcast Corporation, the primary center for the transcription and recording of South African music in the twentieth century, had earlier decided that all their recordings of early South African jazz had no real value, and proceeded to destroy much of the archive. The second message was that musicians in exile (largely of African and mixed racial descent) would not be willing to talk with White South African researchers. There was no point pursuing a research project on South African jazz in exile because no one would talk to me as a White South African.

Despite that understanding, I was to have an absolutely amazing experience listening to the music of Abdullah Ibrahim for that seminar in the music library at what was then the University of Natal. I would like to encourage you to listen too. Much of Abdullah Ibrahim's prolific output is commercially available either in the name of Dollar Brand or Abdullah Ibrahim and can be purchased online (see Rasmussen's *Discography* (2000a) for a complete listing of compositions and recordings, and commercial websites to purchase his music). The recordings by Abdullah Ibrahim (and later Sathima Bea Benjamin) were an integral part of the library's collection. In order to listen to this music, however, I recall having to sign my name against every single cut of music I listened to. Somehow I managed to make cassette copies of a small body of Abdullah's recordings, and I remember spending an entire weekend just soaking up the extraordinary sounds of Dollar Brand/Abdullah Ibrahim, and reading whatever I could find about the ties between music, spirituality, and political liberation that this musician poured into his music. "South African sunshine, see how the guns shine . . . hit and run, hit and run, freedom comes through the barrel of a gun." These are the words that run through my mind when I reflect on that period of my life. They intermingle with my experiences of hearing the brilliant sounds of *isicathamiya* competitions in Umlazi, and with trying to learn to gumboot dance between declarations of states of emergency, of having a constant sense that state security forces were in surveillance (both genres discussed in Part II). The apartheid government justified its harsh rule with images of both the "*swart gevaar*" (the danger of being overcome by Black people) and the related "*rooi gevaar*"—the fear of communists. Sometimes Black people were construed as dangerous because they were all assumed to have communist intentions. These images were used to justify security-force occupation of Black **townships**; but it was hard to reconcile such images with the kinds of personal contacts I was making in those same places. I never dreamed at the time that I would ever actually meet Abdullah Ibrahim, or indeed, that he had a wife and musical partner who was so remarkable a singer and human being.

In 1989, while I was a graduate student at New York University in New York City I enrolled for a seminar on jazz under American jazz scholar, Lewis Porter, in which we were required to undertake a project tied to the Jazz Archives at Rutgers University in Newark, New Jersey. I decided to follow up on the undergraduate experience and see what I could find out about the musicians that I knew were living or performing somewhere in New York City. I found files on Abdullah Ibrahim, Hugh Masakela, Miriam Makeba, and then on Sathima Bea Benjamin. In these files I discovered that Abdullah and Sathima had established a record label, Ekapa (meaning at or from the Cape). There was a phone number and an address with the label name. I knew little about how jazz communities actually operated in New York City but remembered Ballantine's caution that these musicians wouldn't speak to White South Africans. Wishing to respect the distance I believed they desired, I decided to just call the record company rather than approach the musicians directly. What I did not understand at the time was that for many independent labels the record label was run out of the musician's own home. I suddenly realized when I called the number that I was actually speaking to Abdullah Ibrahim himself! I nervously told him what I was trying to do, he asked me endless questions, and then told me to call back in a couple of days. I did so, and he invited me to come to one of his performances in the Alice Tully Hall at Lincoln Center in New York City, and to come to the Green Room after the performance to meet him.

Less than a year later, Nelson Mandela was released from prison, and the ban on the African National Congress and other liberation movements working inside and outside of South Africa was lifted. South Africans living in New York City celebrated Mandela's release in the Riverside Church located on Riverside Drive near Columbia

University. (John D. Rockefeller built this ecumenical church in the 1930s to house the man that Rockefeller wanted as his personal pastor.) Abdullah Ibrahim was standing outside the door greeting people when my husband and I arrived. We hugged. Abdullah and Sathima both performed at that event. Afterwards, Abdullah told me to call him at his home the following week. Sathima answered the phone because Abdullah was performing in India. This was the first of many, many conversations I would have with this exceptional woman over more than a decade. The first call, however, occurred just as I was beginning to think about working with South African women, and not just its great men. Sathima agreed to meet me in the Chelsea section of Manhattan a few days later, but I was not to bring a tape recorder. We would just talk.

Though Sathima and Abdullah had been living in the Chelsea Hotel since the late 1970s, as a kind of "strategic retreat" until they would be able to return to South Africa, I met Sathima at a neighborhood diner, a place to which we have returned many times. I had brought a list of questions, as she requested, and I asked the first one. There was no need for any more. Sathima overflowed with words, beautifully strung together, deep, filled with metaphor. Some of the words were poetic; others were imbued with pain and struggle. For about two hours, Sathima spun her narrative. When she finished I staggered out of the diner, wondering how I would ever remember what she had so willingly told me. For the next 48 hours I did nothing but make notes from the memory of that conversation, notes to which I have returned many times in thinking about my first encounters with this woman from Cape Town, the city in which we were both raised, but the place that in many ways constituted itself so differently because of the different time periods and social spaces in which we spent our childhood.

Sathima left South Africa less than a year before I was born. She was born before apartheid was legalized, but into a community that the government later classified as "Coloured," i.e., of mixed race. By the time I was born, these classifications were deeply entrenched in society, both by habit and by the force of law. It has taken me a long time to begin to understand the ramifications on both of our lives of living in a society that sought to keep people apart, by whatever means necessary, purely because of skin color and family heritage, and indeed, to rethink the deeply ingrained ideas about the "naturalness" of racial classification so pervasive in South Africa (and indeed in many other parts of the world). Let us return to the Cape Town of Sathima's childhood, to explore how she came to know and respect the music of American musicians like Billie Holiday, Duke Ellington, and Nat King Cole.

Life in Cape Town

> Cape Town is a beautiful place, with mountains, the sea, a perfect climate, exotic birds, flora and fauna, and gorgeous sunrises and sunsets. There seemed to be music in the air, always. Is that possible, or is that just the memory I carry? (Sathima Bea Benjamin interview with Lee Hildebrand, January 25, 1987)

> There was music everywhere. First you would hear the horses coming down the street and then you'd hear them shouting, "*aartappels en uiwe*" (potatoes and onions). They're singing the price and everything. There was always so much

> music, people just using their voices naturally. It was everywhere. (Sathima Bea Benjamin, personal communication with Carol Muller, March 16, 1990)

Those who visit Cape Town cannot but help feel in awe of the beauty of the place. It is something of a truism amongst South Africans that you have not seen South Africa until you have been to the Cape. Situated in the area where the Indian and Atlantic Oceans meet, the coastline around the Cape has been explored and written about at least since Portuguese explorers first encountered it in the late fifteenth century. Founded as a refreshment station called the Cape of Good Hope by the Dutch of the Dutch East India Company starting in 1652, the city is nestled between the ocean and the mountain. Without doubt, Cape Town remains one of the most visually stunning pieces of urban topography in the world. Those who live in the city have long demonstrated enormous pride in belonging to, or coming from, this place. But Cape Town is also remembered as being a place filled with melodious strains, not just on stage or over the radio, but in the streets themselves.

The cultural and political history of the city of Cape Town has nevertheless been woven out of narratives of slavery, colonial immigration, the decimation of indigenous peoples through warfare and disease, an ongoing interaction between Islam and Christianity, racial and nationalist power struggles, the emergence of the South African

Slave Musical Performances from the Seventeenth Century (Excerpted from Martin 1999: 58–61)

As early as 1676, the Governor of the Cape was said to have a "slave orchestra," and in 1800 H. Lichtenstein included an account of an evening at the house of a Mr. Van Reenen during which "a concert by the slaves took place." They played marches and dances on all sorts of European instruments, from violin and flute to bassoon and French horns. Wealthy burghers (citizens) kept slave orchestras who learned music by ear, entertained their children and guests on every occasion, and allowed them to indulge in dancing, which was one of the favorite pastimes at the Cape. On these occasions they played European dance music in fashion at the time: waltzes, quadrilles and postillions.

Slaves also performed among themselves in the dancing houses in the country. All sorts of non-European instruments could be heard, including a single-headed cylindrical drum (possibly the ancestor of the Cape **ghoema** drum) and a three stringed lute with a calabash resonator which might be the ancestor to the **ramkie**, the instrument copied by Khoikhoi from slaves from Malabar. Slave boys from Madagascar and Mozambique brought their stringed instruments to the Cape. They danced to music of their own tribes, to European music, and were influenced by the music of military bands. It is not clear what music was played at the "rainbow balls" frequented by slave girls and free coloured women, male officers and merchants.

The taverns were the meeting place of sailors, lower class colonists and slaves. They drank, gambled and were entertained by slave musicians. Slaves played on violins, flutes, trumpets, oboes, harps, and ramkies. The first true Cape songs were probably composed in tavern culture: in 1707 punishment was meted out to a man called Biron "for singing dubious ditties half in Malay and half in Dutch in the streets of Cape Town."

language of **Afrikaans**, and also of annual rites of celebration. Vivian Bickford-Smith et al. have published a book on the social history of twentieth-century Cape Town (1999). Denis-Constant Martin's work (1999) on New Year Celebrations in the city amongst people classified as **"Cape Coloured"** provides a rich sense of the history of Cape Town, particularly in terms of slavery, and the impact of Islam and Christianity, and indeed of English and American minstrelsy, amongst a host of other cosmopolitan influences, on twentieth-century Cape performances. Finally, Zimitri Erasmus (2001 [2002]) who teaches at the University of Cape Town has edited an excellent collection of essays on Coloured identity in post-apartheid South Africa. It is a book well worth reading if you are interested in the politics of racial identities in the contemporary world.

Without delving too deeply into the histories, it is important to have some understanding of the cosmopolitan and creolized nature of Cape society as it developed from the mid-seventeenth century to the present. The major European forces to colonize and inhabit the Cape were the Dutch, the English, the French, the Portuguese, and the Germans, though until 1948 when the Afrikaner Nationalist government took power, it was largely the Dutch and English who competed for control of what has become the city. Both were seeking a halfway house on the sea route from Europe to the East. The real richness and diversity of the city evolved, however, with the importation of slaves from East and West Africa, but more importantly from Madagascar (the island east of South Africa), India, present day Indonesia, and Ceylon. The first slave to reach Cape Town was a man named Abraham from Batavia, and he came just twelve months after the Dutch arrived to settle the Cape of Good Hope as a refreshment station. Slavery was outlawed by the British in 1808, but not actually abolished in the Cape until 1834. Even after that, there was a group of 5000 "prize Negroes" that were sent to the Cape from 1808 to 1856. They were trained for a period of fourteen years and then released into domestic work or agricultural labor.

The Khoikhoi (later merged with the San to form a group called the **Khoisan**)—indigenous peoples who were pastoralists—inhabited the Cape prior to the arrival of the Dutch. In contact with the European settlers who increasingly moved into the interiors of South Africa, the Khoikhoi were largely wiped out as a separate group, but they were not actually treated as slaves by the colonists. Instead they lived on European property, intermingling with Europeans, as indeed did the imported slaves. As a result the cultures of the three groups became integrally entwined. There were also groups of "free Blacks" at the Cape during slavery. These were people of **Asian** and African descent who were largely either ex-slaves or ex-convicts, though some came as free persons. They were mostly excluded from the occupations of White colonists; they could not farm because they were unable to acquire credit, though some purchased their own slaves. A good percentage of these free Blacks were actually Muslim (mostly of Indonesian origin), and despite initial bans on religious rituals performed by Muslims, these followers of Islam played a critical role in the spread of Islamic belief in the Cape particularly amongst the slaves. Cape Islamic traditions and beliefs continue to be transmitted in contemporary Cape society. Like Sufi Muslims elsewhere in the world, Cape Muslims integrated secular musical performance into their religious rituals. From the outset, however, the place where all Cape residents met together was in the taverns: wine, women, and song were the elements that have bound many of those who lived in the windy city together over the last four centuries.

Figure 10.1 Three participants in the New Year's Carnival, Bo-Kaap, Cape Town, January 1996, taken by Carol Muller.

There are three reasons for discussing some of the early patterns of settlement and social interaction in the Cape: it is important to recognize first, that Cape culture has always been a Creole culture, i.e., a culture that has blended the old and new, the powerful and the less powerful, the local and the foreign; and second, that sexual relations across cultural and racial groups were an integral dimension of the first European settlements in the Cape, and that the people now called "Cape Coloured" were some of the first inhabitants of this new culture; third, the archival record suggests that these slaves and their Cape Town descendants were brilliant musicians, able to hear and replicate in their singing and instrumental performances almost any musical repertories.

Perhaps the most significant imported musical culture to shape Cape Town's performance life in the twentieth century, and indeed to South Africa as a whole, was nineteenth-century American and English minstrelsy.

Denis-Constant Martin provides a brief history of blackface minstrelsy in Cape Town,

Figure 10.2 Marching through the streets in the center of Cape Town, New Year's Carnival, January 1996, taken by Carol Muller.

following Erlmann's earlier work on the travels of Orpheus McAdoo and the Virginia Christy Minstrels, an African American jubilee group who visited South Africa in the 1890s. Minstrel groups were actually White actors, singers, and comedians who impersonated Black performers from the southern United States. Faces were painted black, and the outfits worn by these men were exaggerated, colorful, and "dandy." Songs were accompanied on violin, cello, tambourine, banjo, and "the bones." Minstrelsy in the city was preceded by Serenaders, first spoken about in 1848 with the visit of the "Celebrated Ethiopian Serenaders" who performed at the "Ethiopische Club" in Cape Town. An advertisement in August 1862 told of the upcoming visit of the "Christy Minstrels," organized in 1842 for performances in London and New York.

This is not the place to spell out the contested history of minstrelsy as it was performed in the United States or Europe. Here you might wonder why minstrelsy appealed to not only people of European descent, but also functioned as a model of Black performance culture in South Africa amongst people now called "Coloured" or those of Black African descent. Despite the fact that blackface minstrelsy stereotyped and caricatured slave performances in the United States, elements of minstrelsy were incorporated into what is now remembered as twentieth-century Black performance culture, including *isicathamiya*, gumboot dance, and perhaps most importantly, into the New Year's Celebrations of so-called "Coloured" people who have a carnival still colloquially identified as the "Coon Carnival." Denis-Constant Martin suggests that the themes of the shows appealed in the mid-nineteenth century because they addressed contemporary concerns about social, economic, and cultural issues. In addition, he argues that while the term "coon" is offensive to many outside of South Africa, for those who participate in this musical culture, the word represents the thrill and excitement of the New Year's Festival. In the words of one of the troupe's composers and performance coaches, "the minute you talk Coon, he sees New Years day, he sees satin and the eyes and mouth with circles in white, the rest of the face is black, like the American minstrels" (Martin 1999: 4). Clearly these performers insist on defining terms according to their own local meanings.

"Cape Coloured" as Racial Classification

In the initial years of twentieth-century Cape Town, a period described by Sathima Bea Benjamin as "relaxed apartheid," people of color could mix fairly freely with those of European descent, as long as they adhered to the social hierarchies based on race and class that were implicitly marked in social interaction. Sathima recalls, for example, that two social principles were inculcated into her as a child of mixed race, (a) know your place and (b) do not look for trouble. This was not only true once the Afrikaner Nationalists came to power in 1948, but was also an effective strategy under British governance prior to that. For example, it was under the British that "Cape Coloureds" were removed from the Common Voters' Roll in 1936. These two social principles, knowing your place and not looking for trouble, manifest themselves in the style of dance band music played by Coloured musicians for community dances of their own people. It was music that refrained from breaking free of the musical rules and structures. This contrasted markedly with the kind of improvised and experimental jazz that people like Abdullah Ibrahim, Kippie Moeketsi, Johnny Dyani, Chris McGregor and indeed, Sathima were interested in making in South Africa in the late 1950s.

By the mid-twentieth century, to be classified "Colo[u]red" came to mean something slightly different from its use in mid-century America. While in nineteenth-century South Africa and America, "Colo[u]red" simply referenced all people not of European descent, in the twentieth century several new words were used to classify people of African and mixed racial descent in both countries. By the 1950s, the apartheid government had created two separate racial categories. "Coloured" applied to all those of mixed race regardless of their individual or collective histories (the term largely referred to those based in the Cape). "Bantu" was a term for the majority of people living in South Africa who were dark skinned and spoke Bantu languages including Zulu, Xhosa, Sotho, and Tswana.

Within the space of about twelve years, 1950–1962, Cape Town the Mother City changed for people of color from evoking a profound sense of place and home, to being a space of exclusion, fragmentation, transgression, and boundary marking. This was the experience of the young Sathima and all those who participated in Cape Town's avant-garde jazz community, those who were interested in making music without racial or national boundaries. Apartheid legislation intentionally sought to keep people categorized as "Coloured" (or Black African) out of White space. State enforcement of these laws played a critical role in the transformation and often destruction of these communities, and of jazz performance itself. These laws played out in the Cape in quite specific ways as they impacted upon people categorized as Coloured.

The 1950 Population Registration Act (amended in 1966) defined "Coloureds" as persons not native or European, or persons married to a man or woman *classified* as Coloured. The Immorality Act (passed in 1927 and amended in 1950 to include a ban on interracial marriages) made all sexual relationships across what was called the color bar illegal. The Group Areas Act (1950) required different racial groups to live together in specific areas, seeking to separate out the "Coloureds" from "Europeans" to preclude any further racial mixing in Cape Town specifically (though it had ramifications in the rest of the country as well). The Separate Amenities Act (1950) forced racial segregation in all public venues. The newspapers in the 1950s and early 1960s are replete with articles expounding on the implications of apartheid legislation for Coloured people. These include forced divorces, the break up of families because some members are classified "Coloured" and others "European," and the problem of the "science" of race that appears to be neither scientific nor historical in the South African context. Naming "Coloured" identity became a means to divide, rule, and marginalize rather than to unite and empower.

Those assigned the racial category of "Coloured" have responded to the label in different ways. While in the United States, race is still largely considered a "natural" category, increasingly in South Africa, there are those who question the naturalness or usefulness of such labeling, and who would prefer to be identified through categories other than race. Racial categorization has quite consistently been thought by some to be a construction, a mere label, used to oppress people of mixed or non-White racial heritage. Race, after all, is only skin deep. So one finds in the period that many "Coloureds" rejected the label and sought to "pass" for White or to identify through other social categories, including class or education because, like the notion of *metissage* in the Caribbean, to be labeled "Coloured" has not translated into a positive identification.

Sathima's family heritage adds a new twist to the question of being labeled "Cape Coloured" because they were not Cape Coloureds in the historical sense of the term. Half her family hailed from the remote Atlantic island of St. Helena. Sathima's father Edward Benjamin's family had immigrated to Cape Town from St. Helena when his mother, later known as Ma Benjamin, was a young girl. The Benjamin family arrived on boats in the Cape Town harbor and settled with other St. Helenians. This group of immigrants lived in three places in the city: District Six before its destruction, the Rondebosch-Claremont suburbs, where Sathima spent her early childhood, and Athlone, a Coloured area where she lived in her late teens and early twenties with her mother. Many St. Helenians of Sathima's father's generation kept themselves apart from others of mixed race who were called "Cape Coloured." Unlike some Cape Coloureds who spoke Afrikaans, who were part of the working class or variably employed, and danced to live band music on weekends, St. Helenians aspired to participation in a milieu of English language middle class cosmopolitanism and respectability. Some preferred to identify themselves as British, and, certainly, most were proud that their birth certificates initially stated, of "mixed St. Helenian" rather than Cape Coloured descent. Culturally, they kept themselves apart from others of mixed race. On weekends, St. Helenians gathered the extended family to play cards and sing around the piano. Most were church-going Christians. This would change with the next generation, which sought to assimilate into Cape society on the one hand, but were forced to identify themselves as Cape Coloured from the late 1940s.

One of the most chilling moments in young Sathima's life was the day she signed away her identity as St. Helenian and replaced it with the government category of "Cape Coloured." Sathima was living with her father's mother, Ma Benjamin, on the day a government official came around to the house with census forms and required the elderly woman to sign that she agreed to be classified as Cape Coloured in what was becoming an increasingly divided society. Proud of her St. Helenian roots, the elderly Ms. Benjamin could not do it. She came in tears to her granddaughter and asked her if she would please sign the piece of paper. The official told Ma Benjamin that in the eyes of the government, "St Helenian" did not exist. Everybody who was not White or African would now be in the same boat. The young girl was not fully aware of the politicized nature of these issues at the time. She was already a Cape Coloured in her mind, because she attended a Coloured school, lived in a neighborhood of people of mixed race, and she was interacting with Coloured children every day. But she realized that this must be something serious because she had never seen her Ma cry before. She dutifully signed the paper. Under the Population Registration Act of 1950, the St. Helenian side of the family officially became Cape Coloured. From that time onwards, like those classified as White, they were required to carry identity cards that categorized them as such. Unlike for Whites, however, that identification would have severe consequences for Coloured individuals and communities throughout South Africa.

In a home environment—both public and private—where young Sathima Benjamin and her sister Joan were often made to feel like they were "charity" children, or not White enough, music worked as an inclusive medium. It was through the sounds of singers far away, brought close to home through the radio in her grandmother's home that Sathima would let her mind and imagination wander, daydreaming the hours away. At first, she aspired to sound like the White women singers, Joni James and Doris Day, though right from the start her friends recall she had her own style of singing: a deeply emotive, naturally nurtured voice that loved to scoop and play with pitch. The words mattered too, and as she had been taught to respect the daily utterances of the men in her household, so she always paid heed to the sound of the words and their message in the songs that she sang. Singing was the one way, however, that the young girl could get someone to sit down and listen to what she had to say!

CHAPTER 11

Sathima Bea Benjamin's Cape Town

Popular Culture in the Post-World War II Era

Sathima Bea[trice] Benjamin was born to Edward Benjamin and Evelyn Henry in Johannesburg on October 17, 1936. Her father Edward had gone to Johannesburg to find work, and though she was seven months pregnant, Evelyn had boarded the train in Cape Town and headed north. Baby Beattie arrived more than a month early. "You were born like Jesus," Sathima's mother later told her. "We had no clothes for you," and so the woman who ran the boarding house where Evelyn was staying had torn a sheet into long strips and wrapped the newborn baby in swaddling clothes. Disappointed that she was not a boy, Sathima's father refused to look at her for the first two weeks. When he did finally look, he saw a similarity between his new daughter and his sister, Beattie. So the newborn was named Beatrice Benjamin, later shortened to Bea.

Little is known about Sathima's mother's family heritage. Sathima's grandmother, Francesca de la Cruz, was of Filipino descent and living in the diamond mining town of Kimberley. Francesca de la Cruz died in the 'Flu Epidemic of 1918. Evelyn Henry was thus orphaned at a young age, and sent to stay with relatives in Cape Town where she ultimately met Edward Benjamin, Sathima's father. The couple had two daughters, Beattie and Joan, and a son Maurice (who died). They divorced when Sathima was about five and the girls went to live with their father and his new wife. The loss of their mother so early in life was traumatic for these young girls. As an adult Sathima would attempt to overcome her mother's absence in two ways. First, she vowed that her children would always have a mother to care for them, and second, for several years in exile, she consistently began each live performance with an evocative rendition of the old African American spiritual, "Sometimes I Feel Like a Motherless Child." You will already have listened to an extract of such a performance on the CD, track 11.

After Edward Benjamin divorced Evelyn Henry, she married a second time and from the two marriages had eight more children, two of whom passed away in their childhood. Perhaps because of his stronger family structure and ability to support his two girls, Bea and Joan lived with their father and his new wife until Bea was nine years old when it was discovered at school that the Benjamin girls were being severely beaten by their father's second wife. At this point they were sent to live with their paternal grandmother, Ma Benjamin, who had a large house in the Cape Town middle class but informally segregated suburb of Claremont. Life changed once she and her younger sister Joan went to live with Ma Benjamin. Though she was a strong and opinionated woman, Ma Benjamin's home in Claremont provided a measure of discipline, security, and a sense of their extended St. Helenian family for the two Benjamin girls. The family subsequently lost the house with Group Areas legislation in which Claremont was declared a suburb for Europeans only, and people of mixed race were required to move to Coloured areas of the city. Now allowed to return to South Africa, Sathima has purchased an apartment in the historically "White" part of Claremont, an important mechanism for reclaiming a place for herself in post-apartheid South Africa.

Singing and daydreaming were the mechanisms the young Benjamin girls used to survive the traumas of their early childhood. Sathima described this period of her life with Ma Benjamin to Francis Davis.

> My parents were separated by the time I was 5 . . . I was raised by my grandmother who was very strict, very strict, very proper, very British in her ways, though she was quite dark, quite African-looking. I was a very lonely child, and music was my solace, along with daydreaming, which I indulged in constantly. (*Philadelphia Inquirer*, November 19, 1986)

From an early age, then, musical sounds stimulated the young girl's imagination and shaped her dream world. Music was the vehicle of escape from the harshness of everyday life. The melodies were beautiful, and the words soothing. The combination of sound and text moved the young girl emotionally, and it created a trance-like space where her heart, mind, and soul could wander to any place imaginable. Music was something that this young girl from Cape Town could hear in the more conventional spaces of live and mediated performances, but also in the sounds of the natural world, in the strong wind, the crashing waves, and the pounding downpour of rain. Without doubt music has long facilitated a sense of belonging, a sense of warmth, support, and joy for Sathima.

Certainly, in Cape Town of the 1940s and 1950s, the sound of music was everywhere, not just on the stage, or in the movies, though these were certainly important places for musical performance, but out on the streets and in your home. Earlier, I cited two statements of Sathima's about the musicality of Cape Town's soundscape. In 1936, the year Sathima was born, there was an article written in the *Cape Standard*, one of the daily newspapers aimed at a Coloured audience. It talks about the people who walked the streets selling a popular fish in Cape Town called *snoek* and conveys something of the musicality of these people.

> Many changes have taken place now the Malay fish hawker, with his high-pitched call, who sold his fish from baskets yoked across his shoulders, has disappeared. His place has been taken by the horse and cart hawker with his characteristic fish horn. The sailing boat has changed places with the motorboat and other sundry changes have taken place. (*Cape Standard*, June 8, 1936, p. 3).

For Sathima, an important musical sound coming from the natural world was the noise of the wind. Cape Town is known for its powerful winds, and in many ways the wind continues to shape what it means to live in Cape Town. Certainly, when you leave the city, you long for the sound of the wind and the strength of its blowing. If you have never experienced the force of a windstorm, it might be hard to imagine just how the wind can carry sounds that are like music to your ears. But Sathima has vivid memories of those sounds, and she sings about their power in one of her most profound compositions, "Windsong" (discussed below).

The more conventionally defined musical renditions could be heard on the radio and through live performance at home, singing in the church, and at school. There was always live music on the streets, live and mediated musical performance in "bob" parties (see below) and the cinema/"**bioscope**" on Saturdays, and the live dance band sounds of teenage bop clubs. So a song first heard in a movie on a Saturday afternoon could be heard repeatedly in the following week. It could be heard over the air, on record, and performed live in a cover version by local dance bands or in subsequent talent contests held at the cinema and fundraising events organized in various churches and community halls. In the section that follows, we will examine these sites of musical performance, particularly as they intersected with Sathima's own experience.

The young girl's British popular music heritage came through the St. Helenian part of her family. Sathima vividly recalls gatherings in the 1940s and 1950s in which family members sang the popular songs of the 1920s and 1930s, accompanied on the piano by her grandmother. During the week while everyone undertook their household chores, Sathima remembers hearing Ma Benjamin humming tunes she played on an old phonograph she had in the house. Many of these melodies, like "Ah! Sweet Mystery of Life" or "The Roses of Picardy" had been popular in Ma Benjamin's own youth: they derived from operettas, Tin Pan Alley, and music-theater. On Sundays, someone in the family who could play the piano would come to the house, and everybody would sing along. On occasion, the family would gather for a more spirited celebration and dance the night away to the sounds of these old tunes streaming out of the gramophone. Sathima remembers the tunes of many of these songs.

> You see, one thing about these melodies from the '20s and '30s, they were wonderful melodies . . . Having grown up in Cape Town, where I heard these melodies being played, you see, the melodies were so real with me. They played in my head. (Sathima Bea Benjamin, personal communication, April 9, 1990)

Sathima archived these melodies in her memory, and in 1999 she returned to Cape Town to record eleven of these songs with a Cape Town trio, but in a jazz rather than straight style of performance (eight of the songs appear on *Cape Town Love*, 1999, all now available on iTunes, keyword Sathima Bea Benjamin). The pianist is Henry February, an early mentor who had invited Sathima to join his group, the Nat King Cole Trio, in the late 1950s. The bass player, Basil Moses, began playing dance band music and jazz in Cape Town in the 1960s. February died in 2004, but Moses remains active in the Cape Town jazz and dance band scene.

Sunday was the day Bea and her sister Joan participated in another repertory of

***Music from the Streets of Cape Town* (CD)**

This is the name of a commercially available CD (further details can be found in Appendix 3, under heading "Cape Town: dance bands, pop bands, and Cape culture bands"). It functions almost as something between the emcee at a variety show and a cultural tour guide through the city. There are examples of all kinds of interesting street music, including music of the New Year's Festivals, dance band music, and Cape Jazz. The liner notes include a map of the city center, marking out the spaces in which you might hear this music if you were to visit.

music: that of the Wayfarer missionaries who held Sunday School classes in Ma Benjamin's garage. Sathima recalls the wonderful melodies of the old English hymns, "Onward Christian Soldiers," "The Church's One Foundation" (which she now hears in her mind as a jazz tune), and "Joy, Joy, Joy, With Joy My Heart is Ringing." (Many of these songs were also sung at school, as part of the National Christian Education policies of the apartheid government.) All the neighborhood children attended Sunday School with Bea, Joan and the two White missionaries from America. After lunch, the children would join the congregation for the eventide service. Though Ma Benjamin never attended, she was rigid about the girls going regularly to church. Sathima fulfilled her church duties until she was about fifteen. Typical of both cinemas and churches in Cape Town at the time, seating arrangements were segregated. Whites sat in the front and Coloured members sat further back. One day, Bea decided that she would sit in the forbidden zone. Perhaps predictably, she was immediately informed that she should either move to the appropriate place for Coloureds or leave the building. Stunned by the cold reality of racism in the church community, Bea left and never returned.

Sathima was more fortunate than many of the jazz musicians she later performed with. For a brief period, her father paid for piano and theory lessons. When he left Cape Town to live in London for a few years, there was no money to pay for the lessons. Sathima recalls that she preferred to express herself in songs she heard others singing, rather than at the keyboard reading music. In this context her musical training was more compatible with that of her friends, most of whom were self-taught, and learned by careful listening and imitation. In her late teens Bea even went to opera lessons, but the style did not appeal to her sense of a good singing voice. She found the vibrato too contrived: her preference remains for a more natural-sounding voice. One of Sathima's friends, Vincent Kolbe, told quite a different story about his early musical training. He recalled:

> As a young boy I learned to play music, which many of us did, because you always had a relative or a neighbor or a friend who played in these carnivals, and there was guitars and instruments all over the place throughout the year. And these same people would play at dances and at parties in homes before hi-fi. And I learnt that way; you know someone would show you how to play the drum or how to play the bass or how to play a chord on the piano, and that was good enough for the next party. (Nixon 1997 20)

The radio played all day long in Ma Benjamin's home but, Sathima recalls, no one was ever permitted to sit down and listen. The sounds emanating from the radio were the accompaniment provided for daily chores. From the age of about ten Sathima used to keep a pen and notebook hidden in her grandmother's wind-up Victrola, the source of so many good melodies. Whenever she heard a tune she really liked playing on the radio, she would quickly scribble down the words—Ma Benjamin did not think the young girl should be wasting her time with the music. She could not afford to buy the sheet music or fakebooks herself. Instead she would listen to a song over and over, until she had a handle on the text. This was in the years before the radio moved from commercial to state-control. These were the days when, according to Ms. Benjamin, radio stations used to play all the music you heard in America. You could hear it in South Africa. Through the radio she listened to American and English popular music and jazz by the likes of Duke Ellington, Nat King Cole, Ella Fitzgerald, Doris Day, Joni James, and Billie Holiday. Sathima absorbed all of these styles and voices as music that is now an integral dimension of her childhood memories.

One of Sathima's closest school friends is a woman named Ruth Fife. Though she lived close by, the Fife family was not St. Helenian, and operated quite differently from the Benjamin household. The Fifes played the European classical repertory at home, while Ma Benjamin refused to listen to it; in fact, the Fife home is where Sathima both heard European classical music, and was exposed to a family who were politically active. For people of color, any kind of political awareness would lead to conflict with the apartheid government. Sathima remembers one year in her high school days: it was April 16, the public holiday in South Africa that celebrated the arrival of Jan Van Riebeek, the Dutchman who first settled in the Cape. In this particular year, Ruth Fife's brother, the Mathematics teacher at the school, had handed out leaflets protesting the celebration—because of the impact of European settlement in the Cape and the lack of acknowledgment of the integral place of Coloured people in that history. Fife's brother was also in a relationship with a woman of Indian descent, not allowed in the apartheid regime, so he was forced into political exile, forced to leave the country for his political beliefs. He went to live in Nigeria.

In addition to the music of men and women selling flowers, fish, and vegetables on the street, Christmas and New Year were the times set apart in Cape Town for street processions and musical performances. Like many of her peers, Bea would watch the live performances of Coloured street bands and choirs at Christmas time and over the New Year holidays. There were Malay choirs, and brass bands called Christmas Choirs, and minstrel groups. Sathima recalls that she would often follow the groups as they paraded through town, and at times got lost in the process. There was something so magical about these processions, that musicians and followers alike often experienced the performances in trance-like states. Historian Bill Nasson cites the experience of a resident of Cape Town's historic District Six. Mr S. D., an elderly retired fruit hawker, recalled:

> I tell you, when we were little we would follow [the bands and choirs] to wherever they went . . . we would try to get near to them and walk with them. They sang up close to us . . . I wanted to touch [them] . . . They was something, really beautiful, they wasn't far away on radio. They was here, our choirs, singing for us. (In Nasson 1989: 302)

The sound recording was the most common form of musical transmission in postwar Cape Town. This was the primary medium through which jazz musicians in particular listened closely to the music from England and America. Though Bea could not afford to buy seventy-eight disks of her favorite performers until she began teaching, three of her jazz colleagues tell wonderful stories of the impact of film and sound recordings on local culture. Vincent Kolbe explains that musicians did not just play exact renditions of the music they heard in the cinema or on these disks. They drew on the images on record covers to construct hair and clothing styles. If you were "Cape Town's Dizzy Gillespie," you took the album cover of Gillespie to the barber and had the appropriate haircut, and then you went to the tailor who would cut you an outfit that duplicated what you could see on the album cover. Harold Jephta, one of Cape Town's best-known Charlie Parker soloists in the late 1950s, recalls that he would use whatever means necessary to buy the latest seventy-eight records of his favorite musicians. He remembers as a young boy telling his mother that he had a toothache. She provided money for a visit to the dentist. Scheming Harry proceeded directly to the record store, and returned home with a Coleman Hawkins record! In contrast to Kolbe and Jephta, close friend and musical cohort Jimmy Adams refused to buy any recordings. He feared that if he owned the records he would listen to them too closely, and lose a sense of his own sound and musical identity. Nevertheless, he regularly borrowed the recordings purchased by Jephta in shaping his sense of the American jazz available in Cape Town.

Later on, in her early twenties, it was through the record collection of Swiss artist, entrepreneur, and friend Paul Meyer that Sathima was exposed to the world of American blues and jazz. In the late 1950s the cost of listening to the recordings was high. Meyer lived in an elite, though politically liberal, coastal suburb of Camps Bay to which Ms. Benjamin, now classified as Cape Coloured, was only allowed to enter if she had a permit to work as a housemaid. To her family's chagrin, Meyer would take the young woman on the back of his motorcycle from Athlone, where Bea was living with her mother, to Camps Bay to hear his records. Both feared being arrested for breaking laws pertaining to racial segregation, like the Group Areas Act. But, Sathima recalls, she was so desperate to hear this music that she was willing to take the risk. Several years after she began singing in public, it was Billie Holiday's voice, heard on record in the backyard of one of Cape Town's most elite neighborhoods that made this young woman realize her own sound held a place in the world of jazz.

In addition to the radio and the wind-up Victrola in her grandmother's home, going to the cinema, or the bioscope as it was more commonly known, was closely tied to Sathima's memories of family life with Ma Benjamin. And it was the bioscope that brought the magic of faraway people and places close to home. The first movie the young girl ever saw was Disney's *Snow White*, which she remembers seeing with the whole family. From then on, the young girl would take her sister and cousins to the bioscope every Saturday for seven or eight years. Sathima's grandmother would give the girls money each Saturday morning. The magical world of the cinema was the place for all to feast their eyes on the dream world made real, and their mouths on the treats they were able to buy: candy, potato chips, and *biltong* (usually dry, salted beef).

> Saturday was your big day for the movies. That's where you would get your big dollop of American culture. I saw the musicals, [and] the westerns. It was almost

> as if you had no choice. My grandmother went to the [horse] races, the whole big house closed down for the afternoon . . . We had three movie houses: one was in Lansdowne, which wasn't too far, we had to walk. In Lansdowne it was called the Broadway, and Claremont was called the Orpheum, and Wynberg was the Gaiety. (Personal communication, July 29, 1999)

In the 1940s, when the young Ms. Benjamin began her regular viewing of American movies, the theater offered more than mere consumption of audio-visual images. For these young teenagers and aspiring performers, Hollywood films provided clearer models of popular performance, particularly by people of color. From the movies, Sathima and her friends deepened their knowledge of jazz performance specifically. *Cabin in the Sky* starring Lena Horne as singer and Duke Ellington as band leader, and *Stormy Weather*, featuring a range of African American jazz performers and variety entertainers, were two of the most popular movies shown in South Africa in the mid-1940s. But there were many others in which people like Billie Holiday, Cab Calloway, and the Ink Spots appeared. In the late 1940s through the mid-1950s several local films on Black South African performance were produced and enthusiastically viewed by largely Black and Coloured audiences. This brought the magic of film life right into the center of everyday life in South Africa.

In the increasingly monitored public environment, the movies were perhaps the only space that allowed a freedom in social (and romantic) interaction between Cape Coloureds in Cape Town in the 1940s and 1950s. There were no other contexts in which young Coloured girls were permitted to appear publicly without their parents. With its mix of reality and fictional material, the program at the theater, much like television in the United States and Britain in the same period, kept the community in touch with the outside world. The darkness of the cinema allowed audiences to sit back, open their eyes to an otherwise inaccessible world of glamor and enchantment, or to keep them closed and to dream.

Historians Nasson (1989) and Jeppe (1990) both argue that "going to the movies" was a ritualized, often boisterous, communal activity in Cape Town's "dream palaces" (mid-1940s through to the late 1950s). Vincent Kolbe, who grew up in the more culturally diverse District Six, comments that in his community Saturday night was movie night. Everyone in the family would dress for the occasion. He would go with his mother and grandmother. They took sandwiches and a thermos of coffee. The standard fare from 7.30 to 11.30 p.m. was a comic strip, the weekly serial (the forerunner of the soap opera), a western, and a love story or musical. Nasson explains:

> The local "bioscope" occupied a very special niche in the recreational life of the community, a place to which both adults and children went in order to be cocooned in the dream world of the flickering screen. Attendance was regular and habitual, as films continually widened their audience appeal and imaginative power to transport people out of themselves, and the humdrum confines of their work and domestic lives at least once a week . . . While [cinemas] tended to be fairly small and unpretentious in appearance, their names—the Star, the West End, the Empire, the British Bioscope—dripped with the promise of glamour or old imperial splendor. (Nasson 1989: 286–7)

Going to the movies in the 1940s was always a grand experience in the Coloured communities in Cape Town. Even though some theaters were segregated, and White theaters definitely more plush than those for Coloureds, these were the places where the entire community gathered.

Sitting in often-crowded cinemas and on hard benches was a common experience for many of these cinema-goers. From these packed seats audiences would frequently audibly engage with the film; as one letter to a local newspaper put it:

> I refer mostly to the talking aloud and passing comments on the players, besides reading aloud subtitles . . . and the sympathy and advise [sic] given out to players by some persons. Some ladies again, bring their babies to the show in the evening. (Cited in Nasson 1989: 286–287)

Amorous couples, and sporadic fights in the plebian cinemas added to the texture of the Cape Town bioscope. Moreover there were the scenes of the audience bringing their snacks with them—from smelly fish and chips to milk chocolates.

In these largely working-class communities, Hollywood films provided the bulk of the entertainment: westerns, thrillers, and horror movies were the favorites for men and boys, while women preferred the musicals and "weepies" as they were called. White audiences of the time opted for British productions. Underscoring the importance of the cinema, almost everyone I have interviewed has stressed that at the time, there was no television to entertain individuals and communities or provide models of performance. (Remember, television only came to South Africa in 1976.) It was the "bioscope" that promised the fantasy and magical sounds that so many Coloured people enthusiastically absorbed, and then performed live for the community in subsequent weeks.

As is true elsewhere in the world, in postwar Cape Town there was a well-established tradition among Cape Town's Coloured movie audiences of combined live and mediated experience in movie theaters. Audience members recall singing along with popular songs that accompanied "Tom and Jerry" cartoons, for example. At the time, the words and music would appear on the screen, encouraging collective participation. "Just a Song at Twilight," a tune Ms. Benjamin vividly remembers from her childhood, was one of these songs. Many local theaters also staged elaborate live variety acts and hosted talent competitions. The Gaiety Bioscope ran an advertisement in 1936 that read:

> A Gala Week
> The Gaiety Bioscope will have a real Gala Week for their patrons and predict full houses. It is advisable to be early to secure seats. Chandu the Magician and the Western drama, Sharpshooter [will be the features] . . . The Two Black Crows [clever, eccentric dancers and singers] in their tap dancing and singing will entertain in a clever interlude . . . The Moffie [homosexual/cross-dresser] Concert Party will appear on Wednesday evening.

The Gaiety was the theater where Sathima first appeared in public as a singer when she was about eleven years old. Retrospectively, she suggests there were three levels in which American and British films shaped her individually and musically. She identified with child stars of the movies, and recalls that her aunt even braided her hair in the style of girl stars of the period. Film culture inculcated a particular notion of romance and romantic love that, even if she was never to really find it in daily relationships, she could express desire for in song. For the young Sathima, the emotional force of romantic love she witnessed in the realistic images of the cinema was enhanced by the rich sounds of film melodies. Many of these old tunes remain archived in Sathima's memory, and have become an integral aspect of her current performance repertory. Sathima reinvents these "straight" melodies with a jazz sensibility that enables her to reflect temporal displacement as a musical attribute.

Sathima entered a talent contest held one Saturday afternoon at intermission. Urged to enter by her sister Joan and close school friends, Sathima made them promise that if she did so, they would not tell Ma Benjamin who would have been horrified to know that her young granddaughter was appearing on stage. Bea won the talent contest. The prize: eight free tickets to the movies. This was the first of many talent contests that young Sathima would win in her teenage years. At the time she sang the popular songs of Doris Day, Joni James, and others. "Mr. Wonderful" and "Somewhere over the Rainbow" were her two signature tunes for her admiring followers. Even though she was singing a cover version of the song, Sathima's close friend Ruth Fife recalls that when she heard her at that first talent contest it was clear that even if she was using the words and melodies of others, Sathima Benjamin already had her own distinctive style. This is perhaps something of the "feeling" described in the introduction to Part III by the Cape Town journalist Howard Lawrence for the *Golden City Post* newspaper.

The content of the films made a deep impact on these talent contests. Vincent Kolbe explains:

> For instance, you had Cape Town's Perry Como, Cape Town's Louis Armstong. The moffies, the gays, always had Cape Town's Marilyn Monroe, Cape Town's Brigitte Bardot. It was all a kind of stage entertainment. Anytime a school or a church had a fundraising thing, the community would get up there and perform. You just had to. (Kolbe, personal communication with Carol Muller, September 1996)

Kolbe also explained how melodies borrowed from locally viewed Hollywood films were incorporated into dance band repertory in Cape Town. When he was not accompanying his mother (and her friends) at the movies, he and his friends would go to the movies at the expense of local bandleaders. As soon as a new film arrived in town, the boys were expected to memorize the words and melodies of a song sung, for example, by Nat King Cole. After the movie, they repeated this information to the bandleader. The next Saturday night Cole's newest song would be played at social dances for the Coloured community. In the dance band context, the tunes were played "straight" to sustain the regular rhythms required of ballroom dance. It was in the live renditions of dance band performances rather than through recordings that the majority of Cape Town's Coloured community remember hearing the "sounds of Hollywood" and American jazz

Cape Town's Coloured dance bands played a varied repertory that sought to articulate and keep up with the tastes of their clients. Their repertory needed to include "Muslim songs, Jewish songs, Afrikaner songs, Portuguese songs, French songs" as they could expect to be hired by a varied clientele. This was not class-specific either. Though carnival music (discussed earlier) is largely considered a working-class or at least "lower" class musical practice by the Coloured elite, even those elite would want to hear carnival music played by a dance band. Nixon writes that the elite would hire a dance band that was expected to play music representing all social classes. Vincent Kolbe recalled that

> [i]t might be a bow tie and black suit sort of occasion. These people would be very elegantly dressed. It would be all very respectable people. At the end of the evening the band would be expected to play a "selection of music" in a "raw and raunchy style." (Kolbe in Nixon 1997: 21)

There were at least three kinds of jazz performance occurring simultaneously in postwar Cape Town: swing band music for social dancing (as outlined in Nixon above), **township jazz**, and the jazz avant garde, which consisted of improvising jazz musicians striving to master American styles while searching for a local jazz sound. The two most important groups in Cape Town in the late 1950s and early 1960s were **Dollar Brand/Abdullah Ibrahim's Jazz Epistles** and **Chris McGregor's Blue Notes** (see McGregor 1995). Many of the personnel of the more experimental jazz styles were usually also those who performed for Saturday night dances in the community. In other words, musicians were able to move between worlds with considerable ease in this period.

While dance bands were not new to the Cape in the postwar era, Vincent Kolbe suggests that musicians went to serve in World War II with their stringed instruments, and returned with brass instruments. Cape Town has a long tradition of music with stringed instruments, fiddles, banjos, ukeleles, and so forth. Those who returned from the War had to then adapt the stringed sounds onto brass instruments, and the saxophone in particular. This is where the "wailing" sound of the saxophone in Cape jazz developed. In the years after World War II dance bands were, therefore, transformed in sound if not in function. Without doubt, the new craze called "jazz" that was spreading around the world had a profound impact on dance band performance history in the Cape. One of the most important post-World War II bands, still in existence (with different personnel) is a group called the Philadelphia Rhythms. They play a style of dance music known as ***langarm*** (literally "long arm," a comment on the style of ballroom dance performed to this music. Think of the tango for example, the long outstretched arms in that genre). Vincent Kolbe told me that many of the musicians who played in these bands had either performed as musicians in the war efforts, or had been trained by those who had "gone North," i.e., to North Africa.

> In the army they learnt music, they could read music. They played in the band. They had a kind of education [that] other people didn't have. They had a kind of sophistication about them. And lots of these original bands, at least the ones I learnt from, were blokes [guys] that had actually been in the army. They were interesting to talk to, and they were very skillful and talented and . . . we learnt our music from them. [We] would play in bands where the bandleader was a Sergeant Major, you know, in the army, you know, disciplined, and he'd count. 123 or quick-step you know. And he would read. And he demanded the best out of you . . . There

> was a kind of pursuit of excellence. The world we lived in was full of hope. (Kolbe, personal communication with Carol Muller, September 1996).

Cape Town's community of popular, dance band, and jazz musicians self-consciously imitated the models seen in films and heard on recordings or aired on the radio. There were several reasons for this. Politically, Hollywood images of America operated in stark relief to the increasing discrimination against and oppression of Cape Coloured people in South Africa from the late 1940s through the early years of "Grand Apartheid." When the music was coupled with the "real" world images brought through the cinema, the resulting audio-visual products were valued because they were associated with a world of high society glamor successfully negotiated in Hollywood by people of color like Dorothy Dandridge, Duke Ellington, and Harry Belafonte. Economically, because films were usually only seen once or twice, and recordings were relatively scarce in the lower income communities of some people of color, owning, or having access to a recording held a certain magical quality for individual musicians.

Vincent Kolbe explained the importance of leisure time to the Coloured working-class people in the postwar period. In his and Sathima's parents' generation, when people lived close to their places of work, what you did in your leisure time was extremely important because it was in that time that the politically oppressed created a world of social gradations and status for themselves. For example, individuals joined sports clubs, a dance band, went dancing, or to the movies. Kolbe outlines a similar kind of transformation of young women through Saturday evening dances: from factory worker to princess:

> So women would work a whole week in a factory, and Saturdays go to a dance with this gown, golden shoes, and a cigarette holder [as they had seen in the movies]. I mean all people, no matter what color you are or where you live, you fantasize on the weekend about being a princess for the night. And men would wear bow ties and black suits. And the music, the dancing hall, and so on. (Kolbe, personal communication with Carol Muller, September 1996)

Sathima recalls that in her teens in the 1940s she spent every weekend dancing in local community spaces with a special dance partner. In addition, many in the community fondly recall the dancing that occurred at "bob parties" in the neighborhood. Bob parties were like African American rent parties, a "bob" equaled ten cents, and was the price you paid to enter the house of the party giver who often had a live band or at the very least a piano player to entertain the guests. All proceeds from the party were used to pay rent, or to cover household expenses. The squares, the waltz, the foxtrot, and the samba were some of the dance styles played by live bands whose rhythms shaped the young girl's sophisticated and quite relaxed sense of musical time. She remembers:

> I used to follow the dance bands and was always hearing the saxophone. So the melodies stayed, but I didn't always know the words. [Now] I do research [in the libraries in New York City] and I find these old things. And then it's a question of running the words over in my head and seeing what I want to do with them, but

> still trying to recapture, you know, those moments I felt in the dance hall, listening to the melody. (Personal communication, April 9, 1990).

On her *Cape Town Love* recording there are at least two melodies that she remembers having danced to in Cape Town in the mid-1950s: "When Day is Done" and "If I Should Ever Fall In Love Again." After dancing the squares and the quadrilles, which became a little wild at times, Sathima recalls that these two songs were used for the slow dances to calm everyone down.

When Sathima began her teacher training she sang in the college choir. Despite her love for singing she realized that she was never asked to perform solos in the cantatas the choir sang. One day she plucked up the courage and asked why this was so. She was told that she scooped too much with her voice. Playing around with the pitch was just the game Sathima loved to play as she sang in the group. Fortunately, the choir director realized how much Sathima loved to sing in the choir, so he never excluded her from performing. Later, when she met up with Abdullah Ibrahim and started to listen seriously to recordings of African American jazz singers and instrumentalists, she would identify her sound and playfulness most powerfully with the music of Billie Holiday. It was not that she tried to imitate Billie's voice, but rather that she heard in her sound an expressive quality that gave this young girl from Cape Town a point of reference.

CHAPTER 12
Sathima Bea Benjamin as Jazz Musician

Sathima's move over into this world of jazz in Cape Town began when she met South African jazz drummer and school teacher-in-training, Sam Isaacs. She was sixteen years old when she first encountered the man who was seven years her senior. Sathima now remembers the first time she saw Isaacs. He was leaning against a wall, smoking a cigarette. "He looked just like a gangster!" she commented. Even though the gangster image did not fit the personal character of Sam Isaacs, it was one of the more prevalent ones in movies shown in the 1940s and 1950s in South Africa. A drummer, Sam played in a trio that had a gig at a skating rink for Whites only. His group played jazz in the style of George Shearing. Though she was not allowed inside because she was Coloured, Bea would sit outside the rink and listen to the music through the windows. Sam would come and meet his new friend at intermission.

Once she began teaching school, Bea and her sister Joan went to live with their mother in Kew Town, a fairly settled Coloured housing settlement in Athlone reserved for men who had fought in World War II. The move into her mother's home was significant because it encouraged Bea's move over into jazz. Her mother, the girl discovered, was a self-taught ragtime pianist who purchased a piano when her daughters Joan and Bea went to live with her. It was through the piano that mother and daughter reunited. This instrument became the center of wonderful evenings spent with Bea and the group of jazz-loving friends she began to gather around her. On occasion the three, mother and two daughters, would go to local hotels where there was always a piano and a place to sing. Self-taught, Eva Green could only play in the keys of C, F, and G, and she always played the melody of old songs like "Up a Lazy River," "Chicago," "Come Back to Sorrento," and "Ah! Sweet Mystery of Life."

Sathima recalls that when she first began to sing with other musicians in public, it was usually at a talent show rather than a pure jazz performance. "You would be on the same bill as local tap dancers, acrobats, it could be anything that people found entertaining. But there were a lot of singers, both male and female, not just in the jazz vein, but doing songs that were popular at the time" she told jazz writer Sally Placksin in 1983. Singers typically performed with a trio: a bassist, drummer, and a pianist, perhaps also a saxophone. In the late 1950s these musicians were listening closely to the music of Americans Louis Armstrong, Sarah Vaughan, and Duke Ellington. They were beginning to really improvise musically at these venues.

Sathima's mother would sometimes go with her daughters to local hotels and venues where such performances took place. While she rarely accompanied her daughter, she would willingly work with some of the local talent. There was one man, Joey Gabriels, an opera singer who sang "Come Back to Sorrento." Gabriels changed his name to Giuseppe Gabriello when he left South Africa to study opera in Italy.

> When the emcees would announce Joey Gabriels, they had their way, the emcees, he would come on and they would announce, he was Cape Town's Mario Lanza or Caruso or whatever, and he would walk. OK we would all be back stage and just walk on the stage and go to the microphone (which probably wasn't working or working and making squeaks) . . . and there comes Joey Gabriels. He would not come from backstage. When they announced him, he came from the back of the cinema. You know, with a big chest and everything, just so pompous and full of conceit. This was all part of the act. He'd get to the stage and walk to the middle and he would take the microphone stand and walk over to the side and put the stand down there, like I don't need this. And he'd just stand there, a gorgeous tenor, you know. It was always the same thing, people always wanted the same thing. He would just get these ovations, he was so flamboyant. (Personal communication with Carol Muller, October 4, 1996)

Many of these shows were also created as fundraising events for local charities and community projects. There are two newspaper articles that talk of Sathima's participation in such activities.

> The Big Jazz Show Has All the Talent.
> Jazz fans were treated to some high-octane music at the Woodstock Town Hall during the week when five leading jazz groups broke loose with a concert in aid of various Peninsula youth clubs. But if you missed the session, not to worry. All these artists have offered to play for "Post's" big jazz night in the Cape Town City Hall in a few weeks time. EVERY PENNY RAISED GOES TO THE CAPE MENTAL HEALTH SOCIETY TO START A BUILDING FUND. ALL WILL BE THERE.
>
> [Picture of Beattie Benjamin].
>
> Blues Buck up Beattie: Beattie Benjamin, another of the artists at the Woodstock show gives with "Mr. Wonderful." Beattie loves singing, especially the "blues" for it does things for her emotions. "Try singing the blues," she advises. It works wonders for you. (*Golden City Post*, April 30, 1958)

> Just Jazz, Just Great: Post Show Aids Kids.
> The city's biggest and best jazz show ever. [Picture of Beattie Benjamin]. Blues singer Beatrice Benjamin had the boys swooning. The Jimmy Adams big band played as well. (*Golden City Post*, July 20, 1958)

Sathima has vivid memories of the audiences at those performances. She recalled:

> that wonderful community of people who loved the music, who got involved . . . It just naturally brought people together, it was happening in Port Elizabeth, and Cape Town. In Johannesburg, you had tons of musicians there. I mean it was so beautiful. You had such a connection. (Benjamin, personal communication, March 9, 1990)

Her memory of Cape performance is that it was completely unmediated. People knew about her vocal abilities by word of mouth because she sang all over: in hotels, clubs, school, and jazz concerts. There were no recordings of Cape Coloured music that made a musician famous, just the live music.

> Your public, they were the critics and they would let you know. "Oh no, you're singing *that*!" They would throw things at you, you know. You really had to be very careful because they could take you off and replace you with someone else who would really do something beautiful. So it was really a tough audience, but also a beautiful audience. Because if you sang something, and you really felt what you were doing, they would respond. You would know it. They were so warm. You could almost hear them breathing with you. That's the way it was. It was always such a rewarding experience. (Benjamin, personal communication with Carol Muller, April 29, 1990)

Aside from these activities, Sathima would spend her evenings in the Kew Town library reading about the African American experience and listening to jazz recordings as part of a Jazz Appreciation Club run by Sathima's friend and jazz pianist, the librarian Vincent Kolbe. Kolbe recalled that the library was the hub of social and artistic activity—he described the community as "bohemian," with several sensitive, artistic schoolteachers in its midst. It was at this library that Sathima listened to African Americans playing jazz on sound recordings, and read the writings of African Americans. Kolbe provided her with books by Richard Wright, Langston Hughes, W. E. B. du Bois, and others. She even found the early autobiography of Billie Holiday, *Lady Sing The Blues: The Searing Autobiography of an American Musical Legend* (1956), before the Nationalist government banned it. It was the time when she began to question her identity. By reading of the experience of a people called "Colored" in the United States, Sathima realized she and her people were not alone in their experiences of the harshness of racism, and that others called "Colo[u]red" were doing the music she was.

Sathima became more directly connected to the local jazz world one day after returning home from teaching school. She was busy picking out a White popular American singer Doris Day tune on her mother's piano and singing along when a man, Bertie

Smith, came to the door selling brooms. He told her he thought that she should become a jazz singer. Furthermore, they were organizing a jazz concert at the Glemore Town Hall in Athlone. Smith invited her to come along and sing and promised to introduce her to the musicians. She was to perform the song "Don't Blame Me." Sathima went to that concert where she met up with Cape Town's community of jazz musicians, all of whom had learned their repertory from repeated listening to jazz records.

> There were people there who could play Errol Garner's solo to every note that Errol Garner played. Cape Tonians are very good at imitating. Excellent. We always had the Cape Town Jerry Lewis, the Cape Town Bing Crosby. I think for a while I was either Doris Day or Joni James, before I went into the other thing [i.e., jazz]. After that concert, after I sang only the one song, "Don't Blame Me," the guys said that were working in the clubs, if I wanted to come and work there, I should just turn up. And I would go. Every weekend my sister Joan and I, we couldn't wait to go into the town, to go to Darryl's nightclub or the Navigators Den. (Sathima Bea Benjamin, interview with the author, New York City, October 4, 1996)

Once Sathima completed her course, she began teaching at an elementary school in Athlone, Cape Town.

Like most of South Africa's Coloured and "African" performers of the era, Sathima participated in local jazz and variety traveling shows prevalent in South Africa before the state clamped down on the freedom of movement of people of color. White entrepreneurs, who talked continually of taking the troupes "overseas," organized the groups. In 1957, at the age of twenty, the young Benjamin joined impressario Arthur Klugman's traveling show, **Coloured Jazz and Variety**, as a singer. More variety than jazz, the Arthur Klugman show was a critical experience for developing Sathima's sense of improvisation, as much a musical as a life skill. Big ideas and equally large failure were not uncommon features of these traveling shows in South Africa in the 1950s. This was the show in which the young woman met Cape saxophonist and big band arranger Jimmy Adams who is central to the early history of jazz band performance in Cape Town. After going as far as Zimbabwe in a bus that regularly broke down, the musicians were left stranded close to the South African border, in Mafeking. Penniless, several of the performers had to entertain local people in order to be fed and housed.

Both Jimmy Adams and Sathima had warm memories of the hospitality of the people of Mafeking at the time. The gig they organized was extremely popular, giving them just enough money to find transportation back to Johannesburg. But it was also the clubs in Johannesburg and Cape Town that supported African performances, such as **Township Jazz** and the traveling jazz and variety shows. There are advertisements for such performances in Cape Town newspapers, like the *Cape Argus*, in January and February 1962. Sathima remembers having performed with **African Jazz and Variety** when it came to Cape Town in the late 1950s, though the primary group she traveled with was Coloured Jazz and Variety. At the time, jazz musicians from Cape Town and Johannesburg were in close contact with each other. The community was quite small, and musicians like Dollar Brand, Hugh Masakela, and Kippie Moeketsi traveled the thousand miles between the two cities quite regularly, as indeed, the traveling shows enabled musicians to work together quite frequently. Sathima Benjamin spent the remainder of 1957 performing with Jimmy Adams at the Bantu Men's Social Center and other venues in Johannesburg, and in Maputo (Lourenzo Marques), Mozambique over the Christmas holidays. While in Johannesburg she and Adams lived in Malay Camp, a housing settlement for people of mixed race, with a group of gangsters. Benjamin recalls the experience (think back to the parallel account by Miriam Makeba in Chapter 6):

> We were all sleeping on the floor, there was like a shebeen (a drinking establishment like a speakeasy) people were coming in so loudly . . . But these people loved artists and musicians, and we'd sing for them . . . We sang at functions in Johannesburg where the gangsters walked in with axes and things, and they said, they had you singing and you couldn't stop until they told you to stop. (Personal communication with Carol Muller, October 4, 1996)

In the mid to late 1950s, there was a moment where Coloured musicians were hired more frequently than white bands in Cape Town clubs because the Coloureds would play for less and because they were more reliable. The clubs ranged in clientele, from being elite dinner-dance venues, to seedy strip joints. The Balailaka and the Navigators Den were two of the less respectable clubs. But it was in the white clubs that jazz was performed, and listened to, more so than in the Coloured communities where band music for dancing was the primary form of "jazz" heard and performed. Of course, all this would change in the 1960s, when no more mixing in public places across the color bar was permitted and white clubs began to import Portuguese and Greek musicians.

The story of Jimmy Adams illustrates the move from dance band to jazz band, and the struggle for jazz musicians trying to play "cross-over" music, i.e., music intended for one racial cateogory of consumers that unexpectedly becomes popular in another racial community, or in this case, was played by a musician from a different racial group. Ethnomusicologist Michael Nixon and social historian Valmont Layne did the core research and interviews with Jimmy Adams before I met him, which were reinforced by my own interviews with Jimmy a few years later. Adams died in Cape Town in 2004.

Jimmy Adams claims to have started the first Coloured jazz band in Cape Town. Adams was one of a few cross-over figures in the Cape Town music scene—cross-over in the South African sense, he was experimenting musically with Black music as a Coloured man. Adams had played the accordion in his father's band since the age of ten. His father, Arnie Adams, ran a Christmas band (see above) and an old-style dance band, both of which had operated since at least the 1930s. As a teenager, Jimmy heard the band of African jazz musician Tem Hawker of Langa—the Black township near Athlone—and fell in love with his music. He told his father of his love for this music and despite his father's reluctance, Adams began to play and arrange music of this kind. He recalls that he was basically living in Langa, walking back and forth to Langa from his home in Bridgetown, near the Coloured township called Athlone. It was in Langa that Adams had lessons with saxophonist Hawker, and worked on jazz theory along with three African jazz musicians, Chris Columbus, Duke, and Ezra Ngcukana's father (these musicians are all discussed in Rasmussen 2003a).

> Adams' work over five years [preparing his band] produced good results. He worked with musicians who have become some of today's leading jazz performers: Tony Schilder was 15 or 16 when he played in Jimmy Adams' band, and Hotep Galeta—still known as Cecil Barnard—was 17 . . . Harold Jephta was another musician who benefited from working with Jimmy Adams. The quality of the music notwithstanding, the band found itself facing misunderstanding, and racism . . . Dancers in the inner city were so accustomed to [traditional ballroom] langarm dance music that Jimmy Adams' band was not a commercial success. Says musician Eddie George: "The Coloured people were not ready for him and so his band was not popular at all. The musicians in his band all became strong musicians . . . But there was no future for jazz in the popular dance scene. Jimmy's band stopped in about 1958/9." (Gassert 1988: 34, cited in Nixon 1997: 22)

In an interview with Michael Nixon in 1995, Vincent Kolbe recalled:

> Jimmy Adams was one of the only guys who could bridge the gap [between Coloured music culture and jazz and the African music world]. Jimmy Adams' was never a very popular band. He played Cole Porter, etcetera, and his smooth style was not so popular in the dance halls . . . (Nixon 1997: 23)

Another musician, Willis Jails, was more cautious. He said his band followed the

> Jimmy Adams style [. . .] our music was very orchestrated, lots of saxophones, two altos and two tenors. In between dance numbers we'd push jazz very subtly. The banjo was definitely out and guitars took over . . . eventually becoming electrified [. . .] Rock'n'roll was taking off but we didn't feel threatened as long as we included it to a small degree in our repertories. We still catered for the older generation's style of music—ballroom. We just adapted a little and compromised where necessary. (Gassert 1988: 34, cited in Nixon 1997: 23)

Sathima's friend Sam Isaacs recalls playing nightly in one of the clubs that had White strippers. Because the musicians were "Coloured," when the stripper began her act, a curtain was drawn to hide the musicians. Ironically, Sam remarked, there was no curtain in rehearsals. The public face of apartheid was replete with anomalies. As was to be expected, while these places hired Coloured musicians (it would later be prohibited) they spent the intermissions with the staff in the kitchen "just like Black American musicians I had read about [including Billie Holiday] had to do in the South," Sathima commented in November 1986.

On returning to Cape Town, Ms. Benjamin continued to moonlight at night and over weekends. The lifestyle did not last long. Moonlighting was illegal if you taught public school. On one occasion a reporter arrived at the school looking for the young jazz singer, because he wanted to write an article on a jazz singer who was also a teacher, an unusual combination for the teaching profession.

The report appeared in *Golden City Post* on August 26, 1958, p. 7:

> HER NAME SPELLS J-A-Z-Z
> Around Cape Town's sleepless night-spots the name of Beatrice Benjamin spells J-A-Z-Z.
>
> It is jazz in its careful, sophisticated moods. Jazz wrapped up in glamour, jazz sung delicately, teasingly, and lovingly. For [Sathima] "Beaty" Benjamin as hundreds of her fans know her, has a way of using her face, her body and hands, to sing a song, thereby enriching its message.
>
> Recently "Beaty" went to the Naaz—Cape Town's plushiest, jazziest, all-race night-club. Her voice, deceptively dreary, sometimes smoky and sad, reached out to the customers as she sang: "It Could Happen to You." Then galloping away with "Fine and Dandy," Beaty whooped it up, eyes closed, forgetfully alone, in a packed night-club. The applause at the end was worth it, for "Beaty" Benjamin has just made her finest statement.
>
> At her most original "Beaty" breaks up the pace of the song and its lines, never losing the beat, and achieves a wonderful personal style that taps the true sources of her power.
>
> Beatrice teaches school by day and sings by night. She has a heart too. Once she sang for a POST charity show to help neglected mental cases.
>
> The fact that she gets engagements in all-White clubs hasn't gone to Beaty's head. On Saturdays and Sundays you can see her, working hard at the "Ambassador's Club" rehearsing. This chocolate gal is just "Fine and Dandy!"

The newspaper article angered the school principal who summoned Bea to his office and reprimanded her for her club singing. Women who sang jazz were not to be trusted and of questionable moral standards. She remembers the principal coming into her classroom to check on her every morning. Sathima was also reprimanded because it was illegal to have more than one form of employment if you worked for the government, i.e., as all public schoolteachers did. Her cousin, Basil Rich, who was also a schoolteacher and guitarist, performed six nights a week at the Navigators' Den, a harbor hangout for jazz musicians and American sailors in Cape Town. He never needed to make the choice between teaching and performing because he never appeared in the newspaper. There was also a significant physical distance between his daily and nightly workplaces (Basil Rich, interview with the author, Cape Town, September 1996).

Much against the wishes of many of those who knew her, Sathima Benjamin decided to leave the relative security of the teaching profession for the more adventurous, but uncertain world of jazz performance. From 1959 she began performing with several ensembles and pianists including the Harold Jephta trio and pianist Henry February's Nat King Cole Trio (February was the pianist with whom she recorded *Cape Town Love* in 1999) in White nightclubs in the Cape Town area. This was about the time she met and first performed with Abdullah Ibrahim.

The new jazz musicians in 1950s Cape Town were a serious group. As Kolbe recalls, "Jazz then was such a religion. No one spoke money then. You sat there reverently" (in Nixon 1997: 22). Kolbe described to Nixon the first jazz concert in District Six, in Cape Town, conducted without White musicians.

> In about 1955, the University of Cape Town Rag (a student group organizing the annual opening festivities of the academic year) decided to include a jazz concert in its program. Probably an imitation of Dave Brubeck's Jazz Goes to Campus. This was at the Weizmann Hall. The white racist musicians who never really jammed, though they could read very well, [dominated] the show. They eventually formed an all white union later . . . And Harold Jeptha, who was the best of our guys, sat with his sax completely ignored.
>
> We were so disgusted, that I approached the priest who said we could have the hall, which was free on Wednesday night. We said we'd charge 5 bob a head and whatever was taken at the door would go to the church. We had a lot of big bands, including . . . the Merry Macs and Dougie Erasmus' big band. It was such a massive success that people are still talking about it. At the wake for Dougie Erasmus (September 1995) all the guys were there and recalled that concert.
>
> The new jazz scene of the 1950s found its operational base in the clubs of Woodstock, a suburb just outside of the city center, which was something of a "grey" area i.e. not so dominated by Coloured culture. There were clubs like the Naaz and the Mermaid, and the Zambezi inside the city center. The Naaz . . . would have white and black musicians playing together, such as Chris McGregor, who played with African and Coloured musicians.
>
> Richer people came to slum in Woodstock. There were quite a few wealthy white jazz fanatics who spent heavily there. They brought their friends. They looked very casual but we knew they were rich . . . The only previous mixing I was aware of was in the Communist Party, but that was all quite Camps Bay, really quite elite. In '50s jazz culture it was a different kind of thing. In the clubs there was mixing to the point of contravening the Immorality Act! Not only was mixed clubbing a problem for the apartheid government, but individuals' relationships were targeted for individual harassment. Maude Damons became a prominent jazz singer from District Six. She ended up in London as the cops were after her and her white lover. Hotep had an older German girlfriend and they had to leave the country. Had it been left to itself, this jazz scene could have developed into something remarkable . . . It was an apartheid casualty. (Kolbe in Nixon 1997: 22–23)

Though Abdullah and Sathima both performed in these nightclubs, the place that these two ultimately created for jazz as an art form was The Ambassadors. By this time, Abdullah was no longer performing with local dance bands, but was developing his own style of jazz performance. The Ambassadors was the space for exploring these new musical (and social) possibilities. Sathima recalled:

> The guy who owned [The Ambassadors] was Dave Saunders, and he was a friend of Abdullah's. He had this lovely space in Woodstock. You had to climb these stairs. He had this space and he had a piano. And Abdullah started. We had thirteen people the first week, we used to do it only on Sunday nights. And after a couple of weeks, we couldn't contain all the people. It was just a place where you went and you sat down and listened. There was no dancing, no food, nothing. And, as I said, there was too much mixing going on at the time when they didn't want people to

> be mixing. So we had to close that down. (Sathima Bea Benjamin, personal communication, April 1988).

In May 1961, one of *Drum Magazine*'s reporters described the Sunday night jazz scene at The Ambassadors.

> The naked light bulb, like the mood, is blue. The only other illumination in the place comes from the glowing ends of cigarettes, or maybe a stray moonbeam filtering down the slopes of Table Mountain and in through a back window.
>
> The chairs are arranged carefully, like pews, and the congregation is as devout as any other Sunday night gathering. In the darkened corner the tall, thin guy with the tight jeans and the size 12 army boots is leading his group through an original composition. The long, bony fingers slide or thump, caress or squeeze the notes out, and the horn, the bass, and the drums, catch the message and pass it on.
>
> Dark as it is, the Dollar is gleaming tonight. This is the real stuff, the pulse beat of the jazz world in the Cape, and Dollar Brand and his group are pumping it out—though this is their night off from six days of cafe-capers with the beatnik gang.
>
> From this center of the jazz scene, which is up an iron staircase near where the Cape's trolley buses get their nightly wash and brush-up, the music world stretches far down the Peninsula, and every other month some new guy with a horn or an alto sax or a bass is coming up from the shadows to catch the ear of the people who know their music.
>
> In the past few years, the Cape has taken over as THE place for music, snatching the laurel from the backrooms and cellars a thousand miles north in [Johannesburg]. Dollar was in at the start of the move south, but he doesn't understand how it happened. Anyone who has been around the Cape long enough to know his music remembers the Big Band age just after the war. But they were all African, fifteen or more, beating it out like ebony Dorseys and Goodmans. Maybe it's the changing mood of South Africa that African music—Cape-wards, anyhow—has faded to no more than a township tin lid. So the Coloreds have taken over, and the mood is softer, sweeter, and more serious.
>
> Dollar and his group are the lone wolves of the Cape Tin Pan Alley, dedicated jazz men all. They play it their way—and if the customers don't like it then that's tough on the customers . . . "Jazz is the real classics," he says. "It's all here, at the Cape. The place is dripping with talent and I'm not sure I ever want to be anywhere else." (*Drum Magazine*, May 1961, p. 46)

Life changed drastically for all Coloured musicians in 1960 in the aftermath of the Sharpeville Massacre and the state of emergency declared by the government. The state clamped down on all performance that catered to mixed ensembles, audiences, or clientele. By the early 1960s it became clear to Abdullah and Sathima, who were now a couple (but not married), that it would be impossible to survive as creative artists in South Africa. Jazz performance, with all its mixing of people, had become a dangerous activity, monitored, and raided by security forces. Sathima remembers:

> I never thought about leaving South Africa. It just happened very quickly and very naturally because the situation got very bad . . . And it started to get very empty. And that is when we moved. We would either have to shut up completely or we'd have to leave. And that's when we decided to leave, in 1961, because it became impossible, not only to do jazz. To do any kind of music. It became very repressive. (Personal communication with Carol Muller, April 29, 1990)

Literally starving for lack of opportunities, they decided to travel to Switzerland where Paul Meyer had promised to help them find work and suitable housing. Abdullah and Sathima left the country after a farewell concert to raise money for their air tickets was held at The Ambassadors. They flew to Zurich, Switzerland, to begin the next phase in their lives as jazz musicians a long, long way from home. This was where they met and recorded with African American jazz greats, Duke Ellington and Billy Strayhorn. Jazz had become a tenuous passport to the transnational community of artists in Europe and the United States for these musicians from Cape Town.

Jazz was not the only genre of performance that emerged out of the popular cultural world of Cape Town. Though he gained fame for his clarinet and saxophone skills, particularly in the style of jazz musician Charlie Parker, Harold Jephta ultimately left South Africa in the early 1960s to study the European classical repertory. Jephta recounted (interview with the author, Cape Town, December 1999) that it was the power of the music of orchestrated film scores that opened the world of European classical music to him. His personal favorites were the monster movies so popular at the time. In the early 1960s Jephta left South Africa for Europe with one of the country's most popular traveling jazz and variety troupes, "The Golden City Dixies." Given the opportunity to study the European repertory at a conservatory in Sweden, Jephta remained in northern Europe playing clarinet for a Symphony Orchestra in Sweden until he was able to return to South Africa in the early 1990s.

Sathima Bea Benjamin and Abdullah Ibrahim followed several South Africans who had left before them, including singer Miriam Makeba, trumpeter Hugh Masekela, and lesser known Ben "Satch" Masinga. Abdullah and Sathima went to Europe. The period of extended movement around the world was not easy. In contrast to the warmth of Africa articulated in her song text, she recalls the move away from home:

> We went to the unknown. That was so shocking. It was so rough and cold. We had to keep moving to survive. We did live in Zurich, but that was like a base and we moved out from there. And the further north we went [to Scandinavia], the further I felt away from home, and I really mean home, deep inside. But, I think, you know, the music always saved me. (Personal communication with Carol Muller, April 29, 1990)

And that music was a South African interpretation and refiguring of the language of American-made jazz. A radio journalist once asked Abdullah Ibrahim if he heard African elements in the American jazz he listened to in Cape Town in the 1950s. Abdullah's reply is poignant. He believes that jazz is "Africa based." For this jazz pianist there was an inherent connection between the sounds of jazz and the music of contemporary Africa.

"For us [in Cape Town], Ellington was never an American. He was just the grand old man in the Village." Similarly, Duke Ellington is reported to have remarked on his arrival in Dakar, Senegal, in 1966, "After writing African music for 35 years, here I am at last in Africa!" Because the South Africans sensed such a strong connection between Cape musicians and African American jazz performers, it is not surprising that the young Sathima Benjamin determined to invite the great Duke Ellington to hear Dollar Brand perform when they were all in Switzerland in February 1963. The story is quite a remarkable one. After leaving South Africa in 1962, Dollar and Beattie ended up performing in a variety of clubs in Switzerland. One night, when Dollar had his band at the Club Africana, Beattie heard that Duke Ellington was in the neighborhood. So she went to his performance, going backstage to try to meet him. She was lucky that night. He suggested that she stay backstage, and wait until the end of the show, which she did. He was taken by more than her sheer tenacity. Prior to meeting her, he had been asked by the US State Department to travel to South Africa. Duke Ellington had refused when he had been told he would have to perform before segregated audiences (Sathima Bea Benjamin, personal communication, April 1997). His meeting up with these two South African jazz musicians, who knew his music so intimately, was clearly a fortuitous moment for all. Duke agreed to hear the Dollar Brand Trio. He stayed for a couple of items, and then turned to the young Benjamin.

> "And what is it that you do?" Ellington asked Benjamin. "Are you the manager?"
> "No," she answered. "But I sing sometimes."
> "Then you must sing," said Ellington with matter-of-fact insistence. "Go and sing." (Hajdu 1996)

The following day, Ellington met with the two South Africans in his hotel in Zurich. At the time he was both a performer and producer for Frank Sinatra at Reprise Records in Paris. He arranged to meet Sathima and the Dollar Brand Trio in Paris three days later. Performing with Dollar Brand were South Africans Johnny Gertze on bass and Makaya Ntshoko on drums. They played six instrumental pieces that were later released as *Duke Ellington Introduces the Dollar Brand Trio*.

The other thirty tracks recorded at that time were never released in Ellington's lifetime. Sathima sings on twelve tracks accompanied on piano by Ellington, Billy Strayhorn or Dollar Brand, and Swedish pizzicato violinist, Svend Asmussen. Ellington had told Sathima afterwards that the record company had thought the pieces were not "commercial" enough. Never having heard the recordings, Sathima came to believe that they had been lost or destroyed. That was until July 1994, when Strayhorn biographer David Hajdu played a cassette copy of the recording to her in New York City. While doing research for his book on Strayhorn, Hajdu had met up with Gerhard Lehner, the studio engineer who was working in Barclay Studios in Paris on February 23, 1963. Lehner had been a soldier in the Nazi army during the Second World War when American soldiers captured him in Russia. Taken a prisoner of war by the Americans, he had been persuaded to work for the US Armed Services Radio Service in Munich. He was subsequently hired as the chief engineer at the Barclay Studios and had been involved with the recording of many of Duke Ellington and Billy Strayhorn's musical sessions.

Lehner was particularly impressed with the recording session Strayhorn and Ellington had with the young South Africans. In fact, because he liked the sound of Sathima's voice so much, he had illegally made a second copy of the morning's work. This was the music that Sathima heard playing in her apartment in July 1994. It would take more than two years before Sathima was able to release twelve tracks of that historic morning in Paris on a CD she has called *A Morning in Paris*. The CD includes twelve American jazz vocal standards, like "Darn That Dream," "Solitude," "I'm Glad There is You," and "A Nightingale Sang in Berkeley Square." The Benjamin–Ellington CD was launched at a live performance Sathima did with several New York musicians, and a Philadelphia jazz violinist, John Blake, in the Recital Hall at Carnegie Hall. Present in the front row were Duke Ellington's flamboyant sister, Ruth Ellington, as well as several members of the Duke Ellington Society.

As it was for several other South Africans, jazz became the couple's means of survival in more than three decades of political and cultural exile from South Africa. More specifically in this period, it was a knowledge of American popular and jazz music, and several fortuitous encounters with African American jazz musicians, that enabled a number of South Africans to settle in England, and the United States in particular. Among others, Miriam Makeba was taken under the wing of Harry Belafonte; both Hugh Masekela and Ben "Satch" Masinga were guided by Louis Armstrong. As is clear from the story above, Abdullah Ibrahim and Sathima Bea Benjamin were greatly assisted by Duke Ellington.

But Europe was not an easy place for these young South Africans, accustomed to warm sunshine, the sounds of English and Afrikaans, and indeed of the Xhosa language with its complicated "click" sounds spoken in the neighboring townships, and the presence of strong, vibrant communities of people. "Europe" and its culture had always been held in such high esteem in Sathima's home, and indeed, by those labeled "European" in South Africa, that she had come to imagine it as something of a mystical space. But the cold reality of Europe was something quite different. Language itself sounded so alien, the people seemed cold and indifferent. Few Europeans had any idea that people of color from South Africa could be performing jazz in its sophisticated inflections. Africa: its people, its pacing, its customary friendliness, and its color and energy, seemed a long, long way away. What saved these musicians in this period was the music itself. Feeling no connection to the society around them, Sathima, Abdullah, and the small group of exiled South African jazz musicians in Europe at the time, sustained themselves by playing their music and engaging with communities of international students living in Europe. This was truly a diasporic community of people, in but not of Europe.

In this mode, Sathima and Abdullah used Zurich as their base from which they moved around Europe, to the United States, and even to South Africa where they returned for the birth of both of their children. Sathima insisted that they had to be born on African soil. The couple moved between South Africa and the northern hemisphere with relative ease until the mid 1970s and the Soweto and related uprisings in 1976. This traumatic event with related uprisings throughout the country, including in Cape Town, was what finally caused Sathima and Abdullah to make public their support of the then banned African National Congress, the organization at the forefront of the struggle against apartheid. On the video *Brother With Perfect Timing* (1988), Abdullah tells a remarkable story about two tunes that he performed in Cape Town in 1976, prior to the June uprising. According to him, these were the tunes titled "Mannenberg" (named after a township in Cape Town that is parallel in significance to Soweto in Johannesburg) and "Soweto." The saxophone solos were being sung to words all over the country, as anthems of anger and resistance to the apartheid regime. Just a few months after the recordings of these tunes were released, the Soweto uprisings occurred. This was the turning point in South African history, when the South African security forces gunned down school children protesting against having to be taught in Afrikaans (the language of White people of European descent, and some Cape Coloureds, but not of the majority of people in the country).

After about fifteen years as jazz migrants, moving between Europe, the United States, and South Africa, Sathima and Abdullah decided to settle in New York City. Sathima has written about her relationship to this city, a relationship she calls a "New York embrace," and that embrace has always been powerfully shaped by the musical relationship she has had, and continues to imagine, with one of New York City's finest jazz musicians, the late great Duke Ellington.

> "A New York Embrace"
> I remember upon arriving in New York on a hot summer's day about a week before the Newport [Jazz] Festival in 1965 that it felt wonderful to me—the energy, the flow, the sight of its many diverse peoples. I was amazed that I did not feel intimidated at all. The excitement swooped me up and it felt good to be here.
>
> We stayed with a dear friend from Nigeria in Greenwich Village for some weeks after our arrival. The same day we arrived we went to meet and hear Duke Ellington at a concert in Harlem. It was all happening so fast—at times it seemed like a dream. Duke introduced us to his dear sister—Ruth—and we were sort of handed over into her care. She helped us to get settled, found us an apartment and later, upon Duke's advice, we decided to apply for the "green card" and settle in New York City . . .
>
> We did several East Coast performances with Ellington. One was at Wolftrap, and another at Cotillion in Baltimore. The last time I sang with Ellington was around Christmas in 1972 at St. Peter's Church in New York. I happened to be in New York at the time. He called and said, "Come and sing 'Come Sunday' with me." That was the last time I saw him as well. I was in South Africa in 1974 when he died.
>
> In 1977 . . . Abdullah and I settled in New York City with our two children, Tsakwe (then six years old) and Tsidi (three months old). Now it was time for me to stop travelling, settle down, and raise my children.
>
> I've been here ever since. (Rasmussen 2000b: 71)

In 1979, with the help of Abdullah, Sathima established the Ekapa label, primarily for the production and distribution of her own jazz recordings. *Ekapa* means "at" or "from the Cape." She remembers how it came about.

> It occurred to me that I could make a record . . . I really didn't know anything about it. I decided to do an album of Ellington songs because I figured, well, they don't

> know me here. Let me do something that is familiar. I was very unsteady with my own compositions, and I was very shy about [them]. Then I did it. I went into the studio. I did it.
>
> And then I sat there with a couple thousand LPs and I said, "What am I going to do with all this?" So I had to get the courage and say, now who are all the critics in this jazz music business? I am going to write a little note, package it, and send it to them. They can either look at it and throw it in the bin, or what, I don't know. I waited six months. I got feedback. I almost fell off my feet. It was so positive, I couldn't believe it . . . I always say I have this little record company. I'm the president, I'm the musician, I'm the messenger, I go to the post office. I do absolutely everything. (Sathima Bea Benjamin, class visit at Marymount College, Tarrytown, NY, October 1990)

It was in New York City, so far from the community of people who enabled Sathima to enter the world of jazz singing, that Sathima began to find her compositional voice. Although she had had songs sitting inside her for many years, it was once she sat in the city that claims to be the center of jazz performance that she mustered the courage to give life to the words and melodies she had held inside for so long. Once she started, new materials began to come to Sathima. Profoundly shaped by the anti-apartheid movement led by the African National Congress in exile and the United Nations in New York City, Sathima's song composition moved over into the explicitly political domain. This is a less prominent dimension of American jazz performance, but its roots can be traced right back to Billie Holiday's powerful rendition of the song "Strange Fruit" so many years prior. And the tradition continued with the bold performances of Abbey Lincoln. The "Liberation Suite" is where Sathima Bea Benjamin made her mark in supporting the struggle against apartheid while she lived in New York City.

From 1979 through 2007, Sathima has produced ten long-playing records or CDs of her own performance. In addition to the more explicitly political lyrics of the "Liberation Suite," Sathima's recordings in the US include a combination of her very personal interpretations of Tin Pan Alley, show tunes, and jazz standards, as well as several of her original compositions that speak of her own vision of jazz, Africa, and its relationship to a sense of South Africanness. The ten recordings are as follows:

1 *Sathima Sings Ellington*, recorded in April 1979 in New York City, with musicians Onaje Allen Gumbs, Vishnu Wood, John Betsch, and Claude Latief.
2 *Dedications*, recorded in January 1982 in New York City with musicians Onaje Allen Gumbs, Carlos Ward, Buster Williams, Ben Riley, and Dom Um Ramao. Reissued by Celeste Company, Japan in 2005.
3 *Memories and Dreams*, recorded in October 1983 at Rudy Van Gelder Studios in Englewood Cliffs, New Jersey with musicians Onaje Allen Gumbs, Carlos Ward, Buster Williams, and Billy Higgins.
4 *Windsong*, in June 1985 at Van Gelder Studios, with Kenny Barron, Buster Williams, and Billy Higgins.
5 *Lovelight*, in September 1987 at Van Gelder Studios with Larry Willis, Ricky Ford, Buster Williams, and Billy Higgins.

6 *Southern Touch*, in December 1989 at Van Gelder Studios, with Kenny Barron, Buster Williams, and Billy Higgins.
7 *Cape Town Love*, in March 1999 at Milestone Studios in Cape Town with Henry February on piano, Basil Moses on bass, and Vincent Pavitt on drums.
8 *The Best of Sathima Bea Benjamin with Friends*, released in 2001 by Enja Records.
9 *Musical Echoes*, recorded in February 2002 in Cape Town with Stephen Scott on piano, Basil Moses on bass, and Lulu Gontsala on drums.
10 *Song Spirit*, a compilation of previously recorded tracks with all of the pianists she has worked with in Europe and the United States. New York: Ekapa SA 003.

Rasmussen (2000b) lists additional recordings Sathima made prior to her production work in New York City.

On occasion, Sathima has organized performances of her own music, sometimes touring to the West Coast, or up the East Coast, to Europe, and since 1990, even back to South Africa. Each time she performs, either live on stage or in a studio, she works with the finest jazz musicians, either in the United States or in South Africa. In the final section of this chapter, we will talk about the critical reception of her music in the United States and South Africa, and indeed, use all the information about Sathima's life and musical experiences as a means to a better understanding and appreciation of her music. Five of her songs are on the CD and introduced briefly in the appendices. If you haven't already done so, listen closely.

Sathima's Singing

So much of this chapter has been about Sathima, the people she grew up with, and the musical communities she participated in. In this final section the focus shifts to Sathima's own voice, in song, and in terms of what she has to say about herself as a jazz musician, as composer, and performer. Briefly, Sathima wrote in 2000 a short piece on what she believes a jazz singer to be.

> Taking a song—remembered or new—and having the freedom to adapt it to your own unique style, vision, and understanding of it, that is my understanding of a jazz singer . . . The magic, the mysticism of that wonderful city [Cape Town], I carry within my soul. I remember songs, smells, sights, people—and it's all music to me. I know my sound, my sense of rhythm and time comes from there—and so it is that I endeavor through jazz singing to give that "sound picture" to the listener. (Rasmussen 2000b: 67)

In 1990 I asked her why she chose to perform jazz specifically. It seemed to be so controversial; an alienating choice in terms of her family and childhood friends.

> I was innately attracted to jazz . . . It happened at a time when I was thinking very deeply about all of this . . . about my own identity. It happened around 1957 through the 1960s. That was a very fervent time at home, and things were happening politically. And I was at such an age when it hit me. I said, "I'm not going to

> take this . . . What am I going to do?" I didn't write my own music then. That's the time I drifted to Duke Ellington's music . . .
>
> All I can say is that jazz came out of a very painful experience. It started with Black people being ripped away, and then innately trying to go back . . . They were denied so many things and were repressed. So the music came out of that. And that we [South Africans] were drawn to it, it just seems natural to me . . . Okay, we weren't ripped away from our continent, but our continent was ripped away from us. And that's why I say it's similar, but not the same. (Benjamin, New York, March 1990)

Defining what jazz in Cape Town in the 1950s was is different from defining jazz in the 1950s United States, for example. Perhaps the history of jazz in Cape Town might be thought of more along the lines of the early influences on African Americans who developed what we now call "jazz." These derive from the music of slave culture in the American South, work songs, religious songs, drumming, vaudeville and variety, combined with the urban blues, and the music that accompanied freed slaves migrating north and to the west in the USA. But there is a difference, because South Africans were clearly absorbing jazz recordings from several periods of early jazz history all at the same time. What that was depended on the availability of sound recordings in South Africa, but also on what was aired on the radio, and what music accompanied films in local theaters. They were combining these sounds with the rich palette of musical sounds important to them locally. So from the Cape Town perspective, there is a different sense of how "jazz" is defined as a category of performance, and indeed, of its history. From the late 1950s and early 1960s, some of that history necessarily has to be written from outside South Africa's geographical borders, because many of the most important musicians playing South African jazz were actually doing so a long way from their original community. This was the music of those who went into cultural and political exile. These differences can be heard to some extent in Sathima's music, though most of the music available for study is the music she recorded some time after leaving South Africa, and a long time after the breakup of the vibrant jazz community of the late 1950s and early 1960s.

Conclusion

To conclude this discussion of Cape Jazz, postwar popular culture, and Sathima Bea Benjamin's move to jazz singing, I return to an earlier reference to the contrast between Sathima Bea Benjamin's life trajectory and my own: though we both claimed Cape Town, South Africa as the city of our childhood experiences, and though it is a city that has profoundly shaped our sense of place in the world, our engagement with that city was fundamentally different. Sathima was born in the same year that my parents were, I was born in Cape Town a year after Sathima left for Europe. While there are many places we remember in common, racial difference fundamentally informed our knowledge and understanding of the world. I grew up in a working-class suburb called Mowbray, in the period after those classified "Coloured" had been moved from Mowbray to other parts of the city. Sathima's home, the one originally owned by her grandmother "Ma Benjamin" was in a more respectable suburb, but it was on the "wrong," i.e., the Coloured, side of the railroad tracks. Ultimately, it wouldn't matter because the family lost their home under the Group Areas Act. A few years ago, Sathima returned to Cape Town and went to find that home. She struggled to identify the exact house because though she knew the road so well, she didn't remember the exact number. Since her family had been turned away, the neighborhood had been "Chelseafied"—the houses had been remodeled according to a local style called "Chelsea" as Whites had moved in. There are many strange twists in the story of my scholarly relationship and personal friendship with Sathima.

It is perhaps fitting that Sathima, her husband, and children have spent almost all of their time in New York City living in the *Chelsea* Hotel. But there is more. Through quite contrasting personal decisions, Sathima and I ended up in New York City in the late 1980s, both of us a long, long way from our sense of home in the grand old Mother City of Cape Town. For Sathima, New York is a vast urban space she has come to know and love because of the memories she has etched upon its landscape. One significant portion of these memories embodies the musical relationship she had, and has continued to nurture imaginatively, with American jazz great, Duke Ellington. My own knowledge and love for the city has similarly been marked by the many conversations I have had with Sathima, and the rare, but always remarkable, performances by Sathima that I have witnessed there. We have both subsequently returned to South Africa on numerous occasions, each of us pulling out our very distant recollections of a bygone era, united in our travel by our common love for jazz, particularly in its South African inflection.

Keywords for Chapters 10–12

African Jazz and Variety a traveling show produced from 1952 by White impresario Alfred Herbert using Black and Coloured musicians performing African-inspired jazz and variety

Afrikaans language that emerged out of colonial encounter in South Africa, largely derived from Dutch, first written in Arabic by Cape muslim clerics

Asian in the apartheid structure in South Africa, Asian largely referred to people from India and Japan; the Chinese came as laborers and intermarried with those called "Coloured."

bioscope the colloquial name for movie theater

Cape Coloured those defined as of "mixed" race

Coloured Jazz and Variety similar to African Jazz and Variety, but focused on traditions coming out of Cape Town's working-class Coloured communities

Dollar Brand/Abdullah Ibrahim's Jazz Epistles and **Chris McGregor's Blue Notes** two of the most important jazz bands performing in the Cape in the late 1950s and early 1960s, both left South Africa to explore the European and even, in the case of Dollar Brand, the American jazz scenes in the 1960s.

ghoema drum performance by slaves from Indonesia and Malaysia in eighteenth and nineteenth-century Cape Town, spawned *ghommaliedjes*, songs with a mixture of Dutch and Malay origins, sung in the Cape

Khoisan short for Khoikhoi or Khoisan, the indigenous people of South Africa

langarm literally translates from Afrikaans to English as "long arm" referencing a particular style of ballroom dancing, akin to the tango. One of the most enduring groups playing this music is the Philadelphia Rhythms in Cape Town. Sathima has a couple of tracks on *Cape Town Love* (1999) that remind her of the old dance tunes she heard and danced to in her childhood.

ramkie small three- or four-stringed guitar, usually plucked; developed by Khoikhoi people in the eighteenth century

townships places close to major urban areas where Black South Africans established living quarters

township jazz refers to both a musical style—the popular, lighter forms of African jazz commonly performed in South Africa's Black townships in the postwar era—and to the late 1950s show created by a White South African, performed by Black South Africans, featuring the transformed sounds of American music to suit local taste

Second Case Study: Shembe Hymns

CHAPTER 13
Mission Hymns and the Founding of the Shembe Community

The focus of discussion on the Shembe hymn repertory is the coastal city of Durban. It is thought that in 1497 Portuguese sea explorer Vasco da Gama made a stop in what is now the port city; it became home to the first British settlers as early as 1685. It did not really begin to develop until the arrival of British settlers Henry Fynn and Frances Farewell in 1824 when they established a trading post in the area. Indian indentured laborers and free passengers came to the region in 1860 and Mahatma Gandhi arrived in 1893. The first missionaries made their base in Natal in 1838. Europeans were in constant engagement with a series of Zulu chiefs north of the Tugela River. Shaka is perhaps the most famous of all.

The 3,200,000 residents of Durban represent all of the world's major religions and a plethora of local spiritual communities. I remember so clearly one Sunday morning in Durban in July 1995, when I had taken a group of overseas visitors to the all-night *isicathamiya* choir competition held in the Beatrice Street YMCA hall. At sunrise, while the competition was in full swing, we left the building and ventured down to the ocean. Though July is mid-winter in South Africa, even at this time of day we found a surprising array of people at the waterfront: Indian fishermen, usually Hindus or Christians; White surfers who may connect to a 1970s charismatic Christian group called the Invisible Church; men and women out jogging who participate in the more conventional Christian, Muslim, or Jewish practices, or perhaps belong to such independent churches as the more evangelical Christian Olive Tree or the modern, global, Hindu-derived Sai Baba communities. A busload of visitors from Johannesburg who traveled for the weekend to participate in a regional *makwaya* (choral) competition by singing the religious works of Handel or Bach had come to the beach to fill bottles with seawater to take home with them and use for ritual purification.

Figure 13.1 Zionist followers baptized in the Indian Ocean, early Sunday morning, July 1995, Durban, taken by G. C. E. Oosthuizen and used with permission.

A handful of men and women stood on the soft sand at the edge of the water, clothed in long robes of blue, yellow, green, or pure white. All of these Zulu-speakers were engaged in the practice of baptism by immersion in the powerful waters of the Indian Ocean. Those in robes of deep blues, yellows, and greens were Zionists; those in white gowns or ***imiNazaretha*** came from ***ibandla lamaNazaretha***, the Church of the Nazarites/Nazaretha—followers of the charismatic prophet **Isaiah Shembe** and his descendants.

On that Sunday in July 1995, we ate breakfast at one of the outdoor restaurants on the beach, then rode by car to **Ebuhleni**, the headquarters of *ibandla lamaNazaretha*, to spend the day witnessing the final ritual events of the July Festival. These included celebrating the dead at the Shembe cemetery, a daily morning service, baptisms in the nearby river, group proposals of marriage and marriage ceremonies, and the sacred dance festival called ***umgido.***

The focus of this chapter is the sacred song and dance repertory of *ibandla lamaNazaretha*. Founded by Isaiah Shembe in about 1911, *ibandla lamaNazaretha* began as a small community, predominantly of women and girls who had been miraculously healed, physically and emotionally, by the spiritual powers of this charismatic prophet. In the early twenty-first century, Shembe's community includes congregations dispersed throughout South Africa and the countries on its borders—Swaziland, Zimbabwe, and Botswana. It claims a rapidly growing membership numbering about one million. Though there are many remarkable dimensions to *ibandla lamaNazaretha*, we focus here on the repertory of spiritual songs composed by Isaiah Shembe and his son Johannes Galilee between 1913

Figure 13.2 Mvangeli Magubane (in green evangelist gown) stands in front of the administrative office where members purchase the hymnal and maps of the holy mountain of Nhlangakaze (both seen behind), as well as marriage and baptismal certificates. Ebuhleni, September 1996, taken by Carol Muller.

and 1940. These songs were written down and later published in an official hymnal called ***IziHlabelelo ZamaNazaretha*** (Shembe 1940). The songs themselves are performed in at least four contexts: in congregational worship (*inkhonzo*), to accompany sacred dance in church festivals (*umgido*), in less formal gatherings of church members and families, and in more **gospel-music**-style settings such as televised performances, on cassettes, CDs, and in world music festivals.

Music and dance occupy a central place in Nazarite belief. A new style of sacred singing and dancing was given to Isaiah Shembe as part of his calling by the ancestors to preach to and heal Zulu traditionalists, and Shembe's authority as a spiritual leader was reinforced by his musical gift. This repertory of religious song is unusual for its time in South African history because it is not merely translations of Christian mission hymns, but rather newly composed poetic forms and texts. The words have spoken directly to the experiences of millions of Black South Africans through the course of the twentieth century. Isaiah Shembe also insisted on dance as an integral dimension of collective ritual practice from as early as the 1920s. This was a radical move because in the early twentieth century, Christian missionaries had forbidden all forms of dance in religious

Figure 13.3 Procession of Shembe members on the annual pilgrimage to the Holy Mountain of Nhlangakaze, January 1992, taken by Carol Muller.

ritual. *Ibandla lamaNazaretha* was one of the first religious communities to reinstate dance.

In this chapter, I examine the hymn repertory, its composition, performance, commodification, translation, and transformation. This discussion focuses on the musical examples on the accompanying CD, drawn from my own field recordings, and related materials on commercially available recordings.

Finding *Ibandla lamaNazaretha*

When I went to Ebuhleni, the Shembe headquarters, in 1991 to do field work for my dissertation, my field assistant, church member Samukelisiwe Nthini, advised me to purchase and wear *imiNazaretha*, the white prayer gown. This naturally led to the assumption that I, too, was a believer, and members often asked me how I knew about *ibandla lamaNazaretha*. Did Shembe appear to me in a dream? Although I was to have a few dreams of Shembe after I began working in the community, it was not a dream but an academic connection that opened up the world of Shembe to me.

Although I grew up in KwaZulu Natal, I had not heard of *ibandla lamaNazaretha* until I joined a class on Contextual Theology at Union Seminary in New York City in the fall of 1989. There I learned about the work of religious studies professor Pippin Oosthuizen, who had long been studying *ibandla lamaNazaretha* and other indigenous or independent church communities. In fact, Oosthuizen had written a controversial book

Figure 13.4 Young Shembe boys playing the Shembe bugles at a wedding celebration in Kwa Mashi, Durban, c. October 1995, taken by Carol Muller.

that examined the Shembe hymn texts as the source of Nazarite theology (1967). I was looking for a religious community in which women were a central part, and one that had its own song repertory.

I traveled to South Africa in December 1989 and made contact with Professor Oosthuizen, who invited me to go to the Nazarites' holy mountain, **Nhlangakaze** ("the big or great reed"), with him and a team of White filmmakers. We were to prepare for the trip by bringing along a thermos of coffee and sandwiches, because no cooking was allowed on the Sabbath. For our feet we brought a couple of pairs of thick socks. Nobody was permitted to wear shoes on the sacred site, even for the walk up the mountain, though White people were allowed to wear socks because their feet were considered soft from wearing shoes.

Nazarite members typically spend time during January on the holy mountain. Some come for the entire month, others for a weekend, or even a single day. While we and some members arrived in motor vehicles, a large group of followers had walked to the mountain from the Shembe headquarters at Ebuhleni over a period of three days at the beginning of January.

A single path runs up the side of the mountain. Lining the path are tents in which people sell goods required for the time on Nhlangakaze. These include perishable and nonperishable food items, dance attire, Zulu-language Bibles, the Shembe hymnbook, photographs of important moments in the life of the church and of the Shembe leadership, prayer gowns, and materials for constructing shelter. All members are required to

Figure 13.5 Unmarried female followers of Shembe prepare for the service that precedes the ritual cleansing of the graves of Shembe members by virgin girls, July 1991, Ekuphakameni, KwaZulu Natal, taken by Carol Muller.

ascend the mountain when they arrive. Typically, they do so in groups, all wearing the white *imiNazaretha* and singing softly as they go. The singing is slow, performed in a call and response format. The year I walked the pilgrimage we sang Hymn 173, *"Livuliwe lel-isango"* (open the gates) all the way. Nobody hurries, pushes, or shouts. One or two of the male leaders guide the members as they climb the rocky crags. Periodically, the group stops to kneel and pray, or to place flowers at particular spots along the way. About half-way up, an ***imbongi*** (praise singer) calls out the praises of Shembe.

Extract from "The Praises of Isaiah Shembe"

Composed by Imbongi Azariah Mthiyane (excerpts)
Recorded in Zulu and translated by Liz Gunner and Mafika Gwala (1991: 66–79)

He is awesome, He is awesome, Our Beautiful Kneeler-and-they-be-satisfied of **Ekuphakameni**
One who overflows with compassion, helper of those in danger.
Broad-shouldered one, never tired of bearing our sins.
Opener of the roads heading for home,
Plume disappearing over there on the mountain, Spring that refreshes the righteous
Hands that radiate like the sun,
Bateleur Eagle, hovering above our own place at Ekuphakameni,

Figure 13.6 Male leaders, three *abavangeli* (evangelists) with leopard-skin shoulder covers waiting between Sabbath services at Ebuhleni, February 1996, taken by Carol Muller.

> Scatterer of the fog and there is light,
> Restrainer of the multitudes—you would not leave them on their journey to Hell.
> Peacemaker with the bulls instead of leaving them to kill each other.

It takes at least a half-hour to reach the top of the mountain, a decidedly otherworldly place. This is where Isaiah Shembe received his calling in a dream to preach to and heal Zulu traditionalists. At the top of the mountain is a large plateau. When we arrived we were amazed to hear what sounded like the musical strains of an organ. A heavy, damp mist covered the area so our vision was limited, but as we moved closer, we could see my colleague Bongani Mthethwa seated at the organ, sounding out the melody and chords of one of the Shembe hymns. The instrument was powered with two large car batteries, its sound amplified by several mounted speakers. Some members were milling around, others were seated in front of the organ according to age, gender, and marital status. Church elders called *abavangeli* ("evangelists") sat on prayer mats on the ground with small baskets in front of them for collecting offerings made to Shembe. A young woman sat on the rock paging through the hymnal. I moved to an outcrop of rock nearby to absorb this dreamlike spectacle around me.

The next day, a Sunday, we returned to the mountaintop for *umgido*, the festival of sacred song and dance celebrated by *ibandla lamaNazaretha*. Below we could hear the young girls preparing to open the festival; they were blowing on the indigenous trumpets peculiar to *ibandla lamaNazaretha* and beating the large bass drums. An occasional

Figure 13.7 Shembe girls' procession with umbrellas to the temple, Paradis, in their special ritual attire. Ebuhleni, KwaZulu Natal, September 1991, taken by Carol Muller.

Figure 13.8 Shembe boys make an offering to their leader, Ebuhleni, July 1991, taken by Carol Muller.

bugle melody sounded out amid the powerful, though slow and deliberate, strands of singing that drifted up from the place where the young girls stood in long lines, ready to make the final ascent, this time to the rhythms of *isihlabelelo samaNazaretha*, a Nazaretha hymn. They would be followed by the men in animal skins and the young boys in either tartan skirts, rugby socks, black boots, and a white cotton headband or in black skirts, rugby socks, black boots, white shirts, and pith helmets. Then came the married women in dense layers of traditional and newly imagined dance regalia.

Each group of dancers sings its own hymn from the Shembe hymnal—although everything is sung from memory while the dance is taking place—accompanied with handclapping, dance rhythms, woodblocks, trumpets, bugles, and drums. Because several groups of dancers are spread along the mountaintop, the overall sense is of a wave of musical sounds, one part blurring into another. It is hard for the outsider to pick out specific words or melodies sung by individual groups. I recall being overwhelmed by a deep sense of calm.

These two experiences—the congregational service on the Sabbath and the sacred dance on the Sunday—made a deep impression on me that weekend in January 1990. I left knowing that field research with *ibandla lamaNazaretha* would be quite different from anything I had ever done before. It would not be easy—at the time I spoke little Zulu and there was not much English among Shembe followers—but it would open up new understandings of what it meant to be South African in the late twentieth century. I would gain deeper insights into the impact of mission Christianity on the peoples of KwaZulu Natal from the mid-nineteenth century, and the response of these people, not only as victims of the colonial encounter but also as people who wished to reshape their own music and beliefs on their own terms. About a year later, I returned to South Africa to begin my research with the followers of third leader, Amos Shembe (younger son of Isaiah and brother of second leader, Johannes Galilee) at Ebuhleni, the current headquarters of the Nazarite religious community previously housed at Ekuphakameni.

Mission Culture

The history of Protestant mission work in South Africa dates to 1737, when Georg Schmidt, a Moravian, opened a mission in the Cape, then returned to the Netherlands in 1742. There followed a fifty-year hiatus in mission work. In 1792, three Moravian missionaries started a new mission in the Cape, building on a nucleus formed around Schmidt's cook, Magdalena, who had continued to teach reading and writing to small groups of converts after Schmidt's departure.

In the following years, missionaries arrived from England, the Netherlands, Scotland, France, and the United States; by the late 1820s, there was a veritable army of Protestant missionaries in the Cape and the interior. Early missions failed, in part, because the Bible and hymns were not available in local languages. The new missionaries turned their attention to producing such translations, creating written forms of vernacular languages, compiling dictionaries, and translating the Bible and the hymnbook.

Throughout Africa, these missionaries established missionary villages—missionary-controlled communities of African people, which had in common the goals of evangelizing, educating, and civilizing Africans. "Civilizing" amounted to little more than Europeanizing

Africans. Replacing traditional music and dance with the European hymn in four-part harmony was a central dimension of the civilizing mission in this period.

Though the number who converted to mission Christianity in the eighteenth and nineteenth centuries was relatively small, the impact of the mission village and its enterprises should not be underestimated. When African converts and their families left the mission villages, they often took a portion of the culture with them, in the form of a vernacular translation of one of the books of the Bible or a hymnal, and quite quickly a new Christian village headed by a local leader would emerge close by.

In Southern African mission work, singing was the most effective method of attracting the attention of those targeted for conversion. Reports from the mission field suggest it was the hymn, more than the sermon, that attracted potential converts. So an important strategy for African mission evangelists was to enter a kraal or homestead in song. With the strands of melody they easily attracted a crowd to whom they would proceed to teach the words and tune. Soon people all over a village would begin to hum and whistle phrases of the hymns.

This did not necessarily mean that everyone understood the meaning of the words, even if they were translated into the vernacular, because quite often the translations were poor. Missionaries failed to recognize that a single word in a tonal language like Zulu or **Xhosa** might have several contradictory meanings depending on its intonation—what kind of tonal motion the speaker produces with each syllable—and the images and metaphors embedded in hymn poetry were quite alien to local experience and poetics. For example, the style of rhyming line endings common to the Protestant hymn was completely foreign to local poetic practices, though it was a common strategy used in translation, transforming texts that were considered poetic in a European language into hideous strains in the vernacular.

Few foreign missionaries grasped the importance, however, of translating more than just the words of their hymns into the vernacular. Christianity has flourished in South Africa in places like *ibandla lamaNazaretha*, the Zionist churches, and the women's *manyanos* ("prayer unions"), where it has rooted itself in local forms. Song, dance, drumming, and a sense of rhythm have been key elements in such transplantation. For the most part, African leaders initiated these processes rather than their European mission counterparts. Put simply, translations of the mission hymn demonstrated a lack of sensitivity to the linguistic and cultural dimensions of African song performance—a failure to understand the value of song and the place of the human voice and oral transmission in indigenous belief systems. Oral transmission relies not only on words but equally on the transfer of cultural values.

The emphasis on orally transmitted messages, on the power of human utterance over readable texts, was key to the success of revivalist styles of prayer, preaching, and hymn singing among largely uneducated African women (Gaitskell 1990). From the 1880s European and American missionary wives in South Africa began organizing weekly afternoon and monthly all-night gatherings for African women. Historian Deborah Gaitskell describes these as "unstructured times of shared testimony, the exposition of biblical verses, and extemporary prayer" (Gaitskell 1990). The thousands of Black South African women who were members of these organizations were regularly involved in preaching, praying, and caring for the sick and needy. The appeal of praying and preaching in the all-night meeting was clearly connected to the lively oral traditions in which African women had been nurtured from birth. In the *manyano*, women extemporized on their own beliefs and experiences. They knew the Bible and hymns—not through reading but through hearing and memorizing what they had been taught by others. Speaking from the heart was highly valued in these religious organizations.

In a manner similar to the nineteenth-century women's *manyano*, contemporary African Zionist worship draws on indigenous modes of singing, dancing, and drumming in re-Africanizing Christianity for largely non-literate or partially literate members. Two anthropologists have written about Zionist singing in South Africa. Research by James Kiernan examines ways in which Zionist songs structure ritual enactment among Zulu-speaking Zionists. John Blacking worked with Venda Zionists in Soweto and the more rural areas of the Northern Province in the 1950s and 1960s.

A handful of African mission converts, of varying relationships to the nineteenth-century mission villages in the Cape, are significant for the hymns they composed in the vernacular. By far the most important is Xhosa-speaking prophet, poet, composer, orator, and dancer Ntsikana Gaba, who died in 1821. Trained as a traditional warrior and royal councilor, Ntsikana had a visionary experience in which what he called a "thing" inside, the voice of Nyengana (that is, the teachings of the early Dutch missionary Van Der Kemp) was calling him to selectively reject aspects of Xhosa tradition, such as polygamy, and smearing the body with ochre, and to selectively incorporate aspects of mission Christianity into his own brand of African spirituality. The Xhosa-speaking prophet rejected the culturally specific elements of European Christianity but accepted the tenets of biblical Christianity. He refused to accept baptism, though he remained with Eastern Cape mission villages and encouraged his rather small group of followers to stay close to these institutions and not return to traditional ways after his death.

This first Xhosa prophet has a clear place in South African religious and musical history because four of the hymns he composed have survived in oral tradition among Xhosa-speaking converts. One of these, "*Ulo Tixo Mkulu*" ("Thou Great God") was published in a Xhosa hymnal in 1876. The most famous of the four, however, is Ntsikana's "Bell," the chant that Ntsikana recited at dawn each day, to call his followers to prayer. The melodies of these hymns, while arranged in the mission structure of four parts (soprano, alto, tenor, bass, or SATB), use the parallel movement of voices derived from Xhosa practices. Ntsikana's hymns also have distinctively Xhosa-sounding melodies. All this suggests that they incorporated elements of both mission and Xhosa musical cultures. Because of this blending, and indeed, of the importance of Ntsikana in Xhosa history as a religious leader who Africanized mission Christianity for his followers, these hymns occupy a central place in Xhosa religious practice, and indeed, in South African music history. A century later, Isaiah Shembe would follow the lead of Ntsikana by re-Africanizing mission Christianity and its ritual practices for Zulu-speaking peoples.[1]

African Religious Independentism

Many of the missions' early converts had connections to the tribal elite. As a result, traditional culture was intertwined with Christian tenets; the countryside was presented as good and wholesome and the city as destabilizing. The conversion experience was, however, not without its discomforts. Christian convert James Matiwane testified in 1881: "We have given up Native dancing, and attend tea meetings, and the like. We have no social gatherings except weddings and such like. The boys and girls have no games; the boys do play at marbles sometimes" (quoted in Hughes 1990: 205). Isaiah Shembe would address these concerns.

In the latter part of the nineteenth century the discovery of diamonds and gold in the area around what is now Johannesburg resulted in the imposition by the colonial government of rigid poll and hut taxation, as well as a harsh system of labor migration. These developments—combined with the racism and colonial attitudes in mission churches and the society at large, the persistence of African spiritual beliefs and of the place of the ancestors in the Christianity practiced by converts, the contested place of polygamy in mission theology, and the central place of health and healing in African spirituality—ignited a significant movement toward religious independence among African Christians. With the translation of the Bible into the principal South African languages of North and South Sotho, Zulu, and Xhosa, African prophets could move away from the control of the mission. Historians of religion have identified two main streams of African religious independentism in this period: **Ethiopianism** and **Zionism**.

Ethiopianism

The exact historical roots of the term "Ethiopianism" as applied to African independent churches in the late nineteenth century are not certain. "Ethiopia" was long used by Europeans to refer to any part of Black Africa; it is mentioned on several occasions in the Bible, and blackface minstrels called themselves "Ethiopian delineators." For Ethiopian Christians, Ethiopia was itself the relocation of Zion. Ethiopianism constituted an early form of African/Black consciousness in South Africa.

In 1892 Mangena Moroke, a Black South African minister in the Wesleyan Church, resigned from that institution over the issue of racial segregation. He formed a new church he called the Ethiopian Church, marking a decisive moment in South African mission history. While others had seceded from mission churches prior to Moroke, his move was a truly enduring one, and it sparked similar moves among African Christians elsewhere, always in protest against mission control and racial discrimination. A short time after forming his church, Moroke fostered an alliance between his community and the African Methodist Episcopal (AME) Church in the United States, the first independent African American church in the United States, though he did not achieve the independence from the US church that he desired for his community.

Ethiopianism signaled for Black South Africans that mission Christianity did not require complete Europeanization; one might convert to biblical Christianity without losing one's cultural identity. The early nineteenth-century figure of Ntsikana was a key symbol of the Ethiopianist movement in South Africa. Many Ethiopianists joined together in 1909 to form the Ntsikana Memorial Association, a cultural, rather than religious, organization that constituted a starting point for the formation of what later became the African National Congress. Out of this movement came the Enoch Sontonga composition, "Nkosi Sikelel'iAfrika" ("God Bless Africa"), adopted as the anthem of the African National Congress in 1925 and now a central part of the South African national anthem.

Text of "Nkosi Sikelel'iAfrika"

(prior to becoming part of South Africa's National Anthem in the 1990s).
Taken from http://www.worship.co.za/sa/nkosi.asp

Zulu	
Nkosi sikelel'iAfrika,	Lord bless Africa
Maluphakanyisw'udumo lwayo;	May her horn be raised
Yizwa imithandazo yethu,	Hear our prayer, Lord
Nkosi sikelela	Lord bless us
Thina lusapho lwayo.	Us your children.
Chorus:	
Woza moya,	Come, spirit
(*Sikelela, Nkosi sikelela*)	(Bless us, Lord, bless us)
Woza Moya oyiNgcwele;	Come Holy Spirit
Usisikelele, thina lusapho lakhe.	Lord bless us, we your children.
Sotho	
Morena boloka Sechaba se heso,	Lord we ask you to protect our nation
U felise lintwa le matsoenyeho	Intervene and end all conflict
U se boloke (2x)	Protect us
Sechaba sa heso. (2x)	Protect our nation.

Zionism

Zionism provided an alternative model of secession, with its roots more clearly located in mission history. A small group of Protestants in South Africa began to connect through the name "Zion," and all identified with faith healing, baptism in a metaphorical Jordan River or the ocean, and with the Pentecostal gift of speaking in tongues. Zionism's beginnings might be traced to an Afrikaner, P. L. le Roux, who worked as a missionary among the Zulu. Le Roux named his chapel the Zions Kerk ("Church of Zion") because they sang *Zions Liedere* ("Hymns of Zion") inspired by the Moravians. Zionism resonated powerfully with African traditional beliefs, so much so that it was easy to forget its European links once it broke away from its center. Zionist hymn singing takes the mission hymn and Africanizes its performance practice.

Isaiah Shembe's religious belief and practice has been variously defined as Ethiopianist, because the texts and performance of his hymns reflect African experience and musical values; as Zionist, because of his healing and other charismatic practices; and as prophetic. He does not fit neatly into any of these categories. Tshabalala (1983), for example, argues for his strong ties to the Wesleyan mission; in my reading of Ranger's accounts of Protestant missions in Zimbabwe (1994), I see elements from all of the missions in Shembe's community. Without doubt, *ibandla lamaNazaretha* was, and remains, an eclectic form of religious community, one derived from Zulu traditional belief but also denying many of its tenets. *Ibandla lamaNazaretha* is a religious grouping that took

Figure 13.9 Married women members march to the beat of the drum to make an offering to Shembe, Ebuhleni, August 1991, taken by Carol Muller.

Figure 13.10 Shembe male follower sitting on his prayer mat in the Paradis temple at Ebuhleni with his Shembe hymnal and Zulu Bible, waiting for the service, Ebuhleni, August 1991, taken by Carol Muller.

the texts of mission Christianity but rejected the messengers and the cultural baggage they brought from faraway places.

Zulu Zionists

Accompanied with drumming, reinforcing rhythmic over melodic qualities, Zulu Zionist singing regularly flows from song to handclapping to body swaying and even to dance, writes anthropologist James Kiernan (1990). Each Zionist community has its own repertory of hymns, though many are drawn from the American Board Mission hymnal and are supplemented with Wesleyan and Episcopal items. The value of hymn singing in Zionist communities is to be found in the ways in which these songs are used in church services. Hymn singing is never planned into the structure of a Zionist service beforehand. Instead, hymns are spontaneously inserted at various points during the service. Kiernan identifies four such moments and the role they play. First, they provide a structure for the meeting—hymns begin and end a gathering and create continuity in a meeting as members move from one item to the next. Second, hymns operate as signature tunes—people begin their contributions to a service by intoning their favorite hymn. Third, hymns are interpolated into a service to forge an opening, if a speaker goes on too long or is tedious. Finally, hymns accompany faith healing.

Venda Zionists

John Blacking's perspective is a contrasting view on Zionist hymn singing based on his work amongst the Venda in the 1950s and 1960s. Blacking's central argument about Venda Zionism is that while Zionists have often been viewed by social scientists as apolitical and cut off from political engagement in South Africa, their worship signifies politically, not in the words as much as in the style of song performance (Blacking 1997). Venda Zionists use both the Psalms and European hymns translated into the vernacular, but their performance practices are quite distinct. Hymns adhere to a verse-refrain format modeled on the European hymn, while the Psalms operate in a more traditional call and response frame with drumming accompaniment. Zionists, Blacking observes, did not sing hymns in the European way; nor were the Psalms sung in a traditional manner. Hymns were sung slowly, allowing individuals to "catch" the Holy Spirit and explore the musical materials in a creative way, while the Psalms were sung at a livelier tempo.

Blacking summarizes the essential characteristics of Venda Zionist singing as follows: it is sung in call and response format, typically in a slow tempo but occasionally increasing speed and incorporating handclapping; the general pitch of a melody rises in a song; melodies are ornamented, slurred, and varied to increase emotional intensity; a thick harmonic texture is created with voices singing in parallel, and making distinctive tonal shifts; and finally, while call and response is the overall form, pieces of a verse can be presented in overlapping, hocket-like phrases; there are no pauses or rests—the stream of sound is thick and constant. Although the start of a hymn might be hesitant as members tune in to its text and tune, once everyone is singing, individuals are free to "let go" with a variety of pitch treatments, including glissandi, ornamentation, slurs, and so

Figure 13.11 Woman member drums the rhythm of *ukusina* at the Ama 14s' all-night meeting, KwaMashu F Section, November 1991, taken by Carol Muller.

forth. Increased emotional intensity is reflected in a faster tempo of performance as a hymn performance progresses (Blacking 1998).

There are significant overlaps in performance practice between what Blacking describes here and the singing of *izihlabelelo zamaNazaretha*. The crucial difference, however, is that the songs of Shembe combine the poetry of the Psalms with the influence of, in particular, Wesleyan hymnody to create a single repertory of song. Blacking's argument that it is the style of performance and not the words of the songs that articulate an Africanist world-view, and thus a political sensibility, works for Venda Zionists. But for followers of Shembe the hymns articulate a political consciousness in both word and performance practice.

Hymn 173 composed by Isaiah Shembe

1. Let us in,
That we may worship Jehovah.
We were prevented,
The gates are now open.

2 Let him in.
Wo! Here is the Zulu [nation],
The descendants of Dingaan
And Senzangakhona.

3 Who opened it,
This gate?
Oh, Liberator of the prisoners.

Hymn 116 composed by Isaiah Shembe

1. You are being called King Solomon,
Child of Dinizulu.
Behold the glory of Jehovah
Is at Ekuphakameni.

2. Come, all you Zulus,
You are being called to Ekuphakameni.
The glory of Jehovah
Is at Ekuphakameni.

3. Come, all you Bhacas,
Come, all you Pondos,
The glory of Jehovah
Is at Ekuphakameni.

4. Come, all you nations,
You are being called to Ekuphakameni.
The glory of Jehovah
Is at Ekuphakameni.

5. You are being called King Solomon,
Child of Dinizulu.
The glory of Jehovah
Is at Ekuphakameni.

Isaiah Shembe's Early Life

Born in about 1870, Isaiah Shembe lived through some of the most tumultuous times for Zulu-speaking people in the late nineteenth and early twentieth century. This included the Anglo-Zulu War of 1879, the annexation of Zululand by the British, the ruthless crushing of the Bambatha Rebellion by the British in 1906, the movement of South Africans away from British control in 1910, and the passage of the Land Act in 1913, which took land from Black South Africans for White purposes. At the time, the region was also riddled with disease and drought, and it had been powerfully transformed by the discovery of gold and diamonds in South Africa from the late 1870s, an event that thrust South Africa into an industrial revolution and rapid modernization. This process forced many Black South Africans into what became one of the harshest structures of migrant labor worldwide, a system that had severe ramifications for people in the South African countryside, many of whom became followers of Shembe. After the Bambatha Rebellion (also

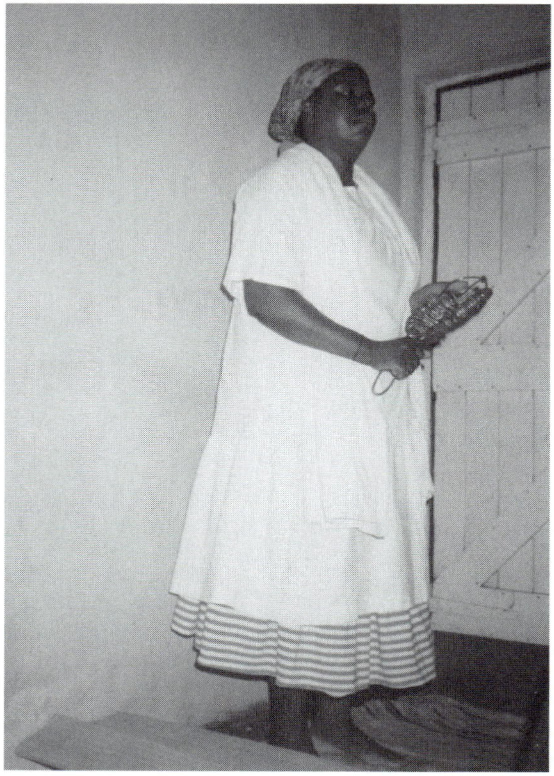

Figure 13.12 Woman shakes the bells to add to the rhythm of the dance, KwaMashu August 1991, taken by Carol Muller.

known as the Zulu Rebellion), Isaiah is reported to have sworn to "revive the bones" of those killed. One member recalls that after being burned by lightning, Shembe was instructed by Jehovah to go to the East, that is, to KwaZulu Natal:

> There are my suffering people. Go and liberate them from their slavery. These people have naked/bare hips. When you will come to them, tell them that they should worship me, their God, the *Mvelingqangi* of their forefathers and the God of their fathers, and that they should take the vow of the Nazarites . . . (Quoted in Hexham and Oosthuizen 1996: vol. 1, 21)

Deeply disturbed by the fragmented position of his people in KwaZulu Natal, Isaiah Shembe was called by the voice of God to go to the mountain called Nhlangakaze in KwaZulu Natal. There are several versions of this founding moment of *ibandla lamaNazaretha*. All accounts agree that while on the mountain, Isaiah Shembe had a vision in which he saw heaven itself. One version suggests that in this vision there were men wearing skins and singing songs without notation. A member, Ms. Mazibuko, told me the story, saying that the songs Shembe heard these old men singing were songs without notes;

Figure 13.13 Mrs. Nthini (at left) claps to the rhythm of the dance, KwaMashu August 1991, taken by Carol Muller.

they were the songs of friends (in other words, not of mission origin), and they were sung by men dressed in what would become Nazarite men's dance attire: the skins of wild animals. The version recounted by the late church activist Petros M. Dhlomo corroborates Ms. Mazibuko's account. Take note of the appeal to the senses of smell, sight, hearing—the stress upon the human body as the mediating vessel of spiritual experience in this excerpt:

> After all these events, he heard a joyful sound of beautiful singing; a mighty clamor arose from the East and came with an awe-inspiring light to him. Shembe rejoiced in his heart, the trees and the rocks shouted for joy, and the grass joined in their cries of happiness. Then Shembe was convinced in his heart: "There comes the real bridegroom, for whom I have been waiting here on the mountain Nhlangakaze." Then Jehovah appeared; he was surrounded by the heavenly hosts and by the saints, who were clad in white robes and had bound golden belts over their chests. Shembe smelled a sweet scent, which made even his bones and the roots of his hair rejoice. It was like a large crowd of people. When they appeared, the grass stubbles shouted: "Holy!" Then the one who had called him from his home country came to him riding on white clouds, which came from the north; [streaks of] lightning flashed over him, crossing one another, and he heard a mighty thundering in the sky. (In Hexham and Oosthuizen 1996: vol. 1, 80)

Figure 13.14 Shembe Youth Choir performs at Amos Shembe's funeral, October 1995, at Ebuhleni, taken by Carol Muller.

All the accounts concur that in this twelve-day sojourn on the mountain Shembe was instructed to preach and to baptize all people. On the last day Jehovah made a covenant for people of African descent in the region: heaven became a space in which African peoples and their cultures were fully incorporated.

Isaiah Shembe's Mission and the Founding of Ekuphakameni

Isaiah Shembe began a mission of travel, moving along the coastline of KwaZulu Natal and the Eastern Cape and eventually into what was Zululand, the area north of the Tugela River north of Durban. In his traveling mode, the prophet's method of drawing people to his community was similar to that of the Christian missionaries. Scholar of African literature Liz Gunner explains:

> While traveling and evangelizing, Shembe and his little group of young men and women would, on approaching a homestead, begin by beating the large round drum used by many Zionists, and they would sing the hymns that Shembe himself had composed. Often the girls would lead the group in, dancing the steps which Isaiah had taught them or which they had devised themselves. Often Shembe would visit the homestead of a chief or headman and hope to extend his influence if he were able to convert a figure of authority. If he did obtain the nucleus of a following he would sometimes leave a woman in charge, a deaconess (*umkhokheli*),

Figure 13.15 A Shembe member and her friend with ice-creams. Ebuhleni, September 1996, taken by Carol Muller.

> and visit again or send an evangelist. Shembe in some ways was able to adapt and use elements of Zulu dance and spectacle to give his own followers a distinctive way of "dancing to the Lord" which could be seen and felt as representing a new, dance-centered expression of African Christianity. He created visual symbols and expressive forms of dance and song that were distinct from the old forms yet related to them, and retained their symbolic power as cultural expressions. (Gunner 1991: 100–101).

Shembe purchased a piece of land in Inanda and called it Ekuphakameni, the elevated place. While it became a kind of mission village it borrowed ideas from the layout of the Zulu royal residence, with separate living quarters for men, women, young girls, and young boys. A school, store, and several sacred buildings were constructed on the site. Space was allocated for both the cultivation of gardens and women's traditional production, including basket and mat weaving. Shembe charged a small rental for anyone wishing to live within the boundaries of his village; all had to abide by a strict code of conduct while there (Roberts 1936). The large majority of his early followers were women. Several years after establishing this village, a colonial official estimated that there were about 400 followers at Ekuphakameni, 90 percent of whom were women and young girls. There was a significant group of single women, left destitute by the dire conditions in KwaZulu Natal, who had no real survival alternatives other than joining Shembe's community. Part of the appeal of the community was the kind of self-sufficiency it

Figure 13.16 Married women with beaded design on their hats. These women are from the southern part of KwaZulu Natal (the cylindrical shape of the hat indicates their place of origin). Women from the northern part of the province wear hats that flare outwards; some of these can be seen in figure 14.12. Photo: Carol Muller.

required of women; part was the stress on ritual performances and sacred dance, with participants all outfitted in festival attire.

Shembe purchased numerous tracts of land and established small temples throughout KwaZulu Natal, the Eastern Cape, what is now Gauteng (the Johannesburg–Pretoria area), Swaziland, and Zimbabwe. He sanctified the landscape with biblical names for his communities—Thesalonika, Judia, Betlehema, Nazareth, Eden, Galilee, and Jordan. Other communities—Bekemesiah, Gospel, eLinde—were named to memorialize Nazarite spiritual history. None of these names appear on official maps; they are known only to those who are members or otherwise connected to *ibandla lamaNazaretha.*

The Bible in *ibandla lamaNazaretha*

The Bible, rather than mission Christianity, was Shembe's source of knowledge about Christianity. The Wesleyan missionaries and their congregations probably introduced him to the Zulu-language Bible. Since he was not raised in the mission culture, he would have read the text without the cultural baggage and theological traditions of the European institutions. Shembe's reading was rather literal, particularly in terms of Old Testament law, which became central to the theological foundation of *ibandla lamaNazaretha*: Sabbath (Saturday) worship is central. Members are required to remove their shoes when on Nazarite ground and to abstain from eating pork and leavened bread, and from having sexual relations. He also noted that the Old Testament vindicated pre-colonial

African practices, including polygamy and animal husbandry, and he recognized how the suffering of the Israelites paralleled the struggles of African peoples against colonial rule and dispossession. For Shembe, the Old Testament authorized pre-colonial African practices, and the New Testament, with its stories of miraculous and dreamlike events, provided models for managing the magic of modernity, embodied in new forms of technology and the mastery of these technologies by Europeans. For example, Shembe himself came to be known as a healer, and a miracle worker, often intervening in extraordinary ways. There are stories about how he enabled his members to purchase land, houses, to keep safe on their daily train rides when there was an upsurge in violence on trains in the 1980s; he also healed women of infertility, and so forth.

Shembe utilized the power he gained from his deep knowledge of the Bible—he could reportedly cite biblical references by chapter and verse to confound and ambush angry missionaries with the tools of their own power. One such story goes as follows:

> On another day he was accused by the pastors (or mission churches) in court. Shembe asked the magistrate to enquire from his accusers whether they would agree that the case be judged according to the Bible. They agreed to this request. Then Shembe asked the pastors through the mouth of the magistrate whether they had studied the Bible. This question of Shembe made them very angry. But in the end they agreed that they had studied the Bible. Shembe asked them to read John 4:37–38. [It reads as follows: "Thus the saying, 'One sows and another reaps' is true. I sent you to reap what you have not worked for. Others have done the hard work and you have reaped the benefits of their labor."] .
>
> When this passage was read, Shembe explained: "We Shembe people follow this way. We enter the work which has been started by others in order to perfect it." The magistrate said: "Go out, Shembe, and preach: but do not enter their place" (Hexham and Oosthuizen 1996: vol. 1, 70).

Other stories are told of similar cases brought against Shembe by jealous missionaries, but each time the judge clears Shembe, ordering him not to enter the territory of the missions. In one account, a White man was sent to kill Shembe for his conflicting interests with the goals of the mission, but the man was overcome by the spiritual power of the Zulu-speaking prophet and let him go. These narratives suggest that there was a clear contest between followers of Shembe and the missions over the terms of spiritual power in the region. Hundreds of narratives exist in the Nazarite archive (now housed at the University of Zululand) about Shembe's power to heal, to provide in times of destitution, and to effect miraculous transformations in all kinds of otherwise impossible situations. Particularly in the earlier history of *ibandla lamaNazaretha*, these narratives are paralleled with the models of action members read about in the Zulu Bible. Shembe's power is thereby authorized and legitimated using the measures of mission Christianity.

CHAPTER 14
Shembe Hymns

IziHlabelelo ZamaNazaretha

Hymn 124/2

Ngohlabelela ngenthokozo	I shall sing with joy
Emzini oyincwele;	In the holy place;
Bajubule abahlangabezi bani	My heavenly escorts will be jubilant
Ngokungena kwami.	With my entrance.

Hymn 54/1

Sitshele ngezwi lakho	Tell us about your word/voice
Nalo masilizwe;	Let us all hear it;
Lingene enhliziyiweni zethu	May it penetrate our hearts
Lisithokozise.	And delight us.

Paradis is the name of the open-air temple at Ebuhleni, the current church headquarters of the followers of Shembe. It is located several miles inside Inanda, just north of the center of the city of Durban. As you turn off the N3 freeway running from north to south along the Indian Ocean coastline, the terrain changes from the borders of some of the most expensive real estate in the region to large sprawling housing, ranging from shacks built out of corrugated iron, plastic sheets, and logs of wood, to more solid structures of cinder block or even brick. People live so close to each other, you can almost hear the conversations of your neighbors in the house behind or on the side of your house. And there are hundreds of outdoor washing lines—ropes strung from one pole to the next with the day's laundry hanging out to dry in the bright sunshine. When you turn left off the main road through Inanda toward Ebuhleni, the landscape becomes less densely populated. The road is rougher and dust hangs in the air.

Figure 14.1 A woman sells goods on the side of the road at Ebuhleni: these include vaseline petroleum jelly and sunlight soap, both important for purification purposes, September 1996. Photo by Carol Muller.

Up the steep slope the taxis and buses scramble, drawing closer to the sacred site of *ibandla lamaNazaretha*, to the gates of Ebuhleni, and eventually to Paradis itself. When you arrive at the gate, you get out of the vehicle, remove your shoes, pull the white *imi-Nazaretha* prayer gown over your body, and proceed into the space allocated by the local chief for the followers of Shembe. As you make your way up the road toward Paradis, you pass between two rows of storefronts. Members are selling food, soap, ice cream, chicken pieces, Bibles, hymnbooks, Vaseline petroleum jelly, bottles of clean water, photographs of Shembe, cassettes and CD recordings of Shembe hymns and sermons. As you approach Paradis you pass by the statue of the Founder, Isaiah Shembe (died 1935). You walk toward the grove of trees surrounded by rocks painted white. If you are a man you enter at the place for men; a married woman, you kneel as you go in through the place assigned for women; and a virgin girl, you find the other young girls with white shawls covering their heads and shoulders who kneel as they enter into Paradis. You find your place and spread the Shembe prayer mat out on the ground. You spread your legs out straight in front of you, and open your hymnbook.

Figure 14.2 Shembe member sells ice-cream cones out of her cooler at Ebuhleni, September 1996. Photo by Carol Muller

If you arrive around 9 in the morning, or on a Saturday around 1 in the afternoon, you will hear the singing of *ibandla lamaNazaretha*. On occasion it is accompanied on an electronic keyboard or car-battery-powered organ; when there is sacred dance, the long trumpets unique to this community sound out a couple of pitches a fourth or fifth apart, and there are the large indigenous drums pounding out the duple meter of the feet of the dance. But it is the singing that begins to move one. At first it seems so far removed from what we might expect from Black South Africans—it is slow, thick textures of human voices, playing with pitch, rhythmic phrases, and text. Each member listens to what those around are singing, most have memorized the words of the songs, and they are free to elaborate in their own ways on the words and melodies of the hymns of Shembe. This is the style of singing known as *izihlabelelo kwakwaShembe*—a Zulu phrase meaning the sacred songs of the place of Shembe.

In the Zulu language, the word *izwi* translates as both word and voice. This is significant because it speaks of the priority given to the human voice in both pre-colonial Zulu belief and its continuity in Nazarite theology. While Shembe displayed deep knowledge of the Bible, it is clear that the word as voice supersedes the mission priority of the word as written. This is amply demonstrated in *izihlabelelo zamaNazaretha*, the repertory of hymns he composed. The Zulu word *isihlabelelo* may be translated in several ways. The noun *isihlabelelo* may refer to a "hymn" though the more conventional translation references the Psalms of David found in the Old Testament; it may mean the repertory of songs that mothers compose for their children, which are sung at significant moments in the life of a child, such as puberty and marriage. At a more abstract level, the word connotes the idea of an individual, personal voice. The Psalms convey the strongest sense of the individual voice in the Bible, the voice of praise and struggle, of anguish and jubilation. It is a voice quite different from that of most other Old Testament books, which provide spiritual histories and accounts of the battles of the Israelites collectively rather than individually.

To more fully illustrate Nazarite beliefs about the place and power of song in the lives of *ibandla lamaNazaretha*, I have selected three types of narratives told in the community. While the focus of the narratives is not song itself, but the extraordinary power of Shembe, song is used as a vehicle of spiritual power and transformation. It emerges from the mouth of Shembe, and of birds, and even the stars because ultimately Nazarite song invokes ancestral presence. The verb *hlabelela* refers to the singing of birds (that is, high-pitched sounds), or of people in chorus or recitation (Doke et al. 1990). Birds suggest ancestral presence, because in their capacity to fly they mediate between those in heaven and those on the earth. A similar case can be made for sacred dance, as discussed at the end of this chapter.

The first type of narrative tells of Isaiah Shembe's ability to raise the dead to life. Liz Gunner (1990) collected two such stories, both concerning the resurrection of dead children. The first is excerpted from a sermon preached by a woman named Ma Ciya.

> When the child had been wrapped around, he said, "I will bear it again. I will give birth to it a second time." He counted the months, just as it is for a woman who is pregnant. He said the first month, and then the second. He counted the months speaking, murmuring, singing the hymn (No. 71), which says:
>
> My Lord you loved me
> Before the mountains were firm
> In ancient times you anointed me
> I am the beginning of your journey.
>
> When he had finished counting the ninth month, he opened his larynx. He said, "Today I am giving birth to that child anew." The child began to cry and it cried like the young of a sheep. As it was crying like that Shembe said, "Hey, the child of a human doesn't cry like that!" He said, "Cry like the child of a human." (Gunner 1990)

The second version is an excerpt from a sermon preached by Shembe himself on December 21, 1929:

> On the fifth night as the mother sleeps, stars appear shining round the child. A voice says, "Where is that child's death?" Another voice answers, "It has been drunk by his mother." The stars sing, they shine on the top of his head and a great star shines with particular brightness. The stars then become birds, they fly around him, bring him back to life, and then these heavenly beings disappear. (Gunner 1990)

Figure 14.3 Shembe woman gets married at home in KwaMashu, surrounded by gifts wrapped in woven grass mats, 1995, taken by Carol Muller.

Figure 14.4 Shembe women attend marriage at home of KwaMashu bride, 1995, taken by Carol Muller.

Nazarites also recall Shembe's power as a healer. Soweto member Ms. Mazibuko told of how Shembe healed her own mother from a series of miscarriages. Shembe's promise to give Mazibuko's mother children was embodied in the birdsong that her father heard while he prayed for the safe birth of his child.

Mazibuko recalled:

> So my father says when he was praying under those trees, he used to hear the watucal, the snake. Not the snake. Now, the bird. It was singing. When my father prays the bird says, "Twiree, twiree, twiree." When my father stops praying, the bird stops. Every day when my father prays. Now my mother was pregnant. When my mother went to hospital, my father went to pray again under the tree, calling Shembe. "Now my wife is in hospital. [S]he is going to have the baby. I pray you please to be with my wife. That she must deliver that child, give birth to it right away. I don't want the child to die anymore." Then the bird was singing there with my father. After my mother got the baby, when my father went to pray, the bird was no more there. It was finished now because now it means that Shembe is send[ing] the bird there to be with my father. (Quoted in Muller 1999: 102)

Finally, there are stories told in *ibandla lamaNazaretha* of the overwhelming power of Shembe's own singing voice. In 1918, he was traveling toward the mountain of Nhlangakazi. He stopped along the way to stay in the homestead of the family of a young boy, Ephraim Fulela. Fulela recalls the experiences as follows:

> I went to my mother and asked: "Who is this man there in the hut?" She said, "Shembe." There I saw him for the first time. At 1:00 p.m. a man came out and called for a prayer meeting. All went out for the devotions to the place outside the village where the chief used to hear court cases . . . the entire family of the chief went there.
>
> One of Shembe's companions read the liturgy from the book. Then Shembe rose and started to sing, not having said a word. His singing swept all the people away from the place; only the [two] men remained there. [The people] escaped into the forest. Shembe pointed with his hand to them and all those who had escaped fell down. Then he proceeded with the service.
>
> When he was speaking, a haze emanated from his mouth and shed light on the whole Nyuswa country, it was brighter than the sun. When he had ended his talk, this light returned to him, and only the sun was shining over the country. I thought that all people must have seen this light, but it was seen by me alone. At that time I was too young to join this church. (Quoted in Hexham and Oosthuizen 1996: vol. 2, 84)

There are numerous such reports of Shembe's use of song in a range of situations. For the Nazarites, as for the Zionists, the singing voice summons spiritual power for healing, for raising the dead, in baptism, when in conflict with mission communities, in dreams predicting death, for dancing, to cast out demons, to elicit spiritual power in battles to purchase land, and to reinforce Old Testament law, especially regarding the Sabbath. Song in dream spaces signaled the presence of heavenly beings dressed in white robes,

Figure 14.5 Beadwork on hat of married woman, KwaMashu, 1995, taken by Carol Muller.

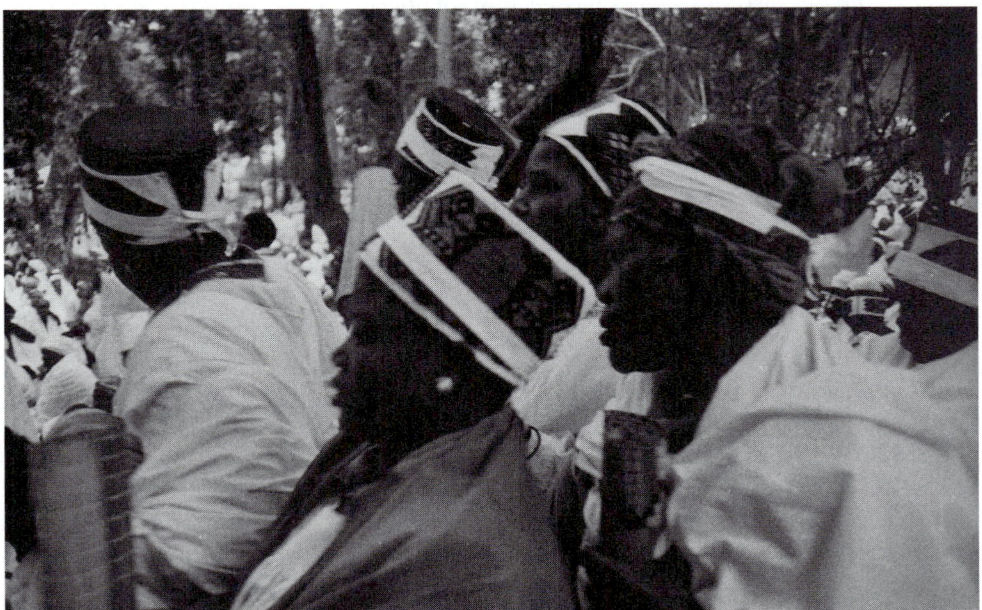

Figure 14.6 Married women waiting for the inauguration of fourth leader Rev. Vimbeni Shembe, at Gospel, December 2005, taken by Carol Muller.

and it offered protection, much as the white robes worn daily by Nazarite members are believed to guard the body against danger.

Composing *IziHlabelelo*

While Shembe's hymn repertory has a direct historical connection to the hymn as defined by the European and American mission in KwaZulu Natal, the way in which song composition is described is quite different from the contemporary European practice. European composition is based on writing; in Shembe's narrative, the body is the site of creation. Prior to composing his own songs, Shembe relied on the hymn repertory of the Wesleyans for ritual purposes. Wesleyan hymnody is recognized as being the inspiration for several hymns in the Nazarite repertory.

The first Nazarite spiritual song, or hymn, came to Isaiah in 1910, when he arrived in KwaZulu Natal. He received the second hymn in 1913, on the holy mountain of Nhlangakaze. It was not until 1920, however, that he began to compose Nazarite hymns prolifically. Shembe began having compositional song visions once he was more settled at Ekuphakameni; he composed the bulk of his songs between 1920 and 1935, the year he died. Shembe gave three more hymns to women after his death. The remaining hymns were composed by Galilee Shembe between 1936 and 1976, the year he died.

The human voice as the compositional vessel, rather than writing, is central in Shembe's compositional process. According to Galilee, Isaiah Shembe received many of his spiritual songs while walking along paths in KwaZulu Natal, and frequently they came to him in visions. Sundkler records Galilee's recollections of how his father composed (or received) new songs.

> [Isaiah] would hear a woman's voice, often a girl's voice singing new and unexpected words. He could not see her, but as he woke up from a dream or walked along the path in Zululand, meditating, he heard that small voice, that clear voice, which gave him a new hymn. He had to write down the new words, while humming and singing the tune, which was born with the words. With Is[aiah] Shembe it was the rhythm that moved in him even while he was sleeping; it was the rhythm that first came to the surface and had to be caught and written down. This rhythm expressed itself in two or three words to be sung to the accompaniment of the beat of drums, and the feet of the dancing faithful. He found the chorus, and he built the hymn on this foundation. Waking up from his sleep, he still carried within him the rhythm of what he had heard in the dream dimension of life. (Galilee Shembe quoted in Sundkler 1961: 186–187)

There are three elements in this description that I suggest are critical to the composition and performance of *izihlabelelo zamaNazaretha*, and that set them apart from what Sundkler calls the "hymn-carpentry" of the Christian mission: the relationship between words and rhythm; the human body, rather than writing, as the compositional medium; and the female voice as the vessel of transmission.

The female voice in song composition underscores the central position that young virgin girls occupy in *ibandla lamaNazaretha*, a position paralleled in pre-colonial Zulu

Figure 14.7 The installation of fourth leader Rev. Vimbeni Shembe, Gospel, southern KwaZulu Natal, December 1995, taken by Carol Muller.

Figure 14.8 Installation of Rev. Vimbeni Shembe, December 1995. These are the married women who attended the ceremony. Photo: Carol Muller.

Figure 14.9 Nazarite virgin with flowers at the installation of fourth leader, Rev. Vimbeni Shembe. Gospel, December 1995, taken by Carol Muller.

communities (Muller 1999: chs. 2, 3, and 6). They have a special relationship, in myth and ritual, to the church founder. The articulation of the voice heard inside Shembe as female resurfaces in a comment made in one of the narratives about the sound of Isaiah Shembe's own voice at the time of his baptism by Pastor Lushigah of the African Baptist church on July 22, 1906:

> After a time it became evident that this man (Shembe) did not stand by himself but that Jehova was with him. When they asked him to lead the service, he intoned the hymn of the Wesleyans . . . Shembe was singing with a very fine voice, even a girl would not have been able to sing like him." (Khaya Ndelu cited in Hexham and Oosthuizen 1996: vol. 2, 32)

It is the voice like that of a girl that signals the extraordinary spiritual powers of the prophet. This point ties to the earlier definition of *isihlabelelo* as the songs a mother sings to her children. Metaphorically, Isaiah takes the voice of a woman, a mother, and sings to his/her spiritual children.

Figure 14.10 Shembe members walk towards the site where Rev. Vimbeni Shembe is to be installed as fourth leader of *ibandla lamaNazaretha* in December 1995, taken by Carol Muller.

There is one hymn in the hymnbook, Hymn 92, where Isaiah writes in the voice of a young girl. In English translation it reads, "I will dance the sacred dance with hope/I am a Nazarite maiden/I shall fear nothing/Because I am perfect (a virgin) . . ." While other Zulu-language composers claim that song composition occurs through the medium of dreams and visions (see Ballantine 1999, Muller 1999), only Shembe hears these messages through the medium of a female voice, pointing once again to the special relationship Shembe had with his female membership.

Initially, the words and rhythms of these hymn visions were written down either by Shembe or an assistant. In time, his followers copied the written texts into their own books, which included hymns, miracle stories, prayers, sermons, and letters from Shembe. When Shembe's son Johannes Galilee assumed leadership, he had these texts written into a single book. Galilee himself had several compositional visions, and these songs were included in the published hymnal. University educated, the younger Shembe clearly understood the power and value of the book in European culture and the importance of having African literature available in the vernacular. W. H. Shepherd printed the first version of the Nazarite hymnbook in Durban in 1940. That volume included 220 hymns; the more recent publication contains 242 hymns. Along with the Zulu translation of the Bible, *Izihlabelelo ZamaNazaretha* created a new set of practices and cultural truths outside of mission control. The hymnbook in particular constituted an innovative and more culturally coherent set of theological texts for people of African descent in twentieth-century KwaZulu Natal than the mission was ever able to provide.

The images of song composition created in Galilee Shembe's dreams and visions differ

Figure 14.11 Mvangeli Magubane at the installation of Rev. Vimbeni Shembe, December 1995, taken by Carol Muller.

markedly from those of his father. The images in Galilee's dreams/visions corresponded to his experience as a teacher: they came as words on a chalkboard. More recently, controversial Nazarite songwriter and arranger Nathoya Mbatha has a vision of song composition that has shifted even further (see Muller 1999: ch. 5, for further discussion):

> When I am dreaming, or when I am just sleeping, it happens that I see myself in front of people, singing and all that . . . When I wake up, I wake up and go to a keyboard or an organ or a tape if it's necessary, and tape what I have seen . . . In the dream, it happens that I am with the choir, or I'm alone, sometimes in the forest or bush, seeing myself singing and a lot of people who are seated down . . . They are just an audience. (Mbatha quoted in Muller 1999: 134)

A century after Isaiah Shembe's experiences, Mbatha's vision is clearly modeled on a gospel-style performance, not connected to the world of the ancestors but emerging from the social space in which he longs to perform: on a stage in front of an audience. Here the young man is alone but he is dreaming of gospel performance stardom.

Figure 14.12 Married women singing at Rev. Vimbeni Shembe's installation as fourth leader of *ibandla lamaNazaretha*, December 2005. The woman with the glasses in the right corner just off center is Ntombemhlope Mthethwa, wife of (now deceased) organist Bongani Mthethwa. Photo: Carol Muller.

Nazarite Ritual

There are two frames in which *izihlabelelo* are habitually performed in *ibandla lamaNazaretha*. Isaiah Shembe and his son Galilee conceived of religious worship in both the European congregational format (***inkhonzo***) of the Protestant church, with the book as the primary ritual object, and as African-derived sacred dance, with the body as the vessel of spiritual power. The way in which the hymns are performed in these two environments reflects these different modalities. In *inkhonzo* they are performed in the context of fixed liturgy read from a book. In sacred dance festivals or ***umgido*** the hymns are sung from memory. There is no visible presence of the book in this context.

I will qualify this distinction, however. Though on the one hand *inkhonzo* might seem to be a purely European invention borrowed by Isaiah and Galilee Shembe, Mthethwa (n.d.) argues that *ukukhonza* (to worship) was not uncommon in pre-colonial Zulu culture. This was the mode of interaction between a local king or paramount chief and his subjects. Those visiting the king/chief would sit quietly around the man while he exchanged words with the visitors. There would often be a pot of beer available and each person, including the king, would take a sip from the pot. The practice was equated with basking in the sun—the sun was the king, and the people basked in his presence. It was a practice that easily transferred into the mission structure of worship where members were expected to sit quietly while the minister preached. On the other hand, dance is an integral dimension of worship in the Psalm texts of the Old Testament. Once again, Zulu cultural memory is reinforced with the example and exhortations of the mission Bible.

Inkhonzo—congregational worship

In Paradis, the open-air temple at Ebuhleni, services are held every morning at 9 a.m., and in the evening at 6 p.m. The word *ekuphakameni* means "elevated place" or "place of spiritual upliftment" and "heaven." Each time you come to Ebuhleni (the temporary site of Ekuphakameni) you enter the metaphorical gates, at which the Angel of the Lord stands, and walk to Paradis for the daily or Sabbath services. Once you are sitting inside the boundaries of Paradis you have the sense of being in a remarkably serene and exquisitely beautiful place. Trees form a canopy over the area; you hear the birds singing in an otherwise silent environment; and all inside inhabit a space of respect for each other and adoration of their leader. The sweet voices of the birds signal ancestral presence. Adorned in white prayer gowns, the *ibandla lamaNazaretha* community resembles the image of heaven Isaiah Shembe saw in his dreams and visions.

Members begin to gather at about 8:30 a.m. Clad in the white *imiNazaretha*, the young girls come with their heads draped in long white shawls, married women with the traditional top-knot adorned with Nazarite beadwork. Men typically wear bands of furry animal skin around their heads. All come bearing a handmade prayer mat, a Shembe hymnbook, and a Zulu Bible, both books often wrapped in a towel.

These services convey a deep sense of reverence. An aura of peace quite unusual in the larger political context permeates the scene. At about ten minutes to the hour, the bell rings. All members, wherever they are, kneel down in silent prayer when they hear the bell's first ringing. After the final ringing, everyone knows to gather their goods and to enter into Paradis through openings determined by gender and marital status. Within a periphery of white-painted stones, members sit in a circle around Shembe, men and boys on one side, virgin girls on the other, and married women and unmarried mothers seated directly opposite. Senior members of the community, including *abamshumayeli*, *abavangeli*, and *abakhokheli* (ministers, evangelists, and women leaders), take their places in the inner circle. The organ, introduced by third leader Amos Shembe into congregational worship in the late 1980s, sounds out through amplifiers attached to trees. It is situated at the boundary between the place for men and women, directly in front of Shembe. At 9 a.m. one of the male leaders begins the liturgy for the Morning Prayer.

Morning Prayer

In this excerpt (CD track 16) you hear three kinds of vocalization: the liturgy read by the leader, the responses of the congregation as recitation, and stanzas of the hymn sung for the Morning Prayer. The congregation hums together at the end, and goes into a time of collective prayer. The evangelist ends the prayer with "*Ameni*."

The Morning Prayer was written out by Isaiah Shembe but printed by his son, Galilee, when the hymnal was first published in 1940. In the early years of the church, the services were conducted according to the practices of the Wesleyan Separatist Church that Isaiah had attended. It opened with prayer by a lay preacher, followed by a hymn, and a Bible pas-

Figure 14.13 Carol Muller stands at the "gate" to Ebuhleni (though there was no fence at the time), which marks the entrance to the holy site and church headquarters of *ibandla lamaNazaretha.* Ebuhleni, September 1996. Photo by Carol Muller.

sage read by a second preacher. Another hymn was sung, and then the minister preached his sermon. The structure of the liturgy in later years presented divergences from this early pattern, with the solo voice of the leader dominant, interspersed with single stanzas of the Morning Hymn and collectively recited passages interspersed in the liturgy.

The text of the early part of the liturgy is based on the words of Psalm 23, the Shepherd's Psalm, but rewritten to speak to the needs of the local community. Liturgical portions are numbered. The recorded excerpt is transcribed in Appendix 5. Translation by Bongani Mthethwa with Carol Muller.

Nazarite Hymns as Written Texts

Considering that the Zionists, *manyano* women, and *ibandla lamaNazaretha* are all religious communities whose constituency is largely illiterate or only partially literate, it is perhaps surprising that books, reading, and published liturgy occupy such a central place in Nazarite daily and Sabbath ritual. From reading the text of the Morning Prayer

Figure 14.14 Funeral service of third leader, Rev. Amos Shembe. Members crowd around the statue of church founder Rev. Isaiah Shembe at Ebuhleni, the church headquarters, October 1995, taken by Carol Muller.

and hearing the audio example it should be evident that *Izihlabelelo ZamaNazaretha*, the hymnal of *ibandla lamaNazaretha*, is the key ritual object at this service. You may also have realized that this book is not read in quite the same way by Nazarites as it might be by those immersed in a culture of literacy. What you see by reading is not what you get in performance. If you look at the book without reading or understanding its Zulu texts, the Nazarite hymnal strongly resembles the format of standard Protestant hymn and prayer books—each hymn is divided into several stanzas of standard length and number of lines, and some have several stanzas with a repeating refrain. *Izihlabelelo*, however, are very rarely performed straight through, without seemingly endless cycles of repetition. It is in this repetition that the most sacred musical quality, a sense of rhythm, is articulated. As Oosthuizen (1967: 154–155) argued in his book on the Shembe hymns, "rhythm and word go together . . . the turning over and over of one idea in a sermon [or a hymn] is the rhythm of repetition."

The hymnbook contains more than just the songs. It opens with a photographic image of Isaiah Shembe. This photographic image, the representation of the founder, was believed by many followers in the early years to have the capacity to heal in the absence of the founder, who died before the hymnbook was published. Such interpretation of the photographic image of Shembe in the hymnal is much like his appearances in the dreams of members, that is, the seemingly magical experiences of new technologies are conflated with the equally extraordinary occurrences in which one's ancestors or Shembe himself appears in a dream.

Figure 14.15 Many videographers and photographers capture the moment of Amos Shembe's funeral and Nelson Mandela's presence at Ebuhleni, October 1995. Photo by Carol Muller.

The photograph of Shembe is followed by an index of hymn titles and three liturgical texts: the first for the Morning Prayers, the second for the Evening Prayers, and the third and most substantial for the Sabbath Prayers. As you heard on the recorded example, a male leader reads the liturgy in the congregational worship, with brief spoken responses from the congregation scattered throughout; all sing together the individual stanzas of hymns for each liturgical piece interspersed in the text; and finally the congregation sings the fragments of song as a whole at the end of the liturgical reading. It is important to take note of the distinct differences in the mode of performance in each kind of vocal utterance. The main body of the liturgy is read as printed without repetition, while the hymn stanzas are sung with the greatest number of repetitions. Here a single line of text can be repeated for several minutes in multiple versions, which seems to signal the power of song in Nazarite spirituality. For it is through singing, not through the rapidly read liturgy, that each individual voice finds its own place in the larger ritual fabric. It is through song that members utter the inspired words of Shembe, and they do so with the most sacred of musical principles, a densely layered, overlapping, slow tempo, repeating rhythm. The words embody the rhythms; rhythm conveys the numinous and non-material force of Nazarite spirituality (Oosthuizen 1967).

The texts themselves speak of a complex process of cultural and religious negotiation. I have already written about the way in which Isaiah Shembe named and sanctified the landscape with names derived from the Old and New Testaments. Not only does Shembe sanctify the landscape with names from the Bible, but in the hymn texts he reconfigures biblical narrative to coalesce with local experiences. This was revealed in his sermons but is most poignantly demonstrated in the words of *izihlabelelo*. Three examples illustrate how this negotiation is revealed in the *izihlabelelo* texts. In the first set of texts, Shembe uses a biblical text that is localized by the style of performance in some instances, or in both the style and text in other cases.

Hymn 152

1. Jerusalema, Betlehema *Izazi zisitshelile* *Umsindisi uselezelwe* *Ebetlehema eBetlehema.*	1. Jerusalem, Bethlehem The wisemen have told us The Savior has been born In Bethlehem, in Bethlehem.

Hymn 58

1. Baba wethu osezulwini *Ngisebusweni bakho,* *Aliphathwe ngobuNgcwele* *Lelogama lakho.* Chorus: *Umoya wakho mawuze Nkosi* *Ubaphilise abantu bakho.*	1. Our Father who is in heaven I stand before you, May your name be holy That name of yours. Let your spirit come, Lord, And heal your people.

Hymn 80

1. Nkosi kuyisisusa sakho *Ukwakhiwa komuzi wase Ntanda;* *Namhla sesiyabonga* *Ebusweni bakho.*	1. Lord it is through your will The Village of Ntanda was built; Today we give thanks In your presence.
2. Nawe Betlehema Juda *Muzi omncinyane,* *Bongake kanye nathi,* *Ngokwakhiwa kwakho.*	2. Even you, Bethlehem of Judah, The smallest village; Give thanks with us, Because you have been built.
5. Yebo Betlehema Juda *Muzi wakakhosazana,* *Mawuhlobe ngeziqhamo* *Umsinele uJehova.*	5. Yes, Bethlehem of Judah, Village of the maidens, Be adorned with blossoms, And dance for Jehovah.

The second text illustrates the way in which the style of the biblical Psalms has been absorbed into the Nazarite hymn. Compare, for example, Psalm 106 with Hymn 60:

Hymn 60	*Psalm 106*
1. Give thanks to Jehovah Because he is righteous His mercy is everlasting, Because he is righteous.	1. Give thanks to the Lord for he is good; his love endures forever.

Figure 14.16 Shembe member purchases the poster of the holy mountain of Nhlangakaze, updated with the four heads of *ibandla lamaNazaretha*: founder Isaiah; successor Galilee; third leader Amos; and his son, Vimbeni. Ebuhleni, September 1996. Photo by Carol Muller

The third example introduces the political and economic struggles of African peoples into Nazarite theology:

Hymn 79

3. Phakamisa amasango akho *Singene sidumise,* *Kade wawusimemeza* *Uthi asizodumisa.*	3. Lift up your gates That we may enter and praise, You have long been calling us Saying we must come and praise.
4. Phakamisa amasango akho *Wozanini zizwe nonke,* *Nize kudumisa uJehova* *Amzini wase Mthwalume.*	4. Lift up your gates! Come, all nations, Come and praise Jehovah At the village of Mthwalume.

Figure 14.17 Two married women followers of Shembe, the woman on the left has her white *imiNazaretha* prayer gown and the white *inansook* (prayer shawl) covering her body. She is also wearing a photographic image of Shembe on a chain around her neck. Both women wear the characteristic beadwork that covers their hats. The shape of the hats indicates both women come from south of the Tugela River, i.e., the Natal part of KwaZulu Natal. September 1996, Ebuhleni. Photo by Carol Muller.

Hymn 120

1. South Africa vuka	1. South Africa, wake up!
Zokhele izikhuni zakho	Rekindle your fire logs
Zisondele zonke izizwe	So that all the nations may come closer
Ziwothe umlilo.	To warm themselves at your fire.

Inkhonzo Song Style

Several months after I began my field research in *ibandla lamaNazaretha*, I was called to the office of church secretary Petros Dhlomo. He wanted to know how the work was proceeding. To test my assurance that all was well, he asked me to sing the melody of one or two of the more popular Nazarite hymns. I remember the panic that set in, not because I was unable to memorize a tune, but because I had been sitting amongst the virgin girls in temple worship and had never heard a single melody sung by those around me. The problem was not that there was no melody; it was that from my position in the temple, none of those whom I had captured on my tape recorder were singing a melody. Instead, they freely sang a range of "responses" to the call of the male song leader, who sang the melody but was seated in front of the male church members at some distance from where the young girls were located. I sang the melody as best I could, but it was difficult, because there was no one else to sing with me, to pick up parts of the melody and sing in a call and response pattern. Mr. Dhlomo smiled, he never asked me to sing along in front of him again!

Typically, during Nazaretha worship, the men sang the melody, and the women improvised in word and tune, around the lower male voices. This gendered division of musical labor is described by South African musicologist Percival Kirby in his discussion of one of the oldest melodies in *izihlabelelo* sung to Isaiah Shembe's text, "Lalela Zulu."

"Lalela Zulu," Hymn 183

1. Lalela Zulu *Lalela abantu bengiphethe* *Ngezwe lethu.*	1. Listen Zulu [nation] Listen, hear our people nagging me About our land.

The song was recorded by Hugh Tracey, founder of the International Library of African Music (South Africa), perhaps as early as 1939 but issued on the commercial label Gallotone (South Africa), in the Sound of Africa Series in 1948. Kirby comments:

> There is no doubt that in Shembe's hymn, "Lalela Zulu," we have authentic Zulu choral music such as the early pioneers in Natal must have heard. This hymn is of great interest, for its music dates back at least to the days of Chief Mpande (1840–1872).
>
> The main melody is pentatonic, as might be expected of **Nguni** music, and it is executed by baritone voices. But at times, deeper voices, which normally sing in parallel with the others, double the melody in the lower octave. The "embroideries" sung by the women are of a comparatively free nature. (Kirby 1968: 249–250)

From the way Kirby describes this recording, shaped at least in part by Tracey's placement of the microphones to stress the melody in the lower voices, one might easily conclude that the "melody" was the most important musical parameter and the women's voices were merely ornamental. But five decades later, my own research among and recordings of Nazarite women singing suggests an alternative interpretation. On one hand, a series of CDs and cassettes have been professionally recorded and sold in the commercial and Nazarite marketplaces in the last decade. For the most part, these embody the official sound of *izihlabelelo* along the lines of Tracey's recording, with a male leader who intones a melody and a relatively homogeneous choral response that overlaps with the line of the leader. On the other hand, the recordings I have made sitting amongst married women and unwed mothers in their all-night meetings, and amongst virgin girls in congregational (*inkhonzo*) contexts of hymn performance, provide a different perspective, suggesting that listeners' "readings" of a performance depend on where they are sitting in a service and what musical values they bring to the performance.

Nazarite Musical Examples

I have suggested that a basic distinction between the music of South Africa and the rest of the continent, particularly in the western part of Africa, is that complexity in traditional African music was expressed in the human voice in South Africa rather than in the drumming ensembles so common to West Africa. As you listen to the traditional style of *izihlabelelo* on tracks on the CD, think about what you consider the most outstanding musical characteristics of these performances. Look for **call and response**, **cyclicity**, **overlapping phrases**, **tempo**, **rhythm**, **melody**, **cross-rhythm**, **syllabic treatment of text**, **melodic contour**, **bass voices**, **counterpoint**, **pentatonic versus heptatonic scales**, **tone color**, **pitch treatment**, **and harmony**. (All these musical terms are defined at the end of this chapter.)

How do the voices interact? What kinds of repetition do you hear? How do singers treat intonation, rhythm, and the relationships between voices? Has the music been written as a guide to singing, or is it freely improvised?

Now listen to an excerpt of *isicathimaya* (track 1 or 2), identify the outstanding musical characteristics and compare the musical style of the male close-harmony groups with that of Isaiah Shembe's *izihlabelelo*.

In the traditional *izihlabelelo* style, the "embroideries" sung by the women, freely woven in and around the "main" melody-words-rhythms intoned by the leader, are the sum total of the musical texture. Without the more homogeneous response of the lower voices described by Kirby, the musical texture created by the voices of girls and women is constituted from layers and layers of individual voices, freely playing with the rhythm of words, breaking up poetic phrases, repeating syllables, inserting vocables. The tempo is slow, the text is spun out syllable by syllable, fragment by fragment, overlapping, breaking off, starting up again, sometimes newly improvised, at other times copied from another line. In this frame of singing, each individual voice matters, each utterance contributes to the overall fabric of the song. The resulting effect of the interaction of voices is what Nazarite members call the rhythm of *izihlabelelo*. No two performances of a song are ever the same; your memory of each performance depends on what voices you could hear from wherever you were seated.

The Nazarites claim that this "rhythm" is what distinguishes their performance of *izihlabelelo* from any other kind of hymn singing in South African mission churches. If you are familiar with the lining out practices in some parts of the United States, you will probably hear some musical similarities between those of the South and those from *ibandla lamaNazaretha*.

A typical mission hymn text would be sung straight through from beginning to end, with minimal repetition of words or music. In contrast, as has happened with African jazz (see West 2002 and Ballantine 1993), a Nazarite hymn is typically sung with far more improvisation from the church members and continually staggered entries through cycles of repetition. A member may take a fragment of the song text and improvise with the rhythm of the phrase, adding syllables, extending or contracting the phrase. There is also considerable overlapping of melodic material, resulting in an extremely dense musical texture. Members exercise enormous latitude in performance—far more so than we have become accustomed to, for example, in the *isicathamiya* choral performances of

Joseph Shabalala and Ladysmith Black Mambazo. (As we discussed in Chapter 4, they adhere to a strict, one-line-each, leader–chorus format and, generally speaking, only the leader is allowed to improvise.) The relative freedom of the female voice singing *izihlabelelo zamaNazaretha* works in stark contrast to the model of the civilizing mission, the European hymn. Poorly translated into vernacular languages, heedless of aesthetic sensibility, the mission hymn was ordered into four voices—soprano, alto, tenor, and bass—all required to move within a strictly controlled set of rules. Galilee Shembe chose not to have the hymns arranged in the mission model of four-part harmony when he codified the texts into book form, largely because that musical style is typically performed without any kind of body motion. According to Bongani Mthethwa (personal communication, 1991), there is a saying in *ibandla lamaNazaretha*: "*iculo elingasukumi lifile*," which means a song that does not "stand up" (that is, make you dance) is dead.

Umgido: Festivals of Sacred Dance

The central importance and power of *umgido*, the festivals of sacred dance, cannot be overestimated in *ibandla lamaNazaretha*. Shembe introduced these dance festivals into his community as early as the 1920s. It was a radical position for an indigenous religious group, because even then the mission position was to forbid all forms of traditional dance in religious contexts. But as Esther Roberts reminds us from her research with Shembe in the 1930s, dance was one of the factors that contributed to the rapid growth of Shembe's movement in KwaZulu Natal from its earliest days, and the "concluding days of the [July] festival are devoted almost entirely to dancing. The red-skirted girls and the [boys] in kilts and pleated skirts usually play a more prominent part than the others" (Roberts 1936: 106).

Now that you have listened to the CD tracks with the traditional style for singing *izihlabelelo*, you might be wondering just what exactly excites the Nazarites about singing in this style. The music is slow and repetitive, it seems to take a long time to get through the words, and to the outsider, it seems to lack a good, toe-tapping beat. It is quite hard to connect emotionally to this musical style. If you were to go to Ebuhleni or one of the other Nazarite temples and watch *umgido*, you might begin to think the same thing about the dance festivals. Once you have seen an hour of the dance, with each of the groups represented in their visually stunning dance attire, it all begins to look the same. This was the kind of comment I overheard made by one of the filmmakers when we were up on the holy mountain in January 1990. This sense one has of being a complete outsider, of simply feeling that you are unable to make any meaningful engagement with a music or dance repertory is not uncommon when you participate in the world of music as a global phenomenon. To use this sense of alienation from the repertory productively, however, you must reflect on the purpose of *izihlabelelo zamaNazaretha* and *umgido*. While the dancers are visually spectacular, the goal of the performance is not to create a visual and musical spectacle, but rather to have as many members as possible participate in the process of singing and dancing together. To thread your voice into the larger fabric of song, to move your body in the same rhythms as the man, woman, boy, or girl standing on both sides, in front and behind you, and to do it in a style and manner that is culturally consistent is where the true power of this repertory lies.

Figure 14.18 Married women dance toward Shembe with great joy, Ebuhleni, August 1991, taken by Carol Muller.

This idea resonates with John Blacking's discussion of Zionist singing as having a more African than European sensibility that I mentioned earlier. Both Zionist singing, drumming, and body movement, and Nazarite song, using the words of their own founder and not a far-off European or American composer, naming places that people know locally, and articulating these words and sounds through the body moving in sync with hundreds of other bodies, some known and others complete strangers, are radical gestures. But it is only significant to those who participate or who abide by similar sentiments. This sensibility is quite different from that of the popular music industry, which, in order to generate profits, has sought to find music with a common denominator and to reach the widest possible audience. In this commercial frame, the audience pays to have the performers move them emotionally, to perform aural and bodily tricks for them, and to be visually and aurally spectacular.

As cultural outsiders the closest we might come to engaging with the sounds of *ibandla lamaNazaretha* as performed for *inkhonzo* or *umgido* is to acquire some understanding of how the music and dance work and have meaning for their participants. For the Nazarites, dance is not just entertainment. It invokes the presence of the ancestors and its rhythm serves to unite the living with the dead. It is, in fact, a form of prayer. Oosthuizen claims in his 1967 work that

> dancing before the Lord and repetitive singing are expressions of worship indigenous to the Zulu and foreign to the European. The sacred rhythm wants to come to

> expression in sacred dance. This is the way contact is made with the supernatural world. The pure expression of numinous power is in rhythm, poetry, music, and movements in dance. (1967: 154–155)

At the beginning of this chapter I gave a partial description of *umgido* on the mountain of Nhlangakaze, focusing for the most part on the uniforms worn and musical instruments used to accompany the singing and dancing of *ibandla lamaNazaretha*. In this section, we will spend a little more time thinking about the idea of rhythm, and the process of collective dance itself. Here I draw on my research with Nazarite women. I was extremely fortunate to have Khethiwe Mthethwa, Bongani Mthethwa's daughter, explain to me the process for participating in *umgido* of the married women in the early 1990s.

> The leader starts to sing—and everyone follows the leader of the song. After about a minute, she [and others] form a line and start to dance—very slowly, until all are in unison. And they dance following the song. The others—those who aren't dancing—start to clap, taking the rhythm of those who are dancing. When they have the good rhythm for that song, when the drumbeater feels that those who are dancing and those who are clapping are in full unison, [s]he will take the cue and start to beat the drum, and have to pick up the right rhythm.
>
> After a very long time, maybe about ten minutes or so, again, the one who is blowing *izimbomvu* [long alpine horn-like instrument peculiar to *ibandla lamaNazaretha*] should blow it in a key that will be in harmony with the whole key used in the song.
>
> The people who are in control of the rhythm are the dancers, because those who are clapping look at the [dancers' feet]. And according to the way they are dancing, they clap. The drumbeater too, will look at the way they dance, and beat according to the way they dance. If there is a foot that is stronger, maybe the right foot is stronger than the left that [beat] should be heard in the drum. So the strong beat is heard in the drum, so the drumbeater should be in unity with the dancers. Everything is in rhythm.
>
> When the one who had started the song feels they've warmed up enough—the warm up is the repetition of the first two lines [of the hymn text] (that maybe about thirty minutes of the song), she'll change to the third and fourth lines of the song, which are faster and with more variations. When she changes, everything will be quiet. Everything breaks and they all listen to the changing.
>
> Everyone will sing from the start. Then those clapping come in according to the right rhythm, and the drumbeater follows, and the blower comes in, and everything is in unity again. But faster this time. When the dance is at its climax, there may be a trumpet blower coming in, blowing according to the rhythm. (Personal communication, December 1992)

This description shows *umgido* as a social and musical process. While there were many advantages to outsiders writing about African music, one of the problems was that quite often these outsiders only want to find out about the music and not about the music's connection to other dimensions of African art and life. In the last part of this section on *umgido* we discover a profound connection between the different expressive forms and spiritual practices embodied in *umgido* performance, particularly in its culmination in the pilgrimage to the holy mountain of Nhlangakaze. Walking to the mountain, singing, dancing, and the exquisite beadwork sewn together by Nazarite girls and women all combine conceptually and spiritually through the ideas of the path and the mountain.

Expressions of the Path

In Nazarite belief, walking to the mountain of Nhlangakaze earns one an imprint of the mountain on your feet. That imprint is recognized when you arrive at the gates of heaven. Those who have the mountain imprint, and their families, will be allowed to enter the gates of heaven; all others will be excluded.

Walking the path to the holy mountain is always accompanied by singing. Walking and singing are conceptually connected because both involve traversing a path. The path for physically walking is obvious, but the path for singing is perhaps not as clear. In Zulu, the word "melody" is translated as "the way/path of the words." There is no melody without a text; because Zulu is a tonal language, all melodies are determined by the words of the text.

Women dancing *umgido* map out the symbolic pathways to heaven in a physical manner. Their dance steps, for example, are made from slow, controlled movements in which the feet move in a left-right, left-right-right-left duple rhythm. This is a highly rhythmic pattern derived from regular left-right walking in everyday life. Furthermore, dance is a form of prayer, the way in which the living invoke and invite the presence of the ancestors.

In women's singing for *umgido*, such as Khethiwe Mthethwa describes above, a transcription of the melodic paths sung by the leader and the rest of the women suggests that, through the medium of song, women symbolically climb the holy mountain. As Khethiwe's description suggests, in the typical performance of song for *umgido*, the leader begins the song by setting out the pitch, content, and shape of the melody. The women respond to this initiative by finding their individual vocal places on the melodic path. One hears several points of entry for these voices. The shape of the leader's melody is created by starting in the lower pitches and ascending through a series of melodic intervals that decrease in size. Then she levels out, repeating pitches in the high range, exploring the timbral possibilities of a repeating pitch. The other women join her in this exploration. On a recording, the leader's voice is submerged with the voices of the others for a few minutes, then she enters strongly again. This time she creates a kind of mirror image of the path she followed in starting the song. Here she takes the women back down in pitch to the starting note, with increasingly larger intervals. They all return to the original starting pitch. All the voices and instruments except the drum are silent until the leader takes the next couplet of text and starts the process over again, following the same melodic pathway.

A similar image—of a vertical ascent, a plateau, and a vertical descent—is commonly featured in the beadwork women create for their dance attire, particularly that worn by married women on their traditional hats, which consist of the weaving together of dried grass and a woman's own hair. This beadwork is traditionally given by a husband to his wife after the birth of their first child; the birth of a child signals the blessing of the ancestors and the incorporation of the wife into the husband's ancestral lineage. Bon-

Figure 14.19 Beadwork on a married woman's hat; the design is frequently in the shape of the mountain. Ebuhleni, September 1996, taken by Carol Muller.

gani Mthethwa has written on the way in which this beadwork has been transformed in *ibandla lamaNazaretha* to signal a woman's spiritual relationship to Shembe rather than the romantic love of a man and woman. The colors signify particular spiritual qualities: white is purity, red is forgiveness. The outline of much of the women's beadwork is a kind of music writing that outlines the spiritual experience women have through song, another iteration of the sacred path.

Carefully examine the photographic image of the beadwork on the woman's hat. Then compare it with the transcription of musical pathways created by a song leader and her community. Both have the diagonal ascent, leveling out, and diagonal descent. This image is filled in with a polyphonic mix of visual and vocal color, pattern, and texture; the straight lines of white beadwork resemble the non-melodic instruments, the repetitive pulses of the drums, handclapping, and dancing feet; finally, there is the moment at the end of the textual couplet, in musical terms, a cadential moment, in which everything drops out except for the drumbeat. This moment of transition is signaled by the double strand of beads between the two mirror images of the beaded mountain that encircle the head of a woman. The musical transcription similarly repeats to complete the second couplet of a four-line stanza of text.

Recent Changes in *IziHlabelelo ZamaNazaretha*

In *ibandla lamaNazaretha*, spiritual and musical leadership are intertwined. Song is the vessel of spiritual power, so to be given new songs by the ancestors is a sign that an individual has been selected and blessed by the ancestors. Though Isaiah Shembe was best known outside his community for his abilities to heal the sick and to assist the needy, inside he is also warmly remembered for the song and dance repertory he bequeathed to his followers. His son Galilee left a much smaller body of songs but made his mark by compiling the Shembe repertory in a publishable book form. Amos Shembe, Galilee's brother, took the song repertory in a new direction: in the late 1980s he had Bongani Mthethwa introduce organ accompaniment into *inkhonzo* singing. This was not just because the organ is considered a church instrument; it was also an attempt to modernize the sounds of *izihlabelelo* in an effort to keep the next generation of Shembe youth interested in retaining their membership of *ibandla lamaNazaretha*.

To the outsider, bringing an organ into a church might not seem a particularly noteworthy event. But introducing a keyboard instrument with fixed pitch was a radical departure for the Nazarites. A note played on the organ always sounds the same, requiring everyone to tune to its pitch rather than finding the pitch that is comfortable for their voices. The organ clearly introduced a whole new way of performing *izihlabelelo zamaNazaretha* into the community. The new way of performing these treasured hymns caused enormous consternation among the older members of the community, and many did not approve of the aging leader's initiative.

Until Amos Shembe introduced the organ into congregational worship, freedom of voice, pitch, harmony, rhythm, and tonality were dependent on the vocal range and skill of each song leader for every new rendition of a hymn. While there was a song leader who intoned a call, the congregation freely responded, by listening to what was being sung around them. Without a fixed pitch reference point, members could explore the tone quality of a pitch, and it was easier to modulate upwards in the course of performance, gradually increasing the emotional intensity of the song. But with an organ and organist, the flexibility and freedom allowed to the individual voice was curtailed, though not completely destroyed.

Bongani Mthethwa explained that the community was not accustomed to singing with keyboard accompaniment, and the song leaders continued to lead and not to submit to the pitch provided by the organ. This problem was solved in two ways. To accommodate the practices of song leaders, who determined starting pitch, tonality, modulations, and tempo, the organ was fitted with a pitch adjuster. In addition, Amos Shembe instructed Bongani Mthethwa to form a choir of young people who would sit around the organ and lead the Nazarite congregation.

Changes to the Hymn Repertory (see CD tracks 18–22)

Below is an overview of CD tracks 18–22, which exemplify the changes that Shembe style has undergone in recent years.

1 Congregation singing with organ accompaniment.

2 Bongani Mthethwa and KwaMashu Temple Choir, piano accompaniment to SATB arrangement.

One of the consequences of the KwaMashu choir and the organ accompaniment, in addition to Amos's concern for keeping the children of Shembe members active in *ibandla lamaNazaretha* in the early 1990s, was the spawning of Nazareth Baptist Youth for Shembe choirs, performing the classic repertory and South African gospel-style religious songs.

3 KwaMashu Youth Choir gospel style.

This rendition was performed at the Blessing of Mshumayeli in KwaMashu in 1991.

Compare the gospel rendition, or even Bongani Mthethwa's Youth Choir arrangements with *izihlabelelo* for *umgido*. This is where the difficulty lies, in the rhythm itself. It is hard to imagine dancing *umgido* to gospel arrangements. Although the music may appeal more to the uninitiated listener, it is a far cry from the rhythm of the older style.

4 KwaMashu Youth Choir rehearsal of classic "*makwaya*."

This piece uses tonic sol-fa.

5 Youth choir rehearsal, singing in SATB style.

The choir learns to sing in fixed voices. The style is less personal, lacking possibilities for improvisational exploration. The bodies have become stiff, at least for the more formal Shembe hymns.

6 Nathoya Mbatha.

The "rhythm" of dance is gone: here is an individual performing with multi-track recording technology. He sings alone, makes his money alone, while giving praise to Amos Shembe for the miraculous way in which the project has succeeded.

In July 2002 I returned to Ebuhleni, primarily to get permission from Rev. Vimbeni Shembe to publish an English translation of the Zulu-language hymns of Shembe and to see what new music had appeared at the religious site. I was not disappointed. Blaring out at the edge of the village stores were startling new sounds of Shembe members loudly proclaiming their belief in Shembe. The volume of the music, the recording technology, and the acoustical space demanded by these new sounds all spoke to a newly found sense of place in the fully democratic South Africa of the early twenty-first century. The youth were no longer expressing their commitment to Shembe in the muted tones of twentieth-century Nazarite worship, the softer tones of a docile Black community under the apartheid regime. As I suggested in Chapter 7 might be the case with *isicathamiya*, the youth are claiming new public spaces for their voices, and the volume has been turned all the way up. Nobody came to silence the blaring sounds of Shembe worship coming from the large black speakers mounted on the sides of the store. Instead, there was a steady stream of customers ready to buy the latest in the bright sounds of Shembe gospel music. I happily joined the line to purchase.

Keywords for Chapters 13–14

bass voices the lowest voices of a musical texture, typically sung by men

call and response a common performance style in African and African American music where a leader sings a melodic "call" and a group/choir responds, often with a musical phrase that copies or expands on what the leader has sung

counterpoint when several melodic lines are performed note against note, i.e., it is common to the keyboard music of J. S. Bach's fugues

cross-rhythm often thought to characterize musical performances in Africa, it involves one line of music in duple meter performed at the same time as another line in triple meter for example, creating a certain rhythm tension between the two lines

cyclicity a musical structure often found in Southern Africa in which a melodic/rhythmic line repeats endlessly, without a clearly articulated beginning and ending. It is often thought of as the opposite of the more linear structure of music from other parts of the world

Ebuhleni the current Shembe headquarters

Ekuphakameni the original Shembe headquarters, also used to refer to heaven

Ethiopianism a late nineteenth-century form of religious independence which allowed for varying degrees of assimilation of European culture; begun in response to mission Christianity

gospel music in South Africa, gospel music takes its cue from the United States, but is sung in local languages, and has its own body of locally composed songs

harmony how notes sounding simultaneously blend together, in a consonant or dissonant manner

ibandla lamaNazaretha the congregation of Nazaretha, the religion founded by Isaiah Shembe

imbongi a Zulu praise poet (like a griot)

imiNazaretha the white prayer gown worn by followers of Shembe that identifies them as Nazaretha

inkhonzo congregational worship style among followers of Shembe

Isaiah Shembe founder of *ibandla lamaNazaretha*; succeeded by son, Johannes Galilee; succeeded by Galilee's brother Amos; and present leader Vimbeni. Londa Shembe, son of J. G. Shembe, sought to lead after death of J. G., but was murdered

izihlabelelo zamaNazaretha the hymns of the Nazaretha composed by Isaiah and Johannes Galilee Shembe and compiled into a hymnal in 1940

melodic contour the shape of the melody, as it moves up (higher pitch) and down (lower pitch)

Nguni collective term for Bantu-speaking peoples in South Africa, including the Zulu, Xhosa, Swazi, Pedi, and Sotho

Nhlangakaze literally means the first big or great reed, name of holy mountain of Shembe

overlapping phrases typical of call and response forms, where the response to the leader's call starts before the leader has completed the musical phrase. So the response overlaps with the call

pentatonic versus heptatonic scales musical materials using either five or seven pitches

pitch treatment how pitch is articulated—by sliding up or down from a note, by ornamenting the note with additional pitches, and so forth

rhythm the patterns of stressed and unstressed beats in a musical utterance

syllabic treatment of the text one pitch per syllable of text

tempo the fast or slow pace at which music unfolds

tone color or timbre refers to the particular quality of pitch, regardless of what "note" is being performed, i.e., tone color accounts for the different quality of sound between a violin and a cello, or between the oboe and a clarinet, of a piano and an organ for example

umgido festivals of sacred dance in *ibandla lamaNazaretha*

Xhosa a language and people who speak one of the "click" languages, related to the Zulu language. Nelson Mandela is Xhosa-speaking

Zionism religious independent movement that arose out of the Zions Kerk and is also related to Zion City in Illinois, United States

Afterword

CHAPTER **15**

Final Reflections

> I was born with the songs of Zulu rainmakers in my ears, they sang to end the drought, which burnt the land for ten years in South Africa . . . I remember how my nanny would tell me that if I listened to the wind, I would hear the voices of my life. I listened and I heard Prof talk about justice, I heard Piet talk about hope, I heard Dubula Manzi, the old medicine man, talk about courage. I heard Maria [talk about love] . . . These are the voices of my life, the voices of Africa; the voices I carry with me as Duma and I set out together to bring our country closer to each other. (Derived from *The Power of One*, 1992)

The Power of South African Music

The Power of One is the name of the 1989 novel by Bryce Courtenay, and the 1992 Hollywood feature film directed by John G. Avildsen. It is an emotionally evocative narrative told in the first person by a young boy of English descent who is born on a farm in South Africa. It is not a film that made a significant impact on South Africa or its people—I was not even aware of it though I was living in South Africa when it was released. Nevertheless, in some ways, the film is useful for the ways in which themes in its narrative have formed the foundation for much of my discussion of South African music in this book.

The plot of the film is filled with the optimism of discourses of racial and cultural reconciliation—the idealistic belief in the capacity to forge a nation out of enormous differences—linguistic, cultural, educational, and economic. In summary, the story is as follows. The main character is a boy, PK, who spends his early years with his best friend, a Black South African whose mother is PK's Nanny. PK is orphaned at the age of seven and sent to boarding school. It is in this school that the boy begins to witness many of the horrors of life in South Africa, initially under the racist policies of the British segregation (prior to 1948), and later the even harsher system the White Afrikaner called "apartheid." PK meets up with a German piano professor after he goes to live with his grandfather, but the pianist is put into prison for failing to inform the British-controlled South African government that he was still in the country. While the "Prof" is visiting South Africa, the Nazis kill his family in Germany (including his grandson, who was the same age as PK) because they stood up against Hitler, implicitly suggesting that standing up to Hitler paralleled the courage it would take to resist the apartheid regime.

Taught to box by a Black South African prisoner (played by Morgan Freeman) PK is instilled with a burning desire to seek justice for all South Africans. Prof and the young boy decide to work with the prisoner on composing a song for all the Black prisoners to sing when an important White official visits the prison. Because most Whites do not understand African languages, they are not aware that the words of the song supposedly to honor the apartheid official is actually a song that invokes a pan-African unity. The narrative is simple, perhaps a little idealistic, and certainly open to much critique. That is not my purpose here.

The Power of One celebrates the idea of "one" in several ways. It is about the capacity of an individual like PK to make a difference in the lives of so many. It speaks of the impact of a single song in forging unity between people of different languages and cultures, albeit of a single race. And it speaks to the power of song as a force of national reconciliation and unity. To conclude this book, I use the story of *The Power of One* to restate themes of the film that resonate with this book on the one hand, and to address questions that the personal style I have used in writing this text might raise on the other hand. In a very real sense, we might wonder how one person's experiences and story might speak to larger historical, musical, social, even political processes. Can one person's narrative represent anything larger than itself? I begin by highlighting themes in the film that are generated in the narrative of this book and then address the question of larger representation.

The human voice

The film opens with an unaccompanied solo voice, echoing through the vast expanses of the map of Africa, which is represented in a hand-drawn outline of the African continent. The map is almost empty—a few animals are scattered on its surface. We can interpret the image from several perspectives. It could represent the lack of knowledge the average film viewer has of the African continent; it might reference the way in which the first European colonists saw the continent—as *terra nubilus*—land without inhabitants, open to occupation. The map may even symbolize a desire to start afresh in a post-colonial world, expunging the horrors of the past, a desire that can ultimately not be realized. At the very least, the map opens up to the story of a White boy born in Africa.

In the film, as in South Africa itself, it is the human voice and not the drum that signals the sounds of place and identity. The singing voice is, nonetheless, a hybrid. By hybrid I am not simply referring to a natural category, but one often shaped by struggle and emerging out of violence and silence. Throughout the film, PK's narrative voice intermingles with the singing voices of Black South Africans. These are human voices that have encountered European tradition, absorbed it, and made it sound South African by incorporating local languages, timbres, and intonations germane to the region. The real South African voice is not pure, but a voice in constant encounter with other voices, other languages, other sounds. Its authenticity lies in its peculiar kind of hybridity, and a constantly evolving sound, structure, and timbre.

Colonial history

Running over the map at the start of the film are printed words, words that tell of the arrival of Europeans in that part of the world: the French, the Dutch, and the Germans who left Europe in the 1680s because of religious persecution and traveled to South Africa. They spent 250 years fighting with the English (and local Africans, though the filmmaker does not mention this) for control of the land. At this moment, the soloist is incorporated into a mixed voice choir, singing in a call-and-response structure. Throughout the film, the words are foreign to the American viewer—mostly in Zulu, or sung simply as sounds that evoke a particular kind of ambience as does much "world music" produced by the popular music industry—but the strange sounds are arranged in a familiar structure. Very soon, we hear the autobiographical voice of PK as he begins the story of his evolving relationship to South Africa, and indeed, of his sense of being South African rather than English. The voice starts out with a British accent, but gradually changes in the film to sound more typically White South African, shaped by its interaction with the sounds of Afrikaans, Xhosa, Zulu, among other languages spoken in the region and in the natural world.

Segregation and apartheid

The narrative covers the middle years of the twentieth century, when South Africa moved from British control and the rules of segregation to the rise to power of the Afrikaner Nationalists in 1948, and runs through about the early 1970s—if we judge by the age of the main character as the story progresses. It does not take us to the end of apartheid, or beyond. In this its historical usefulness is limited, but like so many foreign-made films of the 1980s and 1990s that address South Africa, they do so through the experiences of the harshness of these years for South Africans, particularly Black South Africans.

The body

An integral part of achieving political liberation in 1994 was the recuperation of the human body. The body beaten, abused, even destroyed under apartheid is very much alive in musical performance. Even singing, which in our world often uses only the voice, emphasizes the body. Group singing in the film consistently involves exuberant clapping, body swaying, and eye contact. As we read in Chapter 9 and could see in the *Gumboots!* video, the body is a central dimension of South African performance for many of its citizens. Singing is a very physical act.

Song

The song composed by the pianist and PK serves to resolve differences—not by forcing everyone into a monophonic rendition, or even one in the four-part harmony of Caluza's

Quartet, the 1930s recording used in the soundtrack. Rather, the composition allows for call and response, for several groups to sing their own melodies in a larger harmony with other groups. Each sings their part and does it in their own way, but ultimately, the voices blend together to create a rich musical texture. Different voices weave their parts into a single entity. Singing the song, voices engaged with each other, becomes a metaphor for nation building. Singing this song gives each singer a glimpse into the political possibilities of unity in diversity, of "many cultures, one nation," the idea that underpinned the birth of the "new South Africa" in the 1990s.

Middle class mission music

Reuben Caluza's Double Quartet traveled to England from the city of Durban to record their music in the 1930s (see recording listed in Appendix 3 under *makwaya, Caluza's Double Quartet*). This recorded example is drawn from the scholarly reissue of this historic recording by ethnomusicologist Veit Erlmann. It is a remarkable document. If you can locate the CD, listen closely to the excerpt, for it encapsulates a moment of encounter: Black South Africans encountering the culture of American missionaries in KwaZulu Natal. If you listen to the piano accompaniment on other tracks of the CD, you will hear echoes of secular ragtime. If you focus on the voices, you hear the SATB arrangements of the mission hymn brought to South Africa and introduced to Black South Africans as the model, the *isawundi* (sound) of civilized music. In this recording, the voices seem a little strained, the African voice striving to assimilate into European ways. By the end of the twentieth century, African voices have found a comfortable place for themselves in the "classic" repertory of Europe.

In terms of numbers of people participating, more Black South Africans have sung the European Baroque and classical vocal repertory over the last 150 years than those of European descent in South Africa. This begs the question about the nationality of, for example, Handel's *Messiah* in the twenty-first century. We can easily identify its European origins, but with less certainty, its consumption and performance in the contemporary world. In the early 1990s Sam Tshabalala, who worked for Radio Zulu at the time, translated the text of *The Messiah* into the Zulu language. This translation was performed on national television, live in city halls in several communities, and on radio for South Africans. To whose culture does *The Messiah* belong? In South Africa the answer is a complicated one, suggesting, as the film does in other ways, that in South Africa racial and cultural stereotyping from a European or American perspective becomes a messy process.

Transnational collaboration

Borrowing culture from beyond South Africa's geopolitical borders has certainly characterized the history of South African musical traditions in the twentieth century. Some of the outside culture has been assimilated because it was imposed, some in more neutral forms of borrowing. In the film we are shown the compositional process of the unity song. It was a combination of three unlikely characters: the European classical skills of the German Prof, the Zulu language and conducting skills of PK, and most certainly the words were the ideas of the prisoner who taught PK to box. Like Paul Simon's *Graceland* project, the song in the film is an interracial, intergenerational, and intercultural musical collaboration, a pooling of resources, at some times more equitably than others. There are times in the twentieth century when borrowing has come through people copying recorded music that has traveled from the global metropolitan centers—New York City, Los Angeles, London, and Paris—to South Africa. There is ample evidence of this process in Chapter 2. Without access to appropriate models locally, South Africans have copied, imitated, and typically transformed the foreign sounds into local languages. But they have also indigenized the sounds of these borrowed structures—transforming them into genres of performance unique to South Africa—*maskanda*, *mqashiyo*, gumboot dance, *kwaito*, and *mbube* are just a handful of examples of this process.

Africa as resource

We learn from the film that Africa is not just a place of copies and appropriations. In the mind of the highly cultured German pianist, Africa is also a resource, not to be exploited but valued. He urges PK to learn to read the signs of the natural world as a resource for original thought. PK heeds the pianist's advice, and it is this capacity to read the signs of the natural world in South Africa that enables him to define himself as South African rather than British. But it is also the specificity of his experiences living in South Africa that marks him as different from his British compatriots.

Global travel

PK comes to know the German pianist because he is a global traveler, performing his skilled interpretations of European classical music the world over. He stops over in South Africa and has to stay a while because his travel is interrupted by the events unfolding in Europe in what we now call World War II. So one of the primary forms of cultural encounter is through the world travels of performers from Europe and the United States. But it is not only the Europeans coming to South Africa. Later in the film, PK is granted a fellowship to study at Oxford University in England. Unlike others, however, PK ultimately turns down the scholarship to forge a place for himself and others in South Africa. The point is that various forms of travel have shaped South African culture, both internationally and within the country, between town and countryside. We saw in Chapters 3 and 4 how music has created the connective tissue in these travels, either as live or mediated performance.

Individual versus collective

Each time we are taken into the township of Alexandra or into the prison in Barberton in the film, we are shown images of Black South Africans performing. Here all performance is live and collective, there are no individual musicians walking the streets alone; even the pennywhistle players in the middle of the film are performing as a group. Each plays an individual melody, but all perform on the same common ground. We know from earlier in this book that individual musicians were quite common on the streets of South

Africa in this time period, but what the filmmaker is presenting to us is a stereotype of African performance—that it is always collective. It is a stereotype projected from within the Black community and outside of it, and can at times make it quite difficult for individual musicians to record their music alone.

Orality and literacy

PK recalls at the start of the film that in his early childhood he was taught by his mother about the ways of England, in which there were books and music, and by his nanny whose knowledge of Africa came directly from the wisdom of her people. One of the ways in which PK is urged to help his fellow South Africans in Alexandra township is through literacy training, specifically by teaching a group of people to read English. The idea is that to engage with the contemporary world, to be able to read its signs, one has to have a command of the English language, as both spoken and written language. But the prisoners are not taught the song of unity by reading, though the piece was written, but rather through forms of oral and aural transmission. They learn by listening. In several places in this book we have caught a glimpse of the coexistence and at times tensions between orality and literacy, core characteristics of South African performance in the twentieth century.

The peculiarity of the hybrid

Finally, we have learned that South African identity and its musical performance in the post-colonial world is a hybrid identity, not purely African or European. The film strives to portray a sense of the possibilities of new national formations that can emerge from sharing cultural ways, composing new music by blending different musical styles into a new acoustical fabric. In fact, neither a distinctive sense of Europeanness nor of Africanness makes complete sense in South Africa; both have been somewhat redefined in contact with the other. There are, too, multiple forms of national identity. As we have seen in several instances the meaning of the word *nation* has shifted dramatically for some in South Africa; no doubt for others it still retains something of its nineteenth-century inflection—the Zulus belong to the Zulu nation, the Afrikaners to the Afrikaans nation. For others, just to be South African and not culturally or racially categorized is an adequate category of identity.

South Africa in Africa

In Chapter 1 we began to explore the nature of South Africa's relationship to the region of Southern Africa and to the continent of Africa as a whole. For so long, it seemed to have remained isolated, cut off from travel to and engagement with the rest of the continent. To meet other Africans, South Africans often had to travel abroad, to England, Europe, or the United States. While Africa has certainly opened itself up to South Africans since the early 1990s, and South Africa has had to open its borders to people from other parts of Africa, the relationship is tenuous and, at times, fragile.

This is beautifully illustrated for me in a CD, *South Africa—Rainbow Nation* (1996).

Ostensibly a celebration of the African-ness of all South Africans, it is a CD of only four or five songs. One is titled "Viva Madiba" (Long Live Mandela), a song in praise of Mandela as the father of the nation; a second is a reissue of Miriam Makeba's now famous "Click Song," sung in the New York City Town Hall in the early 1960s. That song begins with Miriam Makeba's youthful voice telling the story of the place of the song in her "native land," of the "African peoples" in that land. In that story, African was the opposite of European. But "African" now means something else because, as *The Power of One* suggests, all people born in Africa are indeed Africans, regardless of skin color or culture. The trouble now is how to define South Africa's relationship to the Africa beyond its borders. This CD embodies the complexity of that relationship: the CD is cut in the shape of Africa, but it is the South African flag that covers the entire continent. The question remains: to what extent will South Africa now become the dominant force in Africa, musically, culturally, economically, and politically? There are many signs of the opening up of the continent and the Southern African region to South Africa—culturally, economically, and politically. And South Africa has opened itself to the in migration, both legal and illegal, of many from elsewhere in the continent, many who don't speak local languages, whose lives are transient and economically uncertain. What should South Africa's place in Africa be, what is her responsibility to the peoples of Africa, are questions that many grapple with, both inside and outside of South Africa. Not everyone is comfortable with the consequences of that kind of role and responsibility.

The Power of One?

I began this book with a discussion of two influential individuals in twentieth-century South African music history. One was Solomon Linda—one man with a song that has moved into the collective memory of millions in the world, through its reiteration and transformations by others in the United States during the course of the twentieth century. The other was Hugh Tracey—one man with a mission to record as much of the music of Africa as financially possible, a vision to save in the face of change, to archive the richness of what was, in many cases, a fast-fading art form. With assistance from many in England and the United States, he was able to achieve his vision. I end by asking the question, what is the power of one ethnomusicologist in conveying a sense of South African music and culture in the twentieth century for readers in far-flung places? How representative are my experiences as a White English-speaking South African woman now living in the United States? It has to be said that they are quite peculiar. In my generation, few White South Africans ever crossed the boundaries between White urban spaces and Black townships. Then again, that is not unique to South Africa. Racial, linguistic, class, and social differences are clearly marked on the landscapes of many cities and rural areas around the world. My hope is that through reading this book you have opened your minds to the experiences of South Africans I have encountered and written about; that your ears are tuned to the music these men and women have made, a small portion of which is available on the CD; and that you have participated at least imaginatively and from a distance in the vibrant and always changing musical traditions of twentieth-century South Africa.

APPENDIX 1

A Guide to African Music

A Music of Encounters, North, South, East, and West

African Music: Early Encounters

The earliest written record of sub-Saharan African peoples is mention of "pygmies" in the account of a Fourth-Dynasty Egyptian expedition to discover the source of the Nile. This record is preserved in the tomb of Pharaoh Nefrikare, and was composed by Herkouf, the Pharaoh's commander. Herkouf tells that they went into "a great forest west of the Mountains of the Moon and discovered there a people of the trees, a tiny people who sing and dance to their god, a dance such as had never been seen before" (Turnbull 1968: 15). The Pharaoh ordered the expedition to return with one of these small people. The next mention of pygmies is in Homer's *Iliad*, in which the "Pygmaean race" is mentioned as having been killed by the men of Troy, though again it is not clear if Homer's is a mythical reference (Turnbull 1968: 15).

Though not depicting musical performance as such, Bushmen paintings, some of which are 25,000 to 27,000 years old, have images of ritual performances and of trance dances. In fact, much of this very old artwork on the rock faces of mountains in Southern Africa is thought to articulate the relationship between the spirit world and the everyday life of hunter-gatherers in Southern Africa. Communication between those spheres is induced by song or chant performance (Dowson and Lewis-Williams 1994, and *National Geographic* DVDs on Africa). The last Bushmen rock painters died in the nineteenth century.

In the late 1860s, German linguist Dr. W. H. I. Bleek and his sister-in-law, Lucy Lloyd, began work with a small group of Cape Bushmen convicts, two of whom were prolific storytellers and song performers. They produced a 12,000-page record of the stories, prayers, and songs of the Cape Bushman as recounted by these people (Lewis-Williams 2002). One can only speculate on the age of some of the myths and narratives recounted in this collection though it is thought that the Bushmen have inhabited South Africa for at least 20,000 years.

Hanno's *Periplus* provides another example of an early Western voyage of discovery. Dating to about 500 BC, it survived as a tablet housed in a temple at Carthage, inscribed in a Phoenician language. This account makes brief reference to African musical performance on an island on the west coast of Africa: "We could discover nothing in the day time except trees; but in the night we saw many fires burning, and heard the sound of pipes, cymbals, drums, and confused shouts. We were then afraid, and our diviners ordered us to abandon the island" (Palmer 1931: 2, cited in McCall 1998: 74). Hanno's mention of musical performance is unusual because most ancient narratives of voyages to Africa provide little such information; travelers did not go ashore and engage with indigenous peoples at the time.

The first real records of encounters with African musical performance come from Arabic traders from Mediterranean and Middle Eastern coastal cities. The earliest such account mentions music at the Ghanaian royal courts in 1067. "The beginning of a royal audience is announced by the beating of a kind of drum which they call deba, made of a long piece of hollowed wood. The people gather when they hear this sound" (Davidson 1964: 72 cited in McCall 1998: 75).

The fourteenth-century account of Moroccan traveler Ibn Battuta, who visited the capital of the Malian empire, is particularly important because it provides written documentation of contemporary oral history which claims the existence of griots in that region dating back seven centuries. On returning to his home, Battuta dictated a narrative on his encounters with these griots (Hale 1998: 3; McCall 1997). From the fifteenth century numerous Portuguese, Spanish, and English traders traveled into the heart of Africa. Portuguese explorer Vasco da Gama, who traveled round the southernmost tip of Africa, made brief reference to musical performance on the Kenyan coast.

The earliest known report of South African indigenous performance is found in Vasco da Gama's diary about his travels around the South African coast in 1497. This is the first known written description of flutes made of reeds played by "Hottentots," indigenous South Africans living on the western coast of the Cape, near the contemporary town of Mossel Bay. They played on four- or five-reed pipes for the Portuguese travelers. A report by Peter van Meerhoff in 1661 provides the most comprehensive account of these performances. He describes a group of between 100 and 200 flute players, each with a hollow reed in hand, dancing in a circle while blowing their instruments. In the center of the circle was a man grasping a long stick. The reeds were played in harmony with each other, and sounded like trumpets (Kirby 1968: 135–136).

In the seventeenth and eighteenth centuries, numerous missionaries and traders, the Portuguese in Congo, and the French and Dutch in Guinea, produced writings about African music, which were usually disparaging. In the nineteenth century, the idea of Africa and its music in the European mind was definitely one of wild savagery (see McCall 1998). In contrast, South African ethnomusicologist Percival Kirby undertook groundbreaking archival and ethnographic research into South African musical instruments in the 1920s. Kirby examined the earliest known documents, some from as early as the late fifteenth century, describing the instruments, their social uses and value. The book he published (1968 [1934]) is a remarkable resource for the instrumental traditions of African peoples as practiced in South Africa in the early twentieth century; the written records from much earlier suggest that some of these traditions might be traced back several centuries.

In tandem with Kirby's research, British-born musicologist Hugh Tracey began recording the traditional music of Africa, starting in South and Central Africa in the 1930s, and ultimately producing the remarkable *Sound of Africa* series (discussed in Chapter 1).

A handful of nineteenth-century writings on African music include written transcriptions, that is, visual representations of what African music sounded like to the writers. Thomas Bowdich, a writer working for the British African Company, traveled to West Africa to negotiate with the Ashanti. He published a book on that experience, including a chapter on Ashanti music which contains two Ashanti songs transcribed by Bowdich. For his insight into the limitations of European notational symbols to convey Ashanti musical sensibility, and the detail he provides about the musical life of Ashanti people, he may qualify as the first real ethnomusicologist to have worked in sub-Saharan Africa (McCall 1998: 88–89).

A second study is a wonderful piece of nineteenth-century collaborative African musicology about musical life among the Ijebu, part of the Yoruba, in Nigeria. The piece comprises the memories of an African man named Osifekunde (Joachim was his "Christian" name), who was captured by pirates and sold as a slave. Osifekunde ended up in Brazil; thirty years later, he told his story to ethnologist M. A. P. D'Azevac-Macaya. The interviews with Osifekunde took several weeks, and produced the first written account of Yoruba culture. Included in this narrative is a brief section on music with transcriptions of songs performed by Osifekunde (see Lloyd 1968: 277–280 cited in McCall 1998: 89–91).

Other Europeans left musical transcriptions, but perhaps the most significant in shaping European and American ideas of African music in the twentieth century was the music scholar Richard Wallaschek who published a book in 1893 titled *Primitive Music: An Inquiry into the Origin and Development of Music, Songs, Instruments, Dances and Pantomimes of the Savage Races*. In this text, influential for European comparative musicologists of the later nineteenth and early twentieth centuries, Wallaschek incorporated nineteenth-century ideas of social Darwinism into a theory of "primitive" music. Wallaschek used these theories in an attempt to give value to the music of primitive people, countering beliefs current in Europe that the music of primitive peoples like Africans was not to be considered music at all. Wallaschek argued that rather than just being an object of aesthetic pleasure, primitive music was integrally connected to everyday social life. However, his view of African music was that it was music of an earlier stage of human development, and that European music, the music of the present, signaled a higher level of human and cultural development (McCall 1998: 93–97).

Encounters with African Music in the Twentieth Century

This account of the history of African music has privileged written documents over oral narrative as sources of African musical history; the voices of African scholars and individuals have largely remained silent. This should not be interpreted to mean that African people have not had ideas or theories of musical performance in their societies, or that they have had no means of recording or representing their music.

Africans in contact with the Arab world in North Africa, for example, have had their own music theorists for centuries (see, for example, Wright 1978 and Farmer 1957, both cited by Shelemay 1998: 146–147). Unfortunately, there has been very little systematic research, recovery, or analysis of African music writing in sub-Saharan Africa. This means that as outsiders to these performance cultures, we may need to look in different places for these records or forms of representation.

The best-developed example of indigenous African musical notation has been written about by ethnomusicologist Kay Shelemay (all information on Ethiopia here is derived from Shelemay 1998: 146–151). Shelemay studied the musical notation of the Ethiopian Christian church. (Ethiopia became a Christian country in the fourth century, and by the sixth, had a literature and script in the language known as Ge'ez.)

While the earliest parchment texts in Ge'ez derive from the sixth century, the system of music writing emerged much later, in the mid-sixteenth century, following a Muslim invasion of Christian churches and monasteries (1529–1541). Ethiopian church clerics devised a notational system to create written records of the liturgy. Historical sources suggest that the system of notation may have been developed from previous forms of notation that were obliterated by the Muslims in this period. This system of music writing continues to be used and taught in contemporary Ethiopia though it has always operated in conjunction with a vibrant oral tradition; the practice of committing to memory the musical performance is an integral part of monastic training.

In the twentieth century, other kinds of musical notations have been used and created for African musical performance. Tonic sol-fa, the system of notation using the syllables do re mi fa sol la ti do, has been deeply integrated into choral rehearsal and performance in South Africa (Muller 1999: ch. 5) and parts of East Africa (Gunderson and Barz 2000). I have heard tonic sol-fa criticized by Black South Africans because it is of limited use for the study of instrumental music.

Several African countries created national orchestras in a bid to foster a sense of national unity once they gained independence from European colonial powers beginning in the 1950s. This has frequently entailed gathering into a single entity many regional musicians who play diverse styles and use a range of languages and dialects. Completely new hybrid music and dance styles have emerged out of this process, necessitating the creation of an innovative notational system to accommodate musical and linguistic diversity. Standard Western notation has not proved fully adequate for the task, often requiring modification to accommodate specific musical qualities not germane to the European classical or popular tradition. The Ethiopian National Orchestra has developed a complex notational system using pictographs to represent musical elements. For example a turtle placed above a musical note indicates a slow tempo (Shelemay 1983).

Though art music is not a focus of this book, a small but significant number of European- and American-trained composers from Africa have sought to express themselves through the medium of written compositions. Writing art music is a struggle for the African composer, because many outside of Africa expect their music to sound ethnically African. Nigerian ethnomusicologist and composer Akin Euba has been at the forefront of the struggle to find a legitimate compositional space for intercultural composers like himself. To this end he has been one of the organizers of a biannual gathering of composers and scholars at City University in London. Mzilikazi Khumalo is one of a handful of South African art composers, not just writing SATB choral music. Like Euba (Omojola 2001), he has experimented with the problems of combining African traditional musical aesthetics with the forms and aesthetics of European art music. Both have grappled with the challenges inherent in performing African music on Western instruments like the piano or in the symphony orchestra format. White South African Kevin Volans (Taylor 1995) experimented with the sounds of traditional music in his *mbira* works of the 1980s. Using transcriptions of *mbira* music he "classicized" the sounds by performing the transcriptions on retuned harpsichords. The American group, the Kronos Quartet, has made a significant contribution to these intercultural compositional experiments by commissioning new work by African composers, then performing and recording the music for wider consumption.

Oral performance, either transmitted live or recorded in the media of sound and video, remains the most vibrant source of African contemporary and historical performance. In the scholarly world outside of Africa, however, written and recorded words and sounds have been given greater status than those contained in human memory. Human memory, it is claimed, is not as reliable as the written document. While this might be true of individual memories in Europe and the United States, where technologies of writing and computing have become the memory banks of many, it is not the case in parts of Africa that have for centuries nurtured and sustained the human capacity for good memory.

The most outstanding example of the capacity to remember and transmit cultural history is that embodied in the griot/griotte, or jeli/jeliya traditions of West Africa. These are Manding musicians—those belonging to the Mandekan language group, who come from the countries of Mali, Guinea, and Senegambia. The history of their musical traditions, particularly those performed with words accompanied on the *kora*, are documented by Charry (2000), Duran (1994), Hale (1998), and Knight (1991). Manding jeli/griots claim that their ancestry can be traced as far back as the thirteenth century. As mentioned earlier, these oral traditions can be verified by the Arabic documents written in the fourteenth century by Ibn Battuta who first saw griots at the court of Mandinkan ruler Mansa Sulayman (1341–1360). Griots/jeli function as genealogists, historians, spokespeople, diplomats, musicians, teachers, warriors, praise singers, masters of ceremonies, and advisors (Hale 1998).

APPENDIX 2

Key Dates in South African History

c. 100,000 BC	San people settle in Southern Africa
c. AD 500	Bantu-speaking people to present day KwaZulu Natal
1487	Portuguese explorer Bartholemeu Dias sails around Cape of Good Hope
1498	Portuguese Vasco da Gama records passing encounters with Cape, KwaZulu Natal, and Mozambique
c. 1500	Basotho people settle in present day Lesotho
1652	Dutch (Boer) settlement in Table Bay (Cape Town), as refreshment station, Cape also called "Tavern of the Seas"
1688	French Huguenots arrive in the Cape
c. 1690	Boers move into hinterland outside of Cape Town
c. 1750	Nguni people in Swaziland
1779	Boer fight Xhosa at Great Fish River in Eastern Cape
1795	British capture Cape Town from Dutch
1807	No more slaves permitted to be imported to the Cape Colony, though slaves in the Cape are not set free until the late 1830s.
1815	Shaka seizes power in KwaZulu part of KwaZulu Natal, *mfecane/difeqane* (forced migration) begins
1820	British settlers to Eastern Cape
1828	Ordinance 50 allows freedom of movement for Coloureds, may own land and work where they wish
1830s	Voortrekkers (Dutch farmers) begin Great Trek from Cape northwards
1833	Slavery abolished in British Empire
1838	Boers defeat Zulus at Battle of Blood River
1843	Natal a British colony
1840s	First missionaries to KwaZulu Natal
1847–1849	British settlers come to Natal

1851	First sugar cane production in Natal
1852	Boers create Boer Republic of Transvaal, recognized by Britain
1854	Britain recognizes independent Republic of Orange Free State
1857	Diamonds discovered in Griqualand West (now Kimberley); start of industrial revolution in South Africa
1858	British defeat Xhosa after great cattle killing
1860	Indian indentured laborers arrive from India to work sugar cane fields in KwaZulu Natal
1868	British annex Basotholand (Lesotho)
1871	British annex Griqualand West with 50,000 fortune seekers, African labor needed for mines
1875	Formation of Genootskap van Regte Afrikaners (Society of True Afrikaners), an association of those of European descent, wanting Afrikaans to be recognized as official language
1877	British annex the first South African Republic
1879	Anglo-Zulu War, British ultimately gain control of Zululand
1881	Boers defeat British; Transvaal becomes South African Republic
1886	Gold discovered on Witwatersrand, gold rush, Americans and British arrive in droves
1887	British annex Zululand, Zulu king Cetswayo exiled to island of St. Helena
1891	Indian Immigration Law in Natal Colony controls all aspects of Indian life
1893	Indian lawyer Mahatma Gandhi arrives in South Africa, establishes Natal Indian Congress to resist discrimination against Indians
1896	Pass laws introduced to control movement of Black miners
1898	Tensions between British and Boers over miners' rights to franchise
1899–1902	Anglo-Boer War, British burn Boer farms, put Boer women and children into concentration camps, 26,000 die in camps
1902	Transvaal and Orange Free State republics annexed by British, economic reconstruction by British
1904	60,000 Chinese indentured laborers imported to gold mines, mostly repatriated
1905	Abdullah Abdurahman becomes President of African Political Organization founded in 1902, in Cape region
1908	Gandhi leads passive resistance campaign against pass laws for Indians
1910	Union of South Africa formed, Blacks denied vote; Lesotho and Swaziland became British Protectorates
1912	South African Native National Congress, forerunner of the African National Congress (ANC), formed by John Dube
1913	Native Lands Act restricts Black ownership of land to 8 percent
1918	Broederbond, secret society of powerful Afrikaners similar to Ku Klux Klan in USA, formed to protect interests of Afrikaners
1919	Black union, Industrial and Commercial Workers Union formed
1921	South African Communist Party founded, campaigns against pass laws
1922	Army crushes White miners wanting job reservation
1923	First Urban Areas Act restricting entry of Africans into urban areas

1924	Hertzog, champion of poor Whites, workers, and Afrikaner nationalism, becomes Prime Minister
1925	Afrikaans replaces Dutch as second official language
1936	Native Trust and Land Act transfers African and Coloured people from Cape Voters' Roll to separate list; increases land allocated to native reserves from 8 to 13 percent
1939	Split among Whites over support of Europeans in war, some Afrikaners turn support to Nazis, English support Allies
1943	ANC Youth League formed, includes Nelson Mandela, Robert Sobukwe, Walter Sizulu, and Oliver Tambo
1946	India wins United Nations vote of censure against South Africa for discrimination against Indians in Natal
1948	Nationalist party wins over the United Party, Afrikaner Nationalists to power
1949	Prohibition of Mixed Marriages Act passed
1950	Immorality Act forbids sexual relations between Whites and any people of color; Population Registration Act introduces legalized racial classification: White, Coloured, Native, and Asiatic; Group Areas Act divides the country into residential areas based on racial classification; Suppression of Communism Act defines communist as anyone hostile to the government; South African Communist Party dissolves, many join the ANC
1951	Government legislation to remove Coloureds from Voters' Roll; Bantu Authorities Act creates tribal and territorial authorities, retribalizing African population
1952	Native Laws Amendment Act extends influx control to all urban areas and to Black women; Defiance Campaign begins
1953	Public Safety Act enables Governor General to declare states of emergency and rule by decree
1954	Native Resettlement Act allows for forced removal of Black residents from Sophiatown, Johannesburg over five years
1955	ANC Freedom Charter, drawn up by the Congress of the People, adopted
1956	South African Amendment Act removes 45,000 Coloured votes from electoral rolls; Industrial Coalition Act reserves certain skilled jobs for Whites
1957	Union Jack removed as dual official flag of South Africa
1958	First all-White election, National Party wins large majority; women protest the pass laws, about 2000 arrested
1959	Prime Minister Hendrik Verwoerd launches independent "homelands" project; Extension of University Education Bill excludes all non-Whites from White universities, creates separate universities for Blacks, Indians, and Coloureds; Pan Africanist Congress (PAC) formed
1960	Police fire on PAC-inspired march against pass laws, Sharpeville Massacre, 60 killed, 178 wounded; UN Security Council call to end apartheid
1961	South Africa proclaimed a Republic; Albert Luthuli receives Nobel Peace Prize; treason trial of Mandela and other members of ANC ends after four years, all found guilty

1963	General Law Amendment Act allows police to arrest and detain suspects for ninety days without trial; police capture ANC underground leadership including Nelson Mandela, Govan Mbeki, Walter Sizulu, charged with sabotage (punishable by death without appeal); Transkei becomes self-governing
1964	Mandela and others sentenced to life in prison; South Africa banned from Olympic Games participation
1965	Bantu Laws Amendment Act denies 7 million Black people right to live inside South Africa
1967	Defense Amendment Act requires White South African men to undertake military service; Terrorism Act defines terrorism as anything that threatens law and order, gives unlimited powers to arrest, detain, and hold trials without jury
1968	Black Consciousness Movement constituted with Steve Biko as first president
1969	Bureau of State Security established with wide investigative powers, newspapers may not report activities of Bureau
1970	Bantu Homelands Citizenship Act makes all Black South Africans citizens of a tribal homeland, regardless of their place of birth
1972	Bophutatswana, Ciskei, and Lebowa become independent homelands, with KwaZulu part of KwaZulu Natal as semi-autonomous
1976	Television comes to South Africa; Soweto uprising: school children protest Afrikaans as medium of instruction, police fire on children, months of protest countrywide
1977	Steve Biko detained under Terrorism Act and dies of brain injuries suffered in custody
1970–1980s	Union activity, anti-apartheid activity, South African Defense Force activity in surrounding countries
1983	United Democratic Front (UDF) formed to coordinate resistance
1984	Archbishop Desmond Tutu awarded Nobel Peace Prize
1985	Political protesters fired on, indefinite state of emergency declared; Congress of South African Trade Unions (COSATU) formed
1986	Pass laws, Prohibition of Mixed Marriages, and Prohibition of Political Interference Acts all abolished
1987	Political turbulence in KwaZulu Natal intensifies
1988	Church leaders begin to assume place as spokesmen for political organizations
1990	State President de Klerk unbans political organizations including ANC and PAC, announces release of Mandela; Separate Amenities Act repealed; State of Emergency lifted
1994	First free democratic elections held, Nelson Mandela elected first Black president of South Africa
1995	Truth and Reconciliation Commission is called for by Mandela and legislated by South African Government of National Unity with the Promotion of National Unity and Reconciliation Act, No. 24, 1995

1996	The new South African constitution is ratified
1998	Thabo Mbeki (b. 1942) is elected second Black South African president
2002	Launch of the African Union, hosted by South Africa
2003	Development Summit held in South Africa
2004	South Africa hosts the Pan-African Parliament, and the third national elections retain Thabo Mbeki as president
2007	Jacob Zuma elected as president of the African National Congress

APPENDIX 3

Selected Websites and Guide to Recordings

South Africa and Its Music

Selected Websites

These sites are intended to give you starting points in your investigation of South Africa and its music. There is much more available in cyberspace.

South African History

http://www.robben-island.org.za
http://www.sahistory.org.za

South African Record Companies: Commercial and Archival

http://www.gallo.co.za
http://www.mg.co.za (archive)
http://www.oneworld.co.za
http://www.sabc.co.za
http://www.3rdearmusic.com

South African Music and Musicians

http://africanmusic.org
http://www.afribeat.com
http://www.afropop.org
http://www.allaboutjazz.com

http://www.cama.org.za
http://www.johnnyclegg.com
http://www.music.org.za
http://www.putumayo.com
http://www.sheer.co.za
http://www.tunokwe.com

South African Tourism

http://www.owls.co.za
http://www.robben-island.org.za

Purchasing South African Music

Most of the material discussed in the book is available through the major online webstores including amazon.com or barnesandnoble.com.

If you wish to purchase South African music when you travel to South Africa, there are numerous places that now sell South African recordings, but often the best collection available is in the international departures lounge in the Johannesburg International Airport. In addition, if outside South Africa:

http://www.epinions.com has limited stock of major musicians
http://www.kalahari.net has some stock
http://www.oneworld.co.za has more stock on display, but you cannot purchase online from the USA
http://www.nextag.com has limited stock of major musicians

A Guide to Recordings/Resources for Musical Styles and Key Carriers of Style

Most of these styles can be found on the video resource www.youtube.com: type in keyword, e.g., "gumboot dance" or "*pantsula*" or "*mbaqanga*."

This is not a comprehensive list of all that is available, but should be viewed as a foundation for building a personal or university library collection of South African music. It reflects the twenty years of my own gathering of recordings: it is particularly weak in Afrikaans music, currently the fastest growing category of South African music in the international market; and in the genre of art music recordings.

All recordings are on CD (with a shorter list of films—in VHS tape or DVD format—at the end). Many of the tracks from these recordings can be found in online archives like iTunes. Please note: I have provided as much information about publisher, place, and date of publication as is available on the CD—that information is not uniformly produced on all products.

Traditional and Neo-traditional Music

(a) Traditional Instrumental Vocal and Music

YouTube: "Xhosa traditional South African dancing," video clip from 1930s film, plus many more traditional music clips, use keyword searches by genre, language group, or instrument.

Amampondo: *An Image of Africa/Umfanekiso waAfrika*. 1992. Cape Town: Mountclare Productions. CD AM 24.

Andrew Tracey Steelband: *About Time!* N.d. Grahamstown: International Library of African Music.

Nguni Sound: South Africa and Swaziland 1955, 57, 58. Hugh Tracey Recordings, reissued through ILAM, SWP 020.

Nothembi Mkhwebane: *Vukani Bomma*. 1995. Ndebele traditional. Johannesburg: RPM Records.

Umlamu Wami: *Ukufa*. N.d. Zulu traditional. Johannesburg: Gallo Music Productions.

(b) *Isicathamiya*/"The Lion Sleeps Tonight"/"*Mbube*"

There are many Ladysmith Black Mambazo titles available. I have selected three, and provided three copy-cat groups from Cape Town.

Friends of Freedom: *Ingcaluza*. N.d. *Isicathamiya* group from Khayelitsha in Cape Town. CD self-produced and purchased at V & A Waterfront in Cape Town by the author.

Khayelitsha United Mambazo. N.d. Self-produced recording, purchased by the author at the V & A Waterfront in Cape Town.

Khayelitsha United Mambazo: *Amaphiko (Wings)*. N.d. Second self-produced recording, purchased by the author at the V & A Waterfront in Cape Town.

Ladysmith Black Mambazo: *Gift of the Tortoise, A Musical Journey through Southern Africa*. 1994. Johannesburg: Gallo Record Company, CDGMP 40451 R.

Ladysmith Black Mambazo: *Long Walk to Freedom*. 2006. Cleveland, OH: Headsup, HUCD 3109. With several "world" and "popular" artists, including Taj Mahal, Zap Mama, and Lucky Dube.

Ladysmith Black Mambazo: *Shaka Zulu*. 1987. New York: Warner Brothers, 9 25582-2.

Ladysmith Black Mambazo with English Chamber Orchestra: *No Boundaries*. London: Headsup International, 2006.

Lion King: Original Broadway Cast Recording. 1997. Burbank, CA: Walt Disney Records, 60802.

Mbube Roots: Zulu Choral Music from South Africa, 1930s–1960s. 1998. Cambridge, MA: Rounder Records, Rounder CO 5025.

The Tokens: *The Lion Sleeps Tonight*. Originally recorded 1962. Burbank, CA: Walt Disney Records, BB 61051.

Women of Mambazo: *Mamizolo*. 2002. Johannesburg: Gallo Music Productions, CDGMP 40889.

(c) *Maskanda*, *Mbaqanga*, and *Mqashiyo*

Best of Mahlathini and the Mahotella Queens. N.d. Johannesburg: Gallo Music Productions, CDHUL 40274.
Boyoyo Boys: *Back in Town*. 1987. Cambridge, MA: Rounder Records, CD 5026.
Busi Mhlongo: *Urban Zulu*. 2002. West Sussex, UK: Melt 2000.
Busi Mhlongo and Twasa: *Babhemu*. 1994. London: Sterns Africa, SSCD 005.
Indestructible Beat of Soweto. 1986. Compilation of styles recorded in early 1980s in South Africa. Ho-Ho-Kus, NJ: Shanachie Records, 43033.
Johnny Clegg and Savuka: *Heat, Dust, and Dreams*. 1993. London: EMI (UK), Look South Records, CDEMCJ (WF) 5499.
Juluka: *Ya Vuka Inkunzi* (The Bull Has Risen). 1997. No label given. CDCCP (WL) 1127.
Juluka: *Scatterlings*. 1983. New York: Warner Brothers, 9 23898-2.
Juluka: *African Litany*. 1981. Johannesburg: Music Incorporated.
Juluka: *Universal Men*. 1979. Johannesburg: Priority Music, CDMINC (WL) 1095.
Mahlathini and the Mahotella Queens: *The Lion Roars*. C. 1986. Ho-Ho-Kus, NJ: Shanachie Records, 43081.
Mfaz'Omnyama: *Ngiyashisa Bhe!* 1999. Johannesburg: Gallo Record Company, CDAFR 176.
Mfiliseni Magubane: *Woza, Sihambe*. 1994. New York: Celluloid Records, DELC 6211.
Phuzekhemisi no Khethani: *Imbizo*, CDTIG 456.
Tu Nokwe: *Inyakanyaka*. 1996. Johannesburg: Teal Records, CDRBL 247.
Vusi Mahlasela: *The Voice (Ilivi Lebantu)*. 2003. Ato/BMG Records, 79102-21512-2.
Vusi Mahlasela: *When You Come Back*. 1992. Johannesburg: BMG and Shifty Music.
Vusi Ximba: *Threrelina*. N.d. Johannesburg: Paradise Music (BMG Records), CDPDM (SB) 348.
Zulu Jive: Umbaqanga—Urban and Rural Zulu Beats from South Africa. 1983. London: Hannibal Records, 4410.

(d) Gumboot Dance

Janet Topp Fargion and Albert Nene (producers). N.d. *Gumboot Guitar: Zulu Street Guitar Music from South Africa*. London: British Library, Topic World Series.

Religious Music

(a) Gospel Music

Bella: *Elke Dag Met Jesus*. 2006. Johannesburg: New Vision Music.
Holy Cross Choir: *10 Years of Hits*. N.d. Johannesburg: Gallo Music Publisher, CDSZL 149 (J).
International Pentecostal Church: *Mehleng Ya Bofelo*. 1995. Johannesburg: Kariba Records, SJHD 147.
Mthunzi Namba and Friends: *Arise! All ye worshippers*, vol. 1. 1994. Durban: SAREPTA Music, SARCD 016.

Rebecca Malope: *Live at the State Theatre with Pure Magic.* 1996. Johannesburg: EMI, CDFLY(WL)562.
Rough Guide to South African Gospel Music. 2003. London: World Music Network.
Soweto Gospel Choir: *Voices from Heaven.* 2005. Ho-Ho-Kus, NJ: Shanachie.
Spirit of African Gospel. 2000. Arc Music (UK), EUCD1351.
Tales of South African Gospel. 2006. Sheer Sound (UK).
Youth With a Mission: *Ndizelwe Ngokutsha.* N.d. Johannesburg: Youth with a Mission, marketed by Amanxusa Music Productions.
ZCC Brass Band: *Jesu O Lesedi.* No publisher. TELCD 2963.

Historical Styles

(a) Compilations

See http://www.allaboutjazz.com/southafrica/comps.htm for further discussion of general compilations.

From Marabi to Disco: 42 Years of Township Music. 1994. African Classics Series. Johannesburg: Gallo Music Productions.
Long Walk to Freedom: A Celebration of 4 Decades of South African Music. 2002. London: Wrasse Records (all tracks used under license from Gallo Music International, South Africa), WRASS 080.
Township Jazz 'n' Jive. 1997. No place. Music Club, 50041.
Winds of Change: A Journey Through the Key Moments that Gave Birth to a Free, Democratic South Africa. 2004. No place. Cream Music, ACM CD 023/1, 2.

(b) *Marabi*

There are almost no recordings of *marabi* as it was performed in the 1920s–40s, with one or two exceptions. Christopher Ballantine's 1993 book, *Marabi Nights*, published by Ravan Press in Johannesburg, has an accompanying cassette with examples.

From Marabi to Disco: 42 Years of Township Music. African Classics Series. Johannesburg: Gallo Music Productions.

(c) *Kwela*

King Kwela featuring Spokes Mashiyane. 1991. African Classics Series. Johannesburg: Gallo Music Productions, CDZAC 50.
Tebogo: *Kwela Tebza.* 1996. Johannesburg: Teal Records, TELCD 2631.
Nelson Makhokha: *Sophiatown Pennywhistle Special.* N.d. (c. 1995). Johannesburg: Mob Music, CDISA 224.

(d) *Makwaya*

Caluza's Double Quartet. 1930. Heritage Records. Released 1992.
Many choral groups have recorded CDs—from church to hospital choirs.
Holy Spirits: *Kabelo ya ka Entle Thapelo ea Holy Spirits* (Sotho Choral). N.d. Johannesburg: Gallo Music, TELCD 2898 (126)
Original Baragwanath Choir, featuring Nkosi Sikeleli Afrika. N.d. Johannesburg: Roi Music, marketed by Music Team, CDCT(WB) 5.

(e) Protest/"New South African" Music and Spoken Word

Long Walk to Freedom: A Celebration of 4 Decades of South African Music. 2002. London: Wrasse Records (all tracks used under license from Gallo Music International, South Africa), WRASS 080.
The MK Platoon: *Victory. '94 Election Souvenir.* 1994. Recorded at Mint Jam Studios, London. Executive producers Robert McBride and Andrew Kasrils. CDTIG 488.
Place of Hope: Celebrating the New South Africa, Two Worlds Become One. 1996. No place. Warner Brothers, 9 46165-2.
South Africa: Rainbow Nation. 1996. Pretoria: MAC-D, CD cut in shape of African continent.
Voice of Nelson Mandela (Extracts from Famous Speeches). 1999. Johannesburg: SABC Sound Archives.
Winds of Change: A Journey Through the Key Moments that Gave Birth to a Free, Democratic South Africa. 2004. No place. Cream Music, ACM CD 023/1, 2.

(f) Township Pop

AbaShante: *Ayoyo*. 2002. Johannesburg: EMI.
Boyoyo Boys: *Back in Town*. 1987. Cambridge, MA: Rounder Records, ROUNDER CD 5026.
Brenda Fassie: *Greatest Hits*. 2001. CDBREN (WLM) 009.
Brenda (Fassie): *Amadlozi*. 2000. EMI/CCP, CDBREN (WL) 100.

(g) Musical Theater/Film Music

Amandla! Revolution in Four-Part Harmony. 2003. ATO/BMG Records, 79102-21510-2.
Bertha Egnos and Gail Lakier's Ipi-Tombi: Original Cast Recording. 1986. Johannesburg: Teal/Trutone, DOVCD 6.
Duma kaNdlovu (writer and director). *Bergville Stories: The Cast*. 1996. Johannesburg: Downtown Studios. Soundtrack of stage production.
How Long? Gibson Kente's Classic Musical. 1997. Johannesburg: Gallo, CDRED 607.
Little Bird/Sophiatown Partnership: *Sophiatown: Soundtrack to the Movie*. 2005. Recorded in Johannesburg in 2002, film released 2003. Recording released in Johannesburg: Gallo Records, CDCAT001
Neill Solomon: *Gathering of the Beasts*. 1992. Johannesburg: Tusk Music.TFAD 1.

Sarafina! The Music of Liberation. 1988. New York: BMG Records, 9307-2-RC
Sophie Mgcina. 1983. *Poppie Nongena: Original Cast in the Award-Winning South African Musical*. Rykodisc, HNCD 1351.
Wait a Minim! Opened on March 7, 1966 and closed a year later on Broadway at the John Golden Theater in New York City, after 457 performances. See Jeremy Taylor reminiscence http://www.3rdearmusic.com/lyrics/calypso.html. No new recordings reissued, but plenty of sheet music, e.g., *Wait a Minim!: A Musical Entertainment* by Leon Gluckman. Andrew T. N. Tracey Musical Score: Printed music: Musical revues & comedies. New York: Frank Music, ©1966. ILAM has several versions of this and other similar productions available for purchase on CD. See http://www.ilam.ac.za.
Williams, P. and T. Matshikiza. 1996. *King Kong: The Musical*. Johannesburg: Gallo Music Productions, CDZAC 51 R.

(h) African Classical Music: Opera, String Quartets, and Classical Guitar

David Hewitt: *African Tapestry*. 1989. Johannesburg: David Gresham Records, CD DGR 1129.
Soweto String Quartet: *Renaissance*. 1996. Johannesburg: BMG Records, CDBSP (WF) 7009.
Soweto String Quartet: *Zebra Crossing*. 1994. Johannesburg: BMG Records, CD BSP (WF) 2031.
U-Carmen eKhayelitsha—Xhosa-language rendition of Bizet's *Carmen* set in Cape Town. Won Golden Bear award at the Berlin Film Festival, February 2005. Limited circulation of DVD on PAL video system only (see list below). Subtitles in English and Thai.

Post-apartheid

(a) Post-apartheid Bushmen Music

Pops Mohammed Presents Bushmen of the Kalahari. No place. Melt 2000, BW 2128; EFA 89018-2.
Bushmen of the Kalahari. 1995. London: Arc Music, LC 05111, EUCD.
Bushmen of the Kalahari. 2006. West Sussex, UK; Clearwater, FL: Arc Music, EUCD1995; LC 05111.
Namibia: Songs of the Ju'hoansi Bushmen. 1997. Paris: Ocora, 560117.
Namibia: Ju'hoansi Bushmen, Instrumental Music. 2003. Paris: Ocora, 560179 HM 79.
Zen Voyages/Musical Adventures of the Mind: Sands of the Kalahari. 2003. Minnetonka, MN: Liquid Records and Entertainment, LIQ 12146.

(b) Hip Hop and *Kwaito*

African Rap: The Rough Guide, Rappers, Rebels, and Ragamuffins. 2004. London: World Music Network, LC 11067.

Jean Grae: *The Bootleg of the Bootleg*. 2003. New York: Babygrande.
Kwaito: South African Hip Hop. 2000. London: Earthworks/Stern's Music.

White English-language Pop—1960s–1990s

See www.3rdearmusic.com
http://www.rock.co.za/files/sa_classic_songs.html history of classic rock and pop songs 1939–2002 from South Africa
Many of these groups have websites and some have YouTube videos.

(a) General Pop

Best of P. J. Powers and Hotline: 16 Greatest Hits. MFM PJCD 3000.
Claire Johnston: *Africa Blue*. 2005. London: EMI.
EVoid. 1983. Johannesburg: Tusk. CD reissue (2000 on retrofresh). WICD 8012.
Hits of South Africa. N.d. Johannesburg: Gallo Music, reissue, CDGMP 40389 S.
Mango Groove: *Another Country*. 1993. Johannesburg: Tusk Music.
Mango Groove: *Eat a Mango*. 1995. Johannesburg: Tusk Music, WOND 136.
Mango Groove: *Hometalk*. 1990. Johannesburg: Tusk Music, TUCD(F) 14.
Q Cumba Zoo: *Wake Up and Dream*. 1996. New York: Arista Records (BMG), 07822-18931-2.

(b) Local Rock (English and Afrikaans)

Arapaho: *Wild Warriors—The Complete Arapaho*. 2007. Fresh CD (South Africa), FreshCD 151.
Bernoldus Niemand: *Wie is Bernoldus Niemand?* 1995. Johannesburg: Shifty Records (Tic Tic Bang 007).
James Phillips: *Made in South Africa*. 1995. Johannesburg: Shifty Records (Tic Tic Bang).
James Phillips and The Lurchers: *Sunny Skies*. 1993. Johannesburg: Shifty Records (Tic Tic Bang and Free State Music), BANGCD 015.
C Weed. 1999. Johannesburg: Teal Records, Polygram Music.
Koos Kombuis: *Mona Lisa, Die Mooiste Love Songs*. 1999. Johannesburg: Shifty. See review: http://www.cd.co.za/reviews/koosmona.htm.
Best of Urban Creep. 2005. Fresh Music (South Africa), FreshCD 144.

(c) White Folk

Edi Niederlander: *Hear No Evil*. 1989. Cape Town: Mountain Records (Ethnic World Music).
Jeremy Taylor: *Ag Pleez Daddy*. 2005. NP: Folksound Records, CD RED 608.
Landscape Prayers: *Bush Telegraph*. Johannesburg: Sheer Sound, SSCD006.
Syd Kitchen: *City Child*. Tekweni Records.

Afrikaans/English pop

(a) Historical Reissues, and Cross-over

This is a category of South African music that is truly thriving in post-apartheid South Africa. This list does not begin to map out the new directions in Afrikaans-language performance and the growth of festivals celebrating this music.

Boereqanga: *Made in South Africa* led by Nico Carstens. 1996. Cape Town: Lions Head Records.
David Kramer: *Karoo Kitaar Blues*. 2001. Cape Town: Blik Music.
David Kramer: *Klassic Kramer*. 1996. Cape Town: Blik Music.
Jim Muller: *Sy Oorspronklike Keurspele. So Het Hulle Gespeel*, vol. 2. Archivist Rob Allingham (Gallo); Johannesburg: TGE Records at RPM, CDTGE 5 (J).
Musiek Met Feel. Compilation of popular Afrikaans singer-songwriters. Compiled by Naomi LeRoux and Liza Botha. CDEMIM (WL) 065.
Nico Carstens: *22 Goue Treffers*. 1994. Liner notes by Malcolm Lombard. Includes extended discography of works by Carstens for Columbia, HMV, and others; and the works he recorded under the pseudonym Penny Serenaders—recording "Black" music, i.e., *kwela*, *ghoema*, and samba. Carstens recorded extensively on the SABC transcription series for radio broadcast; none of these items are listed in the liner notes here.

Jazz

(a) Compilations

African Jazz Groove. Featuring Sipho Gumede, Dennis Mpale, Sipho "Hotstix" Mabuse, Kalamazoo 2, Joe Nina, Unofficial Language, and many more.
Jazz Offerings from South Africa. 1999. Johannesburg: Gallo Record Company, CDREDD 631.
South African Jazz: The Rough Guide. Hip Kings, Hip Queens and the New Jazz Pioneers. London: World Music Network, RGNET 1045 CD.
Tales of South Africa Jazz: Styles and Influences. Johannesburg: Sheer Sound.

(b) Early Jazz History

(Through the end of the 1970s, some recorded locally, others abroad)
A representative sample, not a comprehensive list of every recording made by individual musicians.

Abdullah Ibrahim: *Fats, Duke, and the Monk*. Recorded 1973. Toronto: Sackville. CD reissue, 1992, SCCD 2-3048.
Buddy Tate Meets Abdullah Ibrahim: The Legendary 1977 Encounter. NY: Chiaroscuro Records. CD reissue, 1996.
Chris McGregor and the South African Jazz Exile's Thunderbolt. PAM, 1997, 405.
Chris McGregor's Brotherhood of Breath: The Memorial Concert. ITM, 1994.

Dark City Sisters and Flying Jazz Queens. 1993. Reissue. London: Earthworks, CDEWV 31, 7243 8 39182 5.
Dollar Brand: *African Space Program*. Recorded 1973, CD reissue, Enja.
Dollar Brand: *Anatomy of a South African Village*. January 1965. London: Black Lion, CD reissue, 1992, BLCD760172.
Dollar Brand: *Round Midnight at the Montmartre*. January 1965. London: Black Lion.
Dollar Brand: *Reflections*. 1965. London: Black Lion.
Dollar Brand Duo: *Good News from Africa*. Recorded 1973. CD reissue, Enja 2048.
Dorothy Masuka: *Hamba Notstokolo and Other Original Hits from the '50s*. African Classics Series. Johannesburg: Gallo Music.
Duke Ellington Presents the Dollar Brand Trio. February 1963 recording, first released 1964; CD reissue by Reprise Records, 1997, 6111-2.
Jabu Nkosi's City Jazz 7: *Remembering Bra Zacks*. Johannesburg: Gallo Music, CDGMP 40718.
Jazz 1962: Cold Castle National Festival Moroka-Jabavu. African Heritage Series, TELCD 2302.
Jazz in Africa, Volume 1. The 1960s Jazz Epistles, first recording. African Recordings Series. Reissued in 1992 by Kaz Records, licensed by Gallo Records Ltd, KAZCD 24.
Jazz in Africa, Volume 2. African Recordings Series. Reissues focused on saxophonist Kippie Moeketsi (d. 1983). KAZCD 28.
Miriam Makeba and the Skylarks. African Heritage Series, vol. 1. Johannesburg: Gallo Music, TELCD 2303.
Miriam Makeba: *Africa*. Novus Series '70. 1991. New York: BMG Records.
Miriam Makeba: *Her Essential Recordings (The Empress of African Song)*. 2006. MANT-DBL502.
Sathima Bea Benjamin: *A Morning in Paris*. 1997. Munich: Enja Records, ENJ-9309 2.
Township Jazz 'n' Jive. 18 South African Urban Swing Classics from the Jivin' 50s. Windswept Pacific Entertainment Company, 50041.
Township Swing Jazz!, vols 1 and 2. African Classics Series. Johannesburg: Gallo Music, CD ZAC 53 and 54.
Very Best of the Manhattan Brothers: Their Greatest Hits (1948–1959). Johannesburg: Gallo Music/Empire Music, CDZAC 77.
West Nkosi: *Sixteen Original Sax Jive Hits*. African Classics Series. Johannesburg: Gallo Music.

(c) Contemporary South African jazz

Readers are advised to check online through a variety of websites for further information on contemporary jazz musicians and the rapid growth of jazz festivals taking place in South Africa. For Abdullah Ibrahim, see Lars Rassmussen's *Discography*, 2nd edition.

Abdullah Ibrahim: *South African Ambassador*. 1997. JazzFest, 2201.
Abdullah Ibrahim: *Township One More Time*. New York: Ekapa, CDEMCJ (WA) 5758.
Abdullah Ibrahim Remixed: re:BRAHIM. Enja Records.
Abdullah Ibrahim Trio: *Cape Town Revisited*. New York: Ekapa.

African Jazz Pioneers. 1989, Gallo GRC Johannesburg; 1990, KAZ Records Ltd, EMI SA, KAZ CD 14.
Elite Swingsters and Dolly Rathebe. 1997. *Siya Gida: We Dance.* Johannesburg: CSR Studios.
Gloria Bosman: *Stop and Think.* 2003. Johannesburg: SABC Studios.
Hugh Masekela: BBC Radio Live in Concert. 2002, recorded October 2001.
Jimmy Dludlu: *Echoes from the Past.* 2000. Johannesburg: Polygram SA.
Kalimba: *Laid Back Sunday.* 2007. CSRMCD 139.
Mafikizolo: *Sibongile.* 2003. Johannesburg: Sony.
Mahube Music from South Africa. 1998. Johannesburg: Steve Dyer Production.
Miriam Makeba: *Sangoma.* 1988. New York: Warner Brothers, 9 25673-2.
Safika: *We Have Arrived.* Imeko Featuring Bra Benny. 1996. African Jazz Classics Series. Johannesburg: Gallo Music, CDRPM 7150.
Sathima Bea Benjamin: *Song Spirit.* 2006. New York: Ekapa Records, 003 (South Africa).
Sathima Bea Benjamin: *Best of Sathima Bea Benjamin.* 2001. Cape Town: EMI and Enja Records, CDSRIK(WL) 7861500.
Sipho Gumede: *Down Freedom Avenue.* Tusk; Kariba Records; B and W Records, B and W CD 1.
Sibongile Khumalo: *Ancient Evenings.*
Sibongile Khumalo: *Live at the Market Theatre.* Recorded May 2 and 3, 1997.
Winston Mankunku: *Crossroads.* 1987. ITM 0033, 1433 CD.

(d) South Africans in Europe

(Very small sample of a much vaster archive)

Chris Joris: *Songs for Mbizo: Tribute to Johnny Dyani.* Torhout: VKH Tonesetters, TS001.
Chris McGregor's Brotherhood of Breath: *Bremen to Bridgewater.* Recent reissue of 1970s performances. London: Cuneiform Records.
Chris McGregor's Traveling Somewhere. Recent reissue of 1970s performances. London: Cuneiform Records.
Haazz and Company: *Unlawful Noise.* With South African free jazz players Louis Moholo and Johnny Dyani. Amsterdam: KGB Records, KGB 7076.
Harry Miller's Isipingo: *Which Way Now?* London: Cuneiform Records.
JazzinZurich. 2004. Zurich: Intakt Records.
Per Henrik Wallin (piano), Johnny Dyani (bass), Erik Dahlback (drums): *Burning in Stockholm.* 2004.
The Very Best of Abdullah Ibrahim. Hoboken, NJ: Music Club, 50140.

(e) Commercial Jazz

(1) Popular swing band singers (1950s through 1990s)

EMI Presents the Magic of Eve Boswell. EMI, 7243 8 57016 2 7.
Margaret Singana: Lady Africa. 1996. Johannesburg: Gallo Record Company.

(2) Cape Town: dance bands, pop bands, and Cape culture bands

Abie Thomas at the V & A Waterfront, vol. 1. 2001. Durban: Third Ear Music.
Band Soft Touch: *At the Waterfront*, vol. 2. N.d. Home produced, M. Abrahms.
Cape Culture Band. 1995. Johannesburg: Teal Records, UPCD 012.
Cape Jazz. Basil Coetzee and Sabenza, et al. 1992. Hamburg: Ethnic World Music, CD MOULP 74.
Music From the Streets of Cape Town. 2 CDs. Johannesburg: BMG Africa, CDSLS(WF)118.
The Rockets: *Black and White*. 1999. Johannesburg: CCP Record Co, CDROCKET (WL) 002.
The Philadelphia Rhythms: *Live at the Goldfinger*. 1997. Johannesburg: BMG Records.

Digital Video Discs/VHS video

Attenborough, Richard (director). 1999 [1987]. DVD. *Cry Freedom: The True Story of the Friendship that Shook South Africa and Awakened the World*. Universal City, CA: Universal Studios.
Austin, Chris. 1988. *Abdullah Ibrahim: Brother With Perfect Timing*. New York: Rhapsody Films.
Austin, Chris and Gill Bond (producers). DVD. *Abdullah Ibrahim: Brother with Perfect Timing*. Oaks, PA: Music Video Distributors.
Bausch, Ike Brooks. 1994. *Zonk!* Vancouver, BC: Villon Films.
Bowey, John. 1998. *African Wave: South African Music and Its Influences*. Princeton: Films for the Humanities and Sciences.
Cappellari, Ciro (director). 2005. *Abdullah Ibrahim: A Struggle for Love*. Berlin: Produktion 1.
Clegg, Jonathan. 2007. DVD. *Johnny Clegg Live, with the Soweto Gospel Choir at the Nelson Mandela Theatre*. Johannesburg: Sting Music, with Rhythm Dog Music.
Dimpho Di Kopane (director). 2003. DVD. *U-Carmen eKhayelitsha*. Fortissimo Films and Mangpong, Thailand.
Erlmann, Veit. 1996. *Nightsong: Performance, Power, and Practice in South Africa*. Accompanies book of same title. Chicago: University of Chicago Press.
Freeman, Morgan (director). 1993. DVD. *Bopha! The Struggle for Freedom Begins at Home*. Hollywood, CA: Paramount Pictures.
Gibson, Angus and Jo Mennell (directors). 1996. *Mandela, Son of Africa, Father of a Nation*. Marina Del Ray, CA: Lion's Gate Films.
Hirsch, Lee. 2002. *Amandla! Revolution in Four-part Harmony*. Santa Monica, CA: Artisan Entertainment.
Hood, Gavin (director). 2005. DVD. *Tsotsi*. Burbank, CA: Miramax Home Entertainment.
Johannes Kerkorrel. 2002. DVD. *Johannes Kerkorrel: 'N Jaar Later in the Staatsteater*. Johannesburg: Kyknet Films.
Kay, Andrew, Clifford Hocking, and David Vigo (producers). 2006. DVD. *Soweto Gospel Choir: Voices from Heaven*. Johannesburg: SABC.
Key, Liza (director). 2004. DVD. *Karoo Kitaar Blues: David Kramer's South African Musical Journey*. South Africa: Key Films, Blik Music.

Kruger, Kevin and Dan Hill (producers). 1996. *South Africa: Rainbow Nation.* Pretoria: Mac-V.

Lindsay-Hogg, Michael (director). 1987. VHS. *Paul Simon, Graceland: The African Concert.* Burbank, CA: Warner Reprise Video, 38136-3.

Little, Steven and Arthur Baker. 1985. *Sun City: Artists United Against Apartheid.* New York: Manhattan Records.

Marre, Jeremy (director). 1998. *Paul Simon's Graceland: Recounting the Journey of a Legendary Music Recording.* Los Angeles: Rhino Entertainment.

Marre, Jeremy (director). 1988. *Rhythm of Resistance: The Black Music of South Africa.* Newtown, NJ: Shanachie Music.

Maseko, Zola (director). 2003. DVD. *Drum.* Johannesburg: Armada Pictures.

Mayfair Productions. 1999. DVD. *Ladysmith Black Mambazo: Live at the Royal Albert Hall.* Shanachie Entertainment Corp. 108.

Nobel, Nigel (director). VHS. 1988. *Voices of Sarafina!: Songs of Hope and Freedom.* Music by Mbongeni Ngema and Hugh Masekela. New York: New Yorker Video, NYV 58091.

Nofal, Emil. 1994. *Song of Africa.* Vancouver, BC: Villon Films.

Nyandeni, Thani and Todd Twala (creators). 2004. DVD. *Umoja: The Spirit of Togetherness.* Johannesburg, South Africa; London; West Gosford, Australia: Sting Music and Red Pepper Films.

Powell, Aubrey (director). DVD. 2000. *Gumboots! An Explosion of Spirit and Song.* Chatsworth, CA: Image Entertainment.

Rifkin, Larry (executive producer). 1997. VHS. *Ipi Ntombi: An African Dance Celebration.* Burbank, CA: PBH Home Video, B3651.

Schmitz, Oliver (director). 2000. DVD. *Mapantsula.* Africa Gold Collection. Johannesburg: Impact Video Distributor.

Simon, Paul. 1988. *Graceland: The African Concert.* New York: Warner Brothers.

Simonson, Eric (director). 2000. *Ladysmith Black Mambazo: On Tip Toe.* N.p. New Video Group (distribution, 2004).

Singh, Anant (director). N.d. VHS. *Sarafina!* With Whoopi Goldberg. Burbank, CA: Hollywood Pictures Home Videos.

Swanson, Donald (director). 1949. *African Jim.* No place. Warrior Films. Re-released 1998, Vancouver, BC: Villon Films.

Uys, Jamie (director). DVD. 1980 and 1988. *The Gods Must be Crazy I and II.* Culver City, CA: Sony Pictures 10649.

Yesterdays. 2004. Oscar-nominated, many film festival awards. First full-length feature film in Zulu language, with English sub-titles. See http://www.southafrica.info, retrieved June 19, 2007.

APPENDIX 4

Themes Common to the Study of African Music

1980s to Present

The study of music in Africa and the study of African music has largely been categorized in two ways: by geographical region and by concept or theme. In this section, I highlight the materials referenced at the end of the book as they pertain to these two kinds of discussion.

There are a few works listed that provide a general overview of the study of contemporary African culture (Barber 1986, 1997a and b; Drewal 1991; Fabian 1997; Hannerz 1997; Thompson 1979). The recently published *Garland Encyclopedia of World Music: Africa* (Stone 1998) provides overview chapters on five musical regions: West Africa, North Africa, East Africa, Central Africa, and Southern Africa (see Cooke 1998, Djedje 1998, Kaemmer 1998, Kubik 1998, and Wendt 1998, respectively; see also Danielson 1996 and Langlois 1996 for additional North African material; Allen 1996 and Coplan 1998 for South Africa. The Garland volume provides additional pieces on individual countries but the coverage is not consistent for the entire continent). Although this volume contains a CD, the recordings are rather limited. They will need to be supplemented with commercially produced sound and video recordings. There are several other volumes that are concerned with popular and traditional music of the continent generally (Bender 1991; Bergman 1985; Broughton et al. 1999; Euba 1988; Ewens 1991; M. Floyd 1999; Graham; 1988 and 1992; Mensah 1998; Njoku 1998; Nketia 1982, 1998; Roberts 1998 [1972]; Schmidt 1994b; Stapleton and May 1990; Stewart 1992). Impey (1998) covers African popular music generally, including discussion of festivals, and the impact of the music industry on African performance. Generally speaking, I shall discuss the literature and recordings on African musical performance as follows: Arabic influences on North Africa; the pygmy sounds of Central Africa; the griot/jali and drumming traditions of West Africa; the loss of Africans to the slave trade and African music in diaspora; competitiveness and the impact of Arabic music from Egypt on East Africa;

the *mbira* traditions of Southern Africa; and vocal music of South Africa. I have selected these themes because they have emerged out of the literature published since 1980.

West Africa

Perhaps because of the significant presence of Africans forced into the Americas through the slave trade, much of what is popularly known in the United States about African music comes from West Africa, the site of much of the slave trade. Frequently, all of African musical production is subsumed under what is specific to the western part of the continent. For example, in the introduction to his landmark study on African drumming and sociability, ethnomusicologist John Chernoff commented in the early 1970s that the most common perception about African music outside the continent is that it was a continent of drummers. Three decades later, the stereotype of Africa remains one of drums and drummers. For those interested in drumming, there are several books and videos that explain drumming techniques as well as the social elements pertaining to drumming ensembles particularly in Nigeria and Ghana (Chernoff 1979; Euba 1990; Locke 1990; Nzewi et al. 2001). For discussion of West African griot/jali traditions, see Charry 2000; Diawara 1997; Duran 1999 [1994], 1995; Eyre 2000; Hale 1998; Jegede 1994; and Knight 1991. Additional pieces on West African popular culture, art music, and individual musicians include: Avorgbedor 2001; Collins 1992; Graebner 1997; Omojola 1997; Schmidt 1994a and b; Veal 2000; and Waterman 1997.

East Africa

There are three broad themes in writing about musical performance in East Africa. The sociability of African (and particularly Ghanaian) drumming ensembles is countered with the stress on competition (see Gunderson and Barz 2000). The impact of religious belief is another theme: for Islam and North African musical culture on the East African coastline see Askew 2002 and Topp Fargion 1999; both Askew and Topp Fargion also have pieces in Gunderson and Barz (2000); for the impact of gospel and mission choir music see Barz in Gunderson and Barz (2000). Additional work in popular music focuses on the guitar (see Kaye 1998; Schmidt 1994b). Topp Fargion's work is specifically focused on women in Taraab as performers and composers.

North Africa

Aside from the general introductory material on music in North Africa (Langlois 1996; Wendt 1998), and music and Islam (Shiloah 1995), there is some discussion of music and trance in the popular imagination (Langlois 1998). My focus in North Africa is with musical performance in two countries: Algeria and Egypt, and with issues of gender, popular culture, and ethnography. Some key works are those by Schade-Poulsen (1999) on men and Algerian popular music, and Danielson (1997) on a powerful woman singer and radio broadcaster, mother of the Arab world, Umm Kulthum.

Central Africa

There are two broad strands of music research on Central Africa in the last two decades: the popular music scene, amply covered in the general texts on African traditional and popular musics cited above, and the music of the so-called "pygmies" native to the central African rainforest. The pygmies have long captured the imagination of Africans and non-Africans alike. Considered some of the original inhabitants of the continent, their relationship to non-Africans has not always been so positive. Turnbull conducted landmark ethnography with a group of pygmies in the 1950s (Turnbull 1962, recently reissued). Michelle Kisliuk (1998), Steven Feld (2000), and Furniss and Arom (1993) have produced the most recent work.

Southern Africa

Several general works relate to music in Southern Africa, though my main focus is obviously on the country called South Africa. Zimbabwe, and the *mbira* as both traditional and popular instrument and musical style, is written about by Berliner (1978), Brown (1999), and Turino (1998, 2000). Wells (1994) writes on traditional music in Lesotho, and Vail and White (1997) have a fascinating piece on the oral transmission of a simple work song in Mozambique. A general overview of South African popular music is provided by Olwage (2008), Lucia (2005) Coplan (1985 and 1998). Individual genres of performance include pennywhistle *kwela* (Allen 2000), South African jazz and vaudeville (Ballantine 1993; Coplan 1985; McGregor 1995; Muller 1996, 2001, 2007a, and 2007b; and Rasmussen 2000a, 2000b, 2002a, 2002b, 2003a, and 2003b), *maskanda* (Davies 1994), gumboot dance (Muller and Topp Fargion 1985, 1999), and *isicathamiya* (Erlmann 1996, 1999; and Meintjes 1990). Women musicians have been the specific focus of several pieces (James 1999; Makeba 1987; Muller 1996, 1999, 2000, 2001, and 2008 [expected]) and male musicians have been given some special attention as well (Ballantine 1993, 1996, and 1999; Erlmann 1996).

APPENDIX 5

Discussion of Musical Examples on CD

Isicathamiya, Tracks 1–2

These two tracks are field recordings of rehearsals of *isicathamiya*. On track 6, Traditional Music Association co-founder Paulus Msimango explains to me what is unusual about this group: they have a woman alto. It is hard to really distinguish her voice from the male singers.

The second example is a recording of one *isicathamiya* group performing at the all night choir competitions held weekly in the YMCA Hall on Beatrice Street, Durban. The group starts out at the back of the hall, and slowly moves forward. Their stepping is quiet at the start, as they move forward to the stage, where the judges are seated. The overall performance moves from soft stepping, synchronized, catlike movements of singers, on to the stage, where the group leader stands in front of the rest of the singers. You can hear the group's supporters applauding at intervals throughout the performance. On a couple of occasions, the applause signals support for a woman—girlfriend or wife—who has approached one of the singers, and claimed him for herself. She stakes her claim by giving him some money, or putting a piece of her own jewelry on to his uniform. About two-thirds of the way through the performance, the singers start to dance together, stepping on the wooden stage in a more pronounced manner. At the end of the song with steps, they form a line and proceed off the stage to the back of the hall.

Track 1: Xolo Homeboys rehearsal

Field recording by Carol Muller, Durban, 1996
Explanation by Paulus Msimango (now deceased)

Track 2: Beatrice Street YMCA, Durban

Field recording by Carol Muller, Durban, 1996

Isicathamiya "praktisa"

Zulu *Maskanda* and Gumboot Dance, Tracks 3–10

These eight tracks provide a detailed soundscape of *maskanda* performance, both as a highly skilled singer-songwriter guitar tradition (Thami Vilakazi) in the style of *isiZulu*, and as the Zulu *maskanda* sounds used to accompany gumboot dance. The *maskanda* style represented here, embodied in the guitar, violin, and concertina, emerged from the southern coastal region of KwaZulu Natal, and is known as *umzansi*.

Blanket Mkhize's guitar playing harkens back to an earlier style, *ukuvamba* (vamping chords), rather than the *ukupika* (picking style) of Thami Vilakazi. Blanket's guitar playing includes the scraping sounds that harken back to the friction musical bow, and forward to the use of the violin, so I have placed his friction style of guitar playing next to the track with the violin playing.

While the musicians who accompany gumboot dance do so by providing a basic rhythmic groove (a largely improvised, heavily repetitive cyclical accompaniment), Thami Vilakazi's *maskanda* style has reached the height of excellent *maskanda* performance. His music is discussed further in the specific tracks below.

Track 3: Blanket Mkhize

Field recording by Carol Muller, Durban, 1996
Zulu *maskanda* guitar with comb

Track 4: Friend of Blanket Mkhize

Field recording by Carol Muller, Durban, 1996
Zulu *maskanda* concertina

Track 5: Friend of Blanket Mkhize

Field recording by Carol Muller, Durban, 1996
Zulu *maskanda* violin

Track 6: "Chuning"

Field recording by Carol Muller, Durban, December 14, 1994
Thami Vilakazi, composer and guitarist
The "*chuning*" here reminds me of the chimes of grandfather clocks present in many White homes in South Africa in my childhood.

Track 7: "Awusho Ndodanba"

Field recording by Carol Muller, Durban, December 14, 1994
Thami Vilakazi, composer and guitarist
Song translation: Sazi Dlamini

Indodana yami	My Son
Awusho ndodana uyitholeph'indawo	Say my son, where did you find it?
Awusho ndodana uyitholeph'indawo	Say my son, where did you find it?
Awusho mfana wami uyitholeph'indawo	Say, my boy, where did you find it?
Awusho ndodana uyitholeph'indawo	Say my son, where have you found a place?
Awusho ndodana uyitholeph'indawo	
Awusho mfana wami uyitholeph'indawo	Say my boy, where did you find it?
Awusho ndodana uyitholeph'indawo	
Musukufihla ndodana	Out with it, my son
Iqondo liyabaqed'abantu	This [sexual disease] wipes out people
Musukufihla mfana wami	Out with it my son
Iqondo likuqondile	The disease is on top of you
Musukufihla mfana wami	Out with it my boy
Ilumbo liyabathath'abantu emhlabeni bo	The affliction takes people away from the face of the earth
Abanye babo abasekho emhlabeni	Some of them are no longer on this earth
Abanye babo bayagula	Some of them are ill
Balel'esibedlela	They are sleeping in the hospital
Abanye babo abasekho emhlabeni	Some of them . . .
Abanye babo bayagula	
Balel'esbedlela	
Abanye babo abasekho emhlabeni	
Abanye babo bayagula	
Balel'esbedlela	
Awusho ndodana uyitholeph'indawo	Say my son, where did you find it?
[Self Praises]	
Zasha phela madoda kuChakide	Men, its burning from Chakide
Ugobekanje bethi bamkakile	Bent like this, they say they have surrounded him
Kwamphosel'uhlamvu	Threw a grain down
Bathi bayaluthatha	They try to pick it up
Bataphuna isitingi senkukhu	They soil their hands with chicken poop
UChakide waphuma kanje	Chakide comes out on the other side
Kwath'angilale [A saying]	[With laughter] I nearly fell sleep
Umahlalel'okade wahlala	The longtime unemployed

Evuk'ekuseni ath'uyemsebenzini	He woke in the morning saying he was going to work
Kant'uyeshebeeni abuyelapho	But he was going to the shebeen and from there
Ayifak'induku	He wielded a stick
Athi kadulelephi izolo	Saying, "Where did you sleep last night?"
Ungabaleki uze ngala	Don't run this way
Uma esekushaya wena	When he's beating you
Uzongixabanisa	You will cause a quarrel
Kubesengathi ubulele kwami	It will seem like you spent a night with me
Kanti angikwazi	Whereas I don't know you
Wangiphika futhi ngikweshela	You refused me when I proposed to you
Hah!	Hah!
Ji!	Ji!

Usehleli phezulu-ke manje	Now he's right on top
UChakide ekhanda kulendoda	Chakide on top of this man's head
Ilibele ukumvimba ubala	Trying in vain to stop him [Chakide]
Abangani bayo	His friends
Bayayibuza ukuthi	They are asking
Ubani lapho wemfowethu	"Who is that there, my brother?"
Hayi khululekani nina	"No, you relax
khohlwani yimina	and forget about me."
Khon'uChakide la	"It is Chakide here."

Track 8: "Kungcono Khona"

Field recording by Carol Muller, Durban, December 14, 1994
Thami Vilakazi, composer and guitarist
Song translation: Sazi Dlamini

Kungcono khona ngizihlalele	It's better that I stay like this
Kunalento engiyibonayo	Than what I am seeing
Kungcono khona ngihlalele Baba	Its better that I stay like this, Father
Kunalento engiyibonayo	
Ngilunge mina ngizihlalele	I am fine if I stay as I am
Kunalento engiyibonayo	Better than what I see around me
Kungcono khona ngizihlalele	It's better that I stay like this
Kunalento engiyibonayo	Than what I am seeing
Kungcono khona ngihlalele Baba	It is better that I stay like this, Father
Kunalento engiyibonayo	Than what I am seeing.
Kungcono khona ngizihlalele	
Kunalento engiyibonayo	
Ngilunge mina ngizihlalele Baba	
Kuna lento engiyibonayo	

[Story]

Akenithulenini phela kenginixoxele	Be quiet while I tell you a story
Ngitholiphepha lapha incwadi encane	I received a paper, a short letter
Ngisukenaye lomuntu la Ethekweni	Having left Durban with this person
Ngimuse ekhaya afik'agilimkhuba	Taking her home only for her to break taboos
Aqomabafana lababelusa izinkomo	Falling in love with herdboys
Ngitheng'isidwaba	I bought the skirt for marriage
Ngithi ngithengelumakhoti	Saying I am buying for the bride
Athi isidwaba siyamusinda	She says the skirt is heavy
Ngeke asifake	She won't wear it
Usekhohliwe ukuthi ufun'umendo	She's forgotten she seeks marriage
Ucabang'ukweqa manje ashon'eGoli	She's contemplating running off to Johannesburg
Uthenengakeqi nje wabanjwa ubaba	But before doing so, my father caught her
Eshuk'igudu la emva kwendlu ngenhla	Rolling a joint behind the house
Wakhuz'ibhadi ubab'ebon'imikhuba	My father was appalled at the spectacle
Abizumana ukuba azombukisa	He called my mother to see for herself
Kuthe kunjalo-ke washaya wachitha	Immediately she ran away
Umakhot'wami lona esebhek'eGoli	My bride to Johannesburg
Uma ngithi ngiyabuza ukuthi kwenzenjani	When I asked her what is wrong
Ahleke kancane nje athi gwegwegwe	She just laughs a little, gwegwegwe
Unginika malini njengoba	What do you give me having
wangithath'eThekwini	taken me from Durban
Wathi uyongithengel'inyama	Saying you are going to buy me meat
Kanti uyongidlis'imfino	But feeding me wild spinach
Awukahle phela khoti ukutheth'ekhaya	Hold on a little, my bride, lower your voice at home
Ubab'uzothini ngoba usafika emzini	What will my father say? You are new in the family
Anginamsebenzi mina ngizobuyel'ekhaya	I don't care, I will go back home
Yeyeni webantu kanti eThekweni kunjani	Oh my, my, how then is Durban?

[Self Praises]

Zasha phela madoda kuChakide	Men, its burning from Chakide
uPhumekanje bathi bamkakile	He went like this when they surrounded him
Wabaphosela uhlamvu	He threw them a kernel
Bathi bayalunqaka	When they caught it
Kanti bathinta isitingi senkhukhu	They touched chicken shit
UChakide waphuma kanje	Chakide comes out the other side
Yini le sekhanda lakho wena?	What's that on your head?
Izinwele zami	It's my hair
Uhleli phezulu wethu?	Is he on top brother?
Ungabe usayiphath	Don't mention it.

Ngilunge mina ngizihlalele Baba	I am alright as I am father
Kunalento engiyibonayo	Better than what I am seeing around me.
Ngilunge mina ngizihlalele Baba	
Kunalento engiyibonayo	

Track 9: Maskanda group accompaniment for gumboot dance, without dancers

Field recording by Carol Muller, Durban, September 1996
Guitar: Blanket Mkhize
Violin, concertina: friends of Blanket Mkhize

Track 10: Maskanda accompaniment for gumboot dance, with dancers

Field recording by Carol Muller, Durban, September 1996
Guitar: Blanket Mkhize
Violin, concertina: friends of Blanket Mkhize
Dancers: Mkhize and sons

Sathima Bea Benjamin, Tracks 11–15

These five tracks have been selected to convey the profound sense of connection many people of color in South Africa felt between their own struggles against racial oppression and those of African Americans in the United States in the twentieth century. Musical performance, and jazz specifically, was a key cultural medium through which the connection in struggle was articulated. The first track is a traditional African American spiritual, a song Benjamin began all of her live performances with in the 1980s. This is an excerpt of a particularly evocative and heartrending performance. The second track evokes the historical connection, made largely through sound recordings and Hollywood films, which Sathima and her peers heard and watched in postwar Cape Town. "I Only Have Eyes for You" is performed by Cape Town musicians in 1999. They remember playing the song in those early years as an integral part of Cape culture. Three of Benjamin's own compositions follow. "Windsong" is a song that evokes memories of what it was like to live in Cape Town, the windy city. The memories were particularly poignant while Benjamin and Abdullah Ibrahim lived in exile in New York City, unable to return to the "Mother City" until the early 1990s. "Nations in Me" and "Africa" carry deep feelings about the struggle in South Africa, about a longing for Africa and a vision of a new nation. The latter song is remarkably prophetic for its time, a period in South African political history, the early 1980s, when there seemed to be little hope for the kind of political transformation that seemed so miraculous in the early 1990s.

Track 11: "Sometimes I Feel Like a Motherless Child"

Traditional
Public domain
Vocals: Sathima Bea Benjamin

Drums/percussion: Billy Higgins
Recorded: Rudy van Gelder Studios, 1985
Reissued: Rasmussen, 2001

Track 12: "I Only Have Eyes for You"

Harry Warren and Al Dubin
Remick Music Corporation (ASCAP)
Vocals: Sathima Bea Benjamin
Piano: Henry February
Bass: Basil Moses
Drums: Vincent Pavitt
Arrangement: Sathima Bea Benjamin
Recorded: Cape Town, 1999
Reissued: Rasmussen, 2001

Track 13: "Windsong"

Sathima Bea Benjamin
Ekapa R.P.M. Publishers (ASCAP)
Vocals: Sathima Bea Benjamin
Piano: Kenny Barron
Bass: Buster Williams
Drums: Billy Higgins
Recorded: Rudy Van Gelder Studios, 1985
Reissued: Rasmussen, 2001

Track 14: "Nations in Me, New Nation-a-Coming"

Sathima Bea Benjamin
Ekapa R.P.M. Publishers (ASCAP)
Vocals: Sathima Bea Benjamin
Piano: Onaje Allen Gumbs
Sax and flute: Carlos Ward
Bass: Buster Williams
Drums: Billy Higgins
Arrangement: Sathima Bea Benjamin
Recorded: Rudy Van Gelder Studios, 1983
Reissued: Rasmussen, 2001

Track 15: "Africa"

Sathima Bea Benjamin
Ekapa R.P.M. Publishers (ASCAP)
Vocals: Sathima Bea Benjamin

Piano: Onaje Allen Gumbs
Bass: Buster Williams
Drums: Billy Higgins
Arrangement: Sathima Bea Benjamin
Recorded: Rudy van Gelder Studios, 1983
Reissued: Rasmussen, 2001

Shembe Liturgy, Tracks 16–17

The first track provides an excerpt of congregational liturgy, hymn singing, and prayers taken from a morning service held at Ebuhleni in September 1996. The last track has the "*Ameni! Oyincwele*" calls, which translated mean "Amen, He is Holy." These are the words used to praise the person of Shembe when he joins the congregation on the Sabbath, and other occasions, after the liturgical part of the service is complete.

Track 16: Ibandla lamaNazaretha, liturgy for morning prayers

Field recording by Carol Muller, Ebuhleni, September 1996
Excerpt of liturgy in Zulu and English translation. We are about six minutes into the liturgical recitation and singing:

31. *Uma wenake uyisizukulwana sika Adam no Eva, okwathiwa kuye ensimini yase Eden lima, ulinde, ubonakala uthabatha isimo sobunja uyazethuka wena ngokungathandi ukusebenza.*
31. If you then are of the generation of Adam and Eve, to whom it was said in the Garden of Eden, plough and watch, you insult yourself by not wanting to work, and are seen to take on the form of a dog.

32. (0:07) *Isilandelo sebandla* [chanted in call and response]
    Nkulunkulu onamandla onke,
    Yise wabo bonke abamkhonzayo,
    Busisa ukuvuka kwethu kwanamhlanje,
    Usigcine ngomsa wakhe. Amen.
32. Congregational response
    God almighty
    Father of all those who worship him
    Bless our awakening this day
    And keep us in your mercy. Amen.

33. (0:19) *Ngokuba kwathiwa umuntu uyokudla umvuzo wezithukuthuku zezandla zakhe, washo uThixo ka Adam.*
33. For it was said that a human being shall eat of the product of the sweat of his hands, thus said the God of Adam.

34. *Wathi uNkulunkulu ngokuqinisa umuntu uyokudla ejulukile. Uyawaphikisa wena lamazwi na? Uyathokoza yini ngawe uNkulunkulu uma udla ukudla ungakusebenzanga ungakujulukelanga ebusweni bakho?*
34. God said emphatically that a human being shall eat only after sweating. Do you oppose these words? Does God rejoice over you when he sees you eating food you have not labored for by the sweat of your brow?

35. (0:38) *Uthanda ukudla ungakujulukelanga. Ubeka isono phezu kwabakuncishayo kanti isono sakho.*
35. You like to eat food that you have not sweated for. You blame those who deny you, when it is rather your own fault.

36. *Amehlo ka Nkulunkulu ayathokoza yini ngawe, uma udla ukudla ungakujulukelanga ukwebile loko kudla.*
36. Do the eyes of God rejoice in you? If you eat food that you have not sweated for, you have stolen that food.

37. (0:52) *Isihlabelelo*
Owasinikela ebuhlungwini bazo
Ngenxa yezono zethu.
Mbukhishwe ubuhlungu bazo, [last two lines repeat]
Ngalelo gama lakho.
37. Hymn
To whose poison you handed us over
Because of our sins.
Remove their poison
Through that name of yours.

38. *Isihlabelelo*
Ibusise Nkosi Baba,
Imisebenzi yezandla zethu,
Singadingi singesweli, [last two lines repeat]
Thina bantu bakho.
38. Hymn
Bless Lord, our Father
The work of our hands
That we will have neither need nor want
We who are your people.

39. *Unkulunkulu akathokozi uma ebona dula ukudla ungakusebenzanga nakancane. Noma uyitombazana uyivila uyavama ukuthakaza ngokuthatha izinto zamanye amantombazane. Wenake ungeneleni esimilweni esibi kangaka na? Sokuba uNkulunkulu akubone usosizini nobuso bakho bunyukubele ngenxa yokulamba.*
39. God does not rejoice if he sees you eating food for which you have not performed anything, even the smallest amount of work. Even you, lazy girl, you frequently make

a nuisance of yourself by taking the belongings of other girls. Why have you taken on such bad character? God sees you in sorrow and your face haggard from hunger.

Track 17: Ibandla lamaNazaretha "Ameni! Oyincwele!"

Spoken at the end of the liturgy
Field recording by Carol Muller, Ebuhleni, September 1996.

Shembe Hymns and Gospel Songs, Tracks 18–22

The remaining five tracks focus on Shembe hymns and represent transformations in the traditional style of performance to hymn singing accompanied on the organ. These arrangements of the hymns in four-part harmony (soprano, alto, tenor, and bass), sung by a youth choir, are intended to help members learn to sing with organ accompaniment, and to foster the creation of a new repertory of gospel-style songs sung to and about Shembe (rather than Jesus, for example).

In track 18, the traditional leader of congregational singing begins singing the song by coming in on the pitch comfortable for his voice. The organist is required to find where the leader has pitched his voice, and to then add chordal accompaniment to this singing. In track 19, we hear the youth choir formed by first church organist Bongani Mthethwa. He has arranged one of the hymns in four-part harmony and plays a more conventional piano introduction and accompaniment for the singing. The next track gives an example of the same youth choir preparing to compete in the annual Youth Choir competition for Shembe members. Here they are learning the more "classical" repertory (that is, conventional four-part harmony) by first learning to sing the piece using solfege, that is, learning pitch using do re mi fa sol la ti do. The next track has a melody you probably know—it is from the Christmas carol, "Joy to the World," transformed into a four-part harmony arrangement with Zulu language words that pertain to praise of Shembe. The last track provides an excerpt from a commercial recording made by church member Nathoya Mbatha in a studio using a keyboard and multi-track recording technique. He is transforming the song style to suit a more youthful audience.

Track 18: Nazarite hymn singing with organ accompaniment

Field recording by Carol Muller, Ebuhleni, July 1991

Track 19: Nazarite hymn with piano accompaniment, arranged in SATB

Field recording by Bongani Mthethwa, c. 1989, used with permission

Track 20: Youth choir rehearsal singing in solfege (do re mi fa sol la ti do)

Field recording by Carol Muller, Durban, November 1991

Track 21: Youth choir performance in "classic" style

Field recording by Carol Muller, Durban, July 1991

Track 22: Nathoya Mbatha's gospel version of Shembe hymn

Mbatha recording used with permission from Mbatha and Rev. Shembe, recorded Richards Bay, c. 1995

Glossary

a cappella sung without instrumental accompaniment

African Jazz and Variety a traveling show produced starting in 1952 by White impresario Alfred Herbert using Black and Coloured musicians performing African-inspired jazz and variety

Afrikaans language that emerged out of colonial encounter in South Africa, largely derived from Dutch, first written in Arabic by Cape muslim clerics

Afrikaners people of European descent who speak Afrikaans

amadoda Zulu word meaning "men"

amadoubles team performances of gumboot dance routines

amantombazane Zulu word for "girls"

apartheid the system of racial segregation legislated by the Afrikaner Nationalists in 1948 in South Africa

Asian in the apartheid structure in South Africa, Asian largely referred to people from India and Japan; the Chinese came as laborers and intermarried with those called "Coloured"

Bantu (languages) "*bantu*" literally means people. Bantu languages in South Africa include Zulu, Xhosa, Ndebele, and North and South Sotho

Bantustan the name for a Black homeland in the apartheid days, the rural reserves where all people of a particular ethnic group were forced to live

Bhaca a largely Zulu speaking people, who live in southern KwaZulu Natal

bioscope the colloquial name for movie theater

call and response a format of performance common in Africa, in which a soloist calls a melodic line, and a group responds, usually by repeating what the soloist has called

Chakide a cunning mythical being, like a trickster, in Zulu mythology

chuning the tuning of a Zulu guitar or concertina

Coloured those defined as of "mixed" race

Coloured Jazz and Variety similar to African Jazz and Variety, but focused on traditions coming out of Cape Town's working-class Coloured communities
concertina a small, simple, and less expensive version of a piano accordion
Ebuhleni the current Shembe headquarters
Ekuphakameni the original Shembe headquarters, also used to refer to heaven
Ethiopianism a late nineteenth-century form of religious independence which allowed for varying degrees of assimilation of European culture; begun in response to mission Christianity
ethnomusicology the field of musicology which examines music as a cultural practice, and which historically is concerned with music outside of Europe
fanakalo the language of command developed among linguistically diverse migrant workers, especially in the mines of South Africa
four-part harmony a style emerging out of the Bach Chorale tradition, where voices are divided by function and register in soprano, alto, tenor, and bass, a structure modified and indigenized in twentieth-century South Africa, e.g., in *isicathamiya* performance
fundamental the basic pitch, usually in the lower register, that produces overtones/partials
Gallo until 2006 when Warner International bought the company and its archives, Gallo Music was the most important recording enterprise in South Africa.
ghoema drum performance by slaves from Indonesia and Malaysia in eighteenth- and nineteenth-century Cape Town, spawned *ghommaliedjes*, songs with a mixture of Dutch and Malay origins, sung in the Cape
gospel music in South Africa, gospel music takes its cue from the United States, but is sung in local languages, and has its own body of locally composed songs
Graceland the controversial album by Paul Simon and several other musicians released in 1986
griot/griotte a traditional poet-historian-musician in West Africa
gumboot dance a neo-traditional dance form developed on the mines by the amaBhaca migrant workers
IBA (Independent Broadcast Authority) established to help South African radio and television become more focused on South African music and culture, and to more fairly represent South Africans in its broadcasting
ibandla lamaNazaretha the congregation of Nazaretha, the religion founded by Isaiah Shembe
ibombing the loud, almost shouting vocal style of early *isicathamiya*
imbongi a Zulu praise poet (like a griot)
imiNazaretha the white prayer gown worn by followers of Shembe that identifies them as Nazaretha
influx control a set of apartheid laws put in place to control the movement of Black South Africans in and out of White space, and urban areas in particular. These were repealed in the early 1990s
inkhonzo congregational worship style among followers of Shembe
isangoma traditional healer
isicathamiya the close-harmony, SATB style performance of Zulu-speaking male migrant workers

isicathulo literally means shoe, also refers to the elite styles of gumboot dance
isingles improvised solo dancing by gumboot dancers
isishameni style of song and dance from the Colenso region of KwaZulu Natal
isiZulu style of *maskanda* performance from northern KwaZulu Natal
isteps the dance routines of *isicathamiya* performers
izihlabelelo zamaNazaretha the hymns of the Nazaretha composed by Isaiah and Galilee Shembe and compiled into a hymnal in 1940
kam Blanket Mkhize plays guitar with a hair comb that he rubs against the strings, much like a violin is scraped
Khoi short for Khoikhoi or Khoisan, the indigenous peoples of South Africa
King Kong the first African musical with Black South African performers, musicians, and narrative. Performed in South Africa, and London in late 1950s
klopskamer the headquarters of each performing troupe in Cape Town's New Year's celebrations
kora a West African harp-like instrument
kwela a pennywhistle style of performance developed on the streets by young boys in South Africa in the 1940s
langarm literally long arm, refers to ballroom dance in Cape Town
makwaya a Zulu version of the word "choir"; refers to mission-derived choral performance
marabi popular music developed in working-class drinking establishments; the forerunner of South African jazz
maskanda literally means musician, refers to Zulu musicians using European instruments
mbaqanga originally called "African jazz," refers to studio-produced Zulu music from the early 1960s continuing through to the contemporary popular music scene
mbira a generic term for the Central African "thumb piano," a metal-tongued instrument popular in Zimbabwe
mbube literally means "lion"; refers to early prototype of *isicathamiya*
moppie upbeat comic song sung by working-class Coloured people from Cape Town, often in New Year's festivities
mqashiyo style of popular music in Johannesburg townships and on radio
music culture all the cultural elements that make up a musical performance, including the social organization of a performance, beliefs about that performance, its material culture, and its history
mvangeli evangelist in *ibandla lamaNazaretha*
nagtroepe night troupes who entertain communities in Cape Town at New Year
Nhlangakaze literally means the first or great reed, name of holy mountain of Shembe
ngoma a dance, song, healing, drumming complex, also refers to particular style of song and dance among Zulu-speaking men
Nguni collective term for Bantu-speaking peoples in South Africa, including the Zulu, Xhosa, Swazi, Pedi, and Sotho
"Nkosi sikelel'iAfrika" a song composed by Enoch Sontonga that was the official anthem of the African National Congress, and has now been combined with "Die Stem" the old South African anthem, to create a new anthem for a democratic South Africa

Ohlange the valley in which Isaiah Shembe created his first community in KwaZulu Natal

overtones/partials tones produced by a resonant lower register fundamental tone, common in musical bow playing

Paradis the name of the Shembe open-air temple

passbook/"*dompas*" the document required by all Black and Coloured South Africans if they were to live in the urban areas in the apartheid era

ramkie small three- or four-stringed guitar, usually plucked; developed by Khoisan people in the eighteenth century

Shembe, Isaiah founder of *ibandla lamaNazaretha*; succeeded by son, Johannes Galilee; succeeded by Galilee's brother Amos; and present leader Vimbeni. Londa Shembe, son of J. G. Shembe, sought to lead after the death of J. G., but was murdered

Sun City the casino in the South African homeland of Bophutatswana where foreign musicians played when they were not supposed to travel to South Africa

township places close to major urban areas where Black South Africans established living quarters

Township Jazz show from late 1950s created by a White South African, but performed by Black South Africans and featuring the transformed sounds of American music to suit local taste

tradition also invented tradition, how cultural ways are transmitted from one generation to the next; if they are invented, it is usually a cultural practice that is self-consciously fashioned at a specific moment in time to meet a political need, such as defining a newly constituted nation

ukusina sacred dance in *ibandla lamaNazaretha*

umgido festivals of sacred dance in *ibandla lamaNazaretha*

umshumayeli preacher in *ibandla lamaNazaretha*

Umzansi the area south of the city of Durban

wimoweh the word used to replace "*mbube*" when the song traveled to the USA in the 1950s

Xhosa name for the family of "click" languages (related to Zulu) and the people that speak them. Nelson Mandela is Xhosa-speaking

Zionist religious independent movement that arose out of the Zions Kerk, also related to Zion City in Illinois, United States

Zulu those who speak Zulu as a first language and who identify culturally as "Zulu"

References

Books and Journal Articles

Abrahams, Randall. *Spinning Around: The South African Music Industry in Transition.* Pretoria: Human Sciences Research Council, 2003.

Allen, Lara. "Circuits of Recognition and Desire in the Evolution of Black South African Popular Music: The Career of the Penny Whistle." *South African Journal of Musicology* 25 (2005): 31–51.

——. "Music, Film, and Gangsters in the Sophiatown Imaginary: Featuring Dolly Rathebe." *Scrutiny 2, Issues in English Studies in Southern Africa* 9/1 (2004): 19–38.

——. "Commerce, Politics, and Musical Hybridity: Vocalising Urban Black South African Identity During the 1950s." *Ethnomusicology* 47/2 (2003): 228–249.

——. "Kwela: The Structure and Sound of Pennywhistle Music." In *Composing the Music of Africa: Composition, Interpretation, and Realization*, edited by Malcolm Floyd, 227–264. Brookfield, Vermont: Ashgate, 1999.

——. "An Archive of Black South African Popular Music: Recently Released Reissues." *British Journal of Ethnomusicology* 5 (1996): 177–180.

Allingham, Rob. "Township Jive" and "Hip Kings, Hip Queens." In *World Music: The Rough Guide*, edited by Simon Broughton et al. London: Penguin Books, 371–395.

Anderson, Benedict. *Imagined Communities: On the Origins and Spread of Nationalism.* London: Verso, 1983.

Andersson, Muff. *Music in the Mix: The Story of South African Popular Music.* Johannesburg: Ravan Press, 1981.

Ansell, Gwen. *Soweto Blues: Jazz, Popular Music and Politics in South Africa.* New York: Continuum Books, 2004.

Arom, Simha and Susanne Furniss. "An Interactive, Experimental Method for the Determination of Musical Scales in Oral Cultures." *Contemporary Music Review* 9/2 (1993), 7–12.

Askew, Kelly. *Performing the Nation: Swahili Musical and Cultural Politics in Tanzania.* Chicago: University of Chicago Press, 2002.

Avorgbedor, Daniel. "'It's a Great Song!' Halo Performance as Literary Production." *Research in African Literatures* 32/2 (2001): 17–43.

Badsha, Farzanah. "Old Skool Rules/New Skool Breaks: Negotiating Identifies in the Cape Town Hip-Hop Scene." In *Shifting Selves: Post-Apartheid Essays on Mass Media, Culture, and Identity*, edited by Herman Wasserman and Sean Jacobs, 131–144. Cape Town: Kwela Books, 2003.

Baines, Gary. "Catalyst or Detonator? Local Music Quotas and the Current South African Music 'Explosion.'" *Social Dynamics* 24/1 (1998): 66–87.

Ballantine, Christopher. "Looking to the USA: The Politics of Male Close-Harmony Song and Style in South Africa During the 1940s and 1950s." *Popular Music* 18/1 (1999): 1–17.

——. "Joseph Shabalala: Chronicles of an African Composer." *British Journal of Ethnomusicology* 5/2 (1996): 1–37.

——. *Marabi Nights: Early South African Jazz and Vaudeville.* Johannesburg: Ravan, 1993.

Barber, Karen. "Preliminary Notes on Audiences in Africa." *Africa* 67/3 (1997a): 347–362.

——, ed. *Readings in African Popular Culture.* Bloomington, IN: Indiana University Press, 1997b.

——. "Popular Arts in Africa." *African Studies Review* 30/3 (1986): 1–78.

Battersby, Jane. 2003. "'Sometimes it Feels Like I'm Not Black Enough': Recast(e)ing Coloured Through South African Hip-Hop as a Postcolonial Text." In *Shifting Selves: Post-Apartheid Essays on Mass Media, Culture, and Identity*, edited by Herman Wasserman and Sean Jacobs, 109–130. Cape Town: Kwela Books, 2003.

Bender, Wolfgang. *Sweet Mother: Modern African Music*. Chicago: University of Chicago Press, 1991.

Bergman, Billy. *African Pop: Goodtime Kings*. Dorset, UK: Blandford Press, 1985.

Berliner, Paul. *The Soul of Mbira: Music and Traditions of the Shona People of Zimbabwe*. Berkeley: University of California Press, 1978.

Bickford Smith, Vivian, Elizabeth van Heyningen, and Nigel Worden, eds. *Cape Town in the Twentieth Century*. Cape Town: David Philip, 1999.

Blacking, John. *Music, Culture, and Experience*. Edited posthumously by Reginal Byron. Chicago: University of Chicago Press, 1995.

Broughton, Simon, et al., eds. *World Music: The Rough Guide*. New York: Penguin Books, 1999.

Brown, Duncan. "Orality and Christianity: The Hymns of Isaiah Shembe and the Church of the Nazarites." In *Oral Literature and Performance in Southern Africa*, edited by Duncan Brown, 199–215. Oxford: James Currey, 1999.

Brown, Ernest. "The Guitar and the Mbira: Resilience, Assimilation, and Pan-Africanism in Zimbabwean Music." *World of Music* 36/2 (1994): 73–117.

Bryant, A. "Zulu-English Dictionary." Unpublished manuscript in Killie Campbell Library, University of Natal, South Africa, n.d.

Chamber of Mines. *The Miner's Dictionary in English, Afrikaans, and Fanakalo*. Johannesburg: Central News Agency, 1974.

——. *1938 Miner's Companion in English, Afrikaans, Sesotho, and Mine Kaffir*. Johannesburg: Central News Agency, 1938.

——. *1920 Miner's Companion in Zulu*. Johannesburg: Central News Agency, 1920.

Chapman, Michael. *Southern African Literatures*. London: Longmans, 1996.

Charry, Eric. *Mande Music: Traditional and Modern Music of the Maninka and Mandinka of Western Africa*. Chicago: University of Chicago Press, 2000.

——. "The Grand Mande Guitar Tradition of the Western Sahel and Savannah." *World of Music* 36/2 (1994): 21–61.

Chernoff, John. *African Rhythm and African Sensibility: Aesthetics and Social Action in African Musical Idioms*. Chicago: University of Chicago Press, 1979.

Cockrell, Dale. "Of Gospel Hymns, Minstrel Shows, and Jubilee Singers: Toward Some Black South African Musics." *American Music* 5/4 (1987): 417–432.

Collins, John. *West African Pop Roots*. Philadelphia: Temple University Press, 1992.

Comaroff, Jean. *Body of Power, Spirit of Resistance*. Chicago: University of Chicago Press, 1985.

Cooke, Peter. "East Africa: An Introduction." In *The Garland Encyclopedia of World Music: Africa*, edited by Ruth Stone, 598–609. New York: Garland, 1998.

Coplan, David. "God Rock Africa: Thoughts on Politics in Popular Black Performance in South Africa." *African Studies* 64/1 (2005): 9–27.

——. "Popular Music in South Africa." In *The Garland Encyclopedia of World Music: Africa*, edited by Ruth Stone, 759–780. New York: Garland, 1998.

——. *In The Time of Cannibals: Word Music of South Africa's Basotho Migrants*. Chicago: University of Chicago Press, 1994.

——. "Ethnomusicology and the Meaning of Tradition." In *Ethnomusicology and Modern Music History*, edited by Stephen Blum, et al., 34–60. Urbana: University of Illinois Press, 1991.

——. *In Township Tonight! South Africa's Black City Music and Theatre*. New York: Longman, 1985. New edn to be published 2008, by University of Chicago Press.

Courtenay, Bryce. *The Power of One: A Novel*. New York: Ballantine Books, 1989.

Danielson, Virginia. *The Voice of Egypt: Umm Kulthum, Arabic Song, and Egyptian Society in the Twentieth Century*. Chicago: University of Chicago Press, 1997.

——. "New Nightingales of the Nile: Popular Music in Egypt Since the 1970s." *Popular Music* 15/3 (1996): 299–311.

Davidson, Basil. *The African Past: Chronicles from Antiquity to Modern Times*. New York: Grosser and Dunlap, 1964.

Davies, Nollene. "The Guitar in Zulu Maskanda Tradition." *World of Music* 36/2 (1994): 118–137.

De Certeau, Michel. *The Practice of Everyday Life*. Translated by Steven Randall. Los Angeles: University of California Press, 1988 [1984].

Diawara, Mamadou. "Mande Oral Popular Culture Revisited by the Electronic Media." In *Readings in African Popular Culture*, edited by Karen Barber, 40–47. Bloomington, IN: Indiana University Press, 1997.

Dje-dje, Jacqueline. "West Africa: An Introduction." In *The Garland Encyclopedia of World Music: Africa*, edited by Ruth Stone, 442–470. New York: Garland, 1998.

Doke, C. M., et al. *Zulu-English, English-Zulu Dictionary*. Johannesburg: University of the Witwatersrand Press, 1990.

Dowson, Thomas A. and David Lewis-Williams, eds. *Contested Images: Diversity in Southern African Rock Art Research*. Johannesburg: Witwatersrand University Press, 1994.

Drewal, Margaret. "The State of Research on Performance in Africa." *African Studies Review* 34/3 (1991): 1–64.

Duran, Lucy. "Birds of Wasulu: Freedom of Expression and Expressions of Freedom in the Popular Music of Southern Mali." *British Journal of Ethnomusicology* 4 (1995): 101–134.

——. "Music Created by God." In *World Music: The Rough Guide*, edited by Simon Broughton et al., 243–259. New York: Penguin Books, 1999 [1994].

Erasmus, Zmitri. 2001 [2000]. *Coloured by History, Shaped by Place: New Perspectives on Coloured Identities in Cape Town*. Cape Town: Kwela Books.

Erlmann, Veit. *Music, Modernity, and the Global Imagination*. New York: Oxford University Press, 1999.

——. *Nightsong: Performance, Power, and Practice in Black South African Performance*. Chicago: Chicago University Press, 1996.

——. Sleeve notes to *Caluza's Double Quartet: 1930*, by Reuben Caluza. Wiltshire, England: Heritage Records, 1992.

——. *African Stars: Studies in Black South African Performance*. Chicago: Chicago University Press, 1991.

Euba, Akin. "Text Setting in African Composition." *Research in African Literatures* 32/2 (2001): 119–133.

——. *Yoruba Drumming: The Dundun Tradition*. Bayreuth, Germany: Eckhard Breitinger, 1990.

——. *Essays on Music in Africa*. Bayreuth, Germany: Iwalewa Haus, Bayreuth University Press, 1988.

Ewens, Graeme. *Africa O-Ye!: A Celebration of African Music*. London: Guinness, 1991.

Eyre, Banning. *In Griot Time: An American Guitarist in Mali*. Philadelphia: Temple University Press, 2000.

Fabian, Johannes. "Popular Culture in Africa: Findings and Conjectures." In *Readings in African Popular Culture*, edited by Karen Barber, 18–28. Bloomington, IN: Indiana University Press, 1997.

Farmer, Henry George. "The Music of Islam." In *The New Oxford History of Music, Vol. 1*, edited by Egon Wellesz, 421–477. Oxford: Oxford University Press, 1957.

Feld, Steven. "The Poetics and Politics of Pygmy Pop." In *Western Music and Its Others*, edited by Georgina Born and Desmond Hesmondhalgh, 254–279. Berkeley: University of California Press, 2000.

Floyd, Malcolm, ed. *Composing the Music of Africa: Composition, Interpretation, and Realization*. Brookfield, Vermont: Ashgate, 1999.

Floyd, Samuel. *The Power of Black Music: Interpreting its History from Africa to the United States*. New York: Oxford University Press, 1995.

Gaitskell, Deborah. "Devout Christianity? A Century of African Women's Christianity in South Africa." In *Women and Gender in Southern Africa Until 1945*, edited by Cherryl Walker, 251–272. Cape Town: David Philip, 1990.

Garafalo, Reebee. *Rockin' the Boat: Mass Music and Mass Movements*. Boston: South End Press, 1992.

Gassert, Richard. "Bop 'Til You Drop: An Oral Study of Popular Music Cultures in Cape Town from the Late 1940s to the Early 1960s." Unpublished Honors essay, University of Cape Town, 1988.

Graebner, Werner. "Whose Music? The Songs of Remmy Ongala and the Orchestra Super Matimila." In *Readings in African Popular Culture*, edited by Karen Barber, 110–117. Bloomington, IN: Indiana University Press, 1997.

Graham, Ronnie. *The World of African Music: Stern's Guide to Contemporary African Music, Volume Two*. London: Pluto Press, 1992.

——. *The Da Capo Guide to Contemporary African Music*. New York: Da Capo, 1988.

Gunderson, Frank and Gregory Barz, eds. *Mashindano! Competitive Music Performance in East Africa*. Dar Es Salaam: Nkuki wa Nyota Publishers, 2000.

Gunner, Liz, ed. *Politics and Performance: Theater, Poetry, and Performance in Southern Africa*. Johannesburg: Witwatersrand University Press, 1994.

——. "The Dead Child Returned to Life: The Sermon as Oral Narrative in Isaiah Shembe's Nazareth Baptist Church." In *D'Un Contre . . . A L'Autre: La Variabilite dans la Litterature Orale*, edited by V. Gorog-Karady, 192–201. Paris: Editions du CNRS, 1990.

Gunner, Liz and Mafika Gwala, eds. and transl. *Musho! Zulu Popular Praises*. East Lansing, MI: Michigan State University Press, 1991.

Gutsche, Thelma. *The History and Social Significance of Motion Pictures in South Africa*. Cape Town: Howard Timmons, 1972.

Hadebe, Jonney. Program Notes for South African Railways Gumboot Dance Performance, n.d.

Hajdu, David. *Lush Life: A Biography of Billy Strayhorn*. New York: Farrar, 1996.

Hale, Thomas. *Griots and Griottes: Masters of Words and Music*. Bloomington, IN: Indiana University Press, 1998.

Hamm, Charles. *Putting Popular Music in Its Place*. Cambridge: Cambridge University Press, 1995.

Hannerz, Ulf. "Sophiatown: The View from Afar." In *Readings in African Popular Culture*, edited by Karen Barber, 164–170. Bloomington, IN: Indiana University Press, 1997.

Hexham, Irving, ed. *The Scriptures of the AmaNazaretha of Ekuphakameni: Selected Writings of the Zulu Prophets Isaiah and Londa Shembe*. Translated by Londa Shembe and Hans-Jürgen Becken, with an essay by G. C. Oosthuizen. Calgary: University of Calgary Press, 1994.

Hexham, Irving and G. C. Oosthuizen, eds. *The Story of Isaiah Shembe*. Translated by Hans-Jürgen Becken. Lewiston, NY: E. Mellen Press, 1996.

Hexham, Irving and Robert Papini, eds. *The Catechism of the Nazarites and Related Writings*. Translated by Hans-Jürgen Becken and Phyllis Zungu. Lewiston, NY: E. Mellen Press, 2002.

Hofmeyr, Isabel. "John Bunyan, His Chair, and a Few Other Relics: Orality, Literacy, and the Limits of Area Studies." In *African Words, African Voices: Critical Practices in Oral History*, edited by Luise White, et al., 78–90. Bloomington, IN: Indiana University Press, 2001.

Holiday, Billie and William Dufty. *Lady Sing the Blues: The Searing Autobiography of an American Musical Legend.* New York: Penguin, 1984 [1956].

Hughes, Heather. "'A Lighthouse for African Womanhood': Inanda Seminary, 1869–1945." In *Women and Gender in Southern Africa Until 1945*, edited by Cherryl Walker, 197–220. Cape Town: David Philip, 1990.

Huskisson, Yvonne. *Black Composers of Southern Africa: An Expanded Supplement to Bantu Composers.* Edited by Sarita Hauptfleish. Pretoria: Human Sciences Research Council, 1992.

——. *The Bantu Composers of Southern Africa (with Two Supplements).* Pretoria: Human Sciences Research Council, 1983.

Impey, Angela. "Resurrecting the Flesh: Reflections on Women in Kwaito." *Agenda* 49 (2001): 44–50.

——. "Popular Music in Africa." In *The Garland Encyclopedia of World Music: Africa*, edited by Ruth Stone, 415–437. New York: Garland, 1998.

International Library of African Music. *Proceedings of the [South African] Symposiae on Ethnomusicology.* Grahamstown: Rhodes University, 1980ff.

James, Deborah. *Songs of the Women Migrants: Performance and Identity in South Africa.* Edinburgh: Edinburgh University Press, 1999.

Jegede, Tunde. *African Classical Music and the Griot Tradition.* London: Diabate Arts, 1994.

Jeppe, Shamiel. "Aspects of Popular Culture and Class Expression in Inner Cape Town ca., 1939–1959." Unpublished master's thesis, University of Cape Town, 1990.

Jeske, Lee. Sleeve notes to *Solo Monk*, by Thelonius Monk. New York: Sony Music Entertainment, 1992.

Kaemmer, John. "Southern Africa: An Introduction." In *The Garland Encyclopedia of World Music: Africa*, edited by Ruth Stone, 700–721. New York: Garland, 1998.

Kaye, Andrew. "The Guitar in Africa." In *The Garland Encyclopedia of World Music: Africa*, edited by Ruth Stone, 350–369. New York: Garland, 1998.

Kiernan, Jim. "Canticles of Zion: Song as Word and Action in Zulu Zionist Discourse." *Journal of Religion in Africa* 20/2, 1990: 169–179.

Kirby, Percival. *The Musical Instruments of the Native Races of South Africa.* Johannesburg: Witwatersrand University Press, 1968 [1934].

Kisliuk, Michelle. *Seize the Dance! BaAka Musical Life and the Ethnography of Performance.* Oxford: Oxford University Press, 1998.

Knight, Roderic. "Music Out of Africa: Mande Jaliya in Paris." *World of Music* 33/1 (1991): 52–69.

Kubik, Gerhard. *Africa and the Blues.* Jackson, MS: University Press of Mississippi, 1999.

——. "Central Africa: An Introduction." In *The Garland Encyclopedia of World Music: Africa*, edited by Ruth Stone, 650–680. New York: Garland, 1998.

Langlois, Tony. "The Gnawa of Oujda: Music at the Margins in Morocco." *World of Music* 40/1 (1998): 135–156.

——. "The Local and the Global in North African Popular Music." *Popular Music* 15/3 (1996): 259–273.

Layne, Valmont. "A History of Dance and Jazz Band Performance in the Western Cape in the Post-1945 Era." Unpublished master's thesis, University of Cape Town, 1995.

Levine, Laurie. *The Drumcafe's Traditional Music of South Africa.* With CD. Johannesburg: Jacana Media, 2005.

Lewis-Williams, J. David. *A Cosmos in Stone: Interpreting Religion and Society Through Rock Art.* New York: Alta Mira, 2002.

Lipsitz, George. *Dangerous Crossroads: Popular Music, Postmodernism, and the Poetics of Place.* New York: Verso, 1994.

Lloyd, P. C. "Osifekunde of Ijebu." In *Africa Remembered: Narratives by West Africans from the Era of the Slave Trade*, edited by Philip Curtin, 217–288. Madison, WI: University of Wisconsin Press, 1968 (1845).

Locke, David. *Drum Damba: Talking Drum Lessons.* Crown Point, IN: White Cliffs Media, 1990.

Lucia, Christine, ed. *The World of South African Music: A Reader.* Cambridge: Cambridge Scholars Press, 2005.

Makeba, Miriam, with James Hall. *Makeba: My Story.* New York: New American Library, 1987.

Malan, Jacques P, ed. *South African Music Encyclopedia.* 4 vols. Cape Town: Oxford University Press, 1979–1986.

Marlin-Curiel, Stephanie. "Sampling the Past: Sound, Language and Identity in the New South Africa." In *Shifting Selves: Post-Apartheid Essays on Mass Media, Culture, and Identity*, edited by Herman Wasserman and Sean Jacobs, 55–78. Cape Town: Kwela Books, 2003.

Marre, Jeremy and Hannah Charlton. *Beats of the Heart: Popular Music of the World.* New York: Pantheon, 1986.

Martin, Denis-Constant. *Coon Carnival: Cape Town, Past and Present.* Cape Town: David Philip, 1999.

McCall, John. "The Representation of African Music in Early Documents." In *The Garland Encyclopedia of World Music: Africa*, edited by Ruth Stone, 74–99. New York: Garland, 1998.

McCord, Margaret. *The Calling of Katie Makanya.* Cape Town: David Philip, 1995.

McGregor, Maxine. *Chris McGregor and the Brotherhood of Breath.* Flint, MI: Bamberger Books, 1995.

McMurtry, Mervyn. "'Doing Their Own Thane': The Critical Reception of Umabatha, Welcome Msomi's Macbeth." *Ilha do Desterro* 36 (1999): 309–336.

Meintjes, Louise. *Sound of Africa! Making Zulu Music in a South African Studio.* Durham: Duke University Press, 2003.

——. "Paul Simon's *Graceland*, South Africa and the Mediation of Musical Meaning." *Ethnomusicology* 34 (1990): 37–73.
Mensah, Atta. "Compositional Processes in African Music." In *The Garland Encyclopedia of World Music: Africa*, edited by Ruth Stone, 208–231. New York: Garland, 1998.
——. "Jazz—The Round Trip." *Jazzforschung—Jazz Research* 3/4 (1972): 124–137.
Molefe, Z. B. and Mike Mzileni. *A Common Hunger to Sing: A Tribute to South Africa's Black Women of Song 1950–1990*. Cape Town: Kwela Books, 1997.
Moodie, Dunbar. "Mine Culture and Miner's Identity on the South African Gold Mines." In *Town and Countryside in the Transvaal: Capitalist Penetration and Popular Response*, edited by Belinda Bozzoli, 176–197. Johannesburg: Ravan Press, 1983.
Mthethwa, Bongani. "Syncretism in the Hymns of Ibandla LamaNazaretha." Incomplete doctoral dissertation, University of Natal, n.d
Muller, Carol, ed., translated by Bongani Mthethwa, assisted by Sazi Dlamini and Carol Muller. *The Hymns of the Nazaretha. Composed by Isaiah and Galilee Shembe*. Pietermaritzburg: University of Natal Press, forthcoming, 2008.
——. "Musical Echoes of American Jazz: Towards a Comparative Historiography." *Safundi* 8/1 (2007a): 57–71.
——. "South African and American Jazz: Towards a Polyphonic History." *History Compass* 5/4 (2007b): 1062–1077.
——. "Archiving Africanness in Sacred Song." *Ethnomusicology* 46/3 (2002): 409–430.
——. "Capturing the 'Spirit of Africa' in the Jazz Singing of South African-born Sathima Bea Benjamin." *Research in African Literatures* 32/3 (2001): 133–152.
——. "Sathima Bea Benjamin Finds Cape Jazz to be Her Home Within." In *Sathima Bea Benjamin: Embracing Jazz*, edited by Lars Rasmussen, 21–37. Copenhagen: The Book Trader, 2000.
——. *Rituals of Fertility and the Sacrifice of Desire: Nazarite Women's Performance in South Africa.* (CD Rom). Chicago: University of Chicago Press, 1999.
——. "Sathima Bea Benjamin, Exile and the 'Southern Touch' in Jazz Creation and Performance." *African Languages and Culture* 9/2 (1996): 127–144.
Muller, Carol and Janet Topp Fargion. "Gumboots, Migrants, and Fred Astaire: South African Worker Dance and Musical Style." *African Music* 714 (1999): 88–109.
——. "A Preliminary Study of Gumboot Dance." Unpublished honors thesis, University of Natal, Durban, 1985.
Muller, Carol and Sathima Bea Benjamin. *Musical Echoes*. Durham, NC: Duke University Press, forthcoming, expected 2008.
Murray, Jon, Jeff Williams and Richard Everist. *Lonely Planet South Africa, Lesotho, and Swaziland*. London: Lonely Planet Publications, 3rd edn, 1998.
Nasson, Bill. "'She Preferred Living in a Cave with Harry the Snake-Catcher': Towards an Oral History of Popular Leisure and Class Expression in District Six, Cape Town, c. 1920s–1950s." In *Holding Their Ground: Class, Locality, and Culture in 19th and 20th Century South Africa*, edited by P. Bonner, et al., 286–295. Johannesburg: Witwatersrand University Press, 1989.
Ndebele, Njabulo. "Memory, Metaphor, and the Triumph of Narrative. In *Negotiating the Past: The Making of Memory in South Africa*, edited by Sarah Nuttall and Carli Coetzee, 19–28.
Nixon, Michael. "The World of Jazz in Inner Cape Town, 1940–1960." *Proceedings of the Symposium on Ethnomusicology #14, July 1997*. Grahamstown: International Library of African Music, 19–23.
Nixon, Rob. *Homelands, Harlem, and Hollywood: South African Culture and the World Beyond*. New York: Routledge, 1994.
Njoku, J. A.-K. "Art Composed Music in Africa." In *The Garland Encyclopedia of World Music: Africa*, edited by Ruth Stone, 232–253. New York: Garland, 1998.
Nketia, Kwabena. "The Scholarly Study of African Music: A Historical Review." In *The Garland Encyclopedia of World Music: Africa*, edited by Ruth Stone, 13–73. New York: Garland, 1998.
——. *The Music of Africa*. London: Victor Gollancz, 1982.
Nkosi, Lewis. *Home and Exile and Other Selections*. New York: Longmans, 1965.
Nuttall, Sarah. "Stylizing the Self: The Y Generation in Rosebank, Johannesburg." *Public Culture* 16/3 (2004): 430–452.
Nuttall, Sarah and Carli Coetzee, eds. *Negotiating the Past: The Making of Memory in South Africa*. Cape Town: Oxford University Press, 1998.
Nuttall, Sarah and Cheryl-Ann Michael, eds. *Senses of Culture*. London: Oxford University Press, 2000.
Nzewi, Meki, et al. "Beyond Song Texts—The Lingual Fundamentals of African Drum Music." *Research in African Literatures* 32/2 (2001): 90–104.
Olwage, Grant, ed. *Composing Apartheid*. Johannesburg: Wits University Press, 2008.
——. "John Knox Bokwe and Black Choralism." In *The World of South African Music: A Reader*, edited by Christine Lucia, 309–318. Cambridge: Cambridge Scholars Press, 2005.
Omojola, Bode. "African Pianism as an Intercultural Compositional Framework: A Study of the Piano Works of Akin Euba." *Research in African Literatures* 32/2 (2001): 153–173.
——. *Nigerian Art Music, with an Introductory Study of Ghanaian Art Music*. Ibadan and Bayreuth, Germany: Bayreuth Studies in African Music, 1997.

Oosthuizen, G. C. E. *The Theology of a South African Messiah: An Analysis of the Hymnal of The Church of the Nazarites*. Leiden: E. J. Brill, 1967.

Palma, H. R. *The Carthaganian Voyage to West Africa in 500 B.C.* Bathurst: J. M. Lawani, 1931.

Papini, Robert. "Carl Faye's Transcript of Isaiah Shembe's Testimony of His Early Life and Calling." *Journal of Religion in Africa* 29/3 (1999): 243–284.

Peterson, Bhekiziwe. "Kwaito, 'Dawgs' and the Antimonies of Hustling." *African Identities* 1/2 (2003): 197–215.

Pewa, Elliot. "Musical Competition." Unpublished master's thesis, University of Natal, 1994.

Phillips, Ray. *The Bantu in the City: A Study of Cultural Adjustment on the Witwatersrand*. London: Faber and Faber, 1938.

Placksin, Sally. "To Me Music is Such a Direct Way for One Heart to Speak to the Other." In *Sathima Bea Benjamin: Embracing Jazz*, edited by Lars Rasmussen, 11–20. Copenhagen: The Book Trader, 2000.

Pongweni, Alec. "The Chimurenga Songs of the Zimbabwean War of Liberation." In *Readings in African Popular Culture*, edited by Karen Barber, 63–72. Bloomington, IN: Indiana University Press, 1997.

Ranger, Terence. "Protestant Missions in Africa: The Dialectic of Conversion in the American Methodist Episcopal Church in Eastern Zimbabwe, 1900–1950." In Thomas Blakely et al. (eds.), *Religion in Africa*. London: Heinemann and James Currey, 1994.

Rasmussen, Lars. *Jazz People of Cape Town*. Copenhagen: The Booktrader, 2003a.

——. *Mbizo: A Book about Johnny Dyani*. Copenhagen: The Booktrader, 2003b.

——. *Cape Town Jazz: 1959–1963: The Photographs of Hardy Stockman*. Copenhagen: The Booktrader, 2002a.

——. *Joe Mogotsi, Mantindane: "He Who Survives"—My Life with the Manhattan Brothers*. Copenhagen: The Booktrader, 2002b.

——. *Abdullah Ibrahim: A Discography*. 2nd edn. Copenhagen: The Booktrader, 2000a.

——. *Sathima Bea Benjamin: Embracing Jazz*. With two CDs. Copenhagen: The Booktrader, 2000b.

Reader's Digest. *Illustrated History of South Africa: The Real Story. Expanded third edition, completely updated*. Cape Town: Reader's Digest, 1994.

Richmond, Simon, et al. *Lonely Planet: South Africa, Lesotho, and Swaziland*. Victoria, Australia: Lonely Planet Publications, 2002.

Roberts, Esther. "Shembe: The Man and His Work." Unpublished master's thesis, University of the Witwatersrand, 1936.

Roberts, John S. *Black Music of Two Worlds: African, Caribbean, Latin, and African American Traditions*. New York: Schirmer, 1998 [1972].

Rossi, Michael. "Perspectives on Saxophone Performance Practices in South Africa." *IAJE Jazz Research Proceedings Yearbook XXXI* (2001): 12–18.

Rycroft, David. "Zulu Melodic and Non-Melodic Styles." In *Proceedings of the Fifth Symposium on Ethnomusicology*. Grahamstown: International Library of African Music, 1984, 10–14.

——. "Stylistic Evidence in Zulu Song." In *Essays on Music and History in Africa*, edited by K. P. Wachsmann, 213–241. Evanston, IL: Northwestern University Press, 1971.

SABC. *South African Broadcast Corporation Annual Reports*. Johannesburg: SABC.

Sarno, Louis. *Bayaka: The Extraordinary Music of the Babenzele Pygmies*. New York: Ellipsis Arts, 1995.

Schade-Poulsen, Marc. *Men and Popular Music in Algeria: The Social Significance of Rai*. Austin, TX: University of Texas Press, 1999.

Schmidt, Cynthia. "Interview with John Collins on Cultural Policy, Folklore, and the Recording Industry in Ghana." *World of Music* 36/2 (1994a): 138–147.

——. "The Guitar in Africa: Issues and Research." *World of Music* 36/2 (1994b): 3–20.

Shelemay, Kay. "Notation and Oral Tradition." In *The Garland Encyclopedia of World Music: Africa*, edited by Ruth Stone, 147–163. New York: Garland, 1998.

——. *Music, Ritual, and Falasha History*. East Lansing, MI: Michigan State University Press, 1989.

——. "A New System of Musical Notation in Ethiopia." In *Ethiopian Studies Dedicated to Wolf Leslau*, edited by S. Segert and A. J. E. Bodrogligeti, 571–582. Wiesbaden: Otto Harrasowitz, 1983.

Shelemay, K. and P. Jeffrey. *Ethiopian Christian Liturgical Change: An Anthology*. 3 vols. Madison, WI: A-R Editions, 1993.

Shembe, Galilee, ed. *IziHlabelelo ZamaNazaretha*. Durban: WG Shepherd, 1940.

Shifrin, Thelma. "South Africa: Idealism or Blackmail?" *Musical America* July 1989: 21.

Shiloah, Ammon. *Music in the World of Islam: A Socio-Cultural Study*. Detroit: Wayne State University, 1995.

South African Library. *The Book of Books: Catalogue of an Exhibition of Bibles Held in the South African Library, June–September 1986*. Cape Town: South African Library, 1986.

Stapleton, Chris and Chris May. *African Rock: Pop Music of a Continent*. New York: Obelisk, 1990.

Steingo, Gavin. "South African Music After Apartheid: Kwaito, the 'Party Politic' and the Appropriation of Gold as a Sign of Success." *Popular Music and Society* 28/3 (2005): 333–357.

Stephens, Simon. "Kwaito." In *Senses of Culture: South African Cultural Studies*, edited by Sarah Nuttall and Cheryl-Ann Michael, 256–273. Cape Town: Oxford University Press, 2000.

Stewart, Gary. *Rumba on the River: A History of the Popular Music of the Two Congos*. London: Verso, 2000.

——. *Breakout! Profiles in African Rhythm*. Chicago: University of Chicago Press, 1992.
Stone, Ruth, ed. *The Garland Encyclopedia of World Music: Africa*. New York: Garland, 1998.
Sundkler, Bengt. *Bantu Prophets in South Africa*. London: Oxford University Press, 1961 [1948].
Taylor, Timothy. *Global Pop: World Music, World Markets*. New York: Routledge, 1997.
——. "When We Think About Music and Politics: The Case of Kevin Volans." *Perspectives in New Music* 33/1 (1995): 504–36.
Thomas, Jeff. "Ingoma Dancers and their Response to Town: A Study of Ingoma Dance Troupes Among Zulu Migrant Workers in Durban." Unpublished master's thesis, University of Natal, Durban. 1988.
Thompson, Robert F. *African Art in Motion*. Los Angeles: University of California Press, 1979.
Titlestad, Michael. *Making the Changes: Jazz in South African Literature and Reportage*. Pretoria: UNISA, 2004.
Tomaselli, Keyan. "Mandela, MTV, Television and Apartheid." *Popular Music and Society* 17/2 (1993): 1–19.
Topp Fargion, Janet. "Consumer-Led Creation: Taarab Music Composition in Zanzibar." In *Composing the Music of Africa: Composition, Interpretation, and Realization*, edited by Malcolm Floyd. Brookfield, Vermont: Ashgate, 1999.
Tracey, Hugh. *African Dances of the Witwatersrand Gold Mines*. Johannesburg: African Music Society, 1952.
——. *Lalela Zulu: 100 Zulu Lyrics*. Roodepoort: African Music Society, 1948.
Trewhela, Ralph. *Song Safari*. Johannesburg: Limelight Press, 1980.
Tshabalala, M. Z. *Shembe's Hymnbook Reconsidered, Its Sources and Significance*. Unpublished master's thesis, University of Aberdeen, Scotland, 1983.
Tucker, Percy. *Just the Ticket! My 50 Years in Show Business*. Johannesburg: Jonathan Ball Publishers, 1997.
Turino, Thomas. *Nationalists, Cosmopolitans, and Popular Music in Zimbabwe*. Chicago: University of Chicago Press, 2000.
——. "The Mbira, Worldbeat, and the International Imagination." *World of Music* 40/2 (1998): 85–106.
Turnbull, Colin. *The Forest People*. New York: Touchstone, 1962.
Vail, Leroy and Landeg White. "Plantation Protest: The History of a Mozambican Song." In *Readings in African Popular Culture*, edited by Karen Barber, 54–62. Bloomington, IN: Indiana University Press, 1997.
——. *Power and the Praise Poem: Southern African Voices in History*. London: James Currey, 1991.
Veal, Michael. *Fela: The Life and Times of a Musical Icon*. Philadelphia: Temple University Press, 2000.
Wallaschek, Richard. *Primitive Music: An Inquiry into the Origin and Development of Music, Songs, Instruments, Dances, and Pantomimes of Savage Races*. London: Longmans, Green, 1893.
Wasserman, Herman and Sean Jacobs (eds.) 2003. *Shifting Selves: Post-Apartheid Essays on Mass Media, Culture, and Identity*. Cape Town: Kwela Books.
Waterman, Christopher. "'Our Tradition is a Very Modern Tradition:' Popular Music and the Construction of Pan-Yoruba Identity." In *Readings in African Popular Culture*, edited by Karen Barber, 48–53. Bloomington, IN: Indiana University Press, 1997.
Watkins, Lee. "Tracking Down the Narrative: The Poetics of Identity in Rap Music and Hip-Hop Culture in Cape Town." Unpublished master's thesis, University of Natal, Durban, 1999.
Wells, Robin. *An Introduction to the Music of the Basotho*. Morija, Lesotho: Morija Museum Press, 1994.
Wendt, Caroline Card. "North Africa: An Introduction." In *The Garland Encyclopedia of World Music: Africa*, edited by Ruth Stone, 532–548. New York: Garland, 1998.
West, Gerald. "From the Bible as Bola to Biblical Interpretation as Marabi: Tlhaping Transactions with the Bible." In *Orality, Literacy, and Colonialism in Southern Africa*, edited by Jonathan Draper, 57–90. Atlanta: Society of Biblical Literature, 2003.
White, Luise, Stephan F. Miescher, and David William Cohen, eds. *African Words, African Voices: Critical Practices in Oral History*. Bloomington, IN: Indiana University Press, 2001.
Zaretti, Joan. *Carnegie Hall Presents Global Encounters. South African Sounds, Teacher's Guide and Accompanying Compact Discs*. New York: Carnegie Hall Education Department, 2002.
Zonk! An African People's Magazine. Johannesburg,1950s.

Video Recordings on African Music (place and name of USA distributor given)

Absa, Mousa Sene. *Ca Twiste a Popenguine*. San Francisco: California Newsreel, 1993.
Anderson, John. *King of Jazz*. Hollywood, CA: MGM Studios, 1930.
Avildsen, John. *The Power of One*. Burbank, CA: Warner Studios, 1992.
Ba, Ndiouga Moctar. *You Africa! Youssou N'Dour and Super Etoile: The African Tour*. San Francisco: California Newsreel, 1994.
Balmer, Paul. *Africa I Remember: A Musical Synthesis of Two Cultures*. New York: Filmmakers Library, 1995.
BBC Productions. *Under African Skies: Mali, the Music of Life*. Princeton: Films for the Humanities and Sciences, 1997.
Bischoff, Peter. *Listen to the Silence: A Film About African Cross-Rhythms as Seen Through Ghanaian Music*. Princeton: Films for the Humanities and Sciences, 1996.

De Villiers, Violane. *Mizike Mama*. New York: Interama Video Classics, 1992.
Drewal, Margaret. *Yoruba Ritual*. Accompanying video to *Yoruba Ritual: Performers, Play, Agency*. Bloomington, IN: Indiana University Press, 1992.
Genini, Izzi. *Gnaouas (Morocco)*. New York: Icarus, First Run Films, 1990.
Haydon, Geoffrey and Dennis Marks. *Repercussions: A Celebration of African-American Music*. Chicago: Home Vision, 1994.
Knight, Roderic. *Jali Nyama Suso: Kora Player of the Gambia*. Tivoli, New York: Original Music, 1992a.
——. *Music of the Mande*. Tivoli, New York: Original Music, 1992b.
Kruger, Kevin and Dan Hill (producers). *South Africa: Rainbow Nation*. Pretoria: Mac-V, 1996.
Kubik, Gerhard. *African Guitar: Solo Finger-Style Guitar Music, Composers and Performers*. Cambridge, MA: Rounder Records, 1995.
Lough, Robin. *African Sanctus: David Fanshawe's African Journey*. Robin Lough & Associates, 1994.
Minnelli, Vincente (director). *Cabin in the Sky* (originally released 1943). Santa Monica, CA: MGM/US Home Video, 1999.
Morin, Bertrand. *The Lost City of Zimbabwe*. Princeton: Films for the Humanities and Sciences, 1993.
Raeburn, Michael. *Zimbabwe: Music with a Past*. Princeton: Films for the Humanities and Sciences, 1997.
Rosellini, Jim. *Diro and His Talking Musical Bow; Adama, the Fulani Magician; Dance of the Bella*. Santa Cruz, CA: African Family Films, 1996.
Simon, Sylvan. *Rio Rita!* Hollywood, CA: MGM Studios, 1942 [1930].
Smith, Larry. *Dagbamba Praise Names and Dances, Stories and Drummer Language*. Crown Point, IN: White Cliffs Media, 1990.
——. *Dagbamba Praise Names*. This and preceding video accompany David Locke's *Drum Damba: Talking Drum Lessons*. Crown Point, IN: White Cliffs Media, 1990.
Soule, Beatrice and Eric Millot. *Djabote: Senegalese Drumming and Song from Master Drummer Doudou N'Diaye Rose*. Montpelier, VT: Multicultural Media (now defunct), 1993.
Stone, Andrew (director). *Stormy Weather* (originally released 1943). Beverly Hills, CA: Fox Home Entertainment, 2005.
Toepke, Alvaro. *The Language You Cry In: The Story of a Mende Song*. San Francisco: California Newsreel, 1999.
A Voice of Egypt: Umm Khulthum. Waltham, MA: Filmmakers Collaborative, 1997.
Yamamato, Hiroshi. *Smithsonian/Folkways Video Anthology of Music and Dance of Africa. Africa, Vols. 1–3*. Tokyo: Victor, 1996.
Zantzinger, Gei. *Songs of the Adventurers (Lesotho)*. DeVault, PA: Constant Springs Productions, 1987.
——. *Mbira dza Vadzimu: Dambatsoko: an Old Cult Center*. University Park, PA: Penn State University Media Sales, 1978a.
——. *Mbira dza Vadzimu: Urban and Rural Ceremonies*. University Park, PA: Penn State University Media Sales, 1978b.
——. *The 1973 Mgodo wa Mbanguzi*. University Park, PA: Penn State University Media Sales, 1974.

Sound Recordings (all African sound recordings listed in Appendix 3)

Inspiration, The. Philadelphia: University of Pennsylvania, 1996.
Monk, Thelonius. *Solo Monk: Original Recording Remastered*. New York: Sony, 2003.

Notes

Preface

1 Even those who label their works as pertaining to "Africa" or "African Music" inevitably create unevenly representative texts—from the *Garland Encyclopedia on World Music: Africa*, to Kofi Agawu's *Representing African Music*. Whatever their real strengths, incomplete representation is certainly a limitation.

1 South African Music: The Lion Sleeps Tonight

1 You can read the full-length story in a range of online sites: most notably http://www.pbx.org/independentlens/lionstrail/song.html; *Time*: "It's a Lawsuit, a Mighty Lawsuit" (http://www.time.com/time/magazine/article/0,9171,725115,00.html); *NPR*: All Things Considered, "Family of 'Lion Sleeps Tonight' Writer to Get Millions" (http://www.npr.org/templates/story/story.php?storyId=5300359).
2 The original recording was reissued by ethnomusicologist Veit Erlmann on *Mbube Roots: Zulu Choral Music from South Africa, 1930s–60s*. Rounder Select B00000038J. CD Release 1990.
3 Several stories circulate about the meaning of the song—Pete Seeger reports that the song is about a lion called "Chaka" who is sleeping while the Whites control the country, but will wake up some day. In this rendition, the lion is the name given to the ferocious leader, Shaka, who consolidated the Zulu kingdom in the nineteenth century but whose descendants were subdued in the Anglo-Zulu War of 1879, and the kingdom divided and ruled by Whites until the 1994 elections.
4 See the two-volume CD of the concert, *The Weavers at Carnegie Hall* (April 1957), released in October 1990 by Vanguard Records B000000EFX.
5 You can hear this rendition on *The Best of the Tokens*, a CD released by RCA Records, ASIN B000002WR2 in August 1994.
6 This performance was recorded and issued as *Miriam Makeba: Africa* (LIVE), by RCA Records. The CD version was released in 1991, and is available on iTunes.
7 *The Lion King* was one of the first full-length films produced in Hollywood to have songs sung in Zulu, increasing its appeal to South African audiences exponentially. And its composer was South African-born composer, Lebo M.
8 For further information on this film see, for example, http://www.pbs.org/independentlens/lionstrail/.
9 Remember that South Africa is the name of the country, Southern Africa is the region—including several countries that lie below the Central African region; West Africa is the region that includes countries on the left bulge of the African continent; North Africa is the area north of the Sahara Desert; and East Africa is the other region of the African continent.

10 *Marabi* is briefly discussed in Chapter 6.

11 How "Southern Africa" is defined varies according to the group engaged in defining: I have included Madagascar here after reading and listening to the CDs of Ron Emoff's recent work in Madagascar—I was struck by the resonance between the sound of Zulu *maskanda* guitar playing, and that recorded by Emoff in the 1990s. I don't take the comparison any further here, though considering the stylistic similarities in the histories of the two forms would be a really useful project.

12 See for example, Bender's *Sweet Mother: African Popular Music*; Graeme Ewens, *Africa O-Ye!*; Ronnie Graham's two volumes, *The World of African Music*; and the *Da Capo Guide to Contemporary African Music*; and Chris May and Chris Stapleton's *African Rock*.

13 This pre-concert exposure is similar to that described by Steven Feld with the *Voices of the Rainforest* recording produced by Feld and Mickey Hart. The Kaluli music was played prior to a Grateful Dead performance on the West Coast (USA).

14 All biographical information on Hugh Tracey is gleaned from the ILAM website, http://ilam.ru.ac.za/ retrieved May 31, 2007.

15 I am of the opinion that *Chopi Musicians* provided the model for subsequent ethnomusicologists, like Paul Berliner and John Chernoff, in terms of how to write their own landmark texts, *The Soul of Mbira* (1978), and *African Rhythm, African Sensibility* (1979).

16 It is my understanding that reflecting and researching the Southern African region as a musical unit is part of what the South[ern] African Music Project (SAMP) is currently undertaking.

17 Unfortunately in Levine's work the past is transmuted into a troubling "ethnographic present"—a present in each language group's musical culture that often draws on work published even before apartheid, a "traditional" present Levine presumes still exists. To this end, she provides an accompanying CD of relevant musical examples drawn from the International Library of African Music archive, a resource that is extremely important largely for its preservation of now lost musical forms and practices. Finally, Levine divides each chapter into "established canon" and "emergent" styles, borrowing from Robin Wells' distinctions made in his work in Lesotho. In the "amaZulu" chapter, emergent styles are defined as *maskanda* and *isicathamiya*, both musical forms that have existed, with clear histories of musical style all their own, for much of the twentieth century (see Chs. 8 and 7 respectively). I wonder if Levine has considered at what moment a cultural or music form/practice can emerge sufficiently to exist not as a bastard of modernity but as a fully-fledged genre in its own right? Some sensitivity to the use and value implied by word usage is really necessary if we are to take Levine's work seriously.

18 A representative sample of this work from the 1980s includes: Allen (1996, 1999, 2003, 2004, 2005), Andersson (1982), Ansell (2004), Ballantine (1993), Cockrell (1987), Coplan (1985, 1994), Erlmann (1991, 1996, 1999), Hamm (1995), James (1999), Lucia (2005), Meintjes (2003), Muller (2004), Muller and Mthethwa (forthcoming, 2008), Nuttall and Coetzee (1998), Olwage (2007), and the Proceedings of the Symposiums on Ethnomusicology (1981 to the present) published by ILAM.

2 Twentieth-Century Political History

1 The racial terminology I have used here represents the words that were used in this time period. Asiatics included those who had come from India—Chinese laborers who arrived in the nineteenth century tended to intermingle with others, and so came to be classified as "Coloured" and for a period of time Japanese visitors or residents were classified as "honorary white." It was not a completely rational system! Coloureds are those of mixed heritage—mixed not referring to Germans who married Italians. Rather, Coloured was the result of mixing people of lighter complexion with those of darker hues. So in District Six in Cape Town, for example, when Italians and Germans had children with darker skinned people their children were classified as Coloured. The words used to refer to people of black African descent change over the twentieth century—from native, to Bantu, to African, to Black. And in post-apartheid South Africa, people of Indian descent or those previously labeled Coloured may opt to identify as Black. Such identification is shaped by political consciousness and choices as much as by skin color or family heritage.

2 *Sophiatown*, the musical, was created by the Junction Avenue Theater Company in Johannesburg in the 1980s. It tells the story of the forced removal of residents from the area close to central Johannesburg and their resettlement a long way from the original site. In 2000, the University of KwaZulu Natal restaged the musical at the request of South Africa's Department of Education and Culture. See http://www.artsmart.co.za/music/archive/715.html retrieved August 5, 2007. In 1986 David Kramer and Taliep Peterson wrote *District Six: The Musical* to tell the story about what had been a vibrant and cosmopolitan community living in District Six, close to the center of Cape Town. Finally, *Ziyabbuya Emkhumbane* (2005) focuses on the Cato Manor community of the early 1960s. The story was co-written by Jerry Pooe and Alfred Nokwe and produced by Pooe in 2005. http://artsmart.co.za/drams/archive/1561.html.

3 Twentieth-Century Entertainment History: Live and Mediated

1. For an updated history of Radio Broadcast in South Africa, see for example, http://pumamouse.com/SABbrbHistory, retrieved August 5, 2007. This outline was adapted from Andersson 1981, Baines 1998, and Hamm 1995.
2. See http://downloads.bbc.co.uk/worldservice/trust/pdf/AMDI/south_africa/amdi_sa2_country.pdf.
3. See Part II for further discussion of these categories of South African performance.
4. See Erlmann (1996) for a detailed discussion of the "unhomely" and "home" in *isicathamiya* texts.
5. See www.gallo.co.za for further information about the recording corporation, which was bought out by Warner in 2006, and is now known as Warner Music Gallo Africa.
6. To fully understand this overview, you will probably have to read a history of twentieth-century sound recording technology—to grasp the changes in technology over the century. There are many such accounts currently available.
7. See http://www.mg.co.za/articlePage.aspx?articleid=272390&area=/breaking_news/breaking_news__business/, retrieved June 17, 2007.
8. Most of the information on South Africa's early film history in this section is taken from Gustche (1972).
9. For further detail on recent developments in South African mass media see the website of the South African Consulate in New York City, http://www.southafrica-newyork.net/consulate/aboutSA.htm.

4 *Graceland* (1986): World Music Collaboration

1. Each of these events, and more, are all well-documented on the worldwide web: Google keywords, e.g., "Live Aid," "Farm Aid," or "Live Eight" for example.
2. You can find video clips of the *Sun City: Artists Against Apartheid* song on YouTube, keyword: Sun City.
3. South African Rob Nixon has written concisely about the sports and cultural boycott (1994: 131–174) against South Africa.
4. Check YouTube for video footage of the Sun City song. "Ain't Gonna Play Sun City" is the name of the collaboratively produced song calling for a boycott.
5. These "homelands" were not recognized as "independent" of the South African government by any organization or country, including the United Nations Organization. It was only the apartheid government and the "puppet" black political leaders in the homelands who thought of them as such.
6. These and similar songs can all be found on iTunes.
7. The *Graceland* album is currently available for purchase on tune lists like iTunes and in CD format.
8. See for example Garafalo 1992, Lipsitz 1994, Nixon 1994, Erlmann 1999, Meintjes 1990, and Hamm 1995. At the time the international press, including *Newsweek*, *Time*, the *Village Voice*, the *New York Times*, and other media were also deeply engaged with the controversy.
9. See Erlmann 1996 for extensive discussion of this history and its performance.
10. See Erlmann 1991 and 1996 for further explanation.
11. See Erlmann's 1988 reissue of *mbube* recordings, *Mbube Roots: Zulu Choral Music from South Africa, 1930s–1960s*. Cambridge, MA: Rounder Records, ROUNDER CD 5025.

5 Representing the Past in South African Music

1. See complete references to these works in the References at the end of the book.

7 Labor Migration: *Isicathamiya*

1. See the documentary film *On Tip Toe* (2002) for a visual clip of this explanation, this time to the filmmaker himself.

13 Mission Hymns and the Founding of the Shembe Community

1. In addition to Ntsikana, a handful of other African Christians wrote spiritual songs that were published by the mission presses. All these new compositions in the published versions were written in the traditional SATB format of the European mission hymn. The first ordained African Presbyterian minister, Tiyo Soga (1829–1871) and his successor, Gqoba, composed hymns for the more European-style congregation. Many of these songs have become an integral part of the *Xhosa Methodist Hymnal*. Soga's son John Henderson Soga was a composer who also wrote two books on black South African history. Bokwe composed his own hymns,

several of which were published by the Lovedale mission press, perhaps the most important mission institution and press in Southern Africa. Nehemiah Tile, founder of the Ethiopian Church in 1884, also composed hymns for his followers. And John Dube, African National Congress founder and contemporary of Isaiah Shembe, was also a composer, though he was better known for his secular works. With the exception of Tile, however, each of these men remained in close contact with the colonial mission.

Index

Abafana Baseqhudeni 100
accordion 49, 53, 61, 69, 114, 119–120, 138, 147, 189
Actor's Equity (US) 54
Adam, Arnie 189
Adams, Jimmy 178, 187–190
Adepoju, Demola 59
advertisements 41, 188
Africa: Africanness 46; African religious independentism 213–214; basic facts about continent since 1994 (box) 8–9; Central Africa 30, 271, 295, 297, 313; earliest records of African peoples 77; East Africa 272, 295–296; historical issues 26, 40, 76, 78, 197, 205, 275–279, 281; North Africa 77, 271, 295–296; population 9; representation of ix–xi, 80–81, 271–272; Southern Africa 8–16, 25, 256, 269, 275, 295–297; themes in study of African music xii, 6–7, 56, 261–267; West Africa 46, 166, 248, 295–296, 312, 313
"Africa" (song) 304–306
African American 10–11, 35, 81, 187, 200, 255, 304
African Broadcasting Company (ABC) 35
African Consolidated Sound Industries 41
African Consolidated Theaters 39
African Dances of the Witwatersrand Gold Mines (Tracey) 137
African Guitar (video) 118
African Jazz and Variety (traveling show) 78, 81, 87, 188, 201, 311–312
African Jazz Pioneers 56–57, 78
African Jim (film) 43, 46
African Methodist Episcopal (AME) Church (US) 214
African music ix–x, 5, 8, 10–14, 193, 195, 248, 251, 271–272, 295–297; characteristics of x; European instruments and forms in 25, 114; guide to 296–273; "Lion Sleeps Tonight" as 7; misconceptions about ix, 5–8; positivism of research into 10; stereotypes of ix; urbanization of, 12, 77
African Music Society 12
African National Congress (ANC) 17, 19, 27 (box), 55, 163, 196, 198, 279; anthem of 23, 313; -led government 10
African popular music 10, 295
African Wave: South African Music and Its Influence (video series) 56 (box)
Afrikaans 9, 14, 19, 28, 36, 41, 44, 48–49, 77, 81, 113, 166, 197, 201, 263, 278, 282, 288–289; -medium universities 13; -speaking White South Africans 13
Afrikaner National Party/ Nationalist government 25, 27, 29, 39, 100, 166, 169, 263, 277, 311

Afrikaners 181, 266, 276, 277, 311
Agawu, Kofi 8
agriculture 26
Allingham, Rob 42, 76
Amandla! Revolution in Four Part Harmony (film) 85
Ambassadors, The (night club) 192–194
American Board Mission hymnal 217
Americanization 77, 81
ancestors 25, 80, 125, 205, 214, 238, 242, 250, 252–254
Anderson, Benedict 33, 159
Anglo-Boer War 26, 276
Anglo-Zulu War 219, 276
ankle rattles 120, 131
Annenberg Center, University of Pennsylvania 107, 110
Ansell, Gwen 76, 85, 97
apartheid: dates of 3; films about 25 (box); forced removals 27, 30, 277; Grand Apartheid 25, 64, 78, 81, 183; legislation 25, (made and unmade 27–29 (box)); mid-1980s 54, 57, 68, 131; music about 25 (box); National Christian Education policies 176; post-apartheid, challenges of 38; racial categories under, 169–170; radio music and 34–38; relaxed apartheid 169; as social engineering 26; and television 48–49, 54–55
appropriation 62, 69, 265
Arabs 271, 273, 295, 296
Argus, The 43
Armstrong, Louis 186, 196
arrangements 6, 19, 61, 102, 156, 176, 255, 264, 308
Artists United Against Apartheid 54, 55, 69, 70
art music 80, 97, 272, 296
Ashanti music 271
Asiatics 27, 29, 30, 277
Asmussen, Svend 195
Astaire, Fred 132, 139, 146, 150
atmospheric theaters 42, 49
audiences 12, 16, 34, 39, 42, 43, 54, 56, 61, 90, 92, 118, 121, 130, 138, 144, 150, 179, 180, 187, 193, 195
Avildsen, John 261
"Awusho Ndodana" (song) 301

Ballantine, Christopher 13, 44, 83–84, 91, 94, 106, 162–163, 237, 248, 285, 297
Bambatha Rebellion 219
Bantu Authorities Act 27
Bantu composers 13, 19, 75
Bantu education 17, 19, 27
Bantu Homelands Citizenship Act 28, 278
Bantu Laws Amendment Act 28, 278
Bantu Radio 27, 34, 35–37, 49
Bantu Self-Government Act 35
Bantu speakers *see* language(s): Bantu languages
Bantustans 9, 26, 36, 55, 78
Bapedi nation 40
Beats of the Heart (Marre) 100
Belafonte, Harry 7, 54, 63, 183, 196
Bengu, John 120
Benjamin, Sathima Bea: children of 197, 201; critics' response to 159, 187; discovers Cape Town jazz 164–167; family of 170, 173, 175, 199–201; grandmother Ma Benjamin 170, 171, 174–178, 181, 200; mother of 173, 178, 185–188; music in childhood of 185–188; in New York 158, 183, 196–197, 201
Berg, Heidi 59
Berliner, Paul 297
Best of Sathima Bea Benjamin with Friends, The 199
Biko, Steve 28, 55, 278
Billboard Top 100 6, 7, 19, 58
bioscopes 43, 49, 175, 178–180, 201, 311
birds 67, 164, 230, 232, 240
Bizet's *Carmen* in Xhosa 46, 80
Black Consciousness Movement 28, 278
Blacking, John 13, 79, 213, 217, 218, 250
Bleek, W. H. I. 261
Bloom, Harry 88, 91, 93
Blue Notes 182, 201
bob parties 183
body movements 44, 249–250; *see also* dance
boeremusiek 40, 49
Bohlman, Philip xii
Bophutatswana 28 (box), 29, 36, 69, 278, 314
Botswana 9, 14, 204
Bouchard, Fred 160
Boyoyo Boys 53, 59, 63, 284, 286
Britain x, 8, 12, 15, 27 (box), 37, 40, 41, 46, 47, 50, 56, 87, 179, 276; British Actors'/Musicians' Unions 54; mining interest in South Africa 24
British Broadcasting Corporation (BBC) 34, 35–36 (box), 56, 70, 291
Brother with Perfect Timing (DVD) 85, 196
Brown, Duncan 16, 297
Brubeck, Darius 78, 162
Brubeck, Dave 78, 162, 192

Brunswick Records 39–40
Bureau of State Security 28 (box), 278
Bushmen rock paintings 80–81, 269
busking 129

Cabin in the Sky (film) 44, 49, 81, 179
cadence 7, 19
call and response 7, 19, 20, 62, 107, 110, 116, 134, 141–142, 143 (box), 161, 217, 247, 248, 255, 256, 264, 306, 311
Calloway, Cab 179
Caluza, Reuben 77, 81, 136, 263–264, 283
Cape Bushmen 80–81, 269
Cape Coloured 156, 166, 167, 169–171, 178, 179, 187, 197, 201
Cape Jazz 45 (box), 157–171, 182, 200; Cape Town rhythm 161; in 1950s 47, 159, 174–179; postwar 180–183; *see also* jazz
Cape Standard 174
Cape Town: cultural and political history of 155–159; District Six 30, 44 (box), 170, 177, 179, 191; Khoikhoi and free blacks in 165–166; New Year holidays in 95–98, 166–169, 176; night club life in 186–192; *see also* Cape Jazz
Cape Town Love (CD) 175, 184, 191, 199, 202
Carnegie Hall 5, 10, 196
Cato Manor 30
CBS (Columbia Broadcast Services) 10
censorship 34, 36 (box), 37
Ceylon 166
Chakide 122–124, 127, 301–303, 311; *see also* Vilakazi, Thami
Chaplin, Charlie 146
Chapman, Michael x, 16
charity rock concerts 54, 69
Chase, Chevy 60
Chernoff, John 296
children 23, 26, 28 (box), 54, 137–138, 171, 176, 179, 229–230, 236, 254–255
Chinese people 30, 201, 276, 311
Chopi xylophone musicians 13
choral music 19, 62, 81, 272; choir uniforms 23; history of 37; Zulu 247; *see also isicathamiya* genre; *makwaya*
Christianity 38, 125, 134, 165–166, 211–214, 217, 223–224, 256, 312; and African religious independentism 213–214; Catholic mass 137; vs. Zulu religious practice 125; *see also* hymns; *ibandla lamaNazaretha* community; missions/missionaries
Christy Minstrels 77, 138–139, 144 (box), 168
Church of the Nazarites/Nazaretha 204; *see also ibandla lamaNazaretha* community; Shembe, Isaiah
cinema 43, 47, 49, 94
Clegg, Johnny 13, 57, 113, 115–117, 119, 128, 284
"Click Song" 267
close-harmony singers 44 (box), 69, 74, 94, 97, 248, 312
clothing 178; of *ibandla lamaNazaretha* community 101; *see also* gumboot dancing: attire for
CNN 24
Cockrell, Dale 136, 138, 139
CODESA I and II 28 (box)
Cold War 34, 49
Cole, Nat King 39, 175, 177, 181, 191
collaboration xi, 42, 46, 54, 57–63, 68, 69, 81, 111, 150, 265; vs. composition 59–60; transnational 264
colonialism *see* Europe: European colonization
Coloured Jazz and Variety (traveling show) 188, 201, 312
Coloureds 27, 169–170, 176, 189, 275; Coloured girls 165; *see also* Cape Coloured
Columbia Records 10, 39, 41
Columbus, Chris 189
Common Voters' Role 169
communism 27 (box), 34, 277
compositional process 60, 106, 234, 264; *see also* dream
Computicket 90
concertinas 29, 86, 97, 112, 114, 119–120, 122, 128, 131, 136, 138, 145, 147, 300, 304, 311
Congress of South African Trade Unions (COSATU) 28, 278
Coon Carnival 95, 97, 98, 168
copies 6, 67, 80
Coplan, David 13, 39, 76, 83, 134, 295, 297
copyright 6, 7, 16
Courtenay, Bryce 261
covers 6, 19, 80
creolization 26, 30
cross-over 17, 19, 56, 97, 189, 289
Crowther, Bruce 159
Cry Freedom (film) 292
cultural boycott 41, 49, 54–56, 65, 69, 79, 325
cultural memory ix, 240
cyclical structure 7, 19

Damons, Maude 192
dance: collective 251; dance band music 169, 175, 176; forbidden by missions 205; and Isaiah Shembe/*ibandla lamaNazaretha* community 212–213, 217, 221, 223; social dancing 40, 49, 77, 161, 182; *see also* body movements; gumboot dancing; *ibandla lamaNazaretha* community: festival of sacred song and dance
Dargie, Father Dave 79
Davies, Nollene 113, 118, 297
Davis, Jr., Sammy 54
Day, Doris 171, 177, 181, 187, 188
D'Azevac-Macaya, M. A. P. 271
Dean, Owen 7
Decca Records 5, 39
de Certeau, Michel 123
Dedications 198
Defense Amendment Act 278
Defiance Campaign 27 (box), 277
democracy 25, 26, 29 (box), 36, 58
Dhlamini, Ezekiel 91
Dhlomo, Petros M. 221, 246–247
diamonds 99, 143 (box), 214, 219, 276
"Diamonds on the Soles of Her Shoes" *see Graceland* album
diaspora 49, 50, 67, 85, 295
Dibango, Manu 5
"Die Stem" (The Call) 30, 31, 313
District Six 30, 44 (box), 170, 177, 179, 191
Dollar Brand 99, 159, 162–163, 182, 193, 195, 201; *see also* Ibrahim, Abdullah
doo-wop 7, 19
Downbeat 160
dream 111, 174, 178–179, 206, 209, 232, 234
Drum Magazine 78, 193
drumming 5, 7, 10, 11, 113, 129, 200, 213, 217, 248, 296, 313
du Bois, W. E. B. 187
Duke Ellington Presents the Dollar Brand Trio 290
Durban xii, 30, 35, 41, 42, 57, 64, 86, 90, 99, 100–109, 112, 113, 119, 121, 122, 126, 131, 132, 134, 136–138, 144, 145 (box), 147, 155, 158, 162, 203–204, 207, 222; *see also* Natal, University of
Dyani, Johnny 84, 97, 162, 169, 291
Dylan, Bob 66, 67

Eastern Cape 9 (box), 34, 222, 224, 275
economic sanctions 28 (box), 30, 79
economy 6, 9 (box), 19, 24, 26, 29, 59, 60
Edison, Thomas 42–43
education vii, 17, 19, 27 (box), 35, 60, 75, 77, 101, 119, 161, 170, 261, 277; of army musicians 182; National Christian Education policies 176; television as educational tool 49
Ekapa label 163, 197, 199, 305
Ekuphakameni 208, 211, 219, 222, 223, 234, 240, 256, 312
elections: 1948 27 (box); 1958 27, (box), 277; 1994 29 (box); 1998 278
Elite Swingsters, The 85, 291
Ellington, Duke 156, 159, 161, 162, 177, 179, 183, 186, 194–196, 200–201
Ellington, Ruth 196
employment xi, 26, 31, 140, 191; *see also* labor; migrant workers
England *see* Britain
entertainment industry 6, 67, 70
Erasmus, Dougie 192
Erlmann, Veit 13, 79, 102, 136, 138, 162, 168, 264, 292, 297
Ethiopia 214, 272
Ethiopian church/Ethiopianism 214, 256, 272, 312
Ethiopian National Orchestra 272
Ethiopian Serenaders 168
Euba, Akin 272, 295–296
Europe 7, 42, 49, 50, 54, 77, 84, 93, 156, 159, 160, 166, 194, 196, 199, 263, 265, 271, 273, 291, 312; early European writings about African music 270; European colonization 11, 19, 262, 272; music of x, 13, 25, 113, 157–158, 271
Everly Brothers 57
exiles xii, 17–19, 30, 39, 41, 53, 54, 77, 161–162, 173, 177, 196, 198, 200, 276, 289, 304
Eyre, Banning 296

fanakalo 141–143, 150, 312
Fanshawe, David 322
February, Henry 172, 191, 305
Fields, Gracie 47, 90
Fife, Ruth 177
films 42–46, 180–181; atmospheric theaters 42, 49; history of in South Africa 42–46; shown in mining compounds 142, 146, 151; terms for 43 (box); *see also* Hollywood
Fitzgerald, Ella 157, 177
Five Roses 122, 128
flutes 8, 84, 90, 165, 270, 305
folk music 29, 40, 49, 76, 97, 134

Ford Foundation 12
four-part harmony 7, 19, 20, 25, 61, 70, 85, 103, 112, 212, 249, 263, 286, 292, 308, 312
France 34, 211
"From Spirituals to Swing" (concert) 10
Fulela, Ephraim 232
fundraising 172, 181, 186

Gabriels, Joey 186
Gaitskell, Deborah 212
Galeta, Hotep (Cecil Barnard) 190
Gallo, Eric 5, 12; and Brunswick Records 39–40; recording South African music 12, 38, 40–42, 65, 76, 77
Gallo Records 12, 38, 40–42, 56, 84, 85, 91, 102; pressing plant 41; reissues 82, 87–88
Gallotone label 92
Gambia, The 114
gangsters 89, 94, 96, 189
Garland Encyclopedia of World Music vii, 295
Gauteng 9, 40, 224
General Law Amendment Act 27 (box), 278
General MD Shirinda and the Gaza Sisters 53, 59
George, Eddie 190
George, Gambi 87, 114, 273
Germany 26, 34, 262
Gertze, Johnny 195
Ghana 8, 270, 296
Gillespie, Dizzy 178
Glebeland migrant worker hostels 102, 106, 130
global economy 6, 19, 59–60
Gluckman, Leon 92, 93, 149, 287
gold 99, 112, 134, 143, 214, 219, 276; *see also* gold mining/miners
Goldberg, Morris 53
Goldberg, Whoopi 64, 86, 293
Golden City Dixies 78, 81, 87, 194
Golden City Post, The 159, 181, 186, 187, 190
gold mining/miners 90, 129, 134, 137, 140–143, 145; booklets issued by Chamber of Mines 146; gang structure in mining operations 141; mine compounds 140, 146; *see also* gold; gumboot dancing: and gold mining
gospel music 255, 256, 284, 285, 312
Graceland album: analyzing 60; "Boy in the Bubble, The" 61; chronology of recording 59; controversy generated by 54, 57–59; "Diamonds on the Soles of her Shoes" 58–59, 65; "Gumboots" 63; "Homeless" 58, 59, 61–65, 67, 69, 110; *see also* Warner Brothers
gramophone 42, 46, 47, 50, 175
Grand Apartheid 25, 64, 78, 81, 183
Green, Eva 185
griot/griotte traditions 273, 295, 296, 312
Group Areas Act 27 (box), 30, 170, 178, 201, 277
Guinea 270, 273
guitar music 86, 100; guitar as *tambo* 113; guitar-like instruments 8, 19; and musical bows 8; styles in *maskanda* performance 113–128; tunings 147, 150, 311
gumboot dancing: aesthetics of performance 147; attire for 138, 140, 146; Collage of thoughts on 143–146 (box); commands/titles of dance sequences 132, 141–142, 146, 148, 150; competitive dimension of 131–134, 136, 138, 140, 142, 146, 148, 150; contemporary performance of 149; and gold mining 129, 134, 137, 139, 140, 141, 145; history of 131, 134, 137; *igumboots* 136, 147, 150; *maskanda* musical accompaniment 146, 147, 148, 150, 151; and minstrel shows 132, 134, 136, 137–139, 147; and mission culture 137; solo performances in 132, 134, 148, 162, 164; sources of 132; terms associated with 136; two kinds of performance 136
Gumboots: Accordion Jive Hits Vol. II 55, 59, 61
Gumboots: An Explosion of Spirit and Song (video) 129
Gumbs, Onaje Allen 160, 198, 305, 306
Gunner, Liz 15, 208, 222, 223, 230
Gutsche, Thelma 42, 43

Hadebe, Jonney 136–139, 142, 146–148, 149
haircuts 178
Halee, Roy 59–63, 70
Hamm, Charles 37, 76
Hammond, John 10
Hannerz, Ulf 134, 295
Hanno 270
harmonic cycle 7, 20
Harrison, Wayne 129
healing 15, 113, 128, 214, 215, 217, 232, 313
Heath, Ted 84
Higgins, Billy 198–199
hip hop 38, 50, 56, 97, 287–88
Hoernle, Winifred 13
Holiday, Billie 198, 199, 305, 306
Hollywood 39, 46, 88, 132, 134, 144, 146, 151, 179, 180, 181, 183, 292, 293; *see also* films
Holst, Gustav 11
homelands *see Bantustans*

"Homeless" *see Graceland* album
homophonic 8, 20
Horne, Lena 179
Hottentots 270
Huddleston, Father Trevor 54, 91
Hughes, Langston 187, 214
Hujah, Jeff 87
human voice 62, 85, 157, 212, 229, 234, 248, 262; female voice 234, 237, 249
humor 134, 138, 146
hunter-gatherers 16, 269
Huskisson, Yvonne 13, 75
hymns 176, 203–257, 308, 313; *see also* *IziHlabelelo zamaNazaretha*

ibandla lamaNazaretha community: the Bible in 207, 211–214, 216, 224–225, 228, 229, 230, 237, 240, 243 (*see also* Shembe, Isaiah: and the Bible); festival of sacred song and dance 209; founding moment of 100, 203–225; liturgy for Morning Prayers 306; narratives told in 225, 230, 236; Nazarite rituals 239–240; virgin girls in 234, 240, 246, 247; youth choir competitions 308; *see also* clothing; Shembe, Isaiah
Ibn Battuta 270, 273
Ibrahim, Abdullah 84, 85, 97, 158–169, 182, 184, 191–197, 201, 276; children of 197, 201; *see also* Dollar Brand
ILAM (International Library of African Music) 11, 12, 13, 14, 21, 283, 287; African music textbook project 12; archive of 11; *Proceedings of the Symposiums on Ethnomusicology* 11; *Sound of Africa* Series (LP recordings, reissued) 11, 12, 247, 271; *see also* Smithsonian Global Sound; SWP Records
illiteracy 33, 99, 142, 241
imagination 17, 47, 171, 174, 296, 297
Imagined Communities: On the Origins and Spread of Nationalism (Anderson) 33
imbongi style 125, 208, 256, 312; *see also* praise singing
imitation 19, 62, 67, 93, 176, 192, 271; *see also* copies; covers
Immorality Act 27 (box), 170, 192, 277
imported musical entertainment 38
improvisation 132, 148, 188, 248, 255
Independent Broadcast Authority 36 (box), 38, 49, 312
independent radio stations 36 (box), 50
independent record labels 41
India/Indians 8, 13, 15, 27 (box), 30, 39, 54, 66, 76, 77, 141, 155, 164, 165, 166, 177, 201, 203, 276, 277
Indonesia 19, 166, 201, 312
Industrial Coalition Act 27 (box), 277
industry 50, 149
influx control 26, 27 (box), 31, 78, 81, 277
Ink Spots 94, 179
Inquiry into the Origin and Development of Music, Songs, Instruments, Dances and Pantomimes of the Savage Races, An (Wallaschek) 271
Inspiration (musical group) 67
Internet x, 9, 17, 41, 73, 74, 76, 82, 155
In Township Tonight! (Coplan) 39
Invisible Church 203
"I Only Have Eyes for You" (song) 161
Isaacs, Sam 185, 190
isicathamiya genre 7, 19, 20, 37, 38, 44, 53, 61–62, 67, 69, 74, 79, 86, 97, 99–112, 136, 149, 163, 168, 248, 255; all-night choir competitions 103; mission hymn 62; SATB style 70, 103, 112
isishameni 13, 20, 86, 313
Islam 38, 165, 166, 296
iTunes xii, 50, 85, 86, 128, 155, 175, 282
izibongo 13, 20, 121, 128
IziHlabelelo ZamaNazaretha (hymnal) 205, 218, 227, 229, 234, 237, 242, 249, 256, 313; recent changes in 253

Jails, Willis 190
James, Deborah 13
James, Joni 171, 177, 181, 188
Jay, Gideon 47–48
jazz x, xii, 10, 13, 20, 36–60, 63, 76–98, 155–163, 169–202, 248; *see also* Cape Jazz; South African jazz
Jazz Epistles 182, 201, 290
Jegede, Tunde 296
Jeptha, Harold 192
Jeske, Lee 159
Jews 77, 181, 203, 299
Jim Comes to Joburg/African Jim (film) 46
jive 37, 55, 59, 61, 69, 83, 84, 89; *see also* *mbaqanga* music
Johannesburg 10, 13, 15, 27 (box), 35 (box), 37–42, 59, 81, 86–94, 97–111, 134, 187–189, 214, 224, 277; Bantu Men's Social Center in 91, 189
Jolson, Al 42
Jones, Rev. A. M. 10, 12
Journal of the Musical Arts of Africa 18

Jowitt, Harold 11
"Joy to the World" (carol) 308
Juluka 57, 100, 119

Kalahari Research Committee 15
Karanga 10
Keita, Salif 114
Kelly, Gene 132, 139, 146, 150
Kerzner, Sol 55, 70
Kethani 121, 128
Kew Town 185, 187
Khayelitsha United Mambazo 67, 69
Khoikhoi people 165, 166, 201, 202, 313
Khumalo, Bakhiti and Vusi 53
Khumalo, Mzilikazi 272
Kiernan, James 213, 217
Kimberley 99, 112, 173, 276
kinetophone 42
King Kong: An African Musical Opera 81, 149
King of Jazz, The (film) 43
Kingston Trio 5
Kirby, Percival 14, 77, 247, 270
Klassic Kramer (CD) 65
Klugman, Arthur 188
Kolbe, Vincent 96, 176, 178, 179, 181, 182, 183, 187, 190–192
kora music 114, 273, 313
Kramer, David 65–67, 69
Kronos Quartet 273
Kruger, Jaco 79
Kubeka, Abigail 87
Kubik, Gerhard 118, 295
"Kungcono Khona" (song) 302
kwaito 38, 41, 50, 80, 97, 265
KwaMashu Temple Choir 254
KwaZulu Natal 218, 220, 221, 231, 233, 254, 255; commercialization of *maskanda* in 120; Umzansi region 118, 121, 128, 131, 146, 300, 314
kwela music 13, 15, 30, 37, 57, 60, 78, 79, 81, 83, 84, 85, 88, 89, 97

labor 89, 102, 131, 140–142, 219, 247; *see also* employment; migrant workers
Lady Sing the Blues: The Searing Autobiography of an American Music Legend 187
Ladysmith Black Mambazo 7, 20, 53, 56–63, 67, 69, 74, 86, 97, 106–112, 136, 138, 249, 283
"Lalela Zulu" (Shembe song) 247
Land Act 219, 277
land ownership 276
langarm 45, 50, 182, 190, 201, 313
language(s): Afrikaans 19, 28 (box), 40, 41, 48, 65, 127, 201, 289; Bantu languages 311; Batswana 14, 29; click sounds 63 (*see also* "Click Song"); Ge'ez 286; Khoisan 14, 15, 313; and national unity x; Ndebele 8, 9 (box), 14, 15, 17, 283; official languages 9, 33, 84, 276, 277, 289; pidgin language in mines 141, 143 (box); and radio 27 (box), 32; Sesotho 8, 14, 23; Siswati 9, 14; Sotho 20, 35, 37, 44 (box), 169, 214, 256, 311, 313; South African English 62; and television 48; tonal 80, 212, 252; translations 205, 211, 237; Tsonga 9, 14, 25 (box); Xhosa 9, 20, 23, 27 (box), 34, 46, 136, 169, 196, 213, 256, 257; *see also* Zulu language
Leeukop Prisoners Choir 67, 70
Lehner, Gerhard 195, 196
Le Roux, P. L. 215
Levine, Laurie 14, 15
license 15, 26, 36, 40, 49, 50, 124
Linda, Solomon 5, 6, 7, 68, 102, 267
Lion King, The 6
"Lion Sleeps Tonight, The" 5–21
Little Steven 55, 69, 70
Lloyd, Lucy 269, 271
LM Radio 18, 20, 36 (box)
local music 14, 36 (box), 38, 40, 49, 50
Los Lobos 57
love 157, 244
Lovedale mission press 326
Lovelight 198
Luthuli, Albert 27 (box), 31, 54, 277

McAdoo, Orpheus 61, 138, 168
McGregor, Chris 84, 85, 97, 169, 182, 192, 201, 289, 291, 297
Madagascar 9, 165, 166
Magubane, Mvangeli 238, 305
Mahlangu, Makhaya 53
Mahlasela, Vusi 284
Mahotella Queens 73, 74, 100, 284
mainstream music 111, 115
Makeba, Miriam 3, 7, 53, 63, 81, 85, 86, 87, 93, 94, 144 (box), 162, 163, 189, 194, 196, 267
makwaya 103, 112, 203, 255, 264; *see also* choral music
Malan, Rian 7
Malay choirs 96, 177; see also *nagtroepe*
Mali 273
Mandela, Nelson 24, 25, 28 (box), 29, 31, 64, 79, 110, 146, 163, 243, 257, 277, 278

Mandela: Son of Africa, Father of a Nation (film) 292
Manding musicians 273
Mango Groove 56, 57, 78
Manhattan Brothers 91, 94
"Mannenberg" (tune) 197
manyano 212, 213, 241
Mapfumo, Thomas 114
marabi music 20, 77, 83, 97, 118, 147
Maree, Daphne 114
marimbas 8
Marks, David 41, 101
Marre, Jeremy 54, 56–63, 66, 70, 75, 100, 101, 106, 112, 293
marriage 27 (box), 28 (box), 63, 126, 170, 173, 204, 205, 230, 277, 278; *see also* polygamy
Martin, Denis-Constant 95, 96, 161, 165, 166, 167, 168, 169
Masekela, Hugh 3, 53, 85, 194, 196
Masinga, Ben "Satchmo" 194, 196
maskanda xi, 13, 29, 38, 45, 49, 68, 73, 74, 86–87, 99–128, 150, 151, 284, 297, 300, 304, 313; commercialization of 120; competitions 119; and gumboot dancing 146–149; technique 117–118
mass media 33, 38, 39, 73, 74, 81; *see also* films; media; radio; television
Matiwane, James 214
Matshikiza, Todd 88, 91, 93
Mazibuko, Cinikile 220, 221, 232
mbaqanga music 15, 20, 37, 49, 64, 65, 73, 74, 79, 85, 86, 97, 100, 120, 147
Mbatha, Nathoya 238, 255, 308
Mbeki, Govan 28–30, 278
mbira instruments/music 8, 20, 114, 273, 296, 297, 313
"Mbube" (song and style) xi, 3, 5–7, 16, 20, 62, 68, 69, 102, 265, 283, 313; South African musical elements of 3; *see also* "Lion Sleeps Tonight, The"; "Wimoweh"
Mbuli, Zenzi 129
Mchunu, Sipho 57, 115, 116, 117, 119, 120, 121, 128
media xi, 3, 20, 34, 38, 50, 54, 56, 79, 273; *see also* mass media
Memories and Dreams 198
memory ix, 5, 17, 30, 123, 146, 156, 159, 175, 181, 187, 211, 239, 240, 248, 267, 272, 273; collective 17
Merry Macs 192
Messiah, The (Handel) 264
Meyer, Paul 178, 194
Mhlongo, Busi 86, 122, 128, 284
migrant workers 13, 37, 38, 64, 102, 106, 119, 129–131, 134, 137, 140, 143 (box), 149, 312; Bhaca workers 134; hostels for 130, 145; *Miner's Dictionary in English, Afrikaans and Fanakalo, The* 141, 142
migration 14, 38, 45, 73, 77, 99–151; of musical styles xi, 99–151; and radio transmission 119–120
minstrelsy 43, 44–45 (box), 95, 144, 166, 167, 168
missions/missionaries 12, 27 (box), 37, 61, 77, 90, 103, 113, 132, 134, 136–139, 176, 203–225; and dance 204–207; mission culture 77, 137, 224; mission vs. Nazarite musical practice 211; Wayfarer missionaries 176
Mr. Smith Wakes Up (film) 42
Mkhize, Blanket 64, 84, 117, 130, 131, 133, 135, 136, 137, 147, 148, 300, 304
Moeketsi, Kippie 84, 91, 97, 169, 188, 290
Monk, Thelonius 84, 159, 289
Moodie, Dunbar 139
Morning in Paris 196
Motloheloa, Forere 53
Mozambique 9, 13, 14, 15, 18, 20, 35 (box), 87, 165, 189, 275, 297
mqashiyo music 74, 86, 97, 265, 284, 313
msakazo (broadcast music) 85, 98
Msimango, Paulos 106, 299
Mthethwa, Bongani 119, 209, 239, 249, 251, 254, 255, 308
Mthethwa, Khethiwe 251
Muller, Carol ix, 236, 237; as ethnomusicologist x; as white South African x
music industry 17, 19, 21, 36, 38, 50, 66, 78, 263, 295
musical bows 8, 20, 114, 115
Musical Echoes 199
musical instruments 14, 15, 77, 138, 270; homemade 116, 118, 119, 164; reed flutes 270; *see also* drumming; guitar music; musical bows; organ accompaniment; saxophone music
musical notation 106, 220, 271, 272
musicals 30, 46, 159, 178, 180
music as universal language 150
music in the streets 37, 88, 165
Music Television (MTV) 49, 54, 55, 70
Muziki (journal) 18

nagtroepe 96, 98, 313
Namajaha, Udokotela Shange 86

Nasson, Bill 177, 179, 180
Natal Mercury, The 139
Natal, University of 78, 102, 106, 119, 120, 122, 130, 163
National Sorghum Breweries 119
"Nations in Me, New Nation-a-Coming" (song) 304, 305
Native Laws Amendments Act 27 (box), 277
Native Resettlement Act 27 (box), 277
Nazareth Baptist Youth 222, 254, 255, 267
N'Dour, Youssou 55, 59
New York City 5, 7, 10, 57, 59, 60, 63, 66, 70, 88, 111, 144, 149, 158, 159, 163, 183, 188, 195–198, 206, 265, 267
Ngema, Mbongeni 64, 70, 74, 86
ngoma 101, 113, 120, 128
Nguni 20, 115, 256, 275, 283, 313; music/dancing 134, 137, 151, 247; song style 7
Nhlangakaze (holy mountain) 205–207, 220, 221, 232, 234, 245, 251, 252, 256, 313
Nigeria x, 8, 59, 177, 197, 271, 272, 296
Nixon, Michael 96, 176, 182, 189, 190, 191, 192
"Nkosi Sikelel'iAfrika" (song) 23, 31, 215 (box), 313
Nobel Peace Prize 27 (box), 29 (box), 31, 54, 278
Nokwe, Tu 86, 122, 128
Nthini, Samukelisiwe 206
Ntshoko, Makaya 195
Ntsikana, Gaba 213
Ntsikana Memorial Association 214
Nuffield Foundation 12, 15
Nyengana, voice of 213
Nzimande, "Bodloza" 119

Oosthuizen, Pippin 200, 204, 206, 221, 225, 232, 236, 242, 243, 250
Oral Literature and Performance in Southern Africa (Brown, ed.) 16
oral transmission 212, 297
organ accompaniment 44 (box), 238, 254, 268, 308
Orpheus McAdoo and the Virginia Jubilee Singers 61, 138, 168
Osifekunde 271
overtones 115–116, 127, 128, 312

Paiva (Mozambique) 15
Pan-Africanists 29, 262, 279; Pan Africanist Congress (PAC) 27 (box), 277
Parales, Jon 159
Parker, Charlie 162, 178, 194
Parnel, Jack 87
pass (*dompas*)/pass laws 26, 27 (box), 31, 314
Paul Simon: Graceland, Recounting the Journey of a Legendary Music Recording (video) 58
pentatonic scale 7, 20, 115, 116, 128, 247, 248, 256
Periplus (Hanno) 270
Phahlane, Mike 92
Phiri, Ray 3, 53, 56, 57, 70, 118
phrase overlap 20
Phuzekhemisi 121, 128
Phuzushukela 120, 128
Pillay, Sonny 87, 91
Placksin, Sally 186
police 26–28, 31, 55, 57, 62, 76, 84, 100, 132, 134, 140, 141, 142, 150, 277, 278
polygamy 214, 225
polyphony 8, 20, 107, 253
Population Registration Act 27, 170, 171, 277
Portugal 24, 113, 165, 166, 181, 189, 203, 270, 275
Power of One (novel/film) 261, 262, 267
praise singing 123; *see also imbongi* style
Princess Magogo (opera) 13
Prohibition of Mixed Marriages Act 27 (box), 28, 277, 278
Prophets of da City 56
Psalms 217–218, 229, 230, 240, 241, 244
Public Broadcasting Services (PBS) 54
Public Safety Act 27 (box) 277
pygmies 269, 297

Rachabane, Barney 63
racism 54, 176, 187, 190, 214
radio: black consumers 37; broadcast history (box) 35–36; commercial 20, 35 (box), 38, 49; community 36, 38, 49; FM transmission 37; local 39, 119; in post-apartheid South Africa 38; Rediffusion Services 35, 50; religious programming 34, 35; traditional music and 37; *see also* language(s); Springbok Radio
Radio Zulu 34, 38, 50, 65, 119, 120, 264
Rathebe, Dolly 87, 91
recordings: Afrikaans 41; foreign 39, 41, 84; independent labels 41, 50, 163; in KwaZulu Natal 86; local pressing 41; in postwar Cape Town 180; of Sathima Bea Benjamin 196–200
Reef Consolidated mines 146
Reprise Records 195
Reuben Caluza's Double Quartet 77, 81, 136, 264
rhythm ix, 7, 19, 54, 56, 57, 59, 60, 62, 63, 70, 75, 84, 86, 89, 96, 97, 100, 101, 103, 112, 115, 116, 117, 120, 121, 131, 136, 138, 148, 159, 181, 183, 199, 201, 211, 212, 217, 218, 220, 221,

229, 234, 242, 243, 248–252, 254, 255, 256; of *izihlabelelo* 248; *see also* Cape Jazz: Cape Town rhythm
Rhythm of Resistance (film/video) 54, 56, 57, 60, 70, 75, 100, 101, 112, 115, 121
Rio Rita (film) 42, 43
Roberts, Esther 223, 249, 295
Rockin' Dopsie and the Twisters 57
rock'n'roll 34, 69, 190
Rosenthal, Hilton 59
royalties 6, 7, 20, 59, 60, 68
rural areas 37, 40, 46, 63, 73, 77, 78, 84, 120, 121, 213, 267

St. Helena 170, 171, 174, 175, 177, 276
Sarafina! The Music of Liberation (feature film, musical, documentary) 68, 70, 86, 287
Sathima Sings Ellington 195, 198
Saunders, Dave 192
saxophone music 45, 63, 81, 84, 85, 160, 161, 162, 182, 183, 194, 197
Schilder, Tony 190
Schmidt, Georg 211, 295, 296
Seeger, Pete 5
segregation xi, 3, 24, 25, 31, 38, 68, 170, 178, 214, 263, 311
self-taught musicians 118, 176, 185
Senegal 59, 114, 195
Senegambia 273
Separate Amenities Act 28 (box), 170, 278
separate development 56
Shabalala, Joseph xi, 20, 53–69, 106; murder of wife of 110
Shanachie Records 86, 284
Sharpeville Massacre 26, 27 (box), 54, 78, 81, 277
Shearing, George 185
shebeen 20, 88, 97, 189, 302; culture 134
Shelemay, Kay 271, 272
Shelembe, Steven 142, 149
Shembe, Amos 211, 222, 240, 254, 255
Shembe, Isaiah 204–257; and the Bible 225; early life 219; as Ethiopianist and Zionist 214; narratives about 225; praises of 208; songs of 218 (*see also IziHlabelelo ZamaNazaretha*); sons of *see* Shembe, Amos; Shembe, Johannes Galilee; *see also ibandla lamaNazaretha* community
Shembe, Johannes Galilee 204, 211, 237, 256, 314
Shembe, Rev. Vimbeni 255, 256, 314
Shembe bugles 207
Shembe singing 115; *see also* Shembe, Isaiah
Shepherd, W. H. 237
Simon, Paul xi, 3, 7, 28 (box), 53, 54–70, 79, 99, 110, 111, 147, 150, 150, 265; and David Kramer 66; motivation for *Graceland* project 60; *see also Graceland* album
Sinatra, Frank 39, 195
Singing Fool, The (film) 42
Sizulu, Walter 28 (box), 278
slavery ix, 77, 165, 166, 220, 275; in Cape Town 275; slave musical performances 165 (box)
Smithsonian Global Sound 12
Snow White and the Seven Dwarves (animated film) 43, 178
social Darwinism 271
Society for Research in South African Music 15
Soga, Tiyo and John Henderson 325
Solomon Linda Evening Birds 5
"Sometimes I Feel Like a Motherless Child" (song) 173, 304–305
Song of Africa (film) 43, 46, 78, 81
Sontonga, Enoch 31, 214, 313
Sophiatown 27 (box), 30, 78, 81, 140, 277, 285
sorghum beer 119, 131
Sound of Africa Series (LP records) 11, 12, 247, 271
South Africa: basic facts since 1994 8–9 (box); constitution 16, 23, 28 (box), 68, 279; English, European, and/or American influence in ix–x; flag 23–24; key dates in history of 275–279; map 2; as nation-state 6, 9 (box), 33, 50, 68; national anthem 23–24, 30, 45, 48, 215; national identity 34, 50, 266; phases of twentieth-century history xi; post-apartheid/new South Africa x, xi, 3, 6, 8, 10, 14, 15, 38, 41, 46, 49, 50, 58, 70, 75, 80, 97, 100, 101, 156, 166, 287, 289; postwar period 18, 43, 46, 49, 81, 157, 159, 161, 163, 165, 167, 169, 171, 173, 182 (*see also* Cape Jazz: postwar); relationship to African continent x, 80; relationship to Southern African region x, 80; relationship to world at large x, 80; segregation period xi, 3, 24, 25, 31, 38, 68, 170, 178, 214, 263, 311; transitional period 3, 29; Union of South Africa created 26, 276
South African Amendment Act 277
South African Broadcast Corporation (SABC) 5, 7, 13, 20, 24, 25, 34, 35–36 (box), 37, 39, 40, 48, 49, 50, 75, 77, 281; Annual Report of 35 (box); SABC-TV 48; Transcription Series 39, 50
South African Defense Force 28 (box), 145 (box), 278

South African jazz xii, 13, 46, 63, 76, 82, 84, 85, 93, 155, 156, 160–162, 195, 196, 200, 297, 313; Township 20, 78, 82, 83, 84, 85, 87, 91, 97, 98, 202, 285, 214; *see also kwela*; *marabi*
South African music: censorship of 17, 34, 36, 37, 40, 41, 76; characteristics of xi, 266; compared with West African music 46, 166, 248, 295–296; historical periods 73, 74, 76, 81; problem of representation 30 (archive 11, 12, 13, 15, 41, 162, 181, 267; originality 43, 80, 81; palimpsest 80, 81; value 79, 80, 82); twentieth century styles xi, 73–80
South African Music Educator's Conference (1985) 130
South African Music Project 15
South African Railways 137
Southern Africa, basic facts since 1994 8–9 (box); as region x, 5–20, 25, 61, 73, 80, 91, 125, 160, 212, 256, 266, 267, 269, 275, 295, 297
Southern African Literatures (book) 16
Southern Touch (recording and aesthetic) 199
Soweto Rhythm Section 59
Soweto String Quartet 65, 70, 287
Soweto uprisings 197
Spoornet 131, 149
Springbok Radio 35–36 (box)
staggered entries 21, 248
States of Emergency 27 (box), 54, 130, 163, 277
Stimela 57, 70
Stormy Weather (film) 78, 81, 179
Strayhorn, Billy 156, 194, 195, 196
Sun City (casino) 54, 57, 64, 69, 314
Sun City: Artists United Against Apartheid 54, 55, 64, 70
Sundkler, Bengt 234
Swazi 256
Swaziland 9 (box), 14, 15, 204, 224, 275, 276, 283, 313
Switzerland 194, 195
SWP Records 11
Syncopation (film) 42

talent contests 175, 181
Tao Ea Matsekha 59
tap dancing 43 (box), 45 (box), 132, 134, 137, 139, 146, 150, 151, 180, 185
taverns 165, 166
taxation 214
technology 18, 37, 40, 76, 82, 225
television 28 (box), 36 (box), 38, 48–49, 50, 54, 55, 67, 74, 75, 87, 120, 179, 180, 264, 278,312
Timbuka (Malawi) 15
Tokens, The 6
"Tom Hark" (recording) 84
tonic sol-fa notation 255, 272
Topp Fargion, Janet 102, 130, 133, 135, 146, 148, 284, 296, 297
Township Jazz 20, 78, 82, 83, 84, 85, 87, 91, 97, 98, 202, 285, 314
Tracey, Andrew 11, 13, 144 (box), 149
Tracey, Hugh 5, 10, 11, 12, 13, 35 (box), 39, 40, 77, 134, 136, 137, 140, 247, 267, 271, 283
traders 270
traditional music 10, 13, 14, 35 (box), 37, 39, 40, 49, 50, 77, 84, 100, 106, 110, 112, 114, 115, 117, 119, 128, 149, 212, 271, 273, 283, 295, 297; *see also* radio
Transkei 27–28 (box), 29, 36 (box), 278
Transkei Radio 37
transnational 7, 12, 21, 38, 39, 70, 79, 85, 130, 194, 264
travel x, 6, 10, 12, 18, 43, 45, 49, 55, 56, 60, 68, 69, 73, 74, 77, 78, 81, 83, 87, 93, 110, 130, 136, 160, 194, 195, 201, 265; in ancient Africa 270
traveling shows 81, 86, 98, 188, 201, 311
Treason Trial 27, 277
tribal identity 37
Truth and Reconciliation Commission 17, 21, 29, 278
Tshabalala, Sam 215, 264
Tucker, Percy 47, 90
Turnbull, Colin 269, 297
Tutu, Archbishop Desmond 28, 31, 110, 278

Ukhozi Radio 38, 50, 119; *see also* Radio Zulu
ukupika 118, 128, 147, 300
ukuvamba 45 (box), 51, 118, 128, 147, 300
umgido 204, 205, 209, 239, 249, 250, 251, 252, 255, 257, 314
Umlazi 102, 130, 163
umzansi style 118, 121, 128, 131, 146, 300, 314
Union of Southern African Artists 87, 91
unison 8, 21, 251
United Democratic Front (UDF) 28 (box), 278
United Nations Organization (UNO) 54, 70, 95
United States 12, 15, 40, 46, 49, 74, 85, 102, 111, 159–160, 168, 196, 199, 214, 267; State Department 12; *see also* African American; New York City
Universal Men (recording) 115

urban areas 9 (box), 20, 26, 27 (box), 29 (box), 31, 37, 46, 50, 54, 73, 81, 99, 113, 121, 126, 136, 142, 202, 276, 277, 312, 314
Vail, Leroy 15, 16, 124, 297
Van Der Kemp (missionary) 213
Van Meerhoff, Peter 270
Van Riebeek, Jan 177
variety shows 42, 43, 44, 50, 87, 176, 188
Vasco da Gama 203, 270, 275
vaudeville 42, 43 (box), 50, 51, 200, 297
Vaughan Williams, Ralph 11
Verster, Francois 7
Verwoerd, Hendrik 27, 31, 36, 277
Vilakazi, Thami 121–127
Villon Films 43, 292, 293
"Viva Madiba" (song) 281
Voice of America radio 21, 36 (box)
Volans, Kevin 162, 273

Wait a Minim! (production) 144, 149, 287
Wallascheck, Richard 271
Warner Brothers 58, 59, 283
Weavers, The (a.k.a. Paul Campbell) 5, 6
websites 97, 163
"Weskusklong" (song) 66
White, Landeg 15
White, Timothy 58
Whiteman, Paul 43
"Wimoweh" (song) xi, 5, 6, 20, 68, 102, 314
Windsong (album/song) 160, 161, 175, 198, 304, 305
Witwatersrand Gold Mines 137, 141, 143 (box), 276
Witwatersrand, University of (Wits) 13, 15
women 23, 27 (box), 42, 62, 119–122, 130, 145, 156, 183, 204, 212, 213, 223–225, 240, 246–253, 277; female voice 234, 237, 249; musicians 86, 122, 220; *see also* Benjamin, Sathima Bea
world music xi, 3, 6, 12, 16, 21, 57, 59, 62, 63, 68, 73, 74, 76, 86, 99, 150, 205; circuits of xi, 99
World War I 77
World War II x, xii, 18, 39, 41, 43, 46, 49, 77, 81, 82, 155, 157, 173, 182, 185, 265; *see also* Cape Town jazz: postwar; South Africa: postwar period
Wright, Richard 187, 271

Ximba, Vusi 121, 128
Xolo Homeboys 299

Yoruba 271
YouTube 3, 18, 73, 155

"Zebra Crossing" (composition) 65
Zimbabwe 7, 9, 10, 11, 12, 13, 14, 15, 60, 114, 188, 204, 215, 224, 297, 313
Zionism (African Christian) 214, 215, 217, 257
Zonk! (film) 43, 44–45, 46, 47, 48, 78, 82, 87, 92, 127, 246
Zonk! The African People's Magazine 87
Zulu language xi, xii, 5, 34, 37, 48, 61, 63, 74, 86, 110, 155, 207, 224, 229, 237, 255, 264, 293, 308
Zulu war dancers 100, 101